# Love as *Agape*

# BMSEC

## BAYLOR–MOHR SIEBECK
### Studies in Early Christianity

*Wayne Coppins and Simon Gathercole*
Series Editors

## ALSO AVAILABLE

*From Jesus to the New Testament*
Early Christian Theology and the Origin of the New Testament Canon
Jens Schröter (2013)

*Israel, Church, and the Gentiles in the Gospel of Matthew*
Matthias Konradt (2014)

*Christian Theology and Its Institutions in the Early Roman Empire*
Prolegomena to a History of Early Christian Theology
Christoph Markschies (2015)

*The Gospel according to Luke*
Volume I: Luke 1–9:50
Michael Wolter (2016)

*The Gospel according to Luke*
Volume II: Luke 9:51–24
Michael Wolter (2017)

*The Glory of the Crucified One*
Christology and Theology in the Gospel of John
Jörg Frey (2018)

*Jesus and Judaism*
Martin Hengel and Anna Maria Schwemer (2019)

*Paul on Humility*
Eve-Marie Becker (2020)

# Love as *Agape*

## *The Early Christian Concept and Modern Discourse*

*Oda Wischmeyer*

Translated by
Wayne Coppins

BAYLOR UNIVERSITY PRESS

Mohr Siebeck

*Cover design* by Natalya Balnova
*Book design* by Baylor University Press
*Book typeset* by Scribe Inc.

Originally published in German as *Liebe als Agape: Das frühchristliche Konzept und der moderne Diskurs* (Tübingen: Mohr Siebeck, 2015) with ISBN 978-3-16-153943-5.

This English edition is published in Germany by Mohr Siebeck under ISBN 978-3-16-160908-4.

Distributors

| *For all other countries* | *For Europe and the UK* |
| --- | --- |
| Baylor University Press | Mohr Siebeck |
| One Bear Place #97363 | Wilhelmstr. 18 |
| Waco, Texas 76798 | 72074 Tübingen |
| USA | Germany |

The Library of Congress has cataloged this book under ISBN 978-1-4813-1574-6.
Library of Congress Control Number: 2021938789

Printed in the United States of America on acid-free paper with a minimum of thirty percent recycled content.

Dedicated to the Philosophical Faculty of the University
of Lund as an expression of thanks for the bestowal
of an Honorary Doctorate in Philosophy

Ἔρος ὃς κάλλιστος ἐν ἀθανάτοισι θεοῖσι

—Hesiod, *Theogony* 120

Οὐ γὰρ ἔρως θεός ἐστι, δ' ἀίδηλον ἁπάντων.

—Pseudo-Phocylides 194

ὁ θεὸς ἀγάπη ἐστίν

—1 John 4.8, 16

Beatus Ioannes cum Ephesi moraretur, usque ad ultimam senectutem, ut vix inter discipulorum manus ad ecclesiam deferretur, nec posset in plura vocem verba contexere, nihil aliud per singulas solebat proferre collectas, nisi hoc: filioli diligite alterutrum. Tandem discipuli et fratres qui aderant taedio affecti quod eadem semper audirent, dixerunt: magister, quare semper hoc loqueris? Qui respondit dignam Ioanne sententiam: quia praeceptum domini est, et si solum fiat, sufficit.

—Jerome, *Comm. Gal.* 5 on Gal 6.10 (Migne PL 26 col. 462)

# Contents

# Editors' Preface

The Baylor–Mohr Siebeck Studies in Early Christianity series aims to facilitate increased dialogue between German and Anglophone scholarship by making recent German research available in English translation. In this way, we hope to play a role in the advancement of our common field of study. The target audience for the series is primarily scholars and graduate students, though some volumes may also be accessible to advanced undergraduates. In selecting books for the series, we will especially seek out works by leading German scholars that represent outstanding contributions in their own right and also serve as windows into the wider world of German-language scholarship.

As Professor Emerita of New Testament at the Friedrich Alexander University Erlangen-Nürnberg and coeditor of Neutestamentliche Entwürfe zur Theologie (NET), Oda Wischmeyer is one of the most prominent scholars of early Christianity in the world today. She is especially well known for her research on Ben Sira, New Testament hermeneutics, the Letters of Paul, and the Epistle of James. Her major publications include *Die Kultur des Buches Jesus Sirach* (BZNW; Berlin: Walter de Gruyter, 1995), *Hermeneutik des Neuen Testaments: Ein Lehrbuch* (NET; Tübingen: Francke, 2004), *Von Ben Sira zu Paulus: Gesammelte Aufsätze zu Texten, Theologie und Hermeneutik des Frühjudentums und des Neuen Testaments* (WUNT; Tübingen: Mohr Siebeck, 2004), *Lexikon der Bibelhermeneutik: Begriffe–Methoden–Theorien–Konzepte* (Berlin: Walter de Gruyter, 2013), *Handbuch der Bibelhermeneutiken* (Berlin: Walter de Gruyter, 2016), *Paulus—Texte und Themen: Gesammelte Aufsätze II* (Tübingen: Mohr Siebeck, forthcoming), and *Der Brief des Jakobus* (KEK; Göttingen: Vandenhoeck & Ruprecht, forthcoming).

The present volume, *Liebe als Agape: Das frühchristliche Konzept und der moderne Diskurs* (Tübingen: Mohr Siebeck, 2015), not only contributes to our understanding of love for God and love for neighbor in the New Testament, but also presents an exegetically informed construction of the New Testament concept of love—which is sharpened through a penetrating comparison with counter, parallel, and alternative concepts—and brings this concept into critical and constructive dialogue with key contemporary visions of love, including those of Julia Kristeva, Martha Nussbaum, Pope Benedict XVI, and Simon May.

With regard to the translator's divided allegiance to the source and target languages, Wayne Coppins has generally attempted to adhere closely to the German wording, while allowing for some adjustments for the sake of clarity and readability in English. In some cases, of course, communication with Oda Wischmeyer has led to more extensive reformulations and occasionally to minor additions or subtractions vis-à-vis the German version, including some new interactions with secondary literature. The following specific points of translation may be mentioned here. I have translated *Weltsicht* and *Weltanschauung* as "worldview," while rendering *Weltdeutung* and *Weltinterpretation* as "world-interpretation." I have usually translated *Gerechtigkeit* as "justice," though sometimes as "righteousness." In most cases, I have translated *Bruderliebe* as "love for brothers and sisters" and *Brüder* as "brothers and sisters."

For help with difficult German sentences and access to secondary literature, Wayne Coppins would like to thank Christoph Heilig, Brandon Wason, and Uta Poplutz. As with previous translations, I am also thankful to Simon Gathercole for his careful reading of the manuscript and his excellent suggestions for improving it. Likewise, I am grateful to Oda Wischmeyer for her feedback on the manuscript in general and for her valuable responses to my specific questions. Finally, thanks are also due to my wife, Ingie Hovland, and my daughters, Sophia and Simone, for creating space in our life for my translation work.

Both editors wish to express their thanks to Elena Müller at Mohr Siebeck and David Aycock at Baylor University Press for their support and guidance in the continued development of this series. Likewise, we are thankful to the many people at Baylor University Press who have contributed to the book with their expertise along the way, especially Jenny Hunt and Cade Jarrell. Finally, a word of thanks is due to our copyeditor and proofreader, Carrie Watterson, for her invaluable help in fine-tuning and polishing this book.

Wayne Coppins and Simon Gathercole
Athens, Georgia, and Cambridge, England
October 2020

# Preface to the English Edition

The German version of the present monograph was published five years ago. It began with an *ethical* interest. My work on the theme of "love as *agape*" was motivated by the perception that German society needed to rediscover the importance of love for neighbor. This need became shockingly clear when the "waves of refugees" from Syria started in 2015 and presented a challenge to German asylum and immigration politics. In this atmosphere, love for neighbor as individual and societal obligation and as Christian inspiration needed to be thematized and justified anew. At the same time, the New Testament call to love one's enemies forms a sharp point of contrast to the current non-culture of hatred for everything different and foreign, which is not confined to German society.

This study led me back to where my exegetical research once began. The analysis of 1 Cor 13 and cognate texts and tradition-historical investigations of the term *agape* brought me into the field of New Testament studies. What attracted me about the New Testament writings, roughly forty years ago, was not by chance grounded in what Paul had stylized with the greatest ambition and emphasis. What I determined in the course of the study, however, was neither a simple déjà vu of my earlier research nor an intensified sensitivity for *agape* in the sense of love for neighbor and enemies in light of recent societal debates and politics. Rather, a more comprehensive understanding became apparent to me. Love as *agape* — I came to see that this concept contains within it a twofold inspiration. The early Christian writers were not only ethicists but also reached for the theological stars. They connected conceptually the love of God for Israel, his love for his Son, his love for human beings, the love of human beings for God and for Jesus Christ, and the love of human beings for one another with the gift of the Spirit and, using the not very sharply delineated Greek term for "affection," they called this universal network of relationships *agape*. What emerged was the great love story between God and humanity, which realized itself in the figure of Jesus Christ. This love story placed love as the most intensive affirming and life-creating relationship in

God himself: God *is* love.[1] Theology as speech about God reaches its actual peak here. At the same time, human beings are drawn into this relationship. They obtain special dignity. More than that, God's love is their life.[2] Without the relation to transcendence, which connects the existence of human beings with God, the *agape* concept of the New Testament cannot be had. For this reason, the *theological* side of the concept merits new attention. Love as *agape* cannot be reduced to ethical normativity and to emotional qualities, to practical help and to empathy. It is not grounded in the sphere of "you shall." It says something about God and about the basis of life for human beings.

This reality of the theological foundation of the *agape* concept is contested from the outset by contemporary Western philosophy and cultural and social studies, which understand themselves as post-Christian. Thus, Simon May, in his new book on love, considers the Christian concept of *agape* to be a dead end.[3] Christian theology and Christian churches, by contrast, are challenged not only to campaign for love as ethos and within the framework of ethics and societal values and norms but also to enter into a critical intellectual dialogue with the post-Christian thought world and to shed new light on the theological and anthropological inspiration of the concept of *agape*.

The present monograph contributes to this dialogue with Christian and non-Christian positions. Although I stand in the Protestant tradition of thought, I give special attention to the encyclical *Deus Caritas Est* of Pope Benedict XVI in this context. This encyclical is an expression of the vital significance of the New Testament concept of love for the worldwide Christianity of our time. Here, a global perspective opens up on that which connects and does not divide persons and continents—a fact that is easily overlooked by essentially post-Christian positions. I hope that the English version of my book will give fresh life to this intercontinental dialogue.

For this reason, I welcome the translation of this study into English. I wish to thank Dr. Wayne Coppins for his very careful and considered translation. He has sharpened and improved the German manuscript in language and substance and also added valuable references to recently published literature. I also thank the editors of the BMSEC series, Dr. Wayne Coppins (University of Georgia) and Dr. Simon Gathercole (University of Cambridge), who have accepted this monograph into their series.

Oda Wischmeyer
Erlangen, Germany
September 1, 2020

---

[1] 1 John 4.8, 16.

[2] This phrasing echoes Johann Wolfgang von Goethe, *West-östlicher Divan*, Buch Suleika, Suleika: "Sag's ihm, aber sag's bescheiden: seine Liebe sei mein Leben."

[3] May 2019, 3–35.

# Preface to the German Edition

In 1930 Anders Nygren, professor of systematic theology at the University of Lund, wrote in the preface to his two-volume work *Eros och Agape* that the question raised for discussion in this work is "one of the most central and yet *most neglected* in the theological field."[1] In the second edition, he could revise this assessment. His work had already found a broad echo, and he referred to numerous studies on the topic in the years between 1930 and 1954.[2] Nygren especially sought to provide a synthesis between dogmatics and ethics. In 1951, in a time that was still shaped by the consequences of Nazi rule and World War II, the Benedictine father Victor Warnach stated that in the present "religious situation" "scarcely a problem . . . is as urgent . . . as that of 'love,' not only in social or political respects but almost even more in personal and pastoral respects."[3] In 1958 the Dominican father Ceslas Spicq presented his major three-volume study *Agapè dans le Nouveau Testament*.[4] His point of departure was the conviction "il est possible d'élaborer une théologie néo-testamentaire en function de la charité."[5] Almost fifty years later, on December 12, 2005, the first encyclical of the professor of systematic theology Joseph Ratzinger, Pope Benedict XVI since 2005, was published with the title *Deus Caritas Est*. In the opening of the encyclical, Benedict writes, "In a world where the name of God is sometimes associated with vengeance or even a duty of hatred and violence, this message is both timely and significant. For this reason, I wish in my first Encyclical to speak of the love which God lavishes upon us and which we in turn must share with others" (§1). In 2009 the decidedly nonreligious French philosopher Alain Badiou

---

[1] Nygren 1982, xiii; cf. 27. For the Swedish version, see Nygren 1930/1936.
[2] Nygren 1982, xiii.
[3] Warnach 1951, 5.
[4] Spicq 1958–1959 (ET = 2007).
[5] Spicq 2007, 1958–1959, 1:5 (ET = 2007, 1:v: "The development of a New Testament theology deriving from charity is perfectly possible").

reached the judgment that in the contemporary world of assurances, promises of comfort, and risk-free matchmaking, love is threatened in its very
nature—a word that Badiou himself, however, rejects as essentialist—and
must be defended by philosophy.[6]

What can New Testament scholarship in 2015/2020 contribute to the
discourse on love? As their *contemporary*, I agree with the retired Pope
as well as with Alain Badiou. Both point to the decisive potential that is
encoded in the word *love*. The potential for hatred, which Europe knows
well from the grand ideologies of the twentieth century with their destructive violence, has returned in the present as religiously grounded hatred in
international politics. And the inspiring, creative, and yet also disruptive
and destructive power of love between two persons is in danger of having
to give way to a new ideology of self-realization.

As a *New Testament scholar*, I see yet another deficit. For some time
now I have noticed a decline in the use of the phrase *love for neighbor* in
our current societal discourse, in which the churches also participate. Likewise, I miss the recourse to the Christian ethical-theological concept of
*agape* in contemporary sociological, philosophical, and cultural-scientific
publications and projects. A movement such as the Aristotelian renaissance, which flourishes especially in practical philosophy; philosophical
ethics; and research on rhetoric, literature, and emotions, and places virtues or emotions such as empathy in the foreground, could be an example of how ancient concepts—and the New Testament concept of *agape*
belongs to these concepts—can have an impact upon contemporary situations. The task of New Testament scholarship is not only to reconstruct or
construct the foundational texts of Christianity ever anew historically but
also to bring them into current societal and scholarly debates—or at least
to create the best preconditions for this.

In the past two generations, New Testament scholarship has sub-
mitted a vast quantity of diverse studies on the topic of *love*. I too have
contributed to this work on multiple occasions. Looking back, it seems
that this tremendous investment of exegetical detailed scholarship has not
been able to prevent Christian love, and love for neighbor in particular,
from belonging among the theological themes that no longer find a place
in public debate. Instead, the topic of *love* appears to be referred to cultural
studies and the humanities. For this reason, I have chosen the format of
a thematic monograph to create a fresh awareness for the topic of love as a
central New Testament theme. The goal of the present study is not only
an up-to-date fine tuning of the historical-exegetical panorama for profes-
sional colleagues but, beyond that, a clear presentation of the contours of

---

[6] Badiou/Truong 2012 (FV = 2009).

the New Testament concept in the context of present-day constructions of love in sociology, philosophy, ethics, and research on emotions. From the time of the Hebrew Bible and the New Testament, love has always been a great or even the great topic of theology and has been perceived as such by philosophy and other disciplines in the humanities. The present book seeks to help this to remain the case also among contemporary scholarly constructions of love.

# Introduction

## From Commandment to Concept

### 1. Occasion and Intention of the Study

The impetus for this study is the perception that in our so-called Western world[1] — which is *linguistically* dominated by terms such as respect, understanding, empathy, emotion, and inclusion; in which the powers of Christian world interpretation and Christian life forms are simultaneously receding *politically*, societally, and religiously; and which is characterized in the *personal* sphere by great uncertainties over what love between the sexes and generations and in the traditional institutions could mean — love for neighbor has a tough time linguistically and materially, and the role of Christian love and mercy as a whole is fading.

In a time in which hatred has simultaneously gained new relevance and attractiveness,[2] I want to think anew about *love*. Here I refer consciously and from the outset to a thematic and historical segment — to the textual corpus of the New Testament. From Plato onward, very different concepts of love have been set forth in the Western world. One of the great and influential concepts comes from the authors of the New Testament.[3] This concept belongs to the first century CE, reaches back in its traditions to ancient Israel, and at the same time continues to have an impact in the Christian conception of love and in Christian churches up to the present.[4] There is

---

[1] This formulation takes into account the fact that the situation looks very different in other political-cultural spheres.

[2] Cf. Benedict XVI 2006, 2 (§1). See also the neologism *Hassprediger* (hate preacher), which was first included in the standard German spelling dictionary (*Duden: Die Deutsche Rechtschreibung*) in 2006.

[3] Thus, e.g., in Kristeva 1987 (FV = 1983).

[4] For literature, see the article on love in TRE 21 (Gerlitz et al. 1991), which provides extensive references to literature with regard to all the individual questions. See also the

probably no other concept of love in the Western world and beyond that has such a historically deep dimension and at the same time continues to have effects in the present in global Christianity. The present monograph is devoted to this concept[5] and its historical contexts. At the same time, I want to contribute not only to the placement of the topic of *agape* in early Christianity but also to the task of bringing the early Christian concept into present-day discourse about love. To attain this end, I will sketch out important contemporary positions on the interpretation of love that have appeared between 1969 and 2011, and confront them with the early Christian concept.

This task is theologically urgent. For in our current post-Christian or—to speak even more generally—post–religiously shaped Western discourses, the Christian concept of love is far from being acknowledged, known, or even still in play.[6] François Bovon wrote about the Sermon on the Mount, the religious *rocher de bronze* (unshakeable element), with an equal measure of understatement and bitterness:

> For exegetes it does not lack a certain tragic sense—in view of their iden-
> tity in communicating with the biblical message—that they must some-
> times conclude that the Sermon on the Mount is irrelevant for today's
> social, political, and human issues.[7]

By contrast, the *intention* of this study is to present anew the New Testament concept of love *in such a way* that it can gain a hearing in the current discussion about love. The theme of love is a central subject that is hotly contested in society and scholarship. Where very different political,

---

bibliography in Helm 2017. Nygren's book on *eros* and *agape* (1982) is probably the theological work with the greatest resonance. On this, see Wischmeyer 2015a.

[5] For classic presentations on the topic, see Warnach 1951; Spicq 1955a; 1958–1959 (ET = 2007).

[6] A good view of the different approaches to the topic of love is provided by Schmölders 1996; Tanner 2005; Düsing/Klein 2009; Jeanrond 2010; May 2011. On the linguistic usage and meaning of *Nächstenliebe* (love for neighbor) in the German language, cf. http://www.dwds.de. For the reference to the standard work, DWDS, I thank Dr. Christine Ganslmayer. For the past century, the following picture emerges: *Nächstenliebe* played a significant role in the scholarly literature of the 1920s and 1950s up to the 1970s, while it was almost not used at all in the 1930s. In fiction the noun occurred with disproportionate frequency in the 1960s. The German archive of texts (DTA: http://www.deutschestextarchiv.de) provides data on the relative frequency of *Nächstenliebe* since 1600. The number of attestations around 1900 is conspicuous.

[7] Bovon 1992, 244 (GV = 1989, 327). Kapl-Blume 2005 has presented an interesting study, which traces the receding of the theological valence of the term between Zedler (1732–1750) and the ninth edition of vol. 8 of the *Brockhaus Enzyklopädie* (1848).

philosophical, cultural, and cognitive scientific concepts strive not only for interpretation, prerogative of interpretation, and personal forms of life, but also for societal and legislative influence,[8] the early Christian view of love has its own, indispensable contribution to make to the discussion.

## 2. The Field of Study

*Love* is, first of all, a term of relation. More precisely, it is the decisive expression for the strongest and closest relationships between humans of a different or of the same sex or age and of different social relationships within or outside of families.[9] As such the term is given diverse interpretations. It is the object of artistic and literary invention and configuration. At the same time, it is subjected to polyphonic philosophical, historical, psychological,[10] sociological,[11] religious, and ethical[12] analysis. The radius of what was connected with "love" was already wide ranging in ancient Near Eastern cultures[13] and Greco-Roman antiquity.[14] Love was set forth in myth and religion and spelled out in philosophy and politics. Love had long since been invoked not only as sexual attraction or primary attraction between the sexes, but also as great feeling, as emotional rush, as destructive possession, and yet also as inner affection, as basis for the institution of marriage and family, as a form of behavior within the family, and as an ethos of family and friendship. Love could lead to a mystical approach to God, and, conversely, love could draw the gods to human beings. Since Homer and Hesiod, within the framework of Greco-Roman religious stories[15] and also in the philosophical myth, the boundary between humans and gods is transcended, whether understood as the gods' and goddesses' desire for love, sung as the god Eros, or imagined as ἔρως in Plato's

---

[8] On this, cf. EKD 2013.

[9] "Love" for things and ideas has been regarded since Aristotle as a derived manner of speech that designates the strength and, perhaps, obsessive inclination to war, nature, art, etc.

[10] For an introduction, see Wulf 2013. This article comprises the following lemmata: love, attachment theory; love, duplex theory; love, evolutionary theoretical approach; love, intensity-indicators model of partner love; love, social-constructivist approach; styles of love.

[11] For an introduction, see Hillmann/Hartfiel 2007, 503–5. Love is defined from the sociological perspective as the ability "in connection with sympathy and attachment to be able to develop . . . intensive, emotional, personal positively experienced relationships to another person or other persons" (503). Opposing terms are "aggression, hate, hostility, egoism, and narcissism" (504).

[12] On the two aspects, see Boyce Gibson et al. 1974.

[13] On this, cf. Bergman/Haldar/Wallis 1977 (GV = 1973).

[14] See the still fundamental article of Waser 1907.

[15] Hesiod, *Theogony* 120: Eros as "the most beautiful among the immortal gods." Cf. Schneider 1966. See further van der Horst 1978, 240–41 on Ps.-Phoc. 194.

philosophical narratives in the *Symposium* and *Phaedrus*.[16] The writers of Israel and ancient Judaism also set forth love as narrative(s). They describe their God as the one who chooses his people, Israel; loves passionately; and expects love from his people. However much the permeability of the divine sphere to the world of humans is imagined in detail, it is invariably thought and experienced in love. In antiquity, love is not restricted to its interhuman components. It is not an immanent entity. Rather, it draws its actual power, its *fascinosum*, precisely from its relation to the spiritual world. It reaches from the divine world into the human world and from the human world into the divine world.

In the process, the phenomenology of love is revealed to be cross-cultural. Much that was ascribed to love was ancient Near Eastern and ancient Greek common property and, correspondingly, known in ancient Israel. In the writings of Israel, it is thematized independently and sometimes configured literarily in a classic way, such as the love between the sexes in the Song of Songs[17] or as the disruptively strong and electing love of the God of Israel for his people in the prophetic books.[18] However, a concise or homogenous concept of love that brought the term and phenomenon into focus cannot be found in the writings of Israel. On the contrary, we encounter a wide variety of ideas about love. It is regarded as the strongest form of the relationship of God to human beings and of human beings to God and can at the same time describe the whole spectrum of relationships of humans to one another.

When the earliest Christian writers speak of ἀγάπη/ἀγαπᾶν, they narrow and focalize the perspective. Something *innovative* arises—a *concept*. In the process, rather than being thematized as an anthropological entity, narrated in its different forms of relationship, described, or normatively taught, love is set forth as the common form of life of the Christ-confessing members of the ἐκκλησίαι θεοῦ—as a social culture that is theologically grounded.

### 3. Results

The results of this study may be briefly summarized in advance with the phrase "from tradition to innovation."

---

[16] Cf. Kany 2013. On concepts of love in archaic and classical Greece, cf. Sanders 2013. On Plato, see Price 1989; Most 2005; Bremer 2009. The interpretation of Plato in Kristeva 1987 is especially impressive.

[17] On this, see Hagedorn 2015.

[18] Cf. the equally complex and violent love metaphoricism in Hos 1–3.

First, the New Testament authors develop their concepts of love from the writings of the Bible of Israel.[19] In doing so, however, they select only certain traditions from the broad spectrum of ideas about love and loving in the Old Testament: first, the theological statements about God's covenantal love for Israel—the great narrative of the Old Testament—and second, the theological-ethical commandments of the Pentateuch on love for God and love for neighbor. They combine these traditions with early Jewish ethical topoi.

Second, Paul and the author of the Johannine writings develop these traditions into their own innovative concepts. In their proclamation of the gospel, they make love the key term of their understanding of God and at the same time recommend it to their communities as an emotional, ethical, and practical attitude—in short, as a new form of life or as the new culture of life together in the communities, the culture of ἀγάπη. With this concentration on community ethics, Paul and 'John' are, in the final analysis, far removed from the conceptual world of their traditions, though they do not abandon these.[20]

The theoretical potential for innovation lies in Christology, which constitutes the new narrative framework of the conception of love. The early Christian authors interpret Jesus' fate of death as the dramatic high point and turning point of the saving love story of God and human beings. By speaking of the God of Israel as the loving father of Jesus, who gives his Son for the salvation of human beings, they not only create a new soteriological paradigm but also change the talk about God, i.e., theology in the narrower sense. They enable from then on a vision of the inner movement in God—a vision whose boldness lies in the metaphorical and emotional potential of the theologoumenon of love and therein can be expressed through a narrative. This vision encompasses the whole time of God. It reaches from the time before creation, when the Son was still with the Father,[21] via the time between Jesus' birth and death and the time of the New Testament writers and communities through to the eschaton. Paul therefore reaches the bold conclusion that love "never ends."[22] It is the bond that connects the members of the communities with the coming world of God already during their lifetimes. The productive impact of the

---

[19] This has been especially emphasized by Feldmeier/Spieckermann 2011, 125–46 (GV = 2010, 126–48).

[20] A fundamental continuity is secured by the fact that the Christ-confessing communities retain the Septuagint as a foundational text ("scripture"). Moreover, what is said here does not apply equally to all writings of the New Testament. For example, James remains wholly bound to the tradition of the commandment of love for neighbor.

[21] Thus, the intimations in the prologue of the Gospel of John.

[22] 1 Cor 13.8–13.

early Christian theology of love in its close attachment to the narrative of
Jesus Christ can be seen in its diverse reception history. The early Christian Trinitarian theologians and the Christian mystics were both able to
develop their thinking on its basis.[23]

Third, the large speculative, ethical, and eschatological concepts of
ἀγάπη stem not from Jesus but from Paul and John. They are developed
further by the Pauline school, especially in Ephesians and Colossians
and later in 1 Clement and by the theologians and community leaders of
the Johannine letters. By contrast, with regard to the topic of "love," the
Jesus tradition that is preserved and literarily and theologically reworked
in the Synoptic Gospels and the Gospel of Thomas is restricted to the
so-called double commandment of love for God and love for neighbor
and to the love for enemies. Both are not innovative in the way that many
exegetes have thought and did not stand alone at the center of the ethics and eschatological hope of the early Christian communities. However, we observe in multiple writings of the second century CE that the
Synoptic Jesus tradition becomes very influential in the course of time,
and the Pauline[24] and Johannine theologies of love simultaneously dimin-
ish in importance. Expressing the point with some exaggeration, love for
neighbor—understood in a nonspeculative way and interpreted neither
theologically nor eschatologically—increasingly gains in significance in
the second century CE. When we speak in the course of this study of the
New Testament or—more broadly understood—early Christian concept of
ἀγάπη, we are therefore summarizing diverse concepts from the corpus
of New Testament texts, whose common inheritance lies in the love commandments of the scriptures of Israel and whose common starting point is
the story of Jesus Christ.[25] In what follows I will introduce the significant
questions and briefly trace the course of this investigation.

## 4. Introduction to the Topic

### 4.1 ἀγάπη (1): Ethics and Beyond

In general, the New Testament texts on love as a whole are primarily perceived and understood as ethical texts, above all as texts on love for neighbor. Accordingly, special attention must be given to this aspect of the New
Testament concept of love.

---

[23] On this, see esp. Kristeva 1987.

[24] On this, see Lindemann 1979.

[25] This connects texts such as James and Romans.

ἀγάπη, love, appears as an ethical entity, i.e., as a constructive form of relationship, behavior, and action between human beings. The basis is the Old Testament commandment of love for neighbor (Mark 12.31 par. following Lev 19.18), from which Luther derived the German neologism *Nächstenliebe*.[26] This translation is very significant, since Luther introduced an emotive-appellative emphasis into the sober Greek "neighbor" when he used *Nächster* (close one) instead of *Nachbar* (neighbor). Since then, we speak of *Nächstenliebe* in German not only when we refer directly to the biblical commandment but also in general when we have 'caritative'[27] actions in view.

The widespread ethically centered perception of the New Testament talk of love draws its legitimation from the texts on love for neighbor and for enemies. If the New Testament concept of love is reduced in this way to love for neighbor as the "Christian" form of love, the converse is also true. The New Testament ethic that became the foundation of later Christian ethical conceptions presents itself on the basis of its central material dimension as an ethic of love—specifically as an ethic of love for neighbor or even of love for enemies. In the course of the history of Christianity, the equation love = love for neighbor = core term of Christian ethics receives such weight that under certain conditions not only are Christian ethics interpreted in the sense of the Augustinian *ama et fac quod vis*, but the whole of Christianity can be understood as a religion of love[28] or of love for neighbor. It is sufficient here to quote Anders Nygren for the Christian self-understanding: "Agape is Christianity's own original basic conception."[29] Accordingly, nothing in Christianity is criticized more strongly than ecclesial power, force, and bondage—in short, lack of love. Forms of sexual abuse, i.e., a perversion of love, as these have been

---

[26] On neologisms in Luther's translation of the Bible, cf. Schilling 2013, 532. The Danish *kaerlighed* is patterned on the neologism of Luther. LSJ, 1420, renders πλησίον with "neighbor" and ἀγάπη with "charity."

[27] On *caritas* as a translation of ἀγάπη, cf. Gurney 2011, 197–217, who provides references to further literature in note 3 of his work. Gurney investigates the question of why More positioned himself so aggressively against William Tyndale's decision to translate ἀγάπη with "love" instead of with "charity." The controversy is situated in the context of More's fight against Luther's theology. More was coauthor of the *Assertio Septem Sacramentorum* of Henry VIII. Tyndale was strangled because of his translation of the Bible and his reformational theology in 1536 and burned afterward; Thomas More had already been beheaded in 1535 because he refused to take the Oath of Supremacy, which placed Henry VIII as supreme head of the Church of England. For the sphere of *caritas* in the sense of labors of love within and outside of Christian communities, see Philippi 1981.

[28] Cf. Goethe on January 4, 1824, to Eckermann on primitive Christianity: "The appearance of the new teaching of love" (Eckermann 2011, 533).

[29] Nygren 1982, 48.

uncovered in different Christian churches in most recent times, appear catastrophic in this context.

The ethical perspective is strengthened through the circumstance that the New Testament authors connect their thoughts on love almost exclusively to the Greek root ἀγαπ-, which the Septuagint translators used for the commandment of love for neighbor. In this way they take a fundamental step away from the general Greek lexis of love.[30] The New Testament authors follow them in this. The Gospels especially use the verb ἀγαπᾶν and understand love on the basis of the commandment "love your neighbor," while Paul and the Deutero-Pauline literature predominantly use the noun ἀγάπη and thus place love in proximity to a *virtue*. However, we must not overlook the fact that in the Septuagint ἀγαπᾶν also stands for emotional and physical love. In contrast to the physical side, the emotional aspect of love is also thematized in the New Testament writings, especially in the Johannine writings. Here the noun and verb appear alongside each other, which leads to a structure that is characterized by a distinctive combination of commandment, virtue, and emotion.

Lexically, the New Testament talk of love and loving thus shows itself to be a version of early Jewish ethics at first glance, for in the Greek lexicon, ἔρως and φιλία mainly function as terms for love, affection, and ties of friendship, while the stem ἀγαπ- is semantically colorless[31] and the substantive ἀγάπη is scarcely used.[32] By contrast, the Bible of Greek-speaking Jews, i.e., the Septuagint, does not use ἔρως at all and uses φιλία only rarely, whereas ἀγάπη, ἀγάπησις, and ἀγαπᾶν appear frequently, especially in the thematic context of love for neighbor.

This initial perception of the close connection between Old Testament–early *Jewish* and New Testament–early *Christian* ethics of love thus leads through lexis and semantics. It deepens and confirms itself on the basis of tradition history, for the fact that the New Testament writings assign a central place to love is due to the commandments of love for God and love for neighbor and is thus first and foremost a result of the Israelite-Jewish tradition, which forms the basis of early Christianity and its own writings. The New Testament authors assign the commandments of love for God and love for neighbor (Deut 6.5 and Lev 19.18) the central place in the Torah. This is not self-evident, for in the Pentateuch itself they do not have this function and are not combined with each other into

---

[30] Wischmeyer 1978; Söding 1992b.

[31] LSJ, 6, provides the following equivalents for ἀγαπᾶν, though without giving equal consideration to non-Jewish Christian and Jewish Christian texts: (1) greet with affection, love, persuade, entreat, caress; (2) to be fond of, prize, desire; (3) to be well pleased, contented.

[32] Cf. Wischmeyer 1978.

a so-called double commandment. Still, in Deut 6.4–5 the commandment of love for God is formulated as the first of all commandments. The commandment of love for neighbor, however, is not as strongly accented. It is simply a member of a longer series of commandments on social behavior in relation to the tribe and fellow members of the people. In the non-biblical literature of early Judaism, the tradition takes the form of passing on the essence of the two different commandments of love in ever new variations and approaches. In the demand for "piety and righteousness,"[33] ancient Judaism can express its notion of obligations to God and to human beings in a concise formula, without making recourse to the commandments. By contrast, the New Testament authors clothe these two fundamental obligations in the double commandment of love.

*Jesus* is connected with the love commandment in a special way in the Synoptic tradition. In the Gospel of Mark, Jesus formulates the double commandment in a prominent place as the "greatest commandment" in the Torah (Mark 12.28–34 par.). Here, the author of the Gospel of Mark stresses the agreement that exists on this point between Jesus and the scribe who poses the question of the greatest commandment. The sayings tradition of the antitheses in the Sermon on the Mount, which Matthew develops, points, however, in the opposite direction. Here, Jesus explicitly interprets the love for neighbor against the tradition as love for enemies (Matt 5.43–48). The author of the Gospel of Luke has his own emphasis. He illustrates and concretizes the double commandment with the story of the merciful Samaritan, which he has Jesus recount in response to the scribe's question about who, then, is "his neighbor." In this way, the evangelist specifies *mercy* as a concrete form of love for neighbor (Luke 10.25–37). At the same time, the story contains a polemical jab against the representatives of the Jewish religion[34] and commends a religious outsider—a Samaritan. A corresponding example story applies to the love of the father for the son (Luke 15.11–32): The father "has compassion" for him (v. 20) and receives the 'lost son' in love. The Johannine writings interpret the commandment of love for neighbor in a quite independent manner by relating it as the commandment of love for brothers and sisters to their fellowships (John 13.31–35; 1 John 2.7–11; and elsewhere). All these different texts have *one thing* in common: they are interpretations of the commandment of love for neighbor as it is formulated in the Torah that experience new authorization through the teaching and proclamation of Jesus; conversely, the linking of Jesus back to the Torah serves to legitimate him as an authoritative teacher.

---

[33] On this, cf. Berger 1972, 56–257; W. Popkes 2001, 171–73.
[34] There is explicit mention of religious agents.

*Paul* never explicitly makes recourse to the ἀγαπᾶν-Jesus tradition. He takes the step from the love *commandment* "of the law"[35] (Rom 13.8–10; Gal 5.14) to the *concept* of ἀγάπη and thereby fundamentally expands the early Christian conception of love from the outset. The thematic text on ἀγάπη in 1 Cor 13 makes especially clear that Paul not only takes up and interprets traditions, but advocates a distinct concept of love. This concept is developed further within the Pauline tradition in Ephesians and Colossians (Col 3.14; Eph 3.14–19). Paul himself, in Galatians, already interprets the love *commandment* as a spiritual *virtue*, which can also be grounded *emotionally*, and as a *concept* of the new form of life and communitarian culture of the Christ-believing communities that he founded in Asia Minor and Greece. He joins in this concept the aspects of the Old Testament love commandment as well as the reciprocal behavior of the community members among one another and toward 'outsiders' with the relationship to God and understands love equally as fulfillment of the law and as a form of life in the Spirit and as the central eschatological virtue, which combines practical, emotional, and 'mystical' or eschatological aspects.

The tradition history of the love commandment has often been presented.[36] The *historical contextualization* of the New Testament concept of love must proceed beyond this narrower tradition-historical question regarding the commandments. For the early Christian concept of love is located from the beginning not only in the line of tradition and in the—narrowly and clearly defined—tradition sphere of early Jewish Torah ethics and in polemical conflict with the varieties of contemporary Jewish Torah interpretation, but also discloses new categories in the context of non-Jewish concepts of virtue in the imperial period. Paul not only quotes the "law" but also writes the "song of songs of love," which manages to do without any recourse to "scripture" and whose middle part is not far removed from the Aristotelian doctrine of emotions (1 Cor 13.4–7).[37] He encourages the Christ-believing ἐκκλησία in Philippi in the style of the virtue ethics of the imperial period (Phil 4.8):

> **4.8** Finally, brothers and sisters, whatever is true, whatever is honorable, whatever is just, whatever is pure, whatever is worthy of love (προσφιλή), whatever has a good reputation, if anything is a virtue (ἀρετή) and if anything is worthy of praise, be mindful of these things.

---

[35] He does not write "of scripture."
[36] For recent literature, see Söding 2014, 497–503.
[37] Cf. Wischmeyer 2012b.

This expansion of the ethical contexts and the concomitant implicit or explicit distancing from the "scripture" of Israel as the exclusive ethical standard is just as clear in the Gospels in a different literary form as it is in the letters of Paul. Beyond the reformulation of the love commandment in different texts of the Synoptic Gospels and especially in the Sermon on the Mount (Matt 5.17–48), Jesus—in the form that the Jesus tradition and its reworking by the Synoptic Gospels shape—engages with the Jewish interpretation of the law of his time in a manner that ranges from critical to repudiating. The Gospel of John designates the love commandment with terminological sharpness and implicit polemic against the Torah as a "new commandment" that Jesus gives to his disciples at the end of his life (John 13.34). The Johannine letters interpret the love commandment pointedly as "old commandment" (1 John 2.7), i.e., as a foundational commandment of their fellowship.[38] Here, the Jesus tradition is so far developed that it is awarded the foundational dignity of antiquity.

At the same time, the New Testament epistolary literature develops, at least in practice, a competitor to the ethical conceptions of the philosophical schools of the imperial period and their significant authors such as Seneca, Marcus Aurelius, and Plutarch, which will then lead equally to an adoption of ethical terms and convictions from the philosophy of the time and to a critical engagement with their concepts in the Christian literature of the second century CE. "Scripture" is the only thing that is cited. However, they live in a world that is full of religions and competing ethical conceptions. After all, the Greco-Roman world is by no means an unethical, amoral sphere that is full of sin, immorality, lack of love, and mutual violence and injustice, as early Jewish and early Christian writers like to polemically describe it (Rom 1.18ff.; 1 Thess 4.3ff.). Rather, from the beginning, the members and leaders of the early Christian communities found themselves to be in competition not only with the ethos and Torah interpretation of the synagogue communities but also with the philosophical schools' high-quality ethical conceptions of life.[39] Here, the concern was with material divergences and convergences and yet also with the terminology, literary forms, textual pragmatics, and degree of normative claim as well as with the types of communal forms and ethos and with the societal reach and so-called lived reality or practicability of the conceptions.

The Johannine letters develop a quite independent conception of life on the basis of love for brothers and sisters: a fellowship of brothers and sisters that is held together by love toward insiders (thus also Paul) and hatred

---

[38] Cf. Wischmeyer 2009a.

[39] Cf., e.g., the Roman concept of friendship: Williams 2012.

toward outsiders (unlike Paul), with the "outsiders" being especially
the "false brethren"—the beginning of the concept of heresy[40] in early
Christianity. Thus, to give one example, in a large city such as Ephesus at
the beginning of the second century CE, Jewish synagogal communities,
early Christian communities of Pauline tradition, groups of brothers and
sisters shaped in a Johannine manner, philosophically guided elite school
groups shaped in a Stoic or Epicurean manner, and different cultic associa-
tions existed alongside one another with various communitarian structures,
while the everyday familial forms of love in the different fellowships were
probably obligated more to the οἶκος concept and thus most likely not
entirely dissimilar to one another structurally.[41]

In summary, the New Testament concept of love is, on the one hand,
founded and focused on the double commandment of love for God and for
neighbor and thus is directly connected to a normative tradition complex
of the ethics of Israel and of ancient Judaism. On the other hand, Paul and
his school work out ἀγάπη as the center of a new ethic of early Christianity, which encompasses elements of virtues and emotions alongside rules
of behavior and action and does not argue in a normative and Torah-based
way but rather communicates in an exhortative and encouraging manner
and is realized in the communities as a communitarian culture. The writings of the Johannine school bring together both possibilities of thematiz-
ing love in the framework of early Christian forms of thought and life. In
this double structure the New Testament concept of love comes into view
for us as a new, distinctive voice in the ethical discourse of the imperial
period and at the same time as a fundamental ethical tradition.

## 4.2 ἀγάπη (2): Social and Institutional Dimensions

The ἀγάπη concept of the New Testament texts does not contain any
explicit social and institutional aspects, as these can be documented since
the second century CE in the *agape* meals of the communities and in the
development of the care for the poor.[42] Paul does not connect his admonitions for the meals in Corinth with his concept of love, nor do we find
such a connection in Acts.[43] In Acts 2.42–47 Luke uses the term κοινωνία

---

[40] Heresy means here αἵρεσις, separation, not offense against dogma, which was not
yet developed.

[41] This is already demonstrated by the mixed marriages with which Paul engages
positively in 1 Cor 7.

[42] Cf. Hauschild 1977.

[43] The stem occurs only four times in the Lukan work: Acts 15.25 in the apostolic
decree (the "beloved" Barnabas and Saul). We evidently find here the same linguistic usage

to designate the social dimension of the solidarity of the community.[44] Aspects of κοινωνία are common meals, common possessions, and common prayer. This term for fellowship, which occurs only here in the Lukan corpus, leads back, however, to Paul. Paul uses κοινωνία on several occasions for the collection[45] and in the context of the Lord's Supper.[46] Alongside it stands the term διακονία, which occurs both in the epistolary literature (Rom 15.31) and in Acts (Acts 1.17 and elsewhere).[47] The building up of the community, the structure of the ἐκκλησίαι, is also not primarily understood as part of the concept of love. Here, the σῶμα concept is guiding.

What is clear, however, is the implicit social and communitarian significance of the ἀγάπη culture to which the New Testament community letters exhort their readers. Alongside the previously presented ethical texts, some rather unspecific recommendations from the epistolary paraenesis point in this direction, such as Eph 4.2, 16 (the community as "body," which builds itself up in love) and Col 3.14 (love as σύνδεσμος τῆς τελειότητος). Second Thessalonians 1.3 invokes the love of the community members for one another, as does 1 Pet 4.8. In 1 Pet 4.9 there is an exhortation to hospitality (φιλόξενοι) and mutual service or help. These motifs can be found already in Paul. In Rom 12.9 Paul exhorts his readers to love without hypocrisy and in 14.15 to love for brothers and sisters (in the context of the strong and the weak in the community).[48] In 1 Cor 16.14 he writes:

**16.14** Let everything (that you do) be done in love.

In this context, the mutual address as brothers or *beloved* brothers[49] and sisters[50] has special significance. In the letters and in Acts we find a familial ethos that could be the foundation for communitarian, social, and institutional developments in the ἐκκλησίαι. In principle, it can be said that the ethical-emotional culture of ἀγάπη, as it was set forth by Paul, the Deutero-Paulines, and the Johannine writings, was conceptualized

---

as in the case of the "beloved son" (Luke 3.22; 9.35; 20.13). The term "love communism" (Troeltsch) has no point of contact in the Lukan semantics.

[44] Cf. Jervell 1998, 154–58 (literature on topic of fellowship).

[45] Rom 15.26; 2 Cor 8.4; 9.13.

[46] 1 Cor 10.16.

[47] Cf. Hentschel 2007; 2010; 2013.

[48] Thus also the exhortation to love for the brother in 2 Cor 2.8.

[49] Very frequently in Acts and in the epistolary literature.

[50] "Sister" occurs four times in the undisputed letters of Paul: Rom 16.1; 1 Cor 7.15; 9.5; Phil 2. Cf. 1 Tim 5.2; and Jas 2.15.

communally rather than individually. It was not set forth as a philosophical
ethic or as an elite ethos but as a concept of lived reality in the emerging
Christ-confessing communities, which, for their part, at least as far as the
Johannine community was concerned, had elitist tendencies in religious
respects.

### 4.3 ἀγάπη (3): Theological and Eschatological Dimensions

The tradition complex of love for neighbor and the communitarian culture
of Christ-confessing communities are important aspects of the New Testament concept of ἀγάπη. Love is, however, *more* than ethical demand,
and ἀγάπη is not identical with love for neighbor or love for brothers and
sisters or communitarian culture. Rather, ἀγάπη also has theological components. The Christian concept of love is only constituted by the three
components of ethics, ἐκκλησία, and theology.

Love is, first, the inner fundamental movement in God, which finds its
strongest expression as God's love for his Son. Second, it is God's love
for human beings, which is realized in Jesus' death for human beings.
Third, it is the love of Christ-confessing members of the early Christian
communities for one another, which picks up the love commandments
of the Old Testament and finds expression as a constructive attitude and
as helping action. Fourth, it is their love for God—though this perspective recedes significantly in comparison with the conceptual world of the
Old Testament.

The roots of the theological dimension of ἀγάπη lie again in the Old
Testament. Love for God can be described as the habitual, essential character of early Christian religion in a certain continuity with ancient Judaism. This is also true for the *love* of God for human beings. By contrast,
love for Jesus Christ and Jesus Christ's love for human beings are part
of the distinctive early Christian theological linguistic and conceptual
world,[51] whose beginnings the New Testament authors since Paul likewise
develop on the basis of "scripture." Beyond this, the combining of the
two commandments of the Hebrew Bible into a double commandment
of love is, as already presented, first attested in the New Testament in the
literary form of a saying of Jesus. The Johannine writings join together
both aspects into a cycle of the love of God via Jesus Christ for human
beings, of the love of human beings for one another, and, again, for Jesus
Christ and for God (John 14). Here, love is expanded into something like
a cosmic principle—the λόγος was with the Father before the beginning

---

[51] Here, 'theology' means the ideational reflection of the early Christian Christ-
religion and its linguistic versions.

of creation—and is at the same time concentrated in the Johannine letters on the love for brothers and sisters of the Johannine communities, which are already threatened by schism, αἵϱεσις, as the de facto antithesis to ἀγάπη.[52] While the speculative expansion of the concept of love into a cosmic principle is only worked out in the Johannine writings, the notion that God loved the world or human beings and 'gave (up)'[53] or 'sent'[54] his beloved Son for their salvation already underlies Paul's letter to the Romans and is then made even more prominent in the Gospel of John. The comprehensive narrative of God's love reaches from the "time before time" until the eschaton.

In summary, the New Testament concept of love cannot be reduced to its ethical and communal significance but has, beyond this, a theological dimension. This is made clear by the double commandment of love for God and love for neighbor and by its adaption in 1 John 4.19:

**4.19** Let us love one another, for he has first loved us.

Here, it must be stated at the same time that a presentation of the early Christian concept of love is something different from a New Testament ethics *in nuce*. ἀγάπη can neither be reduced to ethics, as John the Elder wanted to do, if we can trust Jerome, nor, conversely, are the ethics of the New Testament and early Christian authors exhausted in the reproduction of the commandment of love for neighbor. New Testament ethical instruction concerns the most varied life situations and is not reducible to the behavioral and action form of love for neighbor.

### 5. Historical Interpretation and Critical Dialogue with Contemporary Concepts

I pointed out already at the beginning that the present study goes back to a perception of a threefold deficit.[55] First, in the societal discourse on ethics, "love for neighbor" has been linguistically and materially pushed aside onto the pious or ecclesial-caritative sidetrack. Correspondingly, the phrase "love for neighbor" itself also does not appear (any longer) in general ethical discussions. Second, the religious dimension of love has entirely

---

[52] This is the reason for the role that hatred plays in the Johannine letters.

[53] Cf. John 3.16; Rom 8.32. The basis for the notion or theological motif was probably Gen 22.16, the offering of Isaac (see also Heb 11.17).

[54] 1 John 4.9.

[55] I refer again to A. Badiou, who—on very different philosophical-political premises—makes an analogous experience of deficits the starting point for his "praise of love." See Badiou/Truong 2012.

disappeared from all scholarly discourses on "love/loving," "caritas," and "social action," since in Western scholarly discourse, where philosophical ethics, sociology, and psychology especially make their voices heard, recourse to religious interpretations of the world is obsolete.[56] Third, the converse also applies. Theology, as the scholarly and intellectual articulation of the Christian religion, has de facto lost its place as a participant in these discussions.

New Testament scholarship cannot ignore this situation if it does not want to restrict itself to the task of historical reconstruction but rather seeks to keep the hermeneutical basic datum of the New Testament texts in view—that these are formative (not normative) texts whose direct reception history and *Wirkungsgeschichte* and thus also their material claim and the manner of interpreting them reaches from the time of their emergence into the present.[57] What can the task of New Testament scholarship be in this situation? First and foremost, it must become clear what love for neighbor and ἀγάπη mean in the New Testament texts, how the concept of love leads beyond love for neighbor, and which dimensions of reality and imagination it discloses.

The *conceptualization* then makes it possible to bring the New Testament concept into conversation with current conceptions of love, through which its own contours are worked out more clearly and with which further-reaching critical questions are associated. Thus, what the present study offers is an analysis of the New Testament concept that understands the historical reconstruction not only as the most recent revision of "exegetical positions" but, beyond this, as a basis for processing the further-reaching question of which ethical and theological artefact of the *past* we are dealing with *and* whether we can also see *potential for the present and future* in this concept. This question can first be addressed on the basis of a *comparative* analysis, which looks at the New Testament concept of love from the perspective of current models of love.

---

[56] To name one example, Nussbaum 1999b, 264, writes, "We will, of course, have to rule out, as unavailable any cultural variant that is built on metaphysical beliefs we can no longer accept, or forms of life we can never replicate: in that sense, medieval courtly love is not a live option." Here, the expression "of course" is interesting. It seeks to make any material argumentation superfluous. However, Badiou's insistence on the immanent transcendence of love is a somewhat helpless reaction to the perception that love, also in present-day understanding, cannot be reduced to empathy or social *commitment* as it is by Martha Nussbaum.

[57] Cf. Wischmeyer 2012a. Cf. also the discussion of this essay in Becker/Scholz 2014. To be precise, the responsibility of (Old Testament and) New Testament scholarship in relation to theology as a whole lies here, so long as these scholarly disciplines understand themselves as part of Christian theology.

An exclusive concentration or restriction to the historical reconstruction of New Testament concepts, which can appear natural from the perspective of an exclusively historical and reconstructive understanding of New Testament scholarship, is not advisable, especially in the case of the topic of love. Works such as those of Michel Foucault, Pierre Bourdieu, Giorgio Agamben, Julia Kristeva, and Simon May, as well as the thematically related analyses of Martha Nussbaum and theoretical conceptions such as that of Niklas Luhmann show that it is precisely the *connection* of historical and current analysis, of exegetical interpretation, hermeneutical appraisal, and critical questioning of a concept under the conditions of the present that discloses certain themes, and these themes can play a role in present-day discourse—here the ethical discourse in the broadest sense. The early Christian concept of love is a great and classic concept, which has its specific historical place and its complex reception history, which is carried forward in the present by the Christian churches, and which must be preserved in a scholarly and communicatively effective way by all the disciplines of theology. In the general discourse on love, which receives broad attention specifically outside of theology,[58] it must reposition itself and allow itself to be subjected to critical questioning, and yet, at the same time, it can, in turn, serve as a starting point for questioning other positions and concepts. This last direction in particular is important, for only a conceptual *comparison* in both directions can plumb the depths of the extent to which the early Christian concept of love can represent a voice of its own in the present discourse—motivated by cultural and societal scholarship—on *eros*, emotion, and empathy, and function not only as the object but also as the subject of criticism.

---

[58] Cf. just Pechriggl 2009; May 2011. The presentation of the early Christian conception by A. Pechriggl, however, moves between cliché and a lack of subject knowledge.

# 1

# *The Love Commandment in the New Testament*

## 1. The Commandments of Love for God and Love for Neighbor: Tradition History as Interpretive Method for Normative Tradition

On the one hand, we read the early Christian writings as that which each of them wanted to be read in their own time, situation, and intention—namely, as individual writings: community letter, Gospel, report, revelation. They are expressions of fundamental religious, theological, and ethical convictions and statements of their authors and their environment. On the other hand, we interpret these individual writings of the first "Christians" with the eyes of the early church and the churches that followed not only as individual texts but also as a material unity, i.e., as a structure of texts of proclamation, interpretation, and leadership that are differentiated and individual[1] in detail but coherent in principle and that consciously and intentionally want to be distinguished from other endeavors of a religious and philosophical character. From both perspectives, historical comparison is indispensable. Since the establishment of historical scholarship, the task of interpretation encompasses the work of critical historical derivation and comparison, which is often called historical contextualization today. Both lines of questioning apply both to the individual writings and to the early Christian literature in its entirety. Historical derivation (*Herleitung*) remains an indispensable hermeneutical approach insofar as is not understood in a one-sidedly causal manner as derivations (*Ableitungen*)[2] or associated with the model of natural

---

[1] This word might appear rather inappropriate for the description of ancient phenomena. It is, however, indispensable in light of the variety of religious and ethical conceptions of the New Testament authors.

[2] Understood as "sources" or "influences" and placed into "developmental" schemes.

19

growth.[3] For our topic, it can be accomplished by means of tradition history. This tradition history is fundamental for early Christian ἀγάπη, for *at the beginning of the early Christian concept of love stands the tradition*, expressed in the form of scriptural quotations. The roots of this concept lie in two commandments from the Pentateuch. In the opening formula of one of the great speeches of Moses in Deuteronomy, Moses implores the Israelites:

> **6.4** Hear, O Israel (*Shema' Israel*): The Lord (Yahweh) is our God, the Lord alone (אחד). **5** You shall love the Lord your God with all your heart, and with all your soul, and with all your might. **6** Keep these words that I am commanding you today in your heart. **7** Recite them to your children and talk about them when you are at home and when you are away, when you lie down and when you rise.[4]

The commandment of love for God (part of the so-called *Shema' Israel*) occurs in this strict form only in this text. However, the notion that the Israelites should love (Hebrew אהב, Greek ἀγαπᾶν) Yahweh, their God, appears frequently in Deuteronomy and in later writings of the Tanakh or Septuagint.[5] The commandment of love for neighbor uses the same lexeme, אהב. It does not belong to the Decalogue but is part of one of the most extensive series of commandments and prohibitions in Leviticus:

> **19.17** You shall not hate in your heart anyone of your kin; you shall reprove your neighbor, or you will incur guilt yourself. **18** You shall not take vengeance or bear a grudge against any of your people, but you shall love your neighbor as yourself: I am the LORD (Yahweh).[6]

The commandments and prohibitions summarized in Lev 19.1–18 are introduced by a holiness formula, ended in each case with the pointer "I am the LORD" and concluded with the commandment of love for neighbor. The commandments and prohibitions are close to the Decalogue in parts, whereas parts deal with specifications for sacrifice. The commandment of love for neighbor, which is not part of the Decalogue, has a prominent position in this series but is characterized neither as a summary nor as the most important commandment in the whole series. In 19.34 we hear an echo:

---

[3] Understood as "development."

[4] Trans. NRSV (O.W.'s insertions).

[5] Cf., for an introduction, Spieckermann 2000. Spieckermann points to the significance of love for Deuteronomy: "The theological enrichment . . . also includes the notion of the established and admonished relationship of love between God and Israel" (191). See also Spieckermann 2001b.

[6] Lev 19.17–18; trans. NRSV (O.W.'s insertion).

**19.34** The alien who resides with you shall be to you as the citizen among you; you shall love the alien as yourself, for you were aliens in the land of Egypt: I am the Lord (Yahweh) your God.[7]

Neither of the two commandments is repeated or directly quoted in the writings of the Tanakh. In the early Jewish writings that do not belong to the canon of the Bible of Israel, the demands for love for God and love for neighbor are carried on, without the Torah having to be cited directly. The Torah is living, relevant, and effective. It is read out and is the guide for life. It therefore does not need to be repeated or quoted literarily. The commandments develop their normative authority from their canonical context. Actual *citations* first arise in the New Testament writings, in Paul and in the Gospels. Thus, in Rom 13.9, Paul defines the commandment of love for neighbor as the ἀνακεφαλαίωσις, as the sum of all the commandments "of the law." Correspondingly, in the Gospel of Mark, Jesus defines the commandment of love for God (*Shema ῾ Israel*) and the commandment of love for neighbor as the first and greatest "commandments" (Mark 12.28–34 par.). In the two rather different texts, the concern is with the same topic—with the *proper* "fulfillment of the law" (Rom 13.8). Here, fulfillment does not mean the correct observance of an individual commandment but the summary of all the demands of the Torah, i.e., an ethical centering in a basic attitude, namely, of ἀγάπη.

What is the significance of the citation of Old Testament individual commandments in Paul and the Gospel of Mark? It is only the *selective* and *excluding* aspect that makes the repetition of a sentence or a statement into an actual citation.[8] The *explicit citation* is made possible by the commandment structure of the two statements and the authority that is given to them through this. The citation, however, contains not only the element of affirmation but also and in the first place that of distance. Accordingly, Günter Stemberger writes, "The quotation of a biblical text attests, in distinction from its inner-biblical interpretation or updating, the consciousness of distance from the text that is commented on. Explicit quotations arise only at the end of the biblical [sc. Old Testament] literature (Dan 9.2)."[9] Correspondingly, we find a rich citation culture in the writings

---

[7] Trans. NRSV (O.W.'s insertion).

[8] Cf. Krispenz et al. 2009.

[9] Stemberger 2009, 692. For an in-depth discussion of early Jewish citations in the theoretical context of intertextuality and citationality, see Lange/Weigold 2011, 15–48, esp. 21–23. Lange/Weigold do not, however, use G. Genette's comprehensive concepts but J. Kristeva's definition of the reference to earlier texts by later texts. The distinguishing precision of Stemberger's definition cannot, of course, be reached by Lange/Weigold and is not intended to be. For our topic, however, precisely this distinguishing precision is important.

from Qumran and in the primitive Christian writings. This applies not so much to the repetition, confirmation, and practice of the Torah, but it is an important instrument in the interpretive controversy that flares up over the Bible of Israel between "heretical" Jewish groups such as the "Qumran community" and the "Jesus movement," on the one hand, and so-called "common Judaism," on the other hand. The tradition history draws its relevance from this controversy over the traditions. Thus, the concern here is not with motifs that wander and can be called up from the great reservoir of religious-cultural conceptions and integrated into the most diverse contexts, but rather with formed texts, in oral (tradition) or written (quotation or allusion) form, which are handed down with the goal of supporting one's own argument through the authority of the tradition.[10] The citation creates difference and change, not simply confirmation. In what follows, I will therefore pursue the tradition history of the two commandments in order to be able to present the basis of the love commandments and the history of their interpretation.[11]

Especially with a topic such as that of the love commandments, very detailed analysis may seem tedious. It has its raison d'être, however, in the literature with which we are dealing. Its essential distinguishing features are appeal to tradition, extreme brevity, and claim to religious-ethical authority. A precise tradition-historical detailed analysis does justice to this.

## 2. Basis in the Torah

### 2.1 The Commandment of Love for God

*The commandment to love God* is found in Deuteronomy.[12] The whole book of Deuteronomy is composed as a large farewell discourse of Moses. Moses recapitulates first the history of the wilderness wandering and the revelation of God on Mount Horeb, or Sinai (Deut 1–11), before he proclaims in Deut 12.1–26.16 the so-called Deuteronomic law, a second collection of laws (Deut 17.18) after the so-called book of the covenant (Exod 21–23). The commandment in Deut 6.4 occurs not in the Deuteronomic law but belongs to the second preparatory speech of Moses in the first part of the book (Deut 4.44–11.32). It is paraenetic in character and looks back to the revelation of God on Horeb. The speech is rooted in the idea of the covenant:

---

[10] A motif lacks the element of authority.

[11] The great study of Berger 1972, 56–257, remains fundamental for the topic. Berger distinguishes less clearly among motifs, tradition, and quotation.

[12] For an introduction, see Gertz 2010, 247–60, with an outline on p. 248 and a discussion of the *Shema ʿIsrael* on p. 249. See further Lohfink 1963; Achenbach 1991; Spieckermann 2000.

**5.3** Not with our ancestors did the LORD make this covenant, but with us, who are all of us here alive today. **4** The LORD spoke with you face to face at the mountain, out of the fire.[13]

This introduction is followed by a repetition of the Ten Commandments, which God directly communicated to the people (5.6–22). God communicates the further commandments from 6.1 onward not to the people but to Moses, who mediates them to the people. At the beginning of these commandments, i.e., at a prominent position,[14] stands the aforementioned *Shema ʿ Israel*, which is part of the treaty concept between the God of Israel and the people Israel. The commandment has two parts. The wording of v. 4 permits several interpretations. The Hebrew formulation יהוה אלהינו יהוה אחד can be translated as "Yahweh our God is one." With this Moses formally obligates Israel to *monolatry*: Israel worships only *one* Lord, the God of Israel.[15] Exegetes think here of mono-Yahwism and cult concentration. The translation of אחד as "unique" (*einzig*), which is also possible, modifies the sense of the commandment and transitions to verse 5, which characterizes this worship materially: Israel is to "love" God.[16] This is the mode of *covenantal worship*. How can one envisage this love? Timo Veijola points to the element of loyalty in אהב and assigns the commandment very precisely to the covenant idea. In this context, the commandment of love does not represent a *contradictio in adiecto*. Veijola

---

[13] Deut 5.3–4; trans. NRSV.

[14] Cf. Veijola 2004, 174–93. Veijola assumes that the *Shema ʿ Israel* "once formed the beginning of Deuteronomy" and belonged to the oldest stratum of Deuteronomy, whereas he regards 6.5 as a later comment (175). Nielsen 1995, 85, is critical of this view. We cannot discuss here the stratification and complex and controversial tradition history of the book of Deuteronomy.

[15] Cf. Gertz 2010, 249. Gertz ascribes this interpretation to the older tradition of 6.4–5. Veijola 2004, 177–78, is critical of this view. Cf. Veijola 1992a; 1992b.

[16] Thus, e.g., with great firmness Braulik 1986, 55–56:

The confession "Yahweh is unique (*einzig*) originally does not seek to ward off the disintegration of the unity of Yahweh into different place-bound 'individual Yahwehs.'" . . . It also does not ground his cult at a single place on the basis of Yahweh's nature. . . . Rather, "unique" is a topos of love language (Song 6.8–9). Thus, Deut 6.4–5 proclaims Yahweh's claim to exclusivity in a love relationship. . . . What is meant is a legally enjoined, exclusive relation of loyalty, a complete commitment in obedience, which includes at the same time thankfulness and trust and is realized emotionally in a personal, intimate sphere of experience.

Braulik thus understands verses 4 and 5 as a unit of meaning, whereas Veijola differentiates between the two verses tradition-historically, though he also ultimately translates with "unique" (*einzig*). Weinfeld 1991, 351, confirms the emotional element but stresses that "the practical meaning of the command of love is loyalty and obedience, as it is clear from the continuation."

writes, "The promising commandment of love for Yahweh (cf. Mark 12.28–32) does not mean a sentimental love, but seeks to be understood in the sense of the ancient Near Eastern political treaties, which can also express the fundamental relationship of loyalty and service of the vassal with his suzerain through the demand for love."[17] Thus, Moses can also call for "fear" instead of love in Deut 6.13.

> **6.13** The Lord your God you shall fear; him you shall serve, and by his name alone you shall swear.[18]

Both stances express the ancient Near Eastern understanding of loyalty, which determines the relationship between the God of Israel and his people in Deuteronomy.[19] However, this relationship of loyalty has not only legal character but is also interpreted as a personally obligating and culturally shaping entity when love for God is to be pursued "with all your heart, and with all your soul, and with all your might"—adverbial specifications that also express the inner intensity of the relationship to Yahweh.[20] The justification lies in the uniqueness of the relationship of Yahweh to Israel: "Because the Lord your God, who is present with you, is a jealous God" (6.15).[21] Here, *qanā᾽* (אֵל קַנָּא; LXX: ζηλωτής) is to be understood in a personal and exclusive way as "jealous."[22] We also find this notion of Yahweh as the jealous God who has chosen his people in the Decalogue (5.9). In general, chapter 6 can be interpreted as a commentary on the Decalogue.[23] To the jealous God corresponds the complete devotion and obligation of the covenant people and its individual members ("you" [sg.]). The covenant is a bond of life, love, and faithfulness, which is dangerous, indeed deadly, to break (5.9; 6.15). Deut 7.7–9 then makes clear that with the commandment to love God we are dealing with a reciprocal relationship in which the people react to God's prevenient love:

> **7.7** It was not because you were more numerous than any other people that the Lord set his heart on you and chose you—for you were the

---

[17] Veijola 2004, 189.

[18] Trans. NRSV.

[19] Moran 1963, 77–87. Christensen 1991, 143–44, sets a somewhat different accent and points out that in the case of the love commandment we are dealing not only with an ancient Near Eastern way of speaking but with a central demand of Deuteronomy. For this view, see also Nielsen 1995, 86. Nielsen refers to the proximity to Hosea; cf. also Zobel 1992, 8–87.

[20] Deut 6.5; trans. NRSV. On these specifications, cf. Nielsen 1995, 87.

[21] Trans. NRSV.

[22] Veijola 2004, 190. Cf. also the position of Braulik.

[23] Veijola 2004, 188.

fewest of all peoples. **8** It was because the LORD loved you and kept the oath that he swore to your ancestors, that the LORD has brought you out with a mighty hand, and redeemed you from the house of slavery, from the hand of Pharaoh king of Egypt. **9** Know therefore that the LORD your God is God, the faithful God who maintains covenant loyalty with those who *love* him and keep his commandments for a thousand generations.[24]

In summary, it is clear that the commandment to love God is part of the covenant between God and his chosen people, Israel. It has special significance as the second part of the *Shema 'Israel*. The commandment applies to Israel and the individual Israelites. The love that is called for is the love of loyalty within the covenant. It is, however, not purely legal in nature but is also characterized by personal responsibility and comprehensive obedience toward the covenantal charter, the Torah. In its loyalty it corresponds to the love of God for the people of Israel. In the unconditionality of its loyalty to God and in walking according to the covenantal charter there is indeed an emotional component of affirmation and joy in the law.

### 2.2 The Commandment of Love for Neighbor

*The commandment to love one's neighbor*[25] occurs in Lev 19. The book of Leviticus is "exclusively devoted to the tasks of the priestly-Levitical service and thus to the Old Testament worship service as well as the cultic capacity of priests and lay persons."[26] Chapter 19 occupies a special position in this collection. It belongs to the textual unit of chapters 17–26, the so-called Holiness Code,[27] and is "a collection of commandments and prohibitions of varying content and different forms."[28] Martin Noth finds a certain unifying theme in chapter 19:

---

[24] Trans. NRSV.

[25] On this, cf., in general, Mathys 1990; Neudecker 1992; Ebersohn 1993. Cf. now also Söding 2015.

[26] Kornfeld 1983, 5.

[27] Lev 17–26. On the term "Heiligkeitsgesetz" (Holiness Code), cf. Klostermann 1877. For an introduction, see Gertz 2010, 232–33. The holiness of Yahweh and the holiness of Israel are related to each other: Lev 19.2. The history of the emergence of the Holiness Code is controversial and cannot be discussed here. Two statements correspond to the exegetical majority position: (1) if "this conception of holiness" is rooted "in priestly thinking," (2) it can be the case "that the Holiness Code in legal-historical and literary-historical perspective embodies a conscious continuation and correction of Deuteronomy" (232). Cf. the table in Gertz 2010, 238: the book of Leviticus as part of the supplements of the so-called independent Priestly code (*Priesterschrift*).

[28] Kornfeld 1983, 72. The strata of the chapter cannot be discussed here. In the present text, chapter 19 represents a distinct textual unit, which concludes with the reference to the

The same is true of the contents. It is seen to be relatively self-contained insofar as it deals in general with the right behaviour of individuals (i.e. according to God's will), in the circumstances of daily life within the framework of the community to which he belongs. In detail, however, the different departments of life are arranged very much at random.[29]

According to Noth, the statements in Lev 19.15–18 apply not only to judges, as one could assume on the basis of the mention of court (מֹשְׁפָּט) in v. 15, but to the "legal community 'at the gate,'" to which every fully enfranchised Israelite belonged."[30] For Noth the statements therefore contain "a code of behavior applicable to all Israelites in their relations with other members of the community in which they lived,"[31] i.e., they have a social-ethical legal character:

> **19.15** You shall not act unjustly in court (מֹשְׁפָּט); you shall not be partial to the poor or defer to the great: with justice you shall judge your neighbor (עֲמִית, associate/πλησίον). **16** You shall not go around as a slanderer among your people (עַם), and you shall not profit by the blood of your neighbor (עֲמִית/πλησίον): I am the LORD (Yahweh). **17** You shall not hate in your heart anyone of your kin (אָח); you shall reprove your neighbor (עֲמִית/πλησίον), or you will incur guilt yourself. **18** You shall not take vengeance or bear a grudge against any of your people, but you shall love (אהב/ἀγαπᾶν) your neighbor (רֵע/πλησίον) as yourself: I am the LORD (Yahweh).[32]

Verses 17 and 18 are closely tied to each other and show a clear structure: prohibition, commandment, justification.[33] For the question of how the Hebrew רֵע (neighbor) is to be interpreted, the equivalents of verses 15–18 must be drawn upon. Noth points out that in this text companion, brother, compatriot, and neighbor cannot be distinguished semantically. This means that the "neighbor" is every member of the legal community, and the statement about love for neighbor there "relates especially to behavior in the legal community."[34] In the context of the Holiness Code, Lev 19.18

---

relationship between God's holiness and the holiness of the people Israel (v. 1) and with the corroboration "I (am) Yahweh."

[29] Noth 1965, 138 (GV = Noth 1962, 119).

[30] Noth 1965, 141 (GV = Noth 1962, 122).

[31] Noth 1965, 141 (GV = Noth 1962, 122). Thus also Milgrom 2000, 1654. Milgrom points out that Jesus and Rabbi Hillel interpret "neighbor" universally, whereas Deuteronomy thinks of the fellow Israelite.

[32] Lev 19.15–18; trans. NRSV, modified (O.W.'s insertions).

[33] See Milgrom 2000, 1646.

[34] Noth 1965, 142 (GV = 1962, 122).

has neither an individual-ethical nor emotional connotation, but refers to interactions with compatriots according to the rules of the Israelite legal community. This circumstance explains the sense in which *love can be commanded* there. Jacob Milgrom comments, "How can love be commanded? The answer simply is that the verb *'ahab* signifies not only an emotion or attitude, but also deeds. This is especially true in Deuteronomy, which speaks of covenantal love."[35] Erhard S. Gerstenberger therefore summarizes as follows: Love for neighbor is "wholly a community-related and for that reason 'political' term, and not an individualistic term. Against the background of family solidarity, it refers to the shared connection and mutual responsibility of human beings living in a community of faith."[36] This interpretation gains in plausibility when the consistent translation with πλησίον in the Septuagint is taken into account. πλησίον simply means 'neighbor' and has neither an individual-ethical nor an emotive connotation. Thus, in the context of Leviticus, the neighbor or companion refers to the persons of the Israelite legal community and not to foreigners or resident aliens, for whom there were rules of their own, and certainly not to 'all human beings.' רֵעַ/πλησίον is a group-related term, and Lev 19.18 is a group-related demand. The basis for all varieties of the early Christian reception history of the commandment of love for neighbor lies here.

## 3. New Testament Texts

The two commandments of love for God and love for neighbor never occur together in the Tanakh, and there are no indications of an overarching idea or concept of "love," which could encompass love for God and love for neighbor and systematically coordinate them with each other. The commandments have their own respective places and their different weight in the legal and religious community of Israel. The New Testament writings quote both commandments in new communitarian structures and place them in different combinations and contexts.

### 3.1 The Double Commandment of Love

The commandment of *love for God* from Deut 6.5 is never quoted alone in the writings of the New Testament.[37] It occurs exclusively in connection

---

[35] Milgrom 2000, 1653.

[36] Gerstenberger 1996, 272 (GV = 1993, 248).

[37] On the *Shema'* in Paul, cf. Waaler 2008. For the *Shema'* in Deut 6.4, see pp. 98–114. For the double commandment (Mark 12.28–31 and Matt 22. 34–40), see pp. 216–26.

with the commandment of *love for neighbor* from Lev 19.18, namely only
in Mark 12.29ff. and the parallels (Matt 22.37; Luke 10.27).[38] The situation is different with the quotation of the commandment of love for neighbor from Lev 19.18. This commandment has more weight of its own in the
New Testament writings and is also cited alone—in Gal 5.14 and Jas 2.8,
with an addition in Matt 5.43 and together with the statements from the
Decalogue in Matt 19.19 and Rom 12.9–10.

The so-called double commandment of love in the form of the selective double Torah quotation in the Gospel of Mark is a product of the early
Christian critical engagement with the validity of the individual commandments of the Torah of Israel.[39] Let us begin with the question of the
linguistic form and literary context of the double quotation in the Gospel
of Mark.[40] The exchange over the "greatest commandment" appears in
Jesus' short activity in Jerusalem before the Passover (Mark 11–13). Jesus
enters Jerusalem as the Messiah of peace, "cleanses" the temple from the
money changers' tables and merchants' seats and clashes with the religious and municipal Jewish authorities. His authority (ἐξουσία) becomes
a problem (Mark 11.28–29):[41]

> **11.28** And they (the Jerusalem authorities) said to him, "By what author-
> ity (ἐξουσία)[42] are you doing these (things)?" And who has given you
> this authority that you do these things? **29** Jesus said to them, "I will ask
> you one question; if you answer me, I will tell you by what authority I
> do these things."

Jesus then asks about the authority of John the Baptist. The Jerusalem authorities cannot answer, and Jesus concludes the discussion with the words:

> **11.33** Neither will *I* tell you by what authority I am doing these things.

---

[38] In 1 Cor 8.4 and Jas 2.19, there is a pointer to the first sentence of the *Shema ῾Israel*
(not a quotation) in the use of the short form εἷς θεός (though in Paul in a text that is reformulated in a rather independent way). The second part of the *Shema ῾* is not cited. On this,
cf. Wischmeyer 2004d. A concise examination of the topic can be found in Schnelle 2005b.

[39] For the closely related early Jewish tradition, see below. From the abundant literature, I mention Bornkamm 1957; Burchard 1974; Berger 1972; Fuller 1978; Wischmeyer
2004a, 136–61, esp. 147–54. For the Gospel of Mark, see Yarbro Collins 2007, 565–77
(lit.); Söding 2014.

[40] On all the details, cf. Yarbro Collins 2007, 512–90. For the sake of simplicity, we
will often use the names of the evangelists in what follows. The ascriptions of the evangelists to authors come from the second century CE and are not historically secure.

[41] On this, cf. Scornaienchi 2016.

[42] In German, ἐξουσία can be translated with *Vollmacht* or *Autorität*. *Auctoritas* is the
Latin equivalent of ἐξουσία. Cf. Wischmeyer 2009d.

With this the keyword for what follows is given: Jesus' surpassing authority becomes even more prominent in chapter 12 of the Markan narrative. First, in the form of a parable he presents his fate in the context of the history of God with Israel and with his prophetic interpretation makes himself the Lord of the coming events of his arrest and execution (12.1–12).[43] In a second narrative block, the Jewish political and religious leaders make two failed attempts to force Jesus into compromising interpretations of the Torah.[44] The third exchange leads to a detailed affirmation of Jesus' answer by the inquiring scribe.[45] With this the narrative takes an unexpected turn. Jesus, in turn, then asks the public in the temple a question that concerns the interpretation of the Torah.[46] With regard to this question, Jesus' authority is so decisive that the answer of the Jerusalem authorities is not even mentioned. The textual unit ends already with Jesus' question. In conclusion, Jesus reproaches the scribes. The political and religious Jewish authorities have suffered a complete defeat in the controversy over the correct interpretation of Torah. Jesus has emerged from the dispute over the correct interpretation as master and has proven his authority as teacher.

The individual textual units in Mark 12 all share the topic of *Torah interpretation*. This begins with the parable that closes with a reference to Ps 118 and ends with Jesus' question about the correct interpretation of Ps 110.[47] The textual unit of the *double commandment of love* with its recourse to Deut 6 and Lev 19.18 is situated in this context. Jesus' answer represents the material high point of the chapter. The inquiring teacher of the law not only agrees with Jesus' answer but repeats it in altered form, so that the double commandment receives a singular emphasis and material confirmation (Mark 12.28–34):

**12.28** And one of the scribes came to him, who had heard how they argued with one another.[48] And when he saw that he (Jesus) had answered him well, he asked him, "Which is the first[49] commandment of all?" **29** Jesus answered, "The first is, 'Hear, O Israel, the Lord our God, the

---

[43] This motif does not occur for the first time in the Gospel of John but is already a load-bearing component of the Gospel of Mark from the first passion prediction (8.31) onward.

[44] Mark 12.13–17: Pharisees and Herodians; 12.18–27: Sadducees.

[45] Mark 12.28–34.

[46] Mark 12.35–37.

[47] The short episode with the poor widow in Mark 12.41–44 illustrates the piety that the scribes who are reproached in vv. 38–40 lack (catchword connection: v. 40 and v. 42).

[48] Greek συζητεῖν, "to discuss." On the topic of the controversy dialogues in Mark, cf. Scornaienchi 2016.

[49] Greek πρώτη, "the first," used here in the sense of "importance."

Lord is one, **30** and you shall love the Lord, your God, with all your heart
and with all your soul and with all your mind and with all your strength.'
**31** The second is this: 'You shall love your neighbor as yourself.' There
is no other commandment greater than these." **32** And the scribe said to
him, "Quite right, Teacher, you have truly said that 'he is one and there is
no other except him'; **33** and 'to love him with all the heart and with all
the understanding and with all the strength' and 'to love the neighbor as
yourself' is more than all whole burnt offerings and sacrifices." **34** And
when Jesus saw that he answered thoughtfully, he said to him, "You are
not far from the kingdom of God." And no one dared any more to question him (about the interpretation of the Torah).

The text is very carefully composed, and it pays to read it with corresponding exactness. Four points initially merit attention.[50] First, a Jewish scribe
asks about the "first," i.e., most important, commandment (ἐντολή) of
all.[51] Second, Jesus responds positively to the question but answers without delay not with *one* but with *two* commandments, which he carefully
distinguishes, citing both Deut 6.4 and 6.5 for the first commandment.[52]
Third, the scribe quietly changes Jesus' answer in two respects. As a result,
he places the double commandment over sacrificial practice—an interpretation in the tradition of Hos 6.6 and 1 Sam 16.22, which Jesus had not
given himself. Through this, Jesus' answer receives an additional sense:
love for God and for neighbor stand over and thus consequently possibly
even *against* sacrificial piety. Moreover, the scribe alters the structure of
the two commandments. He isolates and emphasizes the first sentence of the
*Shema 'Israel*, thus stressing the commandment of monotheism, and then
joins *love* for God with *love* for neighbor into a unity. τὸ ἀγαπᾶν, *to love*,
becomes an attitude that stands over the addressees of the different love commandments in the Torah—namely, for God and for neighbor. The scribe
formulates with a noun and thus places the Torah commandments in proximity to the language of Hellenistic virtue ethics.[53] Fourth, the concluding
points refer not to Jesus but to the inquiring scribe. When Jesus testifies
to him that he is not far from the kingdom of God, he brings into play
the term that stands at the center of his own message—not the law but

---

[50] For all exegetical details, cf. Yarbro Collins 2007.

[51] What is meant is the 613 commandments in the Pentateuch.

[52] Matt 22.37 and Luke 10.27 are different. There the *Shema 'Israel* is lacking. The
Leviticus commandment is expanded with a specification: διάνοια. δύναμις is replaced
by ἰσχύς, probably in order to avoid the word sequence διάνοια-δύναμις.

[53] Yarbro Collins 2007, 577, classifies the text accordingly: it is said to have an
"affinity . . . with Greek popular philosophy, probably mediated by Greek-speaking Jews."

the kingdom of God (βασιλεία τοῦ θεοῦ). With this Jesus ultimately makes himself into the authorized interpreter of the will of God.

The decisive contribution of this text lies in the reformulation of the two individual commandments into the double commandment of the scribe, for the so-called double commandment is in the logic of the Markan text not already a creation of Jesus, who, after all, places two commandments alongside each other, but is first created by the Jewish scribe.[54] The reply of the scribe not only repeats Jesus' answer, thereby giving it an elevated significance and validity, but also bears its own dynamic, which develops Jesus' answer further. The starting point was the question about the "first commandment." Jesus answers with the quotation of two commandments, without joining them together[55] or commenting on them materially. The scribe first stylizes Deut 6.4, 5 and Lev 19.18 in such a way that the concern is no longer with *two* distinct commandments but with *one* ethical *basic attitude*, τὸ ἀγαπᾶν, which is superior to sacrifices as an expression of a cultic-ritual religious attitude (the question was not about them at all). The dynamic of the text leads from the standard question about the most important *commandment* to the *virtue* or attitude of ἀγάπη and thus leaves behind the initial question. Jesus' concluding statement explains that this ἀγαπᾶν can be connected with his proclamation of the kingdom of God. Thus, the Markan text, which takes the question of the first commandment as its point of departure, ends surprisingly with the attitude of ἀγαπᾶν, which, in turn, is moved close to Jesus' proclamation of the kingdom of God. The text affirms that there is in this point great closeness and, to some extent, agreement between Jesus and certain scribally educated Jews, so that, on the one hand, Jesus is the authoritative teacher of the Torah—the positive reaction of the scribe is, after all, an expression of the continuity of Jesus with the Torah and thus of his authority as teacher of scripture—and the interpretation of the Torah is not contested at all, and, on the other hand, it is precisely the scribe who finds the attitude of love in the Torah. The framing question, however, remains the question about Jesus' authoritative interpretation of scripture. The love commandments are only the *test case*, albeit the most important one. In the context of Mark 10–12, Jesus achieves here a comprehensive victory over his opponents among the Jewish religious authorities—namely, on the basis of the agreement on the interpretation of the Torah and not through Jesus' rejection, deviation, or reformulation with regard to the Torah.[56]

---

[54] This fact must receive special emphasis, even if one assumes, as Dunn 2003, 584–85, does, that Jesus himself put the two commandments together.

[55] We are, however, dealing with a catchword connection with אהב/ἀγαπᾶν.

[56] Thus in the antitheses of the Sermon on the Mount.

In summary, it does not lie in the logic of the text to characterize the answer of Jesus as 'double commandment of love' and understand it as his original ethical regulation—in the language of Jesus scholarship as a 'genuine' saying of Jesus. The 'double commandment' is first created by the scribe, and this means Mark in his reworking of the tradition.[57] It is not by chance that the answer of the scribe is lacking in Matthew and Luke. It does not belong to the tradition, however that is to be determined. It remains correct that the exclusive compilation of the commandments of Deut 6.5 and Lev 19.18 first occurs in the Gospel of Mark. Since additional source evidence is lacking, Mark 12.29–31 can be evaluated differently with respect to tradition history—as a reworking of the original Jesus tradition, as a community formation, or even as a literary scene that has been shaped entirely by the evangelist. Per Bilde has presented a new study on the quest for Jesus' originality and expresses himself cautiously with regard to the double love commandment: "Still, the formulations that the canonical gospels ascribe to Jesus are rather close to unique . . . , but they are not original and unique in any absolute sense."[58] One will not be able to get beyond this judgment also with respect to the tradition history. At the level of the redaction, however, it is clear that Mark does *not* place the so-called double commandment in the mouth of Jesus.[59]

The Markan pericope is taken up in distinct ways by the other Synoptic evangelists. The author of the Gospel of Matthew remains relatively close to the Markan text (Matt 22.34–40[60]).

**22.34** Now when the Pharisees heard that he had silenced the Sadducees, they gathered together. **35** And one of them, a scribe (νομικός), tested

---

[57] On the tradition behind the Jerusalem controversy dialogues, cf. Scornaienchi 2016.

[58] Bilde 2013, 99–107, on the state of the literature (esp. on G. Theissen, the quote on p. 104).

[59] Cf. the balanced judgment of Theissen/Merz 1998, 388 (GV = 2001, 345): "The twofold commandment fits well into the rest of Jesus' preaching. . . . So, if the twofold commandment to love should be secondary, there was good reason for attributing it to Jesus. At all events, it is characteristic of the Jesus tradition that the commandment to love was extended and intensified, so that it explicitly applies to all human beings. . . . There are also comparable approaches in Jewish writings, but the comprehensive opening up of the commandment to love in the Jesus tradition is without analogy." However, the documentation of the Jewish attestations in Theissen makes clear that the expression "without analogy" is an exaggeration.

[60] For the text, cf. throughout Luz 2005, 75–87 (GV = 1997, 269–85). On the relationship between the Markan version and the Matthean version, see pp. 75–76 (GV = 1997, 270–71). Luz plausibly regards Matt 22.34–40 as a Matthean reworking of the Markan text, whereas he reckons with a "special tradition" for the Lukan version (ET = 76–77; GV = 271). We cannot discuss here the question of the agreements between Matthew and Luke vis-à-vis Mark (the so-called minor agreements).

him and asked, **36** "Teacher, which is the greatest (μεγάλη[61]) command-ment (ἐντολή) in the law (νόμος)?" **37** And he (Jesus) answered him, "'You shall love the Lord your God with all your heart and with all your soul and with all your mind.' **38** This is the greatest and first command-ment. **39** And the second is like it: 'You shall love your neighbor as your-self.' **40** On these commandments hang all the law and the prophets."

Matthew follows Mark in situating the episode in Jerusalem and in the sequence of the episodes in Mark 12. This means that in Matt 22, as in Mark 12, the concern is with the *law* and with its authoritative[62] interpreta-tion by Jesus as teacher of the law (διδάσκαλος) in the conflict with the Jewish political and religious authorities in Jerusalem. In comparison with Mark, four observations are important. First, the opening question of the scribally educated Pharisee is similar to the question in Mark: "Which is the greatest (instead of 'first') commandment in the law (νόμος instead of 'of all')?" The question in Matthew, however, emphasizes the law even more clearly. Second, Matthew—like Luke as well—leaves out the *Shema' Israel*. Third, he alters the concluding formula of Mark, which related precisely to the question that was posed, in a distinctive way: "On these two commandments hang[63] all the law and the prophets." What does this expression mean for the question about the law? With Ulrich Luz the expression can be best rendered in a figurative sense as "to (make something) depend on an overarching principle."[64] With this it is clear that the double commandment does not, for example, nullify the validity of the 248 commandments and 365 prohibitions of the Torah but presents their inner raison d'être. Fourth, Matthew deleted the positive and continuing answer of the scribe. What is said here is that Jesus answers a certain important question regarding the law, which is posed in contemporary Judaism,[65] in a compact way. He is, as elsewhere in Matthew, the authori-tative teacher of the Torah.[66]

---

[61] Luz 2005, 82n71 (GV = 1997, 278n71) points out that the expression "great" com-mandment corresponds more to the Jewish linguistic usage than "first" commandment, though this expression also occurs in Jewish-Hellenistic literature.

[62] Cf. ἐξουσία in Matt 21.23 as point of departure of the episodes in Matt 21.24ff. (par. Mark 11.28 and Luke 20.2).

[63] κρεμάννυμι: "hang." Bauer 1988, 914, wishes to understand the expression pic-torially: "As a door in the hinges, so the whole OT hangs on these two commandments." Luz 2005, 85n96 (GV = 1997, 282n98) rightly rejects this interpretation. Greek doors were not hung.

[64] Luz 2005, 85 (GV = 1997, 282).

[65] On this, cf. Luz 2005, 81–82 (GV = 1997, 277–78).

[66] Cf. Matt 5.17–20. We also find the expression "the law and the prophets" there.

Ulrich Luz has traced further the radius of meaning of ἀγαπᾶν in this version of the double commandment: "Thus with 'to love God' the readers do not think of a feeling, nor do they think about prayers or a mystical flight from the world into union with God. They think instead of knowing the one God and of obeying him in the world. For them the love of God and the love of neighbor are closely related from the beginning."[67] To this corresponds the meaning of love for neighbor: "'love' means practical behavior and solidarity according to the commandments that God has given Israel."[68] With this Matthew adheres most closely to the stipulations of Deuteronomy and Leviticus. There we found the same connection between obedience and love. His handling of the Markan text is more critical and traditional. He retracts the distinctive interpretive features of the Gospel of Mark.

This changes in the presentation of Luke. Luke as a reader and reviser of the Gospel of Mark[69] detaches the narrative episode of the double commandment from the Jerusalem framework and assigns it instead to the second phase of the proclamation of Jesus, his peregrination from Galilee to Jerusalem:[70] Luke 10.25–37.[71] In this way the careful composition and the argumentative line of the collection of controversy dialogues in Mark 12 is severely disturbed—all the other episodes from Mark 12 are retained in Luke 20[72]—and the episode of the double commandment is also removed from its narrative context of the conflict of Jesus with the Jewish authorities in Jerusalem and of the demonstration of Jesus' own authority.[73] On the other hand, the religious backdrop of 'Jerusalem' is narratively present in a new form in the example story of the 'merciful Samaritan.' The author Luke gives the double commandment at the same time a new and very distinct

---

[67] Luz 2005, 83, modified (GV = 1997, 279).

[68] Luz 2005, 83 (GV = 1997, 279–80). Cf. also Luz's more general reflections on pp. 77–81 (GV = 271–76).

[69] On the relationship between the Gospel of Mark and the Gospel of Luke, cf., by way of introduction, Wolter 2016, 12–18 (GV = 2008, 10–16 [lit.]). See further Schürmann 1994, 125–50 (lit.), esp. 136–40. Cf. also Klein 2006, 386–94. Klein assumes that Luke 10.25–29 comes from Luke and that he has also created the dialogue form (388).

[70] Luke 9.51–19.27 ("travel narrative").

[71] On all the exegetical questions, cf. Wolter 2017, 71–82 (GV = 2008, 390–98).

[72] Luke 20.1–8; 9–19; 20–26; 27–40; 41–43; 44–45. Luke 10.25–28 would have had to be inserted between 20.40 and 20.41.

[73] Schürmann 1994, 128, gives as the reason for the change of position that Luke wanted to work out "immediately by way of introduction in 10.25–37 the significance of the love commandment in its importance for the life of the disciples." Wolter 2017, 73 (GV = 2008, 392) appears to question this, without providing his own explanation. The presentation of the source situation in Fitzmyer 1983, 876–90, cannot be documented and discussed here.

interpretation—first, by constructing a new opening question, then, by having the scribe raise a new interpretive question about the commandment, and, finally, by expressing Jesus' answer in a distinctive example story:

**10.25** And behold a certain lawyer (νομικός[74]) stood up, tested him, and said, "Teacher, what must I do to inherit eternal life?" **26** And he said to him, "What is written in the law? What do you read?" **27** He answered and said, "You shall love the Lord your God with all your heart and with all your soul and with all your strength and with all your mind, and your neighbor as yourself." **28** And he said to him, "You have answered rightly; do this and you will live." **29** But he wanted to justify himself and said to Jesus, "Who then is my neighbor?"

**30** Jesus answered and said, "There was a man who went down from Jerusalem to Jericho and fell among robbers, who stripped him and beat him and went away and left him half dead. **31** And it happened that a priest was coming down on that street and when he saw him, he passed by on the other side. **32** And likewise also a Levite: When he came to the place and saw him, he passed by. **33** And a certain Samaritan who was on a trip came there; and when he saw him, he had compassion; **34** and he went to him, poured oil and wine on his wounds and bound them for him, put him on his animal, and brought him to an inn and cared for him. **35** On the next day he took out two denarii and gave them to the innkeeper and said, 'Take care of him; and if you spend more, I will pay you back when I return.'

**36** "Who of these three, do you think, was the neighbor to the one who fell among the robbers?" **37** He said, "The one who showed mercy to him." Then Jesus said to him, "Go then and do likewise."

The opening question of the scribe refers not to the topic of the law, as in Mark 12, but to the question about eternal life.[75] Here, the νομικός asks not about the *nomos* and thus about Jesus' proficiency as a teacher of the law but surprisingly about the *ethos* and thus about himself: "What must *I* do"—the same line of questioning that occurs in the mouth of the ἄρχων in Luke 18.18–20 and that sounds plausible there.[76] Jesus' concluding

---

[74] νομικός is "legal scholar," here then related to the Torah. Cf. Wolter 2016, 311–12 (GV = 2008, 285).

[75] It is possible that this question is thematically connected to Luke 10.19. In any case, chapter 10 represents a high point in the Lukan overall structure. The pericope of the double commandment and the parable of the merciful Samaritan belong to this high point of the activity of Jesus.

[76] In 18.18 Luke uses the Markan text from Mark 10.17, while he changes the Markan text in favor of "eternal life" in chapter 10.

word takes up the opening question: "*Do* likewise!" In Luke it is not the scribe but Jesus who, in his answer to an *ethical* basic question, refers to the *law* entirely as a matter of course and with emphasis. Thus, in the Lukan context, the concern is no longer with the question of Jesus' correct interpretation of the law but with the religious *ethos* that opens up salvation for human beings. In the logic of the text, it is not astonishing that the scribe already knows the answer—according to Luke he does not, after all, ask for the sake of truth but only to see whether Jesus answers correctly. The answer lies in the double commandment of love, which the scribe cites already as *one* commandment—a consequence of the Markan text—by connecting Lev 19.18 to Deut 6.5 simply with "and."[77] With the answer of the scribe, which Jesus affirms, the double commandment of the Gospel of Mark is completely transformed into a unified ethical attitude that claims to reproduce the ethical overall intention of the Torah.

For the evangelist, however, this answer with its reference to ἀγαπᾶν is, in a telling way, not yet the powerful description of the attitude that opens up salvation according to his understanding. Instead, this is first presented with the reference to *mercy* or active compassion (ἔλεος).[78] In order to place special emphasis on this interpretation the evangelist has Jesus recount the example story[79] of the merciful Samaritan.[80] The focus of the entire text is first located here. Luke is not primarily interested in the question of which ethical attitude the Torah is to be subsumed under—the fact that it is ἀγάπη is already just as firmly established for him as the fact that Jesus authoritatively interprets the Torah. He inquires further into the concrete implementation of the applied ethics and has Jesus propagate *mercy* as a manifestation of *love*. The point of departure is the makeshift question[81] "Who is my neighbor?" In Lev 19.18 *rea'* was every member of the Israelite legal community. A query about its meaning was superfluous. Its

---

[77] In contrast to Mark, Deut 6.5 is lacking, since what matters for Luke is only the ethos of ἀγαπᾶν.

[78] ἔλεος is a key term of the theology of the Psalms (חסד); "to 'do'/practice mercy" is a Septuagintism. On the conception of Yahweh's mercy, cf. the sketch of Spieckermann 2001a; Witte 2014.

[79] Wolter 2017, 77 (GV = 2008, 395) specifies the form as "paradigmatic decisions," which "end in a question addressed to the hearers and are not comprehensible without their literary context."

[80] Whether the example story comes from the Lukan special material as a distinctive source of the Gospel of Luke cannot be discussed here. Cf., on the one hand, the very skeptical position of Wolter 2016, 16 (GV = 2008, 14), who understands the so-called *Sondergut*, or special material, merely as a "remainder category," and, on the other hand, the entirely different position of Klein 2006, 43, who wishes to view it "as a unity."

[81] In the flow of the narrative we are dealing, on the one hand, with a makeshift question with which the scribe is characterized negatively ("he wanted to justify himself") and,

translation in the Septuagint with ὁ πλησίον[82] enabled the transfer of the Leviticus commandment to a different social and legal situation. Instead of the Israelite legal community, Lev 19.18 is now applied to the Hellenistic world of fellow citizenship and neighborship. The evangelist appears to experience this world as unclear. The example story of the Samaritan creates new clarity by disclosing the practical-caritative side of ἀγαπᾶν. At the same time, the double commandment is thereby ethicized to a much stronger extent than in Mark and Matthew. Deut 6.5 no longer plays a role in the example story. In his interpretation of the double commandment, Luke follows the path from the *religious-ethical attitude* of ἀγαπᾶν to the *doing* of ἔλεος (Luke 10.28 and 37).[83] With this he leaves the trail of the tradition history: The Torah quotation and ἀγαπᾶν are no longer adequate for him. The Torah quotation no longer speaks for itself; even ἀγαπᾶν no longer speaks simply for itself. Luke fills ἀγαπᾶν with new meaning by opening up a general strategy of action beyond the Torah but not against the Torah—the active loving service of ἔλεος toward those who need such service. Jesus is no longer primarily a teacher of the Torah but a teacher of ethics.[84]

## 3.2 The Commandment of Love for Neighbor

For the early Christian authors, the path led from the double commandment of love to the theme of love for neighbor and to its ethical commentary and concretization. This becomes clear when we follow the quotation tradition of Lev 19.18 beyond the double commandment. It appears in Matt 5.43; 19.19; Rom 13.9; Gal 5.14; and Jas 2.8.[85] Matthew 19.19; Rom 13; and Jas 2.8 do not quote the commandment of love for neighbor together with the commandment of love for God, but they do cite it with statements from the Decalogue, i.e., also with commandments that became central commandments of the scripture in the course of early Jewish scriptural usage. Gal 5.14 is the only text in the New Testament in which Lev 19.18

---

on the other hand, with the opening of a further-reaching teaching of Jesus that makes clear that the mere recourse to the love commandment is no longer sufficient.

[82] Greek: neighbor, fellow human.

[83] Bovon 2013, 52 (GV = 1996, 82), points out the connection between Luke 10.25–37 and the following episode in 10.38–42 (Mary and Martha). The theological component is narratively presented there—the 'love of God.'

[84] On the question of whether the "historical" Jesus created the double commandment, cf. the cautious judgment of Bilde 2013, 99–107 (see the reference to Bilde in section 3.1 above).

[85] First John 4.20–21 may allude to the double commandment. On this, see Waaler 2008.

is exclusively cited and interpreted. I will therefore first present Matt 19; Rom 13; and Jas 2 in a comparative manner. At the outset, we must once again affirm the fact—which is only self-evident at first glance—that Jesus neither "invented" the demand for love for neighbor nor was he the only person to place it at the center of his words and speeches. When love for neighbor according to Lev 19.18 is spoken of in the Jesus tradition, this occurs exclusively in the quotation. With this Jesus is located materially in the neighborhood of diverse early Jewish writings.[86]

In chapters 19 and 20 of his Gospel, Matthew places together traditions that he assigns to Jesus' peregrination from Galilee to Jerusalem. Matthew follows here the narrative context of the Gospel of Mark. The theme of discipleship stands in the foreground, in connection with the question of the rich young man about eternal life (Matt 19.16–22), which leads to Jesus' statement about riches, Peter's question about reward for the disciples' following of Jesus, and to the example story of the workers in the vineyard.[87] Matthew found the episode of 19.16–22[88] in Mark 10.17–22 and left it in the narrative context that it had there. Matthew, however, decisively changed the Markan version at several points, especially in the fact that he has Jesus quote Lev 19.18—the commandment, which is lacking in the Markan text.[89]

> **19.16** And behold, someone came to him and said, "Teacher, what good thing must I do to have eternal life?" **17** And he said to him, "Why do you ask me about the good? There is only one who is good. But if you wish to enter into life, keep the commandments." **18** Then he said to him, "Which ones?" And Jesus said, "You shall not kill; you shall not commit adultery; you shall not steal; you shall not bear false witness; **19** honor your father and mother; and: '*You shall love your neighbor as*

---

[86] Cf. Lange/Weigold 2011, 84.

[87] Mark 10.17–31, cf. Matt 19.16–30. Matthew attaches the parable of the workers in the vineyard, which comes from his special material (20.1–16).

[88] On the text, cf. Luz 2001, 508–23 (GV = 1997, 118–37). Luz points out that the individual episodes of this textual unit belong close together, and an actual attachment first appears in 19.30.

[89] The Lukan version (Luke 18.19–24) remains closer to the Markan text: Lev 19.18 is not cited. Other important changes (against Mark and against Luke): (1) According to Mark and Luke, the man addresses Jesus with "good teacher." Matthew rephrases to the question "What good deed must I do?" (2) Matthew stresses the theme of salvifically relevant commandments with the young man's question "Which ones?" (3) The addition of Lev 19.18 to the Decalogue commandments. (4) The omission of Mark 10.21: "Jesus looked at him and loved him (ἠγάπησεν αὐτόν)," which is also lacking in Luke. It cannot be clarified whether an influence on the mention of the love commandment in Matthew is present here. (5) Matthew adds the expression "If you wish to be perfect" (19.31).

*yourself.*" **20** Then the young man said, "I have kept these; what do I still lack?" **21** Jesus answered him, "If you wish to be perfect (τέλειος), then go, sell your possessions, and give to the poor and you will have treasure in heaven; and come and follow me!" **22** When the young man heard this statement, he went away sorrowful; for he had many goods.

The opening question from Mark 10.17, which Matthew and Luke[90] adopt, resembles the question of Luke 10.25: Jesus is not asked about the interpretation of the law but about "eternal life." Unlike Luke, however, Matthew additionally understands the Markan text as an inquiry regarding Jesus' understanding of the law: Jesus answers with statements from the Decalogue (Exod 20.12–16; Deut 5.16, 20), *to which he adds Lev 19.18*, without making clear that this statement does not belong to the Decalogue. In the logic of the Markan text, which Matthew takes over, what is important is not the commandment of love for neighbor[91] but Jesus' demand to leave everything and follow him, for it is this and only this that the man cannot do. Thus, both Mark and Matthew establish a new and distinctive ethical demand of Jesus — renunciation of possessions and following Jesus. With this the Markan text places following Jesus over the fulfillment of the law in the form of the Decalogue and love for neighbor, and Matthew follows him in this weighting, despite his stronger emphasis on the law.

Rom 13.9 and Jas 2.8 are likewise witnesses to the tradition that developed among early Christian authors of mentioning Lev 19.18 not with the commandment of love for God but together with select Decalogue commandments as the most important commandments of the Torah. Rom 13.8–10[92] belongs in the exhortative part of the letter, which reaches from 12.1 ("I exhort you therefore") to 15.13 and in which different forms and themes are loosely placed together. Paul had already thematized the virtues of love (ἀγάπη) and love for brothers and sisters (φιλαδελφία) at the beginning of his individual exhortations (12.9–10), which he places under the ethical antithesis of good and evil. Under this ethical scheme he also gives recommendations for behavior toward the governing authorities (13.1–7).[93] With the help of the keyword connection of ethical "obligations," he then speaks again of love, though now no longer in a general ethical framework but in connection with the question of the law (13.8–10):

---

[90] Luke 18.18–23, which does not mention the commandment of love for neighbor.

[91] Matthew adds this only for the sake of a certain completeness, for it, like the double commandment and the *Shema ʿ Israel* that is echoed in 19.17 ("there is only one who is good"), already belongs to the most important Torah commandments in the primitive Christian tradition.

[92] Cf. Wischmeyer 2004a.

[93] On this, cf. Wischmeyer 2004c. In general, cf. Jewett 2007, 804–15.

**13.8** Owe no one anything, except mutual[94] love.[95] For the one who loves
has also fulfilled the remaining specifications of the law.[96] **9** For what
is said there, "You shall not commit adultery; You shall not murder;
You shall not steal; You shall not covet"; and if there is any other commandment, this is summed up in this statement, "*Love your neighbor as
yourself.*" **10** Love does not do evil to the neighbor; therefore, love is the
fulfillment of the law.

This text argues in two directions. The first sentence from 13.8 reduces
or concentrates all ethical obligations in house, family, and society to/in
"love." The second sentence draws from this the consequence for the Torah
of Israel, which Paul understands here completely as a set of ethical rules.
If "loving one another" is the actual content of all ethical obligations, then
the whole Torah is also "fulfilled" in Lev 19.18. Accordingly, in distinction from Matt 19, Paul adds Lev 19.18 to the Decalogue specifications
not for reasons of completeness, but, the other way around, he stresses the
central position of the commandment of the love for neighbor, which he
reinforces through the addition of Decalogue commandments. Paul uses
two words to describe this central position—the verb ἀνακεφαλαιόω,
"summarize," and the noun πλήρωμα, "fulfillment." Here too, Paul argues
in the framework of the ethical concept of good and evil. The concluding
point in 13.10 is compressed and formulated *ex negativo*: The law demands
the doing of the good. Since love does only good to the other and not evil, it
is "the fulfillment" of the whole Torah, i.e., its inner tendency.[97] Paul is concerned here not with a possible abolition of individual Torah regulations,
of Torah observance, or in general with an argumentative dispute with the
Jewish understanding of the law in detail (this occurs elsewhere), but very
simply with the statement that ethics does not teach the doing of evil but
of *good*. ἀγάπη does precisely this. The Torah teaches the same thing in
the commandment of love for neighbor and in the Decalogue. Therefore,
ἀγάπη also fulfills the demands of the Torah. Robert Jewett proposes that

[94] Jewett 2007, 808, wants to assign a distinct meaning to ἀλλήλους by taking it
together with τὸν ἕτερον. I relate τὸν ἕτερον to law.

[95] The translation of the second clause follows the *Einheitsübersetzung* ("außer der
gegenseitigen Liebe"). Luther translates "außer daß ihr euch untereinander liebt." The *Einheitsübersetzung* better captures the sense of the argumentation. Cf. Jewett 2007, 806:
"A new obligation is to replace the social dependency on patrons and families, namely
ἀλλήλους ἀγαπᾶν."

[96] I read the participle without an accusative object. "The remaining law" in v. 8 is
listed by way of example in v. 9 and taken up again with the varying repetition "and if there
is any other commandment" (v. 9).

[97] Cf. Jewett 2007, 814–15: "The meaning of πλήρωμα in this sentence is the entire
completion of law, not the sum total of its individual demands."

we understand love here very concretely as the attitude in which the Christ-believing household communities in Rome celebrated their *agape* meal.[98] We can—without it being possible to obtain certainty here—affirm this contextual interpretation if it remains clear that Paul simultaneously understands this situation exemplarily and argues very fundamentally in two directions—namely, ethically on the one hand, and in terms of the interpretation of the Torah on the other. ἀγάπη is the form of their life together *and* at the same time the hermeneutical rule according to which the commandments of the Torah are to be interpreted.

The similarity between the citation of the commandment of love for neighbor and of the Decalogue in Romans and James is only ostensible (Jas 2.8–13):

> **2.8** If you fulfill the royal law according to the scripture, "*You shall love your neighbor as yourself,*" you do well. **9** But if you are a respecter of persons, you commit sin and are convicted by the law as transgressors. **10** For whoever keeps the whole law but trespasses against one of the laws has become guilty with regard to every law. **11** For the one who has said, "You shall not commit adultery," he has also said, "You shall not murder." But if you do not commit adultery but do murder, you have become a transgressor of the law. **12** Speak and act as those who are going to be judged through the law of freedom. **13** For a merciless judgment will come to the one who does not show mercy. But mercy triumphs over judgment.

We encounter here the opposing position within the same discourse—namely, the position of the *equal* validity of all the individual commandments of the Torah. This discourse was already known to Paul when he argued along these lines in Gal 5.3: "I testify again to every man who lets himself be circumcised that he is obligated to do the *whole* law."[99] In this discourse context, there is neither the perspective of a selection nor of a concentration with regard to the commandments of the Torah. What the author of James seeks to argumentatively support is his criticism of the προσωπολημψία, the so-called respect of persons, i.e., the preference for persons with a higher social position, against which he warns in

---

[98] Jewett 2007, 815, finds in these community meals "the precise social context" of Rom 13.8–10. This situational interpretation could explain the theme of chapter 14 (already the argument of 13.13). We know nothing, however, about the Pauline "love feast."

[99] Here we encounter the same semantics as in Rom 13.8 (obligated, i.e., under obligation to keep all the commandments of the Torah).

2.1–7 with a "negative example"[100] from the practice of the community. In 2.8–12 the author develops the example argumentatively. The argument runs as follows: (1) You want to keep the whole "law." (2) You do keep Lev 19.18. (3) But when you, despite this fact, preference influential community members in the community meeting, you contravene the "law,"[101] and your love for neighbor does not benefit you—you are transgressors of the law. (4) Exemplary justification for (3) from the Decalogue: There is not only *one* commandment from the Decalogue, but they are all in force independently of one another. Accordingly, it is of no benefit to keep only *some* commandments from the Decalogue—one must keep them all. (5) Practical admonition and eschatological perspective. Analogous to Rom 13, Christoph Burchard thinks that a concrete social occasion rather than merely a topical admonition is also present here: "The effort . . . suggests that James regards the prohibition as paramount and corrects a dreadful state of affairs that stands in opposition to the law rather than occasional transgressions."[102] This means that the author condemns the social differentiation and early formation of elites in the Christ-believing communities. The confession of love for neighbor is of no benefit if "respect of persons" is practiced. This argumentation goes in a direction that runs counter to that of Rom 13: love for neighbor "alone" is of no benefit. Love is not a hermeneutical rule for Torah interpretation nor a superordinated ethical entity or attitude. Rather, it is simply *one* important commandment among others, which must be done. With a view to Luke 10.30–37, the conclusion of James' argumentation is especially interesting. In a similar way as in Luke, it is not love but active *mercy*, ἔλεος, that stands at the end of the comments on right action—mercy in place of love for neighbor.[103] The extent to which the author of James actually had all the individual commandments of the Torah in view here can be left open. In any case, the ethical course of the overall argument is clear. It is directed not toward individual commandments but, like the Lukan texts, toward mercy.

Gal 5.13–15[104] is then the only text that in the discourse around the intention of the law argues exclusively with the commandment of love for neighbor:

---

[100] Burchard 2000, 97; cf. on the text, pp. 95–109. Cf. now also Wischmeyer forthcoming, ad loc.

[101] What is meant by the perfect, royal, and free law in Jas 1.25; 2.8; and 2.12 is controversial among the exegetes. Cf. the discussion in Burchard 2000, 103–4. In any case, it is not Lev 19.18. Cf. now also Wischmeyer forthcoming, ad loc.

[102] Burchard 2000, 96.

[103] This is not meant in an antithetical sense but as concretion, to which the interest of the author applies.

[104] On the text, cf. Betz 1979, 271–77.

**5.13** For you were called to freedom, brothers and sisters; only (do) not (make) freedom into an opportunity for the flesh but through love serve one another. **14** For the whole law is fulfilled (πεπλήρωται) in one statement, namely: *"You shall love your neighbor as yourself."* **15** But if you bite and devour one another, take care that you are not completely consumed[105] by one another.

The textual unit Gal 5.13–15 stands at the beginning of the rather short ethical exhortations of the letter (Gal 5.13–6.10) and therefore has special weight.[106] Freedom—understood and justified in detail as freedom from the Torah and its commandments, especially from circumcision as presupposition of righteousness before God—is the motto under which Paul places his ethical sketch.[107] But freedom is in danger of being abused.[108] Therefore, it is immediately taken into service anew in v. 13: "through love (ἀγάπη) serve (δουλεύετε) one another." The theme here is not so much love but freedom from the law and the right way of handling this freedom. Hans Dieter Betz has disclosed the logic of the concise text: The Christ-believing members of the Galatian community need concrete help, for "the abolishment of the old rituals and conventions implies that the concepts of sin and guilt no longer apply."[109] Paul wanted to introduce ἀγάπη as the new and only ethical attitude (v. 13). However, in the context of the argumentation against opposing missionaries who were proponents of keeping the Torah, Paul must clarify how ἀγάπη relates to the law. Betz formulates here with equal sharpness and accuracy: "Why then does Paul bring up the matter of the Law again at this point? As far as his own theology is concerned, he could do well without it. Apparently, however, he cannot avoid the matter, because the Galatians are so preoccupied with circumcision and Torah."[110] Paul therefore uses the argument that the one statement from Lev 19.18 "fulfills" the whole Torah—as we have seen, he later uses the same argument again in Rom 13. As in Rom 13, with the conception of "fulfillment," Paul is already concerned in Galatians with "the principle"[111]

---

[105] Following Bauer 1988, 112.

[106] Betz 1979, 253–55, has the exhortations, i.e., the paraenetic portion of the letter, begin with 5.1 and reads 5.1–12 already as the first *exhortatio*. Correspondingly, 5.13–24 is the second *exhortatio* (271). However, 5.1–12 more likely functions as the theological foundation for 5.13–24.

[107] On this, cf. Vollenweider 1989.

[108] Betz 1979, 272.

[109] Betz 1979, 273.

[110] Betz 1979, 275.

[111] Betz 1979, 275. Betz rightly distinguishes between the 'doing or keeping of the Torah,' to which for Paul Christians are not obligated, and the 'fulfillment of the Torah' to which he obligates the Galatians with his ethics of love.

or inner tendency of the Torah, which he finds expressed in Lev 19.18. He then sets forth how this principle is realized in the following catalog of virtues (5.22–23) under the ethical coordinates of 'Spirit' and 'flesh' and under the motto of the 'good' (6.9–10),[112] and not as comments on the law and its implementation in the commandments.

### 3.3 Mutations: Commandments of Love for Enemies and Love for Brothers and Sisters

Lev 19.18 is quoted not only in Galatians but also in the Sermon on the Mount (Matt 5–7). There, however, the commandment of love for neighbor is so strongly altered in three respects that the quotation only forms the point of departure and connection for something new and distinctive. First, the elaboration "as yourself" falls away. Second, we instead find an addition that significantly alters the sense of the commandment. Third, this new commandment is furnished with an antithetical commentary of Jesus, which, in turn, alters once again the meaning of the Leviticus commandment (Matt 5.43–48)[113] and leads from love for neighbor to *love for enemies*.

> **5.43** You have heard that it was said, *You shall love your neighbor* and hate your enemy. **44** But I say to you, *Love your enemies* and pray for those who persecute you, **45** in order that you may be children of your Father in heaven, for he makes his sun rise on the evil and the good and sends rain on the just and the unjust. **46** For if you love those who love you, what reward do you have? Do not even the tax collectors do the same? **47** And if you greet only your brothers and sisters (ἀδελφοί), what do you do that is special? Do not even the gentiles do the same? **48** Therefore, you should be perfect, as your Father in heaven is perfect.

Although the parallel text in Luke (Luke 6.27–36) leads closer to the Jesus tradition underlying the two texts, the conception of love for enemies is shaped by the text of the Gospel of Matthew and is best presented from this text. Matt 5.43–48 presents the last and most important of six antitheses in which Jesus exemplifies his own understanding of the Torah, as

---

[112] Cf. Rom 13.

[113] On the text, cf. throughout Luz 2007, 283–94 (GV = 2002, 400–16), with extensive references to literature (ET = 283; GV = 400). Cf. now also Konradt 2016, 348–380; 2018. Piper 1979 is especially important. Piper reconstructs the tradition history of the commandment of love for enemies. He traces back the commandment to Jesus and pursues its double history in the Gospel tradition and in early Christian paraenesis, as it is encountered in the letters, especially in Rom 12. On this, see below.

Matthew understands it and takes it from the Jesus tradition.[114] Let us make two observations before turning to the analysis. First, the formal and structural proximity to the commandment of love for neighbor is conspicuous. Here, a second commandment (love for enemies) is created, which enters into competition with the first commandment (love for neighbor) precisely by repeating its structure. Second, the material antithesis is inconsistent. Instead of the expected enemy-friend-antithesis, we encounter the enemy-neighbor-dichotomy. Love for *enemies* is not the logical alternative to love for *neighbor*. This is an indication that the sixth antithesis is a construction of the evangelist, who seeks to portray Jesus as the end-time Torah teacher in opposition to contemporary Torah interpretation. To this corresponds the fact that the antithetical formulation "love for neighbor *versus* love for enemy" is not found in the Gospel of Luke (Luke 6.27–36) and does not come from Q.

In light of the significance of the commandment of love for neighbor in Matthew the question initially arises: How do the commandments of love for neighbor and love for enemies relate in Matthew? First, it is clear that Jesus is portrayed as teacher of the Torah here as well as in Matt 19.16–22 and 22.34–40. In all three texts he interprets the Torah with a view to its inner intention, with the Decalogue, the double commandment of love, and the commandment of love for neighbor playing the decisive role.[115] It is also clear that Matthew, along the lines of his traditions—the Gospel of Mark and the Sayings Source Q[116]—assumes that Jesus placed the commandment of *love for neighbor* at the center of his Torah interpretation. All the more important is the sixth antithesis of the Sermon on the Mount, which presents Jesus not in continuity but in *discontinuity* with Lev 19.18. Unlike in Matt 19 and 22, Jesus does not remain within the framework of Jewish Torah interpretation here but presents himself—against the Markan text—with his new interpretation of Lev 19.18 explicitly *against* this. According to Matthew, we hear Jesus' *own* new interpretation of the

---

[114] The theme of νόμος formulated by Matthew in 5.17–20. In Matt 5.21–48, the evangelist has Jesus quote six important Torah commandments or prohibitions—the prohibition of murder and adultery, the dissolution of marriage commandment, the prohibition of false oaths, the so-called *ius talionis* commandment from Exod 21.24 and elsewhere as well as the commandment of love for neighbor from Lev 19.18. In addition to the prohibitions against murder and adultery, the prohibition against false oaths also comes from the Decalogue. Thus, we also find here the familiar constellation of Lev 19.18 and Decalogue commandments, which is expanded through Exod 21.24.

[115] The so-called Golden Rule (Matt 7.12), which does not stem, after all, from the Torah and therefore also cannot be used in the context of the theme of the law, also becomes important only secondarily. Matthew comments here: "For this is the law and the prophets" (cf. 22.40).

[116] On the Q tradition that underlies Matthew, see below.

commandment of love for neighbor here. The specific interpretation concerns the unconditional expansion of the term רֵעַ/πλησίον to the enemy, which results in Matthew having Jesus formulate a new commandment of his own. While it stands in formal continuity to the commandment "love your neighbor," which has been impactfully shortened by Matthew, it brings an end to this continuity materially. With this Lev 19.18 itself becomes obsolete without this being made explicit. For the addition "and hate your enemy," which is not a quotation from the Torah[117] but is meant to disclose the ethically dangerous inner tendency of the commandment of love for neighbor toward mere group ethics, ultimately makes this entirely meaningless, precisely through the fact that the addition is presented as part of the quotation "You have heard that it was said." According to the logic of the text, love for enemies does not simply come alongside love for neighbor but takes its place. The commentary of vv. 46–47 clarifies this mercilessly: Lev 19.18, read in this perspective, is followed by sinners and gentiles and can thus no longer exercise its original function as covenantal action of the people of Israel. According to Matthew, however, the continuity of the two commandments is preserved: Jesus does not abolish the old commandment but newly and authoritatively interprets it.

Another question is connected with this. What does Matthew understand by love for enemies? To whom is the term "enemy" (ἐχθρός) meant to refer? There is only one indication in the text—namely, the parallel elaboration that compares the enemy to those "who persecute you." The term *neighbor*, by contrast, is characterized more closely by *brother/sister*: love for brothers and sisters (φιλαδελφία) appears to be the common interpretation of love for neighbor in the Matthean communities. It is, however, effectively disqualified, since—at least in Matthew's mind—it is also a pagan form of behavior. This gives rise to a problem. The neighbor as the member of the legal community of Israel has become the friend and brother/sister in the group. This weakening or transformation of the political-societal-legal term "neighbor" into the individual-ethical or group-ethical has the consequence that the original sharpness of the demand of the commandment from Leviticus must be reformulated. This occurs in Matthew through the transformation of

---

[117] This antithetical addition comes not from the Jesus tradition but from the evangelist. Substantiation and discussion can be found in Luz 2007, 287–88 (GV = 2002, 402–3). The discussion about whether this is a case of "anti-Judaism" cannot be pursued here. Luz's statement, "No single antithesis expresses as clearly as this one the anti-Jewish front so important for Matthew" (ET = 288; GV = 407) remains unproven, since he himself cannot make out a Jewish front against which the evangelist polemically fights. It seems more plausible to follow Luz's own pointer that Matthew has rhetorically shortened and sharpened the Jesus tradition.

love for neighbor to love for enemies. When we read the sixth antithesis of Matthew closely, we obtain the coordinates of neighbor-brother/sister *versus* enemy-persecutor. And instead of being in the Israelite legal community,[118] or at least in Israel,[119] we find ourselves situated in the early Christian communities and their community experiences internally and toward the outside. The exemplary explanations, which associate enemies with persecutors and neighbors with brothers and sisters, i.e., community members, reflect the perspective of the communities or of the evangelist. In any case, they function as commentary on a saying that had called for *love for enemies* under the community situation of tribulation and persecution. Thus, the evangelist understands the love commandment, further, primarily as inner-community rule[120] when he calls for love toward the persecutors. In light of these considerations, can the saying about love for enemies can be traced back to Jesus, and can Jesus' own specification of 'enemy' perhaps be reconstructed?

For this inquiry the parallel Lukan text must be drawn upon, since it, according to the judgment of the majority of exegetes, more likely leads back to Jesus than the stylistically so concise Matthean version (Luke 6.27–36):[121]

**6.27** But I say to you who are listening, *Love your enemies*, do good to those who hate you, **28** bless those who curse you, pray for those who abuse you. **29** To the one who strikes you on the check, offer the other also; and from the one who takes your overgarment, do not refuse also your undergarment. **30** To everyone who asks of you, give, and from the one who takes your things do not demand them back.

**31** And as you wish that human beings would do to you, do likewise to them.

**32** And if you love (only) those who love you, what do you receive as a return (χάρις)? For even sinners love those who love them (ἀγαπῶντας αὐτοὺς ἀγαπῶσιν). **33** And if you do good to those who do good to you (ἀγαθοποιῆτε τοὺς ἀγαθοποιοῦντας ὑμας), what do you receive as a return? For even the sinners do the same. **34** And if you lend to those from whom you hope to receive something, what do you receive as a return? Even sinners lend to sinners in order to receive

---

[118] Thus the original constellation in the book of Leviticus.

[119] Thus the situation of Jesus himself.

[120] Cf. 1 John.

[121] On the text, cf. throughout Fitzmyer 1981, 630–44; Bovon 1992, 230–45 (GV = 1989, 306–28); Wolter 2016, 276–85 (GV = 2008, 254–61); Allison 2010, 305–86. Allison provides a discussion of the extra–New Testament parallels and the references back to Lev 19.

back the same. **35** But *love your enemies*; do good and lend where you hope to receive nothing back. And your reward (μισθός) will be great and you will become children of the Most High; for he is kind to the ungrateful and the evil.

   **36** Be merciful (οἰκτίρμονες), just as your Father also is merciful.

This text, which is much longer than Matthew's sixth antithesis and less clearly structured both formally and thematically, is part of the so-called Sermon on the Plain in Luke 6.17–49. The Sermon on the Mount and the Sermon on the Plain are based on individual sayings of Jesus and shorter series of sayings from the presumably "written Vorlage,"[122] the so-called Sayings Source Q, which has not been handed down and as such remains hypothetical.[123] Both evangelists have reworked the Jesus tradition from Q[124] into a speech of Jesus. Dale Allison's hypothesis that "the central part of the Sermon on the Plain is not an anthology made up of smaller anthologies, nor was its history as protracted and complex as often imagined; rather, it represents, by and large, the work of a single individual,"[125] is indeed plausible for Luke 6, since Allison can make clear that in Luke 6.27–42 themes are placed together that are thematically related to one another and also occur in other early Jewish and early Christian sources. Moreover, many exegetes assume that Luke has reworked the *Vorlage* to a lesser extent than Matthew. In comparison with Matthew, the Lukan text shows less rhetorical stringency, the commandment of love for enemies is repeated, and the profile of the "enemies" is sketched in a livelier and less narrow way. In addition, Luke takes up sayings in this textual unit that Matthew places at a different point. Matthew places the saying on retribution in Luke 6.29–30 with the fifth antithesis on retaliation, which he created. Luke 6.31, the so-called Golden Rule,[126] occurs in Matthew in 7.12 in the textual units that conclude the Sermon on the Mount. On the whole, the textual unit in the Gospel of Luke has a pronounced ethical coloring. In the Lukan text, the 'enemies' are, on the one hand, persons who act in a violent and hostile way and, on the other hand, simply persons in need or persons who are seeking help,

---

[122] Bovon 1989, 293 (ET = Bovon 1992, 218: "written source").

[123] Scholarship relating to Q cannot be discussed here. On Q, cf., by way of introduction, Hoffmann/Heil 2002. The text of Luke 6.27–36 in the reconstructed version in Q (= Q 6.27–36) appears on pp. 40–43. See also the critical (reconstructing) edition of Robinson/ Hoffmann/Kloppenborg 2000, 56–73.

[124] The wording of the reconstruction in Hoffmann/Heil 2002; and Robinson/Hoffmann/ Kloppenborg 2000, cannot be discussed here.

[125] Allison 2010, 312–13.

[126] On this, see Dihle 1962.

especially those who need credit, without being able to offer financial security. In the Lukan perspective, love for enemies is therefore both renunciation of violence and renunciation of retribution as positive merciful action (v. 36). With this, love for enemies in Luke approaches the interpretation of love for neighbor that Jesus gives in the example story of the merciful Samaritan.[127] The commandment of love for enemies is contoured in a less one-sided way than in Matthew and functions more as an interpretation of the commandment of love for neighbor and less as an outbidding, let alone as an alternative.

Let us return now to the question of the original Jesus tradition. The overwhelming number of exegetes are agreed that the commandment of love for enemies comes from *Jesus* himself.[128] Ulrich Luz regards the commandment of love for enemies in Matt 5.43–44 (= Q 6.27–28) as certainly dominical.[129] Luz has summarized the significance of this text and the works on the reception history of the commandment of love for enemies in a concise and emphatic manner:

> The commandment to love one's enemy is one of the central Christian texts. Not only is it quoted frequently in early Christian paraenesis . . . but also since the Apologists it is regarded as *the* Christian *proprium* and *novum* about which the Gentiles marvel. . . . The central position of the love of one's enemy in the early church reflects the intention of the sayings source and especially of Matthew, who has given it a favored position in his last, conclusive antithesis. Thus he presents the love commandment as the middle of the Christians' "better" righteousness, which he summarizes in v. 48 with "perfect."[130]

The concern here, however, is no longer with love for neighbor but with love for enemies.

F. Bovon reaches a similar conclusion in the context of his comments on Luke 6.27–38: "The *historical Jesus* pronounced the command to love one's enemies and connected it with the promise of adoption, and the justification of the command in God's lovingkindness. . . . On

---

[127] In Luke 10 the noun ἔλεος is used, whereas Luke 6 has the adjective οἰκτίρμων. Both lexemes are widely attested in the LXX.

[128] Cf. esp. Theissen/Merz 1998, 391 (GV = 2001, 347): They regard the Q tradition as "in the core . . . authentic" (GV = 347; ET = 391) They place special value on the statement that the commandment of love for enemies applies in general and is required from the persecuted and not the rulers (ET = 392; GV = 348). They rightly see here the "*distinctive feature of the Jesus tradition*" (ET = 392 [emphasis original]; GV = 348)

[129] Luz 2007, 284 (GV = 2002, 403).

[130] Luz 2007, 285 (GV = 2002, 403).

another occasion he taught that one must renounce resistance . . . , practice compassion . . . , not pass judgment . . . , and measure well."[131] Bovon then reconstructs the growth of the tradition from the oral tradition via the Sayings Source to the Gospel of Luke. According to Bovon, it can be said for Luke that "the compositional skill of the evangelist leads to the addition of the Golden Rule . . . after the love of enemies . . . and the renunciation of resistance . . . , thus juxtaposing it to the call to compassion."[132] By contrast, the Gospel of Matthew integrates the Jesus tradition into the literary form of antitheses. Dale Allison summarizes similarly: "What we are justified in surmising is that Q 6:27–42 probably preserves the general import of some important and characteristic themes in Jesus' teaching, themes that he linked in his discourses."[133]

Despite these weighty exegetical voices, the critical tradition-historical observations of J. Sauer retain their significance.[134] Sauer compares the Synoptic traditions with the Pauline admonitions in Rom 12.9–21 and reaches the following twofold conclusion. First, Paul is said to have "the chronologically oldest statements on the complex of love of enemies and renunciation of retaliation," which come from early Jewish and Hellenistic sapiential spheres of tradition. Second, the sapiential traditional material that was used by Paul in Rom 12 is said to have been placed "in Jesus' mouth" later.[135] I would like to make a differentiation here. Sauer rightly points out that Paul does not know the commandment of love for enemies as such or as a commandment of Jesus. This touches upon the difficult problem of Jesus tradition in Paul, which cannot be pursued here.[136] Sauer also rightly points out that Paul uses sapiential paraenesis, which comes close to the commandment of love for enemies. From this we can infer that the commandment of love for enemies in its ethical intention was not as original and innovative as it has often been assumed to be in Jesus research, which follows the perspective of the Gospel of Matthew here. On the other hand, in the traditions that Sauer draws upon, we precisely do not find the commandment of love for enemies as a contrasting interpretation of the commandment of love for neighbor. Unlike Rom 12, the Synoptic context points not in the direction of sapiential tradition but occurs in connection with the controversy over the correct Torah interpretation, which constitutes part of the activity of Jesus. In the Socratic tradition—which we will discuss below—we find not the idea of love for enemies but the

---

[131] Bovon 1992, 232 (GV = 1989, 310).
[132] Bovon 1992, 233 (GV = 1989, 311).
[133] Allison 2010, 381.
[134] Sauer 1985, 1–28, who provides an extensive bibliography up to 1984 in n1.
[135] Sauer 1985, 28.
[136] On this topic, cf. now Jacobi 2015.

advice to turn enemies into friends. To be sure, the commandment of love for enemies can only be traced back to Q and is thus subject to all caution with regard to "authentic" sayings of Jesus. Here, however, the question is nevertheless unavoidable. Why should a saying that fulfills all the criteria of genuineness be denied to Jesus and ascribed to an unknown group of tradents?[137]

Thus, if we follow the assessment of Luz, Bovon, and other exegetes, we can take up once again the question of what *Jesus* could have meant by *love for enemies*. In any case, the juxtaposition of love for neighbor and love for enemies is to be read in the horizon of Old Testament–Jewish and Greco-Roman binary oppositions between "I"/"we" and "enemy/enemies" or "friend" and "enemy." In the literature of Israel, the "enemy" plays an important role in very diverse material connections.[138] We have already traced previously the tendency toward an ethical coloring and away from the originally judicial meaning of the "legally responsible national comrade" to the person "who needs mercy" in the example story of the merciful Samaritan—a tendency that leads from the group of the members of the legal community of Israel to the individual in need. The Lukan text combines the experiences of political and administrative violence with the needs of socially and financially weak persons. In both directions, the commandment of Jesus calls for renunciation of violence and for mercy.[139] This breadth or also fuzziness of the term "enemy" could correspond to the experiences of Jesus, who lived in a stage of the legal and social fellowship of Israel that was characterized by Roman political, administrative, judicial, and cultural foreign infiltration (*Überfremdung*). Matthew appears to interpret the dominical commandment of love for enemies in a twofold direction—first, in the context of the persecution of the Christ-confessing community and, second, as an especially uncompromising contribution of Jesus to his dispute with the Jewish teachers of the law and as an expression of the "better righteousness," which is a keyword in the Gospel (Matt 5.19). Both directions, the endangerment of the community, on the one hand, and the

---

[137] The commandment of love for enemies is a prominent example for Gerd Theissen's criterion of plausibility. On the one hand, it is very close to the Jewish tradition and, on the other, an expression of personal innovation. Cf. also the echo of the Jesus tradition in Did 1.3.

[138] Cf. esp. Fitzmyer 1981, 637–38 on the conception of enemy in antiquity. Cf. also Foerster 1964 (GV = 1935); Ringgren 1977 (GV = 1973); Dahmen 2011. The New Testament conception of love for enemies can most plausibly be connected to the role of the enemy in individual songs of lamentation and thanksgivings; on this, see Ringgren 1977, 216–18 (GV = 1973, 232–33). Cf. also 4Q449 1,5; 4Q504 1–2 vi 8 (on this, see Dahmen 2011, 90).

[139] A 'song of songs of love for enemies' can be found in Söding 2011, 575–78.

ethical outdoing of Jewish teachers of the law, on the other, mirror community experiences and thus further developments or applications of the Jesus commandment. Here, as often, the Lukan version comes closer to Jesus himself.

However, what Per Bilde says about the question of the originality of Jesus' sayings on the love commandment in general ultimately applies also to love for enemies: "Against this background the double commandment of love, the 'golden rule' and the commandment to love one's enemies cannot be counted as Jesus' original contributions, but rather as his reformulations of earlier Jewish ideas. Still, the formulations that the canonical gospels ascribe to Jesus, are rather close to unique . . . , but they are not original and unique in any absolute sense."[140] The skeptical assessment of Bilde refers, however, to the question of whether Jesus' call to love for enemies was new and without analogy and not to the question of whether Jesus "called" his hearers to love for enemies. This is confirmed by Bilde's judgment rather than called into question by it.

At the same time, Bilde's assessment admonishes us to be cautious with respect to conceptions that seek to understand love for enemies as an ethical *novum*, as the core of Jesus' instruction, and as the high point of New Testament ethics. Here it is beneficial to return again to the philosophical and sapiential analogies to the theme. Plutarch hands down the following anecdotes about the Spartan king Ariston.[141] Ariston comments on an answer of Cleomenes to the question of what a good king should do. Cleomenes had answered, "To do good to one's friends (φίλους) and evil to one's enemies." Ariston, by contrast, said, "How much better, my dear, to do good to our friends and to make friends of our enemies." Plutarch uses the opposition friend/enemy without further concretization, though in a political-military context, and points to Socrates, who is said to have coined this maxim. In Plutarch love for enemies is regarded not as an opposition to love for friends but as its improvement. Jürgen Sauer's reference to Rom 12.17–21 is also important:[142]

> **12.17** Do not repay anyone evil for evil; give thought to what is good in relation to[143] all human beings. **18** As far as it is possible for you, keep peace with all human beings. **19** Do not avenge yourselves, beloved, but

---

[140] Bilde 2013, 104. It is, however, unfortunate that Bilde mentions the very different commandments and rules together. In terms of tradition history, the Golden Rule is clearly removed from the commandment of love for enemies.

[141] Plutarch, *Apophthegmata Laconica*, Ariston §1 (*Mor.* 3.218a). On this topic, see also Reiser 2001; Theissen 2014.

[142] On this, cf. also above.

[143] ἐνώπιον can best be rendered here with "in relation to" (cf. Bauer 1988, 547).

give place for the wrath (of God), for it is written, "Vengeance is mine, I will repay, says the Lord." **20** But if your enemy is hungry, feed him; if he is thirsty give him something to drink; for by doing this you will pile up burning coals on his head. **21** Do not be overcome by evil but overcome evil with what is good.

In his commentary, Robert Jewett documents the connectedness of this paraenetic series of sayings in the writings of early Judaism.[144] However, precisely the consideration of Rom 12 makes clear where the distinctive character of the love for enemies in Matt 5.44 / Luke 6.27, 35 lies—in the juxtaposition to the commandment of love for neighbor, which is shown to be ethically insufficient. The specific feature of the Jesus tradition in the context of early Jewish (and Hellenistic-Roman) paraenesis is not the motif of helping foreigners and, if need be, enemies, but the *clear position statement against "mere" love for neighbor* and thus also explicitly against a highly esteemed Torah commandment. To this extent, the question of whether Jesus' commandment of love for enemies is materially "new" or unique does not at all capture the core of the Matthean text. Jesus is not portrayed here as the creator of a new ethic but as the sovereign—and as such singular—teacher of the Torah.

In the Sermon on the Mount, we find the coordinate system of brothers and sisters in the community on the one side and persecutors of the community on the other side. As we have seen, Matthew interprets the commandment of love for enemies in such a way that love for neighbor relates not only to the members of the community but also includes their persecutors, which means that it is intended to be active toward outsiders in the form of forbearance and suffering. The group of Christ-believing community members presents the framework. The Gospel of John also interprets the Jesus tradition in this coordinate system but moves in the direction of *love for brothers and sisters*. Jesus does not quote Lev 19.18—there is no mention of love for neighbors or love for enemies in the Gospel of John, and the trail of the tradition of both commandments is entirely abandoned—but gives a new love commandment, which refers in the narrative context only to the disciples (John 13.34–35).[145]

---

[144] Jewett 2007, 771–79. Cf. also Zeller 2012.

[145] On the text, cf. Schnackenburg 1982, 53–55 (GV = 1986, 59–61); J. Becker 1991, 537–44 (excursus 11: "Primitive Christian and Johannine Love Commandment"; literature); Thyen 2005, 607–13. See further Strecker 1989, 328–32 (excursus: "The Commandment of Mutual Love").

**13.34** I give you a new commandment, that you love one another, just as I have loved you, that you also love one another. **35** By this all people will know that you are my disciples, if you have love for one another.

The formulation of the "new commandment" belongs in the context of the Johannine passion story (John 13–19), which has two parts. The extensive narrative unit of chapters 13–17 is devoted *ad internum* to Jesus' parting from his disciples. Chapters 18 and 19 narrate the external events of Jesus' arrest, trial, and execution. Chapter 13 begins with the foot washing (vv. 1–20). The announcement of the betrayal by Judas is followed by the contrary announcement of Jesus' glorification. Jesus is so entirely the master of his fate that he proclaims his fate of death, which is sealed with the departure of Judas, as glorification (13.21–35). Part of this proclamation is the "new commandment," which identifies Jesus as a heavenly, already glorified teacher.[146]

Two points are controversial in the commentary literature: (1) Is 13.34–35 a subsequent redactional addition?[147] (2) What does "new" (καινός) mean? The first question can be answered only in the context of a general thesis regarding redaction or textual layers for the Gospel of John.[148] In our context it is sufficient to affirm that 13.34–35 does not disturb the text of 13.21–35 but rather deepens its tendency. The second question is more important. Here, there are two opposing interpretations. Rudolf Bultmann interpreted the adjective eschatologically. According to this reading, Jesus proclaims the behavioral norm of the "new time."[149] The second interpretation understands the "new commandment" in the context of Lev 19.18. This interpretation is definitely to be preferred for the Gospel of John, for the adjective καινός is exclusively used for the commandment of love for brothers and sisters in the Johannine writings.[150] In 13.34 we are dealing with Jesus' own formulation, which is no longer Torah interpretation but rather leaves Lev 19.18 behind and formulates itself a new commandment. Materially, however, the "new commandment" belongs — and this forms a bridge to Bultmann's interpretation — in the end-time, which has already dawned with Jesus' coming.

The author of 1 John discloses this eschatological dimension of the "new commandment" with a wordplay and at the same time expands

---

[146] Not as "new Moses." On ἐντολή, cf. Thyen 2005, 611.

[147] Thus, e.g., Schnackenburg 1982, 53 (GV = 1986, 59).

[148] Cf., by way of introduction, Schnelle 2007, 518–25 (ET = 1998, 485–92). Schnelle assumes the literary unity of John 1–20. The problem cannot be discussed here. Cf. the very balanced position of Broer/Weidemann 2010, 192–98, 197.

[149] Bultmann 1964a, 404–5 (ET = 1971, 526–27). See also Thyen 2005, 610.

[150] John 13.34; 1 John 2.7, 8; 2 John 5.

the circle of addressees from the disciples to the community members (2.7–11):

> **2.7** Beloved, I am not writing you a *new* commandment but an *old* commandment, which you have had from the beginning; the *old* commandment is the word which you have heard. **8** And yet I am writing to you a *new* commandment, which is true in him and in you, for the darkness is passing away and the true light is now shining. **9** The one who says that he is in the light and hates his brother or sister is still in the darkness until now. **10** The one who loves his brother and sister remains in the light and there is no fault in him. **11** But the one who hates his brother or sister is in darkness and walks in the darkness and does not know where he is going, for the darkness has blinded his eyes.

For the author of 2 John, the recourse to the commandment of love for brothers and sisters and the application to the community is already traditional (2 John 5–6).

> **5** And now I ask you, lady (κυρία)—I write to you not as it were a new commandment but that which we have had from the beginning—that we love one another. **6** And this is love, that we walk according to his commandments; this is the commandment, as you have heard it from the beginning, that you walk in it.

Here the eschatological dimension is abandoned. At the same time, the conception of a community ethic that is focused entirely on mutual love is replaced by an apparently simple commandment ethic that is far removed from the ethos of the Gospel of John.[151]

The "new commandment" in John 13 is formulated from a similar attitude as the sixth antithesis in Matt 5.44. Through the wording of *a single* commandment, the hearers or readers in the Johannine community are reminded of the commandment of love for neighbor. This commandment, however, is fundamentally corrected by Jesus—thus in Matthew—or else directly replaced by another commandment—thus in John. The history of the citation of Lev 19.18 has come to an end here. Now the commandment of love for the brothers and sisters from John 13.34 is quoted or alluded to in the Johannine communities.[152] Despite this, the commandment

---

[151] On these connections, cf. Wischmeyer 2009a.

[152] Materially the development in the Qumran texts proceeds in a similar way. Here too, love for neighbor is narrowed to love for the brethren: QD 6.11–7.1 and elsewhere. Cf. Fabry 2011, 68.

of John 13.34 belongs just as much to the history of the tradition of Lev 19.18 as the commandment of love for enemies in Matt 5.44. In both texts, Jesus formulates a commandment in connection with Lev 19.18. The theme of Jesus' Torah interpretation always stands in the foreground: Jesus is the teacher of the Torah. Against this background, the tendency of the Gospel of John becomes even clearer. As I have expressed it in a different context:

> The only "commandment" of Jesus must . . . consistently be read in its narrative context. It is personally and relationally conceptualized and contains clear emotional connections. Rather than transporting Old Testament–Jewish ethical contents, it presents Jesus as the one who opens *new* forms of life together between the disciples.[153]

## 4. Tendencies of the Commandment Tradition: Jesus, Paul, the Evangelists, and the Tradition

Another early Christian writing that is close to the New Testament writings in time but was not received into the canon of the New Testament, the Didache (or the Teaching of the Twelve Apostles), places the double commandment of love at the beginning of the ethical remarks and thereby gives to the two love commandments the dominant place that they never have in the New Testament writings (Did 1.1–2[154]):

> The teaching of the Lord to the Gentiles by the twelve apostles.

> **1.1** There are two ways, one of life and one of death, and there is a great difference between these two ways. **2** Now this is the way of life: first, "you shall love God, who made you"; second, "your neighbor as yourself"; and "whatever you do not wish to happen to you, do not do to another."[155]

---

[153] Wischmeyer 2009a, 219–20.

[154] Text and translation according to Holmes 2002, 246–69; cf. Lindemann/Paulsen 1992, 4–21. For an introduction, see Pratscher 2010 (GV = 2009); see there the editions on pp. 261–63 (GV = 272–73). For the Didache, see Draper 2010 (GV = 2009), with the literature provided there. See also the commentary of Niederwimmer 1989. The dating of the Didache is disputed. Cf. Draper 2010, 8–11 (GV = 2009, 19–21). Most exegetes argue for an early origin in temporal proximity to the Gospel of Matthew and to the Letter of James, i.e., at the end of the first century CE. A date at the beginning of the second century is also possible.

[155] Trans. Holmes 2002, 251.

The profile of the writing is Jewish Christian.[156] The first part of the work, which presents itself as "teaching (διδαχή) of the Lord," consists of ethical commandments, rules, and exhortations. The ethical teaching is ordered according to the pattern of the two ways doctrine. The double commandment of love opens the teaching about the 'way of life' (Did 1.2–4.12), which is followed by the short statements about the 'way of death' (Did 5 and 6). The ethical contents that characterize the 'way of life' are broadly secured in terms of tradition history—through the Synoptic Jesus tradition, especially through the sayings of the Sermon on the Mount and the Sermon on the Plain according to Sayings Source Q, through the recourse back to the second part of the Decalogue, and through ethical exhortations that we mainly know from the paraenetic parts of the New Testament letters.

The commandment of love for enemies from Q 6.27 occurs not explicitly as a quotation or as a distinct saying of Jesus but in Did 1.3 as part of the so-called *sectio evangelica* (Did 1.3b–2.1), in which "elements of the Synoptic tradition"[157] are compiled.[158]

Two points deserve to be emphasized. First, it does not follow from Did 1.2 that we are dealing with a quoting combination of a scriptural quotation (double commandment)[159] and of a saying of the Lord (Golden Rule).[160] Rather, the two statements are treated simply as ethical basic rules that stand next to each other. Their relationship remains undefined. Second, here the double commandment has lost its connection to the theme of "Jesus as the true teacher of the Torah." There is also no connection to the theme of the law. Instead, the double commandment has been taken over, in a leading position, into the reservoir of early Christian ethics. Double commandment, Golden Rule, and commandment of love for enemies are equally regarded as "teaching of the Lord to the Gentiles through the twelve apostles."

This tendency is also found in the eighteenth chapter of the Epistle of Barnabas, where, in the framework of the "way of light," a variant

---

[156] Cf. the concise definition in Draper 2010, 11 (2009, 21–22): "a community (or group of communities) of Diaspora Jews who saw Jesus as the Messiah but were receptive to Gentile Christians. They found themselves in competition with nascent rabbinic Judaism . . . , even if they were closer in their beliefs to the Pharisees than other Jewish groupings."

[157] Niederwimmer 1989, 93.

[158] The discussion about whether Did 1.3ff. is a secondary addition to an originally Jewish two ways doctrine need not be taken up here (cf. Niederwimmer 1989, 93–116).

[159] In addition, the double commandment is shortened and linguistically altered, so that one cannot actually speak of a quotation.

[160] The same applies to the Golden Rule of Q 6.31. It is quoted neither in Matt 7.12 nor in Luke 6.31.

of the two ways doctrine, reference is made in a loose form to the commandment of love for God (Barn. 19.2 in the same formulation as in the Didache) and of love for neighbor (in altered form: "You shall love your neighbor more than your own life" [Barn. 19.5]).[161] The double commandment is as such no longer recognizable. The commandments are also not cited individually. Here, it becomes clear, on the one hand, that the two love commandments have preserved their important position in early Christian ethics, but, on the other hand, that no further impulses proceed from the two commandments as *commandments of the Torah* and that the large thematic contexts of the correct interpretation of the *law* and of Jesus the teacher of the law are not pursued further.[162] The early Christian ethic develops beyond the normative Septuagint citation and also beyond the mere authoritative repetition of sayings of Jesus. The way leads from the law and its commandments—i.e., from the normativity and the citation of normatively understood tradition—to the conception of a distinct ethos in which love is conceptualized as an ethical guiding parameter.

A concluding look at Justin Martyr clarifies and confirms this development.[163] In his *Dialogue with Trypho*,[164] Justin refers, in the context of a hermeneutical-ethical digression,[165] to the significance of the double commandment for Christian[166] ethics (*Dial.* 93.2):

> **93.2** Hence, I am of the opinion that our Lord and Savior Jesus Christ very aptly explained that all justice and piety are summed up in these two commandments: "You shall love the Lord your God with your whole heart and with your whole strength, and your neighbor as yourself!"[167]

For Justin the double commandment of love is the fulfillment of the two highest ethical demands—for justice and piety (δικαιοσύνη καὶ εὐσέβεια). The point of reference is no longer the law but Hellenistic-early Jewish–early Christian virtue ethics. Accordingly, in the continuation

---

[161] Trans. Holmes 2002, 321. For the Epistle of Barnabas, cf., by way of introduction, Prostmeier 2010 (GV = 2009). See also the commentary of Prostmeier 1999, 529–55.

[162] Justin places the double commandment under the double virtue of "justice and piety" (*Dial.* 93.2).

[163] Justin, *Dial.* 93.

[164] The time of origin for this work is between 155 and 161 CE. Cf. Greschat/Tilly 2005, 17–35, esp. 18. For textual editions and literature, see pp. 32–35.

[165] *Dial.* 92.1–94.5 (cf. the structure in Greschat/Tilly 2005, 28–31).

[166] Cf. the polemics against the Jewish dialogue partner in 93.4.

[167] Falls/Halton/Slusser 2003, 144.

of paragraph 93, Justin sets forth love as a concrete form of ethical justice.[168]

With this the path of the two commandments in Christian literature is mapped out. They are placed as ethical basic norms in diverse theological and ethical contexts—thus, e.g., in the monastic rule of Athanasius—and are a component of the Christian ethical inventory.

---

[168] In his *Apology*, Justin places the commandment of love for enemies in a chain of Jesus sayings that are reminiscent of Did. 1 (*1 Apol.* 15.7). Important themes are restraint in interactions between man and woman, abstinence, and mercy. Love of enemies is in no way understood here as *nota evangelica*, or essential mark of the gospel.

# 2

# *Historical Contexts*

## 1. Introduction: Contextualization as Interpretive Method for Historically Adjacent Writings

For our topic, the historical *derivation* could be determined from the tradition history. It has proved to be fundamental for the early Christian concept of ἀγάπη and leads to the location of the conception in the Israelite-Jewish literature. By contrast, the achievement of historical *comparison*—or, understood more broadly, of historical contextualization—lies not so much in possible derivations or attributions but in the sharper grasping of the specific profile of a text, monument, institution, or idea in its historical context.[1]

The relevant questions in this context are: What search terms—ἀγάπη, love, or ethics—prove to be appropriate? What texts should qualify as *contexts* and be drawn upon for comparison? What conclusions are to be expected? Beginning with terminology conceals difficulties. In the introduction, I have already shown that the lexis and semantics of love diverge in Greek literature and Jewish–early Christian literature. The term ἀγάπη will always form the initial stating point. If we focus on ἀγάπη, however, then only the Septuagint and the noncanonical *early Jewish* literature in Greek present themselves as spheres of comparison, for ἀγάπη plays a distinct role, as a lexeme for love, only in this literature. However, a restriction to early Jewish literature on the basis of the lexis would neither

---

[1] See the fundamental study of Troeltsch 1991 (GV = 1981; first published in 1908). Troeltsch defined the categories of criticism, analogy, and correlation as aspects of comparative history-of-religions work. Cf. also Smith 1990. Smith writes, in somewhat ironical manner, about comparison in religious studies: "A comparison is a disciplined exaggeration in the service of knowledge. It lifts out and strongly marks certain features within a field of difference as being of possible intellectual significance, expressed in the rhetoric of their being 'like' in some stipulated fashion. Comparison provides the means by which we 're-vision' phenomena as our data in order to solve our intellectual problems" (52).

satisfy the expectations and possibilities bound up with the German (and English) terms nor adequately illuminate the specific character of the early Christian concept. The early Christian concept of love would stand like an erratic block in the non-Jewish literature of the early imperial period.

This dilemma can be avoided if we go beyond ἀγάπη and use the German term *Liebe* as the basis, which—like the English term "love"—has a very large scope and encompasses at least the semantic range of meaning of the Greek words[2] ἀγάπη, φιλία, ἔρως,[3] and στοργή.[4] This opens up spheres of meaning of love that are, in part, far removed from the range of meaning of ἀγάπη and precisely in this way marks out the contours of the early Christian concept of love contrastively. With φιλία and στοργή we enter the very independent sphere of friendship and comradeship, which stands alongside the concept of ἀγάπη, without being part of this concept.[5] Finally, at first glance, the term ἔρως appears to have no connection to the early Christian writings. It plays no role in the writings of the Septuagint[6] and does not occur in the New Testament. However, the question about concepts of love in the ethical literature of the early imperial period can contribute to the clarification of the question of whether ἀγάπη can have an emotional dimension and perhaps also erotic components in the New Testament.

Thus, we are prohibited from looking only at the lexeme ἀγάπη.[7] This also applies, however, to a presentation of the entire breadth of the Greek lexis for love between *eros* and *agape*, which, on the one hand, is a theme of its own[8] and, on the other hand, corresponds to the terminological expectation in German (and English), despite this breadth, only in part. For the German term (like the English term) is, for its part, shaped in a lasting way by the Jewish-Christian contents of love for neighbor, mercy, humility, etc., which are not connected at all with the lexemes that represent *love* in the Greek vocabulary. Thus, the path via the narrower or broader lexical comparison on the basis of the Greek terminology is not

[2] Notably, C. S. Lewis discussed these four words in his book *The Four Loves* (1960).
[3] Cf. Buchheim 2008.
[4] On the semantics, cf. Görgemanns 2006. Görgemanns distinguishes between ἔρως ("passionate attraction, desire, being in love"), τὰ ἀφροδίσια ("sexual actions"), φιλία ("lasting personal attachment, bound up with the feeling of obligation"); "the verbs ἀγαπᾶν and στέργειν . . . mean loving interaction in everyday life, as well as, in weakened form, 'being satisfied, being content with a person or thing'" (20n52).
[5] On the overlaps in the sphere of Johannine literature, see below.
[6] Exceptions are Prov 7.18 ('sexual love' in the speech of a prostitute); 30.16 (the insatiable love of a woman). In both cases ἔρως has a quite negative connotation. In the LXX ἀγάπ- has sexual and erotic valences of meaning.
[7] Cf. Wischmeyer 1978.
[8] Cf. esp. the classical work of Nygren 1982.

well suited for our line of questioning. The situation is similar for Greek ethics as a whole. From the outset, we are prohibited from drawing on them as "context" for the New Testament concept of love.[9] Rather, instead of ἀγάπη, it is advisable to use the very open German lexeme *Liebe*—or the similarly open English lexeme *love*—as a basis for comparison. This means that we must look, beyond the lexis, for Greek texts that connect the broad topic of *eros*, sexuality, and marriage with the concept of *humanitas* or with basic terms of Greek ethics such as the lawful and the good (τὸ ἀγαθόν),[10] on the one hand, and virtue (ἀρετή),[11] on the other hand.

For such a broader comparison a certain text is especially suitable, namely, Plutarch's *Dialogue on Love* (*Amatorius*).[12] Close to the early Christian texts in time; interested in religion, religions, and ethics; and philosophically influenced by Plato, Plutarch has always been one of the Greek authors who was of special interest for the interpretation of emerging Christianity.[13] Hans Dieter Betz gave a significant impetus for the comparative analysis of the ethical texts of Plutarch and justifies the comparison between Plutarch's writing and early Christian literature in his introduction with reference to its diverse character and processing of tradition:[14] "The closeness between Plutarch and early Christianity can be explained by their sharing in common ethical concerns. Only after this dependence is understood can the original and peculiar features of both sides become clear."[15] Moreover, the dialogue *Amatorius* mirrors the Greek concept of love in its very different aspects. Plutarch is an author who knows how to combine diverse traditions of poetic, philosophical, and religions origins in such a way that a distinct concept emerges, which nevertheless remains concordant with traditions that he regards as important and upon which his own ideas are based—especially Platonism and "ancient Greek

---

[9] On this, cf. the summarizing references of the editors for the keyword *Liebe* in *RAC* 23, 2009, 147, to the lemmas *Eros* (*eros*), *Geschlechtsverkehr* (sexual intercourse), *Homosexualität* (homosexuality), *Humanitas* (*humanitas*), *Nächstenliebe und Gottesliebe* (love for neighbor and love for God). In the broader circle, one would also need to look at love for parents, love for brothers and sisters (Plutarch), friendship (Plutarch and others, an especially popular ethical theme), and others. Dihle 1966 sketched a profound picture of Greco-Roman and early church ethics.

[10] Cf. by way of introduction, Tornau 2008, who also provides reference to relevant literature.

[11] Cf., by way of introduction, Horn/Rapp 2008.

[12] Greek: (*Mor.* 9.748e–771e), Hubert 1971, 336–96; Hembold 1961. Cf. Görgemanns et al. 2006. Cf. also Martin 1978.

[13] Plutarch lived ca. 45–125 CE. See, by way of introduction, Hirsch-Luipold 2000.

[14] Betz 1978, 1–10.

[15] Betz 1978, 8.

religion" and yet also Aristotelian and Stoic ideas.[16] This combination of traditions and new concept, of religious tradition and ethical guidance for life[17] gives Plutarch's dialogue its depth of focus and general relevance. *Amatorius* reads not only as an individual intellectually rich and literarily sophisticated dialogue of Plutarch but also as a reservoir of ethical convictions of Greek traditions. In the accurate formulation of Betz, "Plutarch's ethical writings are storehouses for ethical material of all levels, from archaic customs and rituals to popular morality to philosophical arguments."[18]

From this standpoint the results of the comparison between early Christian and early Jewish texts on ἀγάπη, on the one hand, and *Amatorius*, on the other hand, can be provisionally specified in advance. While the comparison with early Jewish texts finds support in the lexis, *Amatorius* shows which spheres of life belonged to the theme of *love* for Greek tradition and Greek thought and emotions in the early Roman period and which ethical lines of questioning and possibilities could be connected with a concept of love. A comparison with the early Christian concept of love will make clear the distinctive Israelite-Jewish traditions and the new early Christian shaping of love in proximity to and distance from the Greek concept.

## 2. ἀγάπη in the Septuagint

In the Septuagint ἀγάπη/ἀγάπησις[19] is the preferred lexeme for love.[20] Both lexemes are often used for corporeal love, sometimes in the sense of an almost demonic power,[21] sometimes in an erotic sense,[22] and, in addition to these meanings, for love as inclination and attachment, in some cases as the antithesis to hate.[23] In the prophetic literature we encounter a strong concentration on love as a possible form of the intense and at the same time exclusive way God relates to his people and to individual prophets. In the later wisdom writings, ἀγάπη is theologized and placed in the ambit of σοφία.[24] A tendency to become a more loaded term is visible

---

[16] On the details, see the excellent introduction of Görgemanns 2006, 3–38.

[17] On this, see esp. Betz 1978, 1–10.

[18] Betz 1978, 8.

[19] ἔρως only occurs in Prov 7.18 and 24.51 (30.16) for physical love between man and woman.

[20] On the lexemes ἀγάπη/ἀγάπησις, cf. the fundamental study of Spicq 1955a.

[21] 2 Kgs 1.26 (here for love for women *and* for David's love for Jonathan); 13.15; Prov 24.50 (30.15) parallel to ἔρως.

[22] Throughout in Song of Songs: 2.4, 5, 7; 3.5, 10; 5.8; 7.7 (as address); 8.4, 6, 7 (twice).

[23] 2 Kgs 13.15; Eccl 9.1, 6; Ps 108.5.

[24] Wis 3.9; 6.18; Sir 40.20; 48.11; Hos 11.5; Jer 2.2, 33; 38.3; Hab 3.4; Zeph 3.17.

only here. On the whole, the noun in both forms is used rather rarely and cannot be characterized as an important bearer of meaning.

In all the writings of the Septuagint what stands in the foreground is not the noun but the verb. It occurs very frequently and stands for all varieties of love[25] — on the one hand, for love between the sexes,[26] within the family, and between friends, as well as for the relationship to the "neighbor" in the legal community of Israel, and, on the other hand, for the relationship of God to human beings and of human beings to God.[27] ἀγάπη/ἀγαπᾶν predominantly renders Hebrew אהב / אהבה[28] and — like the German (and English) semantic equivalents *Liebe/Lieben* (love / to love) — stands for positive relationships between persons. These relationships can be erotic in nature, have social-caritative character, or designate the connection of personal affection or election, on the one hand, and of personal obligation, on the other hand, that exists between the God of Israel and the Israelites.

A unified concept of love / to love cannot, of course, be found in the collection of writings of the Septuagint, which transports in translation and expansion the works and collections of writings of the Hebrew Bible that come from diverse times and very different authors. In general, the Greek collection of writings mirrors the reality of the different theological, ethical, and anthropological spheres in which love / to love became an important theme for the authors of the Hebrew Bible. The distinctive contribution of the Septuagint lies in the choice of the Greek lexeme, whose significance the translators strongly upgraded:

> As the LXX translators chose to render Hebrew words built from the root '*hb* by forms of *agapáō*, a Greek word which originally was not characteristic, quite clearly *agapáō* acquired its classical meaning initially through translation from the Hebrew. This also indicates that the Hebrew root '*hb* could not be readily expressed either by *eráō* or *philéō* because its fundamental meaning did not correspond to that of these words.[29]

I shall pass over the "profane use"[30] here since the theme of erotic love, which plays a significant role in Song of Songs and elsewhere in the Old

---

[25] This fundamentally distinguishes the Tanakh and Septuagint from the writings of the New Testament. Hebrew אהב/אהבה have a similar semantic sphere as *Lieben* / *Liebe* (to love / love).

[26] On this, cf. Loader 2004.

[27] As a basis, cf. Bergman/Haldar/Wallis 1977 (GV = 1973). On the Qumran texts, cf. Fabry 2011.

[28] See now Oeming 2018.

[29] Bergman/Haldar/Wallis 1977, 103 (Wallis; GV = 1973, 110).

[30] Bergman/Haldar/Wallis 1973, 107 (Wallis; ET = 1977, 99–100).

Testament, is not addressed in the New Testament and corresponding
texts of 'scripture' are also not quoted.[31] However, the difference between
"profane" and "religious" contexts of love should not be exaggerated. Sir
13.15–16 LXX says:

> **13.15** Every living thing loves what is like to it, and every person his
> fellow. **16** All flesh congregates according to kind, and with one like
> himself will a man cleave.[32]

Here, in sapiential fashion, general anthropological, theological-ethical (Lev
19.18), and creation-theological erotic aspects (Gen 2.24) are placed alongside one another. The Psalms are full of verbal formulations that express
the love of the pious for God's justice, salvation, etc. and conversely, the
love of God for what is right, just, etc. In this context, love means "appre-
ciate," "value," "practice," "do."[33] With respect to the love concept of the
New Testament writings, texts that deal with the love of God for human
beings and their love for God are especially important. Both forms of love
are addressed very frequently. Sirach integrates wisdom into this constellation when he says the following about σοφία:

> **4.14** τοὺς ἀγαπῶντας αὐτὴν ἀγαπᾷ ὁ κύριος.[34]

Gerhard Wallis makes a fundamental differentiation when he points out that

> it is not self-evident from the beginning that the concept of love was
> based on God's acts in behalf of his people. Yet, perhaps a clear distinc-
> tion needs to be made between God's acts in behalf of individuals and
> God's acts in behalf of his people as a whole. It could be that originally
> the relationship between God and his people was founded on a different
> principle than God's love for the individual. First of all, the covenant,

---

[31] Knowledge of the Septuagint must be presupposed for the New Testament writings, also, of course, in places where it is not quoted. The view that the early Christian
authors did not know the reality and thematic discussion of affection and love between
the sexes and in the family can be ruled out (see below). This applies to the emotional
side of love in the Old Testament, which Wallis (Bergman/Haldar/Wallis 1977, esp.
107–9; GV = 1973, esp. 115–17) emphasizes (see below). However, the quotations of
Song 4.15 in John 7.38 and 5.2 in Rev 3.20 make clear that early Christian authors
already interpreted the Song of Songs allegorically in a theological-christological sense.
On this, cf. Karrer/Kraus 2011, 2029–33 (J. Herzer and C. M. Maier), with the literature
provided there.

[32] Trans. B. G. Wright in NETS.

[33] Cf. also, e.g., Mic 6.8: the human being is to "love mercy."

[34] Sir 4.14: "those who love her the Lord loves" (trans. B. G. Wright in NETS).

which was initiated by God himself, unites him with his people. But by the very nature of things, they remain distinct from one another. . . . Likewise, the OT does not seem to feel that the relationship of God to the individual was motivated by the bond of love. . . . The affirmation that God surrounds the pious or the righteous with love is also evidently late. It is primarily the Deuteronomist who has considered Yahweh's deeds in behalf of the patriarchs a work of love (Dt. 4:37).[35]

The situation is similar in Deutero-Isaiah:

**41.8** But you, Israel, my servant, Jacob, whom I have chosen, the off-spring of Abraham, my friend; **9** you whom I took from the ends of the earth, and called from its farthest corners, saying to you, "You are my servant, I have chosen you and not cast you off."[36]

God's relationship to Israel is expressed in an especially impressive way in Jer 38.3 LXX:

Ἀγάπησιν αἰωνίαν ἠγάπησά σε, διὰ τοῦτο εἵλκυσά σε εἰς οἰκτίρημημα.[37]

In summary, the holy scripture of Greek-speaking Judaism presented the first Christ-confessing authors with the lexis and the theological and ethical conceptions and rules with the aid of which the early Christian conception of ἀγάπη could be designed.

It becomes clear in the Testaments of the Twelve Patriarchs how far reaching the conception of human love for God and neighbor and of the love of God for the Israelites was in early Judaism and how fluid the boundaries between Jewish[38] and emerging early Christian literature are here.[39] The Testaments of the Twelve Patriarchs are in their final version a Christian text of the second century CE. The vast majority of scholars, however, assume that the present text has a Jewish prehistory. The very frequent mention of ἀγάπη/ἀγαπᾶν in the context of love for neighbor, love for brothers and sisters, love for God, and love of God as well as the

---

[35] Bergman/Haldar/Wallis 1977, 112 (Wallis; GV = 1973, 121).

[36] Isa 41.8–9; trans. NRSV. Cf. Isa 43.4; 44.2; 48.14 and elsewhere.

[37] "I have loved you with an everlasting love; therefore I have drawn you into compassion" (trans. A. Pietersma and M. Saunders in NETS)

[38] Cf. Spicq 1955a, 164–91, on the individual attestations. See also Söding 1995, 56–67 (esp. on the Testaments of the Twelve Patriarchs and on the Qumran texts).

[39] For the text, see de Jonge 1970. For a German translation, see J. Becker 1974. See also the English translation of H. C. Kee in *OTP* 1.

coordination of love for God and love for neighbor points to Hellenistic Judaism: "The interpretation of the love commandment, as it has characteristically shaped the basic stock . . . has its closest parallels in Hellenistic Judaism," writes Jürgen Becker.[40] On the whole, however, the assessment of Robert A. Kugler applies: "As a Christian composition of the second century C.E. it explains the consanguineous nature of adherence to the teachings of Israel's patriarchs, the moral norms of the Greco-Roman world, and trust in Jesus as savior."[41]

### 3. A Greek Concept of Love from the Early Imperial Period: ἔρως in Plutarch

When we turn in what follows to the dialogue *Amatorius*, we move not in the context of religious foundational texts but in the zestful sphere of Greek philosophical-ethical literature, which is fundamentally shaped by Plato's dialogues and combines philosophical investigation with aesthetic shaping and religious deepening. While this literature does not understand itself to be nomothetic, preceptorial, philosophical, or religious in a narrow or exclusive sense, it does aim to contribute on the basis of religion and philosophy to correct insight and, especially, to *right living*. The discursive and fundamentally open structure of the dialogue serves this end.[42] Greek literature, which is to a great extent organized in genres and forms and tied to genres, created two prose genres for the theme of love, ἔρως, in which the theme can be extensively discussed discursively—the literature περὶ γάμους and περὶ ἔρωτος. Herwig Görgemanns[43] has gathered the relevant literature beginning with the Platonic dialogues of the *Phaedrus* and the *Phaedo* in his introduction to Plutarch's *Amatorius*.[44] A glance at this literature makes clear which spheres and values the Greek discourse included[45] and how much the entire discourse on love differed from the early Jewish

---

[40] J. Becker 1974, 25.

[41] Kugler 2010, 1296.

[42] However, Plutarch's dialogues lack the deeply critical disposition and irony of the Platonic dialogues. In *Amatorius*, Plutarch attempts to introduce ironic elements into his position statement on the theme of the dialogue through the sometimes-burlesque framework story (esp. in the conclusion). Cf. also the staged distance from the literary setting of the Platonic dialogues in *Amat.* 749a.

[43] Love is, of course, also a literary subject of epic, drama, and poetry, and then, in a special way, of the Hellenistic novel and later of the Roman love elegy. Cf. also Foucault 1988, 228–32.

[44] Görgemanns 2006, 3–38, esp. 20–25 with nn1 and 55, which gathers the texts and scholarly literature.

[45] The historical development of the topic in the different philosophical schools, which Görgemanns 2006 sketches, need not be repeated here. For Plutarch it is important

concept of love. Plutarch's *Amatorius* brings together the Greek traditions and, at the same time, develops from them an independent conception. In the dialogues περὶ ἔρωτος, love for boys was thematized first, which had been connected since Plato with the idea of *paideia*, the education toward the beautiful and toward philosophical insight. The Stoics took up this concept but joined it with *arete*. Plutarch took over this expanded and transformed conception: The "joining of *eros*, *philia*, and *arete* is the foundation of Plutarch's conception of *eros*. . . . While this had always been a fundamental characteristic in the concept of pedagogical *eros*, this was first formulated programmatically and in catchword form by the Stoics."[46] However, unlike the Stoics, Plutarch avoids the Stoic rejection of the affective side of ἔρως, for πάθος is a fundamental aspect of ἔρως for Plutarch. However, what is even more important for Plutarch is the combination of the "themes of ἔρως and γάμος," i.e., the bringing together of the two literary genres on the topic of love. According to Görgemanns, Plutarch succeeds in connecting the two themes "like no other author" and thus in transferring "the Stoic concept of *eros* to marriage."[47] Thus, it was above all Plutarch who elevated conjugal love to the same level as love for boys and refuted all objections against an upvaluation of love for women and conjugal love. Despite Plutarch's higher evaluation of marriage, "in the middle part of the dialogue, the encomium on *eros*, . . . love for boys and love for women stand alongside one another without distinction," as Görgemanns rightly notes.[48] Here, the traditional high regard for love for boys becomes noticeable. In the subsequent course of the dialogue, however, love for women wins the competition. In 768e Plutarch explains that conjugal eroticism can also lead to φιλία, i.e., a lasting personal relationship characterized by absolute faithfulness (ἀγάπησις and πίστις). In connection with this, there is a clear upgrading of the value of women. This is the case not only with respect to the main virtues of moderation, practical wisdom (*phronesis*), faithfulness, and justice, which were traditionally assigned to the world of men, but Plutarch especially stresses the capacity of the woman for φιλία,[49] which leads to a complete mixing or mingling (κρᾶσις) between man and woman.[50]

---

that he especially builds on Plato and yet also on Aristotle, the Stoics, and some impulses of Epicurus. On Plato, see Most 2005.

[46] Görgemanns 2006, 22.

[47] Görgemanns 2006, 25.

[48] Görgemanns 2006, 27.

[49] Love for children, love for spouse καὶ τὸ στερκτικὸν ὅλως. Görgemanns translates the last of these with "Sinn für liebvolle Geborgenheit" (sense of loving care / feeling of security). See Görgemanns et al. 2006, 123.

[50] On this, cf. Görgemanns et al. 2006, 184n423.

It would, however, fall short of the mark to read Plutarch's *Amatorius* merely as a contribution to the ethical discourse of the early imperial period[51] and the upgrading of the value of marriage.[52] The dialogue—which Görgemanns, following R. Hirzel,[53] calls a "novelistic dialogue"[54]—picks up the Platonic dialogues *Phaedrus* and *Phaedo*[55] not only externally and thematically but in the interpretation of *eros* it also goes, in the tradition of Plato, far beyond the ethicizing pedagogy and 'aids for life' that characterize many texts of the *Moralia* and whose task Hans Dieter Betz rightly designates as "ethical guidance through healing the soul of its illness."[56] *Eros* appears in *Amatorius* not only as an ethical-affective-aesthetic-pedagogical entity but as a *god*. Betz also points to this religious dimension of the dialogues of Plutarch when he writes:

> Plutarch places great emphasis on religion. This emphasis is peculiar because Plutarch seems to have had no illusions about the decline of traditional Greek religion in his time. Observing the superficial religious activities of the masses, he stresses the need for deep religious convictions. Repeatedly the last sections of his writings have a religious theme.[57]

This side of the dialogue, to which Herwig Görgemanns devoted a separate essay,[58] is of special interest to us, for here—as Betz rightly judges—we find a very distinctive contribution of Plutarch to a Greek philosophical-ethical conception of love.[59]

---

[51] Its assignment to the ethical writings by H. D. Betz is not self-evident. It would be just as plausible to assign it to the religious or theological writings. Cf. the selection with commentary in Betz 1975, preface (xii–xi).

[52] Cf. Westbrook et al. 1997 (ET = 2006).

[53] Hirzel 1895, 2: 230–36.

[54] Görgemanns 2006, 17.

[55] Cf. the analysis of Rist 2001. In Rist's judgment, "it is a most unusual document, shedding light not only on ancient social mores, but very specifically on how Plutarch blended and interpreted Plato's various accounts of ἔρως—whether to be found in whole dialogues or in more limited texts." Rist regards Plato's *Phaedrus* as the "seminal Platonic dialogue" (558) for Plutarch's *Amatorius* and places it as follows in the history of philosophy: "Plutarch's dialogue is in part a contribution to an ongoing debate, largely inaugurated by the *Phaedrus* and especially of concern to Epicureans, about the nature of 'real' love (750c) and the proper 'philosophical' attitude towards it" (559).

[56] Betz 1978, 7.

[57] Betz 1978, 7.

[58] Görgemanns 2005; 2013. Cf. also F. Graf 2006.

[59] Brenk 2012, 110–11. According to Brenk, Plutarch incorporates the institution of marriage into Middle Platonism and attempts thereby to bring a new philosophical-religious

First, a sketch of the dialogue will be provided.[60] Here, I can refer only quite briefly to the complex and elegant literary framework. Plutarch forms a double fictional framework. He has his son Autobulus recount to a friend a conversation about *eros*, which Plutarch himself—who is always called 'my father' in the dialogue—is said to have conducted with friends as a newlywed before the birth of the son and which the son knows from the repeated stories of the father. The conversation is situated in an inner narrative framework, which is maintained during the entire reproduction of the conversation, since conversation and inner story are thematically joined. At the time of the conversation about love, Plutarch is residing in Thespiae with his young wife, in order to sacrifice to *Eros* (749b). A rich widow who loved a young man and wanted to marry him has just become the talk of the day there. Plutarch and his friends discuss this current case from different angles but soon proceed to a deeper conversation about love as such. The friends finally learn that the wedding is to take place and leave to attend it. The last word is reserved for the father, i.e., Plutarch himself (771d–e):[61]

> Forward then, by all means forward . . . so that we may . . . salute (προ-
> σκυνήσωμεν) the god. For it's plain to see that he approves and is gra-
> ciously present at this affair.

Thus, *conjugal eros* wins the prize at the end of the dialogue. The scene of this inner story is—not by chance—the sanctuary of the Muses on Helicon, while the time—also not by chance—is the festival of the Erotideia, which is celebrated in Thespiae every four years.

Let us turn then to the course of speeches. As an introduction, Plutarch's friends Protogenes and Daphnaeus discuss the relationship between love for boys and love for women. While Protogenes advocates the classical thesis (750c) that love for boys leads via φιλία to *arete*, whereas love for women exhausts itself in mere physical enjoyment, Daphnaeus (751c) claims that "if union contrary to nature with males does not destroy or curtail a lover's tenderness, it stands to reason that the love (ἔρως) between men and women, being normal and natural, will be conducive to friendship developing in due course from favor (χάρις)." With this the actual theme is formulated: the connection of love for women and marriage with φιλία and *arete*. After some banter about intelligent and dominant women,

---

dimension into marriage. The understanding of marriage of the encyclical *Deus Caritas Est* also belongs in this line, at least in part.

[60] Cf. the outline in Görgemanns 2006, 6.

[61] English translations of Plutarch's *Amatorius* are taken from Hembold 1961.

which is also still due to the inner frame story, Plutarch—in the dialogue of 'the father'—delivers a keynote lecture on *eros* (756a–766d).[62] In conclusion, Plutarch's thesis that conjugal love is the actual fulfillment of *eros* is discussed from different angles (766e–771c).

What is especially interesting thematically is the nature of the middle section devoted to *eros* (756a–766d), which is, for its part, configured in a surprisingly varied way. Plutarch opens his keynote address with an encomium to the god *Eros*, which is based on the traditional religion. From the philosophical, poetic, and religious tradition, Plutarch provides proof that *Eros* is a god, indeed even the first of the gods: "But Hesiod, in my opinion, was more scientific (φυσικῶς) when he depicted *Eros* as the first-born of them all (πάντων προγενέστατον), in order to make him indispensable for the generation of all things" (757f). At the same time, Plutarch vehemently opposes the intellectual fashion of interpreting gods as "emotions, functions, and virtues" (757b). Ares does not mean human anger nor Aphrodite desires (ἐπιθυμία) nor Athena reason (φρόνησις). Plutarch argues with great pathos: "You surely perceive the abyss of atheism (ἀθεότης) that engulfs us if we list each several god on a roster of emotions (πάθη), functions (δυνάμεις), and virtues (ἀρεταί)." Conversely, it is also not permissible to turn the affects into gods.[63] With this argumentative turn, Plutarch joins the discussion of the nature of *eros* with the center of Greek religion, as he interpreted it. The concern now is no longer only with a competition over the theme of love for boys versus love for women but with the fundamentals of Greek belief in the gods. In the process, the topic of the affects is not lost. On the contrary, the strength of the affects requires divine help. In the form of a rhetorical question, Plutarch cries out: "When they desire marriage and an affection that will lead to concord and cooperation (πάθους δὲ γάμου ἐφιεμένου καὶ φιλό-τητος εἰς ὁμοφροσύνην καὶ κοινωνίαν τελευτώσης) is there no god to witness and direct, to lead and to help us (ἡγεμὼν ἢ σύνεργος)?" (757d). Thus, in the case of such an equally powerful and positive affect as love, the Stoic control of the affects is precisely not adequate. Divine guidance is necessary. Plutarch regards the idea that *Eros* is merely an affect as outrageous (δεινός), for we "continue to profit by divinity's love for man (τὸ θεῖον τὸ φιλάνθρωπον)" (758a). Once again, with the help of a quotation from Homer, Plutarch emphasizes that "not without a god does such friendship attain its proper goal" (758c).

---

[62] There is a gap in the text after 766d.

[63] For this tendency, cf. Bendlin/Shapiro 2007 (GV = 2000). Shapiro refers to Apelles, who "was able to create a complete allegory" of defamation with personifications of Ignorance, Suspicion, Envy, Betrayal, Deceit, Remorse, and Truth (ET = 848; GV = 645).

The following discussion of the madness (μανία) of love shows how strong Plutarch regarded love to be. Plutarch presents a synthesis between the forcefulness of erotic madness (ἐρωτικὴ μανία), on the one hand, and its taming and guidance by the god *Eros*, on the other hand (759a–c). This is followed by the actual encomium to the god, to his power, his well-doing (εὐεργεσίαι), and his triumph (759–763).[64] In this encomium Plutarch not only praises *Eros* as god, but he also specifies the character traits of the god that are given to the lovers. Alongside the classic virtues of practical wisdom and courage stand generosity and congenial interaction (762c–d). What is especially interesting is the transformation of the loving soul to "high thoughts, liberality (ἐλευθερία), aspiration, kindness, generosity" (762e). This freedom expresses itself as follows: "A man in love thinks little of practically everything else, not merely companions and relatives, but even laws and magistrates and kings. He fears nothing, he admires nothing, he pays service to nothing" — except for the beloved person (762e).[65]

The encomium is followed in 762a–766b by a ἱερὸς λόγος. Plutarch refers both to Plato and to Egyptian religion and supports with this the previous remarks and gives to them even greater significance: "Plutarch personifies the logos, the speech, as Plato already liked to do. . . . Here, however, Plutarch understands what is owed to the logos not as a demand of inner logic but as a religious obligation. It is . . . sacred speech, which may not be truncated."[66] According to Plutarch's conception — which is expressed here by the friend Soclarus — "the Egyptian tales bear a resemblance to the Platonic doctrine of love" (764a). At the same time, Plutarch establishes connections between the Egyptian and Greek names of gods.[67] For the specification of the nature of *Eros* Plutarch uses, on the one hand, vocabulary from the mysteries: it is the divine *Eros* who "graciously appears to lift us out of the depths and escort us upward, like a mystic guide (μυσταγωγός) beside us at our initiation (ἐν τελετῇ)" (765a).[68] On the other hand, he uses the image of a mirror in order to describe the relationship between heavenly and earthly *Eros*. The heavenly *Eros*

---

[64] Cf. Görgemanns et al. 2006, 763f; on this, see p. 165n283: "The vision of this triumphal procession is portrayed like an allegorical painting." *Eros* is accompanied by φιλία and κοινωνία in his triumphal procession.

[65] Cf. the similarly generalizing statements in Paul in 1 Cor 13: stylistic elements of the encomium.

[66] Görgemanns et al. 2006, 165n288.

[67] For Plutarch's thesis that the Egyptians knew a popular and a heavenly *Eros* and beyond this the sun as a third *Eros*, cf. the notes on 764b–d in Görgemanns et al., 166.

[68] Cf. also the conclusion of the holy speech in 766b.

contrives for us, as in a glass, beautiful reflections of beautiful realities. These are, however, merely mortal reflections of the divine, corruptible of the incorruptible, sensible of the intelligible. By showing us these in the form and hue and aspect of young men radiant in the prime of their beauty, Love gently excites our memory, which is first kindled by this means. (765a)

When people find in the beloved person "a trace of the divine . . . , they are intoxicated with joy and wonder and pay court to it" (765d).[69] It is clear that Plutarch speaks here with recourse to Plato,[70] and Egyptian religion has receded into the background.

After a larger gap in the text, the argumentation continues. In 766e–767b there is another reinforcement of the thesis that love for boys and love for women are equal in their nature, since all striving after love is directed to the beautiful, which can belong to young men as well as women. The further remarks on constancy and faithfulness[71] and on the φιλία of the wife introduce little that is new. The comments on the *arete* of women (769b–e) are significant. Women possess love for "their children and their husbands" as well as the power to bestow "their affection" or "loving care" (τὸ στερκτικόν) (769c). And once again Plutarch describes the "internal amalgamation" or "fusion"[72] of the lovers (769f) and praises conjugal faithfulness.

Looking back, the literary art, the ethical seriousness, and the religio-philosophical depth with which Plutarch handles the theme of *eros* is astonishing and impressive.[73] Despite the literary levity, the sometimes burlesque scenery, and a certain philosophical nonbinding nature, which arises from the juxtaposition of such different spheres as ancient Greek belief in the gods, Egyptian religion, Platonic philosophy, and the language of the mysteries, there arises a great and remarkably lively picture of *eros* between ethical obligation, pathos, enthusiasm, eroticism, *philia*, and *arete*. The traditional themes of love for boys and marriage are united in the new homogenous conception of a love that reaches beyond what is human and connects with the divine world. Plutarch anchors

---

[69] On the mirror motif and the reflection of the divine beauty in the bodies, cf. further 766a.

[70] In what follows Plutarch mentions Plato's doctrine of recollection (*anamnesis*).

[71] The metaphor of change of lordship is noteworthy: "When Love enters as sovereign, men are ever after free and released from all other lords and masters" (768a). Cf. the same metaphor in Paul.

[72] Cf. Görgemanns et al., 184n423 on κρᾶσις.

[73] Here we would also need to point to his other writings on marriage and friendship.

this connection in the invocation of the god *Eros*.[74] Michel Foucault has emphatically pointed out that Plutarch transformed the older Greek binary conception of *eros* — "the first one common, oriented toward the aphrodisia; the second one elevated, spiritual, oriented toward the care of souls," with the former being assigned to love for women and the latter to love for boys — in favor of a unified concept of love:

> Plutarch brings these same Platonic notions into play in an erotics that seeks to form a single Eros capable of accounting for the love of women and the love of boys, and to integrate the *aphrodisia* into it. But in the interest of such a unity, this erotics ultimately excludes the love for boys, for it lacks *charis*.[75]

Jewish and early Christian ethical standards of erotic love distinguish themselves fundamentally from Greco-Roman conceptions in this point. Love for boys and *aphrodisia* have a place neither in Jewish nor in early Christian concepts. The situation is different with regard to Plutarch's high esteem for marriage and the love of the woman. While the prizing of marriage is close to early Jewish texts and New Testament conceptions of marriage, the early Christian ethic beginning with the Deutero-Paulines had to work to understand love as a possible aspect of marriage and to integrate it into its concept of marriage.[76]

---

[74] It is clear that Plutarch regards belief in the god *Eros* to be endangered (see Betz). Thus, the *Amatorius* does indeed have an apologetic dimension.

[75] Foucault 1988, 210.

[76] The encyclical *Deus caritas est* very consciously takes this path further.

# 3

# *ἀγάπη* in the Texts of the New Testament


## 1. Introduction: *Terminological History* as Interpretive Method for Argumentative Texts

It is clear that the noun ἀγάπη functions as a term (*Begriff*) with its own profile and not only as a substantivized summary and semantic shorthand for and repetition of the commandments on love for God and love for neighbor. Paul writes primarily about ἀγάπη and not about the commandments of love for neighbor and love for God. While neither Paul nor the Johannine writings work with terms in the sense of univocal and distinct definitions, texts such as 1 Cor 13 and 1 John 4 are expressions of independent conceptual thinking and phrasing on the theme "love." Here, the lexeme ἀγάπη can indeed be viewed as a "unit of knowledge"[1] that has the function of providing pre-academic definition and regulation for communication about foundations and fundamental terms of behavior. The noun occurs almost exclusively in the New Testament letters.[2] A clear line of demarcation can be observed between the Synoptic tradition of the two Tanakh commandments, on the one hand, and an emerging early Christian terminology of love, which develops — relatively independent of the Synoptic Jesus tradition[3] — in the argumentative-paraenetic letter genre, on

---

[1] Lewandowski 1994, 165–69, esp. 165: "Terms (*Begriffe*) are units of knowledge: Objects are summarized according to characteristics, classes of objects are determined according to traits that distinguish them from other classes." Cf. also pp. 169–73 (*Begriffsbildung*). See further Scholz 2009. Welsch 1994 provides a concise example of how a word develops into a more loaded term for the word or term "postmodern."

[2] Synoptic Gospels: Matt 24.12 and Luke 11.42; John 5.42. Some attestations in John's Farewell Discourses (13.35; 15.9, 13; 17.26) and in Rev 2.4, 19 (letters to the communities in Ephesus and Thyatira) also belong to the argumentative portion of the New Testament texts.

[3] The question of a possible connection is especially posed for 1 Thess 4.9: "for you yourselves are taught by God to love one another." Since θεοδίδακτος is a Pauline neologism, we can only speculate about a possible connection to the Jesus tradition. In terms of

the other hand. Here, what is especially interesting is the extent to which ἀγάπη in Paul functions as a substantival summary of the commands and the points at which a conception of love emerges that makes itself independent of the commandments and discloses and develops distinct, new terminological horizons for the Septuagint word ἀγάπη.

## 2. Pauline Literature

The fact that there is a close connection between the two Tanakh commandments and the terminological formulation of ἀγάπη can best be presented with reference to 1 Thess 4.9 and Rom 13.8.[4] In these texts Paul uses the substantivized infinitive τὸ ἀγαπᾶν as a bridge in order *to refer* directly (Rom 13.8) or indirectly (1 Thess 4.9) to the commandment of love for neighbor. In this connection, Rom 13.8–10 is at the same time a key text for Paul's own concept of love. Starting from Lev 19.18 in combination with the second part of the Decalogue and a generous reference to all "other commandments," Paul interprets love in an equally laconic and practical manner *ex negativo*, in a way that is comparable to the Golden Rule.[5]

**13.10** Love does not do evil to the neighbor.[6]

His interest here is not with love but, as already demonstrated, with the topic of the law. With the following theological judgment, "therefore, love is the fulfillment of the law" (Rom 13.10), Paul creates the theological basis for an ethic of ἀγάπη, which, on the one hand, corresponds to the intention of the law—here Paul wants *continuity*, though this may not be understood as exclusive identity—and, on the other hand, is open for all ethical themes that can be assigned to the category of the good—here Paul wants a *new beginning*. Paul thereby detaches the concept of love from the *commandment structure* of love for God and love for neighbor. More

---

substance, the same thing is said here as in Rom 12.10. The concern is with love for brothers and sisters and not with love for neighbor in general.

[4] On ἀγάπη in Paul, see in general Söding 1995. Söding provides a thorough synchronic terminological analysis for all the Pauline letters. He chooses the perspective of ethics and does not distinguish between the love commandment and the ἀγάπη-paraenesis. He understands his study to be a contribution to the ethics of Paul, which he sees anchored, for its part, in the "saving action of God in Jesus Christ" (285). The "relevance of the Pauline *agape*-paraclesis" (285) both for the dialogue with Judaism and for the ecumenical dialogue is important for Söding.

[5] Cf. Matt 7.12 (*ex positivo*). Cf. Dihle 1962.

[6] Rom 13.10; cf. 1 Cor 13.4.

than that, he detaches his thinking in general from structures of law and commandments and thus from the "law" in the sense of the Torah as the entity that could adequately and exclusively norm the life operations of the Christ-believing communities in commandment sayings. The law as an ethical control mechanism, which works normatively upon the life of human beings in the form of commandments, is replaced by the open principle of the good, which encounters human beings in the form of a listing of attractive forms of behavior that are recommended. Paul describes this in Phil 4.8 in heuristic openness:

> **4.8** Finally, brothers and sisters, whatever is true, whatever is worthy, whatever is just (δίκαια), whatever is pure, whatever is worthy of love (προσφιλῆ), whatever is commendable, if there is any virtue, if there is anything worthy of praise,[7] consider these things (as good).

Here, "justice" is an ethical characteristic among others and not tied to the Torah and its fulfillment, though this neither rules out the fact that the commandments of the Torah continue to be just and good nor does it mean that the basic theological judgment of Paul from Rom 7.12 is no longer applicable:

> **7.12** Therefore, the law is holy and the commandment is holy and just (δικαία) and good (ἀγαθή).

The comparison between Phil 4.8 and Rom 7.12, however, shows that what is just and good is not simply *identical* with the commandment of the law so that it is exhausted therein but is to be sought and found, so to speak, everywhere. Paul is convinced that *new* ethical rules and forms of behavior apply to Christ-believing community members. So long as and insofar as he thinks within the framework of the topic of the law, the new central ethical regulator is no longer the law or the commandment but rather is ἀγάπη, which he finds precisely in the law and which simultaneously opens up the way beyond the law. At the same time, Paul can also present ethics from other perspectives,[8] e.g., from the perspective of the reality of the communities' reception of the Spirit (Gal 3.2–3)—thus in Gal 5.16–6.10—or on the basis of the terminology of the good. Everywhere love is present as a mode of behavior of the Spirit and as a life form of the good, but it receives its decisive function as a controlling ethical

---

[7] ἔπαινος can mean "praise" or "something praiseworthy."
[8] Cf. also the concise discussion of the different approaches to describing Pauline ethics in Löhr 2013.

term from the general early Christian conviction—which Paul takes over
and develops further—that it is the "fulfillment" and "end" of the law as
the ethical regulator.

### 2.1 Galatians 5 and Romans 12 and 13: Love as a Form of Action and a Form of Behavior of the Good

We have seen what continuing significance the commandment saying
has for the tradition and transformation of the Old Testament love commandments, on the one hand, and how innovatively both Paul and the
Synoptic Gospels and the author of the Johannine literature interact with
the commandment sayings, on the other hand. The commandment sayings can stand for the continuity to Old Testament normative ethics, but
they can also express an ethical new beginning. The implicit or explicit
series of imperatives of the Pauline sayings paraenesis are close to the
commandment sayings but represent at the same time a distinct approach
to the theme of "love." Three texts are at the center of interest here—
Gal 5.13–23; Rom 12.9–21; and Rom 13.1–10.

Let us begin with Gal 5 and 6. Paul ends the extensive ethical exhortation in Galatians with the pointed summary in 6.9–10:

> **6.9** And let us not grow weary in doing the *good*, for we will reap at the
> appropriate time if we do not give out. **10** So then, as long as we (still)
> have time, let us do *good* to all, but especially to the household of faith.

The beginning of the exhortation is less clear. However, with Hans Dieter
Betz Galatians 5 and 6 can be defined as a whole as *exhortatio* or as paraenesis.[9] The imperative "stand therefore" in 5.1b opens up this extensive
exhortation, which, in turn, encompasses different formal subparts and
traditions. The ethical exhortation in the strict sense, for which love plays
a decisive role, only begins in 5.13, while Gal 5.1–12 contains concrete

---

[9] Betz 1979, 253, 271, 291. A review of scholarship on the different specifications of
the beginning of the paraenesis in Galatians can be found in Merk 1969. More recent position statements can be found in Nanos 2002. Longenecker 1990, 184, finds the beginning
of the exhortation already in 4.12. His observations on the formulas and clauses in Gal
4.12–20, which signal an interruption in the progress of the text and a new start are accurate
but need not lead to Longenecker's conclusion. Indeed, 4.12–20 does function as an interruption. However, these verses do not do so in an exhortative sense but as reassurance of
the epistolary communication. In that case, the argumentative flow of 4.21–31 is theological
and positional. The general question of the rhetorical genus of Galatians, which Longenecker addresses (185) plays just as little of a role as the question of the epistolographical
genus (cf. the contributions in Nanos 2002).

instructions on the question of circumcision, and Paul thus draws first once more the practical conclusion for the situation of the Galatians, as he interprets it.

**5.13** For you were called to freedom, brothers and sisters;[10] only (do) not (make) freedom into an opportunity for the flesh but through love (ἀγάπη) serve one another. **14** For the whole law is fulfilled in one statement, namely: "You shall love your neighbor as yourself." **15** But if you bite and devour one another, take care that you are not completely consumed by one another.[11] **16** But I say, walk in the Spirit, (then) you will not carry out the desires of the flesh. **17** For the flesh desires against the Spirit and the Spirit against the flesh, for these are opposed to each other, so that you do not do what you want. **18** But if you are led by the Spirit, you are not under the law. **19** But the works of the flesh are evident, which are: sexual immorality, moral depravity, debauchery, **20** idolatry, magic, enmities, strife, jealousy, passionate outbreaks of anger, selfishness,[12] dissensions, divisions, **21** envy, drunken revelry,[13] and things like these, which I foretell you, as I said to you before: Those who do such things will not inherit the kingdom of God.

**22** But the fruit of the Spirit is: love, joy, peace, patience, kindness, goodness (ἀγαθωσύνη), faithfulness (πίστις), **23** gentleness, self-control—the law is not against these (virtues).

In 5.24–6.10 Paul adds other ethical exhortations, which stand, like 5.16, 22–23, under the keyword πνεῦμα. Here Paul combines different ethical figures of justification: Spirit, law of Christ as replacement of νόμος in 5.23, and "the good" as superordinate term for "walking" according to the Spirit (5.25). With respect to love two things become clear in Gal 5 and 6. First, Paul thinks together ἀγάπη and the law. In this respect Gal 5.14[14] is the central statement of the paraenetic part of Galatians. Second, beyond this theological topic, Paul sets forth a new ethos for the Christ-believing communities, which picks up on the community members' experience of the Spirit. It is an *ethos of the good*, which is decisively shaped by ἀγάπη and its practical and psychological manifestations and neighboring phenomena. Gal 5.22 and 23 are the precise expression of this ἀγάπη-ethos.

---

[10] Resumption of the christological affirmation of 5.1, now in the mode of the ethical appeal.

[11] Following Bauer 1988, 112.

[12] Following Baur 1988, 626 (BDR §142).

[13] Consolidation of μέθαι and κῶμοι.

[14] Cf. Rom 13.10.

Hans Dieter Betz points out that the nine substantives in this list are neither "'good deeds' in the sense of Jewish ethics" nor "virtues in the Greek sense of the term."[15] Rather, love, joy, and peace are clearly theologically or pneumatologically grounded entities,[16] which present the basis for the ethos of the Christ-believing communities. Patience, friendliness, and goodness as the positive interpersonal forms of behavior are, so to speak, the human response to the divine gifts. By contrast, Betz wants to understand faithfulness, gentleness, and chastity as "famous virtues from Hellenistic ethics."[17] The combination of the different elements mentioned is especially important for the question of the contours of the love ethics in Gal 5. Paul remains with the loose connection of different forms of behavior and virtues, which may come from different sources[18] and which he brings together under the keyword *love*.

Let us turn to Rom 12. In the short paraenetic series of sentences[19] in Rom 12.9–21, Paul presents a loose web of apostolic recommendations,[20] whose fundamental coordinates are once again ἀγάπη and "the good":

**12.9–21** Let love be without hypocrisy.[21] Abhor what is evil, follow what is *good* (τὸ ἀγαθόν). **10** In mutual love for brothers and sisters be affectionate lovers,[22] rate one another more highly in esteem,[23] **11** do not be sluggish in zeal, be blazing in the Spirit, serve the Lord,[24] **12** rejoice in hope, be patient in tribulation, hold fast in prayer, **13** contribute to the needs of the saints, practice hospitality (φιλοξενία).

---

[15] Betz 1979, 286.

[16] Betz 1979, 287, says that they "represent 'spiritual powers' of the first order."

[17] Betz 1979, 288. Betz hypothesizes that Paul quotes here from a Hellenistic (?) source (288). Here 4 Maccabees would be the kind of work that could be in view.

[18] Cf. the discussion of the origin of the so-called virtue and vice catalogs, which are drawn upon for the specification of the form and tradition of Gal 5.

[19] The verb is lacking in 12.9. Vv. 10–13 form a series of present plural participles without a ruling verb. A plural present imperfect verb first appears again in v. 19b. The participles are understood as imperatives; cf. BDR §468, 2₅ (p. 397).

[20] In 12.3 he stresses, however, his authorization through (divine) grace.

[21] The adverbial style cannot be reproduced. The incomplete sentence can be read as a gnomic saying or as an exhortation. I support the insertion of an imperative (on this, see BDR §128₁₀, p. 106). A different position is taken by Jewett 2007, 755–56, following Wilson 1991, 150. Wilson and Jewett supply an indicative so that v. 9a becomes a gnomic thesis or motto. In the translation of Jewett, 12.9–13 then becomes a love text in which Paul once again defines love conceptually and with the help of examples, as in 1 Cor 13. This interpretation, however, cannot be combined with the plural participles in 12.9b.

[22] This short sentence contains three lexemes for love: φιλία for the brother/sister and φιλία as well as στοργή (love) in the adjective φιλόστοργος. On this, see Spicq 1955b.

[23] Thus with Käsemann 1980b, 343 (GV = 1980a, 333).

[24] On the variant reading καιρῳ, cf. Jewett 2007, 755.

**14** Bless those who persecute (you), bless and do not curse. **15** Rejoice[25] with those who rejoice, weep with those who weep. **16** Be of one mind,[26] do not set your mind on high things but let yourselves be drawn down to low things.[27] Do not become wise in your mind.[28] **17** Do not repay evil with evil, but give thought to what is *good* in relation to[29] all human beings.[30] **18** As far as it is possible for you, keep peace with all human beings. **19** Do not avenge yourselves, beloved, but give place for the wrath (of God), for it is written, "Vengeance is mine,[31] I will repay, says the Lord." **20** But if your enemy is hungry, feed him; if he is thirsty, give him something to drink. For if you do this, you pile up burning coals on his head.

**21** Do not be overcome by evil, but overcome evil with what is *good*.

Robert Jewett classifies Rom 12.1–15.13 as the fourth *probatio* under the heading "Living Together according to the Gospel so as to Sustain the Hope of Global Transformation." With this Jewett follows the textual structure that Paul himself signals when he introduces 12.1 with the ethical opening formula "I exhort you therefore, brothers and sisters." According to Jewett, 12.9–21 is the third part of this *probatio* with the theme "elaboration of guidelines for genuine love."[32] This subdivision also takes up the structure that Paul himself provides. The statements in 12.3–8 are determined by the theme of the different gifts (χάρις, χαρίσματα) that are present in the community. With v. 9 Paul transitions—without setting an overly sharp caesura[33]—to forms of disposition[34] and behavior that he recommends to the members of the community and begins with the exhortation: "Let *love* be without hypocrisy." There follows a semantically,

---

[25] The infinitive is used with imperative force here. Cf. BDR §389, the imperatival infinitive (315).

[26] The participle is interpreted as having imperative force here.

[27] On the translation, cf. Bauer 1988, 1565–66 (συναπάγω). Cf. also E.-M. Becker 2020, 101–2.

[28] Here, Paul uses different forms of φρον-.

[29] ἐνώπιον can best be rendered here with "in relation to" (cf. Bauer 1988, 547).

[30] Cf. Gal 6.10 (see above).

[31] Or: 'Punishment is my job (*Sache*).'

[32] Jewett 2007, 757.

[33] Käsemann 1980b, 343–44 (GV = 1980a, 331–32) sees rather a connection between 12.3–8 and 9–11: "The manifold charismatic ministry of Christians is also described in vv. 9–21" (344; GV = 331).

[34] Käsemann 1980b, 344 (GV = 1980a, 331) rejects this expression (dispositions/ *Gesinnungen*), which was already used by Zahn and Jülicher. The word field of 12.16–17 is shaped by φρον-.

syntactically, and stylistically dense exhortative text,[35] which returns at the end to the opening theme, to what is good and what is evil.[36]

How does Paul deal with the theme of *love* here? The text addresses very different aspects of love, as Paul wishes to recommend it to the Roman Christ communities. In vv. 10–13 it appears in the form of love for brothers and sisters, practical help for the community members and hospitality, i.e., as an active ethos in the circle of the members of the Roman house communities, of those who have the Spirit.[37] This also includes other forms of behavior that are not primarily action-ethical in character such as hope and patience. The Spirit-filled existence that Paul invokes in his exhortation here is characterized further through blessing and shared rejoicing/suffering as charismatically and religiously animated and emotionally agitated (vv. 14–15).[38] In vv. 16 and 17 Paul calls for a disposition of humility, which he sets forth even more clearly in Philippians under the double banner of ἀγάπη (Phil 2.1–11). All these forms of ἀγάπη are assigned to the good. In v. 17 the theme good-evil is repeated, with which v. 21 concludes. In vv. 18–20 evil is added, and the ethical exhortations thus contain, beyond vv. 14–15, an unexpected realistic depth dimension. Where does justice in the sense of vengeance and thus final confirmation of the good and evil remain when the community members exclusively practice ἀγάπη? With Deut 32.35[39] and Prov 25.22, Paul rejects enacting one's own vengeance and leaves it wholly to God. In this way, there arises an equally sharp — directed against avenging justice — and open and coherent profile of ἀγάπη as a way of acting and behaving, indeed also as an intellectual entity — namely, a certain form of insight into what is good for oneself and the other and a spiritual attitude that results from this — that has a spiritual, a community-related, and a personally accountable dimension.

In summary, we can say that Rom 12.9–21 is not a "love text," like 1 Cor 13,[40] but a *text about the implementation of the good* in the life of the Christ-believing communities in Rome. What is good is love and its manifestations. What is excluded is the self-establishment of justice. ἀγάπη and its practical forms occupy the first place. At the same time, Paul sets forth

---

[35] For the structure and stylistic analysis, cf. Jewett 2007, 756ff.

[36] The word ἀγάπη does not even occur once here. The theme of good and evil is pursued further in 13.1–7, while the ἀγάπη theme is treated only at the end in 13.8–10.

[37] This is especially emphasized by Käsemann 1980b, 344 (GV = 1980a, 332). It does not simply give 'liberal' ethics.

[38] Following Sir 7.34.

[39] For the quotation, cf. Jewett 2007, 776.

[40] Jewett reaches a somewhat different judgment because he interprets 12.9 indicatively.

a loose ensemble of forms of action, behavior, and disposition.[41] These are not original,[42] but they make clear in their compilation that Paul interprets the good materially as ἀγάπη. At the same time, it becomes clear that this interpretation is not simply capable of securing a consensus: justice in the sense of vengeance against evil remains unconsidered. Paul makes a strict distinction here—the carrying out of avenging justice for God, the carrying out of ἀγάπη for the Christians. Paul expresses a concluding verdict to this question in 13.10:

**13.10** Love does no evil to the neighbor.

An initial *comparison* of the two texts (Gal 5 and Rom 12) already makes clear the following. First, Paul construes love as an ethical form of behavior from the perspective of the law. With this he builds on early Christian tradition, which understands the commandment of love for neighbor as the "fulfillment" of the Torah. Second, love always also stands in connection with the "good" and is understood as an expression of the doing of the good. Third, love goes back, on the other hand, to the activity of the Spirit. It thus belongs to the new existence of the Christ-believing communities and stands at the head of the "fruits of the Spirit." It opens up the sphere of hope, patience, faithfulness, peace, joy, unity, and loving behavior and action, which Paul presents for their life together in the communities. Fourth, the problem of justice in the sense of vengeance against evil stands at the margin of this ethical sphere.

For this problem, in which love reaches its limits, Paul has two solutions. In Rom 12 he assigns the sphere of punitive justice exclusively to God. In Rom 13 he concretizes this position in a surprising way. Now the ἐξουσία ὑπὸ θεοῦ is the entity that enacts vengeance against evil. It is what exercises the "wrath" (of God). Rom 13.1–7 thus functions as connection text and counter-text to Rom 12.9–21, and it is carried further by Rom 13.8–10. To this extent, Rom 13.1–7 belongs in this context. Again, the concern is with the *good*. Love is thematized again right after this in 13.8–10.

**13.1** Let every person be *sub*ordinated/obedient (ὑποτάσσεσθαι) to the *super*ordinated (ὑπερεχούσαις) authorities.[43] For there is no authority

---

[41] This somewhat infelicitous expression (see the criticism of Käsemann 1980b, 344; 1980a, 331) is meant to stress the intellectual dimension of the text.

[42] Cf. the careful comparison of the individual motifs in Jewett 2007, 765–79. Paul combines traditional Greek, Jewish, and primitive Christian (Jesus tradition!) ethical motifs.

[43] I use "authorities" with reference to Jewett 2007, 780; ἐξουσία can be translated with *auctoritas*. What is meant are the Roman office bearers or magistrates (cf. Jewett

that is not *under* (ὑπό) God, but those that exist are arranged *under* (ὑπό[44]) God. **2** Therefore, the one who resists the authority has set himself (thereby) against an institution of God, and those who resist will draw judgment on themselves. **3** For the magistrates are not a (cause of) terror to the *good* work but for the evil. But do you want not to fear authority?[45] Do what is good, and you will receive praise from it. **4** For it is God's servant (διάκονος) to you for the *good*. But if you do evil, be afraid. For (the magistrate) does not bear the sword to no purpose. For he is God's servant (διάκονος), a judge for (a judgment of) wrath for the one who does evil. **5** Therefore, it is necessary to *sub*ordinate yourself, not only because of (the judgment of) wrath but also because of self-knowledge.[46] **6** For because of this you also pay taxes, for they (the tax collectors) are servants (λειτουργοί[47]) of God who are dedicated to this one task. **7** Pay to all what is owed to them, taxes to the one who collects taxes, customs to the one who collects customs, (show) fear to the one to whom fear is owed, honor to the one to whom honor is owed.

**8** Owe no one anything except for mutual *love* . . .

Robert Jewett specifies the rhetorical position of the text as part 4 of the fourth proof of the *probatio* and gives it the precise heading: "Diatribe concerning Fulfilling Obligations to the Governing Authorities."[48] This section of Romans is also configured carefully and is a short, distinctive passage.[49] In terms of substance, it is, as already mentioned, connected through the theme of the good to the texts that come before and after it.[50]

---

2007, 788: "The Augustan development of an elaborate system of local officials in Rome and the provinces is reflected in Paul's wording"; what is meant are "the local magistrates in Rome," Jewett 2007, 788). Strobel 1956 remains fundamental for this interpretation. On the ethical dimension of the text, cf. Bertschmann 2014.

[44] On the variant reading ἀπό, cf. Jewett 2007, 780. The semantic difference is small (789n74).

[45] The short sentence can best be understood as a question. This is diatribe style. Cf. the questions and the address in the second-person singular in Rom 2. Thus also Jewett 2007, 780–81.

[46] Jewett 2007, 797, pleads with very good reasons for translating συνείδησις here not as "conscience" but as "self-knowledge."

[47] On this term, cf. Jewett 2007, 799–800.

[48] Jewett 2007, 780.

[49] Cf. the analysis in Jewett 2007, 781–82 and 784–85. Similar to 1 Cor 13, we are dealing with a largely independent text, which has been inserted by Paul in an ad hoc manner into an argumentative or paraenetic larger textual context and only partially connected thematically to the larger course of argumentation. For this reason, an overly direct relationship to the situational textual context always remains questionable.

[50] Cf. the discussion of possible glosses or an interpolation of the entire text in Jewett 2007, 782–84.

Only in this respect can it be addressed here in connection with the ἀγάπη-texts in Paul.[51] In Rom 12.21 Paul had excluded vengeance for the Roman Christians. Vengeance is reserved for God alone in his argumentation. Here the Roman magistrates now function as direct servants—servants understood here in the political sense of civil service[52]—of God and enact the punitive and avenging justice that the Christ-believing Roman community members *cannot* enact. The pragmatics of this astonishing assignment of the Roman authorities to God's punitive action of justice, which rewards the good by punishing the evil can be specified in different ways. If we take into account the many collisions of Paul and surely also the Roman Christians with the authorities, then, on a realistic level, we must assume a missionally grounded strategy of appeasement.[53] However, the theological level, which underlies this strategy, remains decisive for the argumentation of Paul. It is *God*, the Father of Jesus Christ, who is Lord over the magistrate. When Paul applies this basic conviction of Israel and ancient Judaism, that God is the Lord, to the contemporary Roman authorities, he emboldens the community members by taking from them the fear of the authorities and domesticating them[54] rather than by presenting them as horrifying as the prophet John will do in Revelation. They are thus not part of what is evil but in principle promoters of the good.[55] Paul does not, however, overextend this conviction. It is not the basis for a positively or negatively accented treatise on the *empire*, as some exegetes suspect,[56] but remains a transitional argument that develops further an idea from chapter 12—the question of punitive justice in the lived reality of the communities—and answers this question as constructively as possible.

[51] The discussion concerning the extent to which Rom 13 is a political text and how the text is to be evaluated in the context of a political ethics cannot be taken up here. On this, cf. Krauter 2009.

[52] Jewett 2007, 794 for διάκονος and 799 for λειτουργοί.

[53] Thus, in a certain way, Jewett 2007, 803, in the context of his interpretation of Romans as preparation for the mission to Spain with its financial and organizational implications: "This pericope is an excruciating example of Paul's willingness to be in the world but not of the world, to reside between the ages, to be all things to all people, all for the sake of the gospel." This applies to taxes as well as to the honoring of the emperor. For the mission "Paul was willing to accept the system that demanded honor for the emperor and his officials."

[54] Jewett 2007, 799, points out the paradox of the statement, the tax collectors of all people are said to be "servants of God."

[55] The early Jewish and early Christian apologists consistently argue along these lines, for only in this way can they appeal to the state powers. Paul must also have thought in this way if he is to have insisted on his trial in Rome. On this complex of questions and the historicity of the trial, cf. F. W. Horn 2001.

[56] On the theme "Paul and Empire," cf. esp. N. Elliott 2008. Cf. now also Heilig 2015.

Then, however, Paul turns his gaze back to the community itself[57] and concludes his thoughts on the relationship between love and law.[58]

## 2.2 1 Cor 13: The Term Love

1 Cor 13 leads into a distinct lexis and textual world. Here it becomes clear that the development of the ethical dimension of ἀγάπη is neither necessarily tied to the topic of the law nor to the topic of the good. In the self-contained thematic text[59] on love in 1 Cor 13, Paul sets forth an ethical program with a specific profile:

**12.31** But strive for the greater charisms. And I am showing you a still more excellent way.[60] **13.1** If I speak with the tongues of human beings and of angels, but do not have love, I am a noisy gong or a clanging cymbal. **2** And if I have prophecy and know all mysteries and all knowledge and if I have all faith so that I can move mountains, but do not have love, I am nothing. **3** And if I distribute all my possessions and hand over my body so that I may boast,[61] but do not have love, I profit nothing. **4** Love is patient, love[62] is kind, it is not jealous; love does not vaunt itself, it is not arrogant, **5** it does not behave improperly, it does not seek its advantage, it does not let itself be provoked, it does not keep a record of wrongs, **6** it does not rejoice in injustice but rejoices in the truth; **7** it bears all things,[63] it believes all things, it hopes all things, it endures all things.

**8** Love never ends; but if there are prophecies, they will pass away; if tongues, they will cease; if knowledge, it will pass away. **9** For we know in part and we prophecy in part. **10** But when the perfect/complete comes, the partial will pass away. **11** When I was a child, I spoke as a child, thought as a child. When I became an adult, I put away childish things. **12** For we see now indirectly,[64] enigmatically, but then face to

---

[57] Cf. Wischmeyer 2004c, 239.

[58] See Wischmeyer 2016a.

[59] On the literary form of 1 Cor 13, cf. Wischmeyer 1981, 193–223.

[60] Textual criticism: Papyrus 46 reads ει τι. On this, cf. Zeller 2010, 405.

[61] Textual criticism: the majority text reads "burn" instead of "boast." Cf. Zeller 2010, 407.

[62] Textual criticism: on the division of the first three stichoi and an additional mention of ἀγάπη in Papyrus 46, cf. Zeller 2010, 410.

[63] Alternative translation: "It covers all things with silence" (cf. Bauer 1988, 1529, with reference to Harnack 1911, 147). Cf. materially 1 Pet 4.8: "Love covers a multitude of sins" (cf. Prov 10.12). With reference to the fourth verb, Harnack's suggestion is plausible, for here an overlap in meaning between the first and fourth verb is avoided.

[64] Literally: "(in a mediated way) through a mirror." What is meant is, not directly but in a mediated way.

face; now I know in part, but then I will know fully just as I am fully known.

**13** But now there remain faith, hope, love, these three; but the greatest of these is love.

In 1 Cor 12–14 love is not thematized in the context of the law but in the crosshairs of community ethics and charisms. The term "love" already occurred in 4.21 with a personal coloring[65] and in 8.1 in a theological statement of principle. Why Paul, with chapter 13, integrates an extensive, literarily sophisticated and thematically homogenous text on the theme of *love* into the tractate on charisms cannot be conclusively explained.[66] The text remains without an actual parallel in the letters of Paul. Apart from love, Paul does not thematize any entity in such a concise way. Despite its clear connections to the context, the chapter remains surprising, thematically and formally prominent and for this very reason exegetes have always given it great attention and held it in high regard.[67] In three textual parts, which are relatively independent formally and thematically, Paul sets forth the picture of love as a comprehensive and extremely intense "striving of the soul toward God and human beings."[68]

In a priamel[69] of religious abilities and values in 13.1–3, which are loosely connected to the theme of charisms in chapter 12, Paul starts by awarding the first prize to love. Not only glossolalia, prophetic gifts, and gnosis—i.e., religious feats that are especially valued in the Corinthian community—but also wonder-working faith, renunciation of possessions, and the voluntary giving up of one's life—i.e., ethical feats that are prized in the Synoptic Gospels—have no significance "without love."[70] Putting the matter pointedly, we could say that religious achievements—which

---

[65] "What do you want? Should I come to you with a rod or with love and in a spirit of gentleness?"

[66] The cross-connections to 1 Cor 8–14 militate against interpolation hypotheses but provide no conclusive explanation for the distinctive characteristics of chapter 13. On the comparative Pauline texts, cf. Wischmeyer 1981, 231–33.

[67] Cf. Wischmeyer 1981, 11–26.

[68] Wischmeyer 2012b, 356.

[69] On the priamel, cf. Wischmeyer 1981, 196, 208–9. See also Race 1982; and Gärtner 2007, 816–17: "Priamels appear in prose and verse and share a formal commonality. The concluding pronouncement (Gnome) in such a series of examples—that can be summarily abbreviated—stands out most as a contrasting or particularizing . . . climax. Particularly distinct is the priamel of values (e.g. . . . . Paul, 1 Cor 13)."

[70] Here the question of an implicit polemic of Paul against ethical values of the Synoptic tradition arises.

can, by the way, also be attested without exception for Paul himself[71] — are worthless without love. In this way, Paul also points multiple times to the love that he himself brings to the communities.[72] But what is this love?

The ekphrasis[73] in 13.4–7 unpacks the term "love" on the basis of its ethical actions and emotional states and patterns of behavior. Generally positive statements about its liberality and love of truth frame a chain of negative characteristics and patterns of behavior that do not belong to love. These negative characteristics can be summarized under the keyword "egoism" and emotional aggression against the neighbor, whereas love operates with constructive affects.[74] For vv. 4–6 it holds true, on the one hand, that "the proprium of this statement of Paul on ἀγάπη, which occurs in this way only here in his writings, is neither the criticism of γνῶσις nor the statement of v. 12 . . . , but the description of the modes of action of ἀγάπη, which . . . places ἀγάπη, despite all differences, closer . . . to a virtue with a Hellenistic character."[75] On the other hand, the reading of Aristotle's *Rhetoric* shows how close virtues and emotions or affects are to each other, so that an ethical reduction to love in 13.4–6 would fall short of the mark. 13.7 presents a transition and at the same time deepens the perspective. Love is not only a constructive affect or virtue but a general ("all") attitude that encompasses the most important "theological virtues" — namely, faith and hope — and thus theologically and ethically reaches beyond charisms and religiously grounded ethos.

Upon this foundation Paul then advances his argument in 13.8–12. This is where the *argumentative* weight of the whole chapter lies. Paul takes up the priamel again, integrates it into a short, apocalyptically[76]

---

[71] 2 Cor 12.12 (cf. the assignment of the "signs of the apostle" to "in all patience," the virtue or attitude that Paul also prizes in 1 Cor 13).

[72] 1 Cor 4.21; 16.24 (this concluding greeting is used by Paul only here); 2 Cor 2.4; 8.7 (reciprocity formula between the love of Paul and the love of the Corinthians); 11.11; 12.15; Phlm 9.

[73] On the ekphrasis, cf. Wischmeyer 1981, 195–96, 210. See also Fantuzzi/Reitz/Egelhaaf-Gaiser 2004, 872: "In the rhetorical terminology of the Imperial period, *ekphrasis* is a description which aims at vividness (ἐνάργεια, enárgeia) (thus in Rhet. Her., Theon, Hermogenes, Aphthonius, etc.), that is, a description which tries to bring its object clearly in front of the readers' eyes: persons, things, situations, cities, seasons, celebrations, etc. . . . The object was not specified until Nicolaus Rhetor (5th cent. AD) as 'primarily statues, visual works (εἰκόνες), and related things.'" Lindemann 2000, 281, 286, advocates the form of the encomium. Cf., however, the critical objections in Wischmeyer 1981, 205–6: "A genuine encomium . . . is certainly not present in 1 Cor 13, for a true expression of praise is not found anywhere." Cf. below on 1 Clem. 49.

[74] Wischmeyer 2012b, 355, on the corresponding remarks on in Aristotle's *Rhetoric* (doctrine of affects). Cf. also Rapp 2012.

[75] Wischmeyer 1981, 230.

[76] The verb "destroy" belongs to apocalyptic semantics.

colored passage with the scheme "now-then" on the eschatological horizon and thus contrasts the temporal limitation of the charisms with the
never-ending duration of love. Thus, the *value* priamel of vv. 1–3, with
the question "what *counts?*" becomes the *eschatological* priamel under the
question "what *remains?*" The relationship to God that the charisms impart
remains fragmentary. Love alone will impart perfect knowledge of God in
the sense of reciprocity. Although Paul, with the comparison of the break
between childhood and adulthood,[77] strives for argumentative plausibility
here, his main thesis of v. 8 — "love never falls (or ends)" — nevertheless
remains a surprising claim in its exclusiveness, though it does pick up the
manifestations of love described in v. 7: in early Jewish writings, faith,
hope, and endurance are forms of existence of the righteous person, who
"does not fall."[78] Thus, love takes up, so to speak, the function of the righteous. Even more surprising than v. 8 is the expression that Paul gives to
the theme of "love" in v. 12. The future love will become mutual perfect
knowledge (ἐπίγνωσις) — presumably between God and the human being,
though this is not explicitly spelled out. It is clear, however, that the concern is with personal knowledge of love that is characterized by an almost
reckless directness: "face to face."[79] Paul already expressed the same idea
in chapter 8 in a programmatic, overly compressed laconic sentence:

**8.1** But concerning meat sacrificed to idols[80] (the following applies): We
know that we all have knowledge (sc. that there are no gods or idols).[81]
(But) knowledge makes arrogant,[82] (whereas) love builds up. **2** If someone thinks that he knows something, he has not yet come to know as it
is necessary to know. **3** But if someone loves God, (for him it applies):
This one is known by him.

Here the possibility of a knowledge of God proceeding from the human
being is fundamentally contested. Not knowledge but love is the appropriate form of behavior in relation to God. Put differently, love *is* knowledge.

---

[77] Paul uses the same scheme of a break between now and then or earthly life and
existence with God in 1 Cor 15. Eschatology is conceptualized in discontinuity.

[78] Cf. Wischmeyer 1981, 119–20.

[79] This contradicts the theological notion of Israel that humans may not and cannot see
God's face (cf. also Paul on Moses and the new vision of God in the Spirit: 2 Cor 3.12–18).

[80] This perspective is the Jewish position in the polemic against the Greco-Roman
divine world.

[81] This sentence may possibly let a quotation shimmer through. Lindemann 2000,
190, discusses the quotation thesis but rightly points out that a "foreign statement" is not
present here. Rather, Paul "writes something that is known to the addressees." It is Jewish
basic knowledge.

[82] Cf. 1 Cor 13.4.

And only it leads to the form of knowledge that is appropriate in relation
to God. Knowledge operates destructively; love operates constructively.
More than that, knowledge proceeds solely from God and has the form
of being personally known as a distinctive form of love. First Corinthians
13.12 repeats these ideas. Thus, Paul turns the early Jewish motif of love
for God into the prevenient love of God for human beings, which is characterized as "being known."[83]

Looking back, we can summarize as follows. First Corinthians 13
represents the most important contribution of Paul to developing ἀγάπη
into a distinct term. The text does not lead, however, to a definition, a
theological systematization, or to a doctrine of love. Rather, the concern is
ultimately always with the situation of the community in Corinth. This is
shown by v. 13.[84] Not only for the eschaton but especially for the present
Paul prizes not the charisms but, in a variation of v. 8, "faith, hope, love."
Moreover, here too, in a kind of priamel, love is again "the greatest." The
exhortation "pursue love" in 14.1 leads back wholly into the practical, and
Paul turns again to the charisms in the worship service.

First Corinthians 13 is one of the rare texts of Paul that provide insight
into his theological thinking beyond direct communication, polemic,[85]
apologetic, and paraenesis. In these texts,[86] he very concisely expresses
distinctive thematic concepts on theology, eschatology, and ethics by
means of early Jewish Greek semantics, stylistics, and theology. It is
always a matter of laconic religious speech forms that say just as much as
they conceal or only provide intimations. Completeness is just as little a
goal as explication. Paul can also say other things about love. In the context of 1 Corinthians, Paul is concerned to specify the highest and truest

---

[83] On this motif, cf. Wischmeyer 2004d. V. 13 works as a gnome. See Thür 2004,
884: "As a nomen actionis the noun γνώμη (not found in Homer or Hesiod), with its
originally extraordinary comprehensive range of meaning must be considered together
with the verb γιγνώσκω (*gignóskō*) [11; 37. 491; 27. 32 (also with regard to etymol-
ogy)]. The verb with its meanings 'to recognize,' 'to form an opinion,' 'to decide'
and 'to judge' falls between two poles: 'the ability to recognize a state of affairs' and
'the consequences of this recognition.' . . . Therefore, its meaning includes orientation in the world and the resulting decision to act." This meaning of *gnōmē* "is attested
from the earliest references to gnome in developed archaic literature . . . to the literature
of the imperial period."

[84] On the possible different interpretations of νυνὶ δέ, cf. Wischmeyer 1981, 153–55.

[85] Niederwimmer (oral communication), however, rightly points out that v. 12 contains a polemic against the high esteem for "gnosis" among a portion of the Corinthian
community. Niederwimmer understands the verse as an excursus on the theme "love and
knowledge."

[86] Cf. 1 Cor 15.35–49; Rom 1.18–32; Rom 2.1–11; Rom 13.1–7. On this, see Wischmeyer 1981, 232–33.

kind of relationship of humans to God as love and to present it in its personal character.[87]

## 2.3 The Triad Faith-Hope-Love

Since his first preserved community letter, Paul places ἀγάπη in the context of the so-called triad.[88] In 1 Thess 1.2–3 he praises the Thessalonians as follows:

> **1.2** . . . unceasingly **3** we remember your work of faith and toil[89] of love and endurance of hope in our Lord Jesus Christ before God, our Father . . .

In this introductory thanksgiving, with which he begins most of his letters, Paul interweaves two traditional series of nouns with each other: faith-love-hope and work-toil-patience. Only the first triad is significant in terms of content and is materially differentiated. The second triad serves to intensify the individual members of the first triad. Patience, however, has more material meaning of its own than toil and work. The early Jewish terminology shines through here. Patience and hope as well as patience and faith are often connected.[90] These connections occur frequently in Paul.[91] The second placement of the triad in 1 Thess 5.8 also shows a slight irregularity:

---

[87] In his comprehensive commentary, Zeller 2010, 419, treats 1 Cor 13 in an almost brusque manner when he says in summary that "the significance of this chapter has been exaggerated beyond measure by interpreters who regard the essential feature of the Christian religion as the ethical." Zeller is correct in three points. First, 1 Cor 13 needs to be read in the context of the question about charisms. Second, we do not find the foundation of a Christian ethic here. Third, the chapter does not contain an explicit soteriology. With regard to the significance of the text, however, I do not agree with Zeller. The significance of the text is already reflected in the history of interpretation. On this, cf. the splendid presentation of the history of interpretation in Schrage 1999, 320–73.

[88] Cf. Wischmeyer 1981, 147–53. For additional literature, see Söding 1992a; W. Weiss 1993; Mell 1999. With his fundamental study, Mell seeks to locate the origin of the triad tradition-historically in the Jewish Christian community of Antioch. In doing so, he distinguishes between a "*pre-Pauline history of emergence and a Pauline history of use*" (206; emphasis original). The tradition-historical construction cannot be discussed here. What is important is the documentation of the early Jewish texts (esp. Wis 3.9) that characterize the theological milieu out of which the early Greek-speaking Jewish Christian communities could develop their theology.

[89] Or: labor.

[90] Cf. Hauck 1967 (GV = 1942). Eph 6.23 connects love and peace.

[91] Rom 5.1–5 (faith, hope, patience, love of God); Rom 8.24–25 (hope, patience); 2 Cor 6.4–10 (patience and love). In verbal form: Rom 12.9–13 (love, love for brothers and

**8** But since we belong to the day, let us be sober, having put on the breastplate of faith and love, and for a helmet the hope of salvation.

Faith and love have a clear relationship to each other here, whereas hope claims a certain place of its own, just as it is, after all, also connected with patience in 1 Thess 1.3. In comparison with these texts it becomes clear that the sharply emphasized triad[92] in 1 Cor 13 is without parallel in its diction and in the complete equality of the three parts. On the one hand, we are dealing with "a felicitous formulation"[93] within the framework of the elevated language of the chapter. On the other hand, for 1 Cor 13.13 we may speak of the "stringency of Paul's formation of theological terms."[94] However, the concern is not with a firm definitional statement on three highest virtues, charisms, or the like. The triad receives this role only in the reception history of the early church.

What light do the two other parts of the triad shed upon love? When Paul, in 1 Cor 13, very consciously—indeed programmatically—places *the value* of love over the Corinthian high esteem for knowledge and ecstatic spiritual gifts and ultimately presents love as the only "remaining" way to God and elevates it over faith and hope (12.31b), this could be understood as a plea for love, which is portrayed in an ethical-affective (13.4–6) or mystical (13.12) way. *Paul, however, is not the teacher of love.* What he seeks to present is the "walking according to the Spirit" and where he seeks to lead the Corinthians[95] is to "a new life" or "a new existence." This existence may *perfect* itself in love, but it is not *exhausted* in it. The author of Col 1.4 provides a good commentary on Paul when he writes in his opening thanksgiving:

**1.3** We thank God, the Father of our Lord Jesus Christ, always when we pray for you, **4** since we have heard of your faith in Christ Jesus and of the *love* that you have for all the saints, **5** through the hope that is laid up for you in the heavens.

Like all commentaries, however, the Deutero-Pauline author, in the act of explaining, also distances himself from the text that he seeks to explain. Texts such as Rom 5.1–11 and 1 Cor 13 show that Paul does not search for clean categories, such as present and future, as does the

---

sisters, hope, to be patient); 1 Cor 13.7 (love, believe, hope, endure). They also occur in the Deutero-Pauline letters, in the Catholic Epistles, and in Revelation.

[92] Delling 1972b (GV = 1969b).

[93] Wischmeyer 1981, 153: "eine glückliche Formulierung."

[94] Wischmeyer 1981, 152: "Stringenz paulinischer theologischer Begriffsbildung."

[95] Note the *way* metaphor in 12.31.

author of Colossians, who assigns faith and love to the present and hope to the future, but seeks to describe the new existence. *This* is his actual topic. The triad and its modifications reveal the framework conditions of ἀγάπη. It is not an end in itself but rather the highest possibility of the new life *alongside* other possibilities. This is shown by texts such as Rom 12, Rom 8, and Gal 5. Rom 12.9–21 spells out the new existence in the form of patterns of behavior, which include "burning in the Spirit" as well as love for brothers and sisters, hope, patience, endurance, and much more that is *good*. This paraenesis stands under the motto:

> **12.9** Let love be without hypocrisy. Abhor what is evil, follow what is good.[96]

In Rom 8.18–30 Paul presents a picture of the eschatological existence of the justified and saved Christ-confessing community members, in which faith and hope as forms of life in the present stand at the center. In Gal 5.1–6 Paul adds love and hope to the central theme of the letter, i.e., faith:

> **5.5** For we wait in the Spirit by faith for the hope for justification. **6** For in Christ Jesus neither circumcision nor uncircumcision is what counts but faith working through love.

## 2.4 Theological Contexts of Love

Other independent motifs are stored around this core of the term "love" in Paul.[97] I have already mentioned some of these motifs. The relationship to the Leviticus commandment has been discussed in detail, as has the rarely used motif of love for God. The short sentences in the framework of the paraenesis that call for love also belong in the context of the Leviticus commandment.[98] As we have already noted, Paul places together faith, hope, and love on multiple occasions in the so-called triad.

Three important contexts can be added to this. First, love is a gift or mode of action of the Spirit.[99] Second, Paul speaks of the love of Christ in

---

[96] There follows before patience etc., first, love for brothers and sisters, heartfelt love, and mutual high regard (12.10).

[97] Cf. Wischmeyer 1981, 228–30.

[98] Rom 12.9 (see above); 1 Cor 14.1; 2 Cor 2.8; Gal 5.13 (see above); Phil 2.2; 1 Thess 3.12; 5.13.

[99] I will not develop this aspect further here. The fact that love can be understood as a charism represents, after all, the basis for 1 Cor 13, even though in 1 Cor 13 love stands over the charisms.

texts with special christological emphasis—in Rom 8.35, 37ff.;[100] 2 Cor
5.14;[101] and Phil 2.1–11. Third, Paul thematizes the love of God for human
beings in Rom 5.5, 8. In advance, one thing applies to all of these spheres.
Here, nothing is explained. No explicit relationships are established.
Love is known from the Septuagint and can at every time be deployed
terminologically with an astonishing taken-for-grantedness—namely, for
every form of mutual intensive positive relationship: between God and
Jesus, between God and human beings, and between humans among one
another. In the process, Paul always understands love as an attitude that
is not simply a natural impulse, does not stand at our disposal, cannot be
retrieved, so to speak, and does not come over human beings, as *eros* does.
Rather, it is given by the Spirit, is thus not under human control, and per
se has a divine component. In Paul, ἀγάπη is therefore never exhausted
in mere self-determined behavior or action. And ἀγάπη is a gift (χάρις,
χάρισμα), not a power. If one thinks in a hierarchy of persons, then God
with the love for his Son sets this flow of love in motion. Christ hands
down this love through the Spirit to human beings, and human beings turn
to one another and to Christ and God in this attitude.[102] Paul sketches this
connection in Rom 5:

> **5.1** Therefore, justified by faith we have peace with God through our
> Lord Jesus Christ, **2** through whom we also have received access by faith
> to this grace in which we stand, and we boast in the hoped-for glory of
> God.[103] **3** But not only this, but we also boast in tribulations, knowing
> that tribulation produces patience, **4** and patience proven character, and
> proven character hope. **5** And hope does not put to shame, for the *love of
> God* has been poured out in our hearts through the Holy Spirit who has
> been given to us. **6** For Christ, at that time, when we were still weak, pre-
> cisely at that time, died for the ungodly.[104] **7** For only rarely will some-
> one die for a just person; for perhaps for a good person someone may
> dare to die. **8** But God proves his own love for us (in the fact) that while

---

[100] On this, cf. Wischmeyer 2009b.

[101] On this, cf. Wischmeyer 2012c.

[102] Thus also Eph 3.14–19.

[103] Following Käsemann 1980a, 122: "Wir rühmen uns erhoffter Herrlichkeit Gottes."
Käsemann 1980b, 131, renders this phrase with "We boast of the glory of God in which
we hope."

[104] Paul expresses three times in v. 6 the idea that Christ died already or "at that time"
for sinners or the ungodly and that this time is now—at the time of the composition of the
letter—past: he uses ἔτι twice and κατὰ καιρόν once. He needs the scheme "then—now"
for his thesis, which works with the logical outbidding: the Romans are protected from
the future wrath since they were already saved as sinners in the past, already live now in
reconciliation with God (v. 11), and therefore could be *all the more certain* about the future.

we were still sinners Christ died for us. **9** How much more, now justified in his blood, will we be saved through him from the (future judgment of) wrath. **10** For if, when we were (still) enemies, we were reconciled with God through the death of his son, how much more, having been reconciled, will we be saved through his life. **11** But not only this, but we also boast in God through our Lord Jesus Christ through whom we have (already) now received reconciliation.

While love does not lie at the center of this fundamental theological text thematically, it forms the theological pattern that underlies the whole argumentation. Rom 5.1–11 is the solemn opening text of chapters 5–8, in which Paul presents, in a way that is singularly detailed and theologically far reaching for his correspondence, "the situation of the Christians" in the tension between the spheres of lordship "of the existing humanity stamped by Adam, which Paul concentrates in death, sin, and law," and the freedom of the Christians precisely from the entities of death, sin, and law.[105] The opening and concluding text are related to each other. Both thematize God's love in Christ.

In the opening text Paul addresses the whole fabric of the relationships between God, Jesus Christ, and human beings as an expression of God's love for human beings and says: While death for a just or good person may be conceivable and understandable, death for an unjust person or sinner can only be an expression of the highest love beyond every plausibility. Thus, Christ has died out of perfect love for human beings, who were sinners.[106] To this can be added the second, implicit argument from vv. 8 and 10, which unveils God's love for human beings as the foundation of the love of Christ. God is the actual lover. Christ was God's beloved Son, his highest good. Christ has not simply sacrificed himself, but God has "handed over" the one whom he loved for human beings. In this argument, Christ is the sacrifice. This twofold love of God and of Christ for human beings is imparted to humans through the Spirit and is thus their new inner life reality (v. 5).

The concluding text in Rom 8.31–39 is just as celebratory as the opening one. Here, Paul invokes the love of God and the love of Christ again and makes a theological assignment in the framework of end-time conceptions:

---

[105] Wischmeyer 2012e, 303 (ET = 2012d, 267). Cf. also the very different interpretive systematization of Jewett 2007, viii: "5:1–8:39 B. The Second Proof: Life in Christ as a New System of Honor that Replaces the Quest for Status through Conformity to the Law. 5:1–11 1. Introduction: Righteousness in Christ Requires a New System of Boasting."

[106] Thus also Gal 2.20 in rather compressed form.

**31** What then shall we say to these things? If God is for us, who is against us? **32** He who did not spare even his own Son but handed him over for us all, how will he not with him also give us all things? **33** Who will bring a charge against the elect of God? God is the one who justifies. **34** Who is the one who renders the verdict? Christ Jesus is the one who died, yet even more, who was raised, who is at the right hand of God, who is also our advocate. **35** Who will separate us from the *love* of Christ? Tribulation or distress or persecution or famine or nakedness or danger or the sword? **36** As it is written, "For your sake we are put to death all day long, we are reckoned as sheep to be slaughtered."[107] **37** But in all these (situations) we gloriously conquer[108] through the one who *loved* us. **38** For I am convinced that neither death nor life nor angels nor rulers nor present nor future nor powers nor height nor depth nor any other (form) of what has been created[109] can separate us from the *love of God, which is in Christ Jesus, our Lord.*

In this concluding text, what is only hinted at in the opening text in chapter 5 becomes clear. The loving God (v. 38) is first the just God who demands justice from human beings and finds injustice (Rom 1.18–3.20) so that the following applies: ὑπόδικος γένηται πᾶς ὁ κόσμος τῷ θεῷ (Rom 1.18–3.20) and οἱ τὰ τοιαῦτα πράσσοντες ἄξιοι θανάτου εἰσιν (Rom 1.31). Christ takes this death upon himself and through this makes life possible for human beings. To make this theological subject matter clear, Paul can, as already indicated, introduce different tools of interpretation:[110] (1) Jesus' death is an expression of God's love for human beings. God "hands over his Son" (Rom 8.32[111]), who is guiltless, i.e., without sin.[112] Here, God is the actor, while Jesus functions as *sacrifice*.[113]

---

[107] Ps 43.23 LXX.

[108] With Bauer 1988, 1677. Jewett 2007, 531 translates "we are supervictors."

[109] Bauer 1988, 925, translates this phrase with "irgendein anderes Geschöpf." But the German word *Geschöpf* refers only to humans and animals (*Kreatur*) and not to cosmic powers and phenomena, which are in view here; cf. Wischmeyer 2009b.

[110] On this, cf., in general, Hahn 2002, 212–21. For the concept of love, the history-of-religions question of whether Paul makes recourse to the sin offering ritual or the motif of place taking does not need to be taken up.

[111] The expression "he did not spare" refers to God's function as judge.

[112] 2 Cor 5.21.

[113] Here the motif of the binding of Isaac (Akedah) could stand in the background. However, it is exclusively a *motif* parallel. If a person-related analogy were to be constructed, then God, as the Father of Jesus Christ, would have to be compared with Abraham and Jesus with Isaac. With this the parallel would be meaningless. Isaac does not die. There is also no material *tertium comparationis*. Abraham's obedience of faith cannot be placed in relation to the love for humans of God, the Father of Jesus Christ.

(2) Jesus' death is an expression of the love of Christ for human beings. Here, Jesus is the actor, Jesus "hands over himself" (Gal 2.20):

**2.20** I live, yet no longer I, but Christ lives in me. And what I now live in the flesh, I live by faith in the Son of God, who *loved* me and handed himself over for me.

Here, the notion of sacrifice is overwritten by the motif of the *voluntary handing over of the self* in the sense of place-taking. Both variants have one thing in common: Jesus' death is understood as a deed of love. This becomes clear in a compressed—indeed, almost cryptic—way in 2 Cor 5.14:

**5.14** For the love of Christ drives us, who judge as follows: one died for all, therefore "all" died.[114]

The distinctive characteristic of this statement lies in the fact that Paul makes recourse here neither to place-taking nor to participation in the sense of the Adam-Christ tool of interpretation for the purpose of making clear the universal scope of the death of Jesus but rather argues "directly on the basis of the motif of the love of Christ, which, for its part, plays a role neither in Rom 5–8 nor in 1 Cor 15."[115] To put the matter pointedly, here we could speak of the universal power of the love of Christ, which places human beings before God in the state of righteousness and opens up life for them.

## 2.5 Ephesians 5.21–33: Love and Marriage

The Deutero-Pauline letters carry forward the Pauline concept of ἀγάπη in different contexts. A further, independent theological development appears in Eph 5.21–33. Gerhard Sellin classifies the author of the letter as follows:

The author of Ephesians is a representative of Pauline theology . . . who knows the community letters of Paul (including Philemon) and presupposes and uses them for his own writing. The time of composition can be specified only approximately, roughly between 80 and 100 CE.[116]

---

[114] For the translation "treiben" (drive), cf. Wischmeyer 2012c. "All" is used with the article in a quotation-like manner.

[115] Wischmeyer 2012c, 330.

[116] Sellin 2008, 58.

Chapter 5 is part of the extensive admonition of chapters 4–6.[117] The author begins in 4.1–3 with a general call to love (4.2):[118]

> **4.1** I, the prisoner in the Lord, exhort you therefore to walk in a manner worthy of the calling to which you have been called, **2** with all humility and gentleness, with patience, bearing with one another in *love*, **3** striving to maintain the unity of the Spirit in the bond of peace.

4.4–16 sketches out a conception of the community in its fundamental unity and of the simultaneous variety of spiritual gifts and services that further develops the Pauline texts of 1 Cor 12–14 and Rom 12. In 4.17–32, the author provides an initial sketch of the new (4.23) community ethos. In 5.1–20 a second sketch, which stands again under the keyword "love," follows:

> **5.1** Therefore, be imitators of God, as beloved children, **2** and walk in love, just as Christ also loved us/you[119] and handed himself over for us as gift and sacrifice to God for a well-pleasing smell.[120]

What follow are individual topical admonitions from the reservoir of Pauline or Deutero-Pauline paraenesis, which is deepened religiously through references to the ethically connoted metaphor of light-darkness. 5.21–6.9 are then devoted to the questions of the *hierarchical ordering (ὑποτάσσειν) in the community and their houses*. The so-called household code (*Haustafel*)[121] contains regulations for wives (5.21–24); husbands (5.25–33); children and parents, especially fathers (6.1–4); and slaves and masters (6.3–9), i.e., for all members of the house. In contrast to the Pastoral Epistles, specific codes for community services are (still) lacking, and the regulations for the houses of community members also stand under the theological horizon of the relationship between Christ and community. The extensive text of Ephesians is based on the shorter text of Colossians (3.18–4.1). Eph 5.21–24 theologically expands the short recommendations of Col 3.18, 19a.[122]

---

[117] For fundamental information on the paraenesis in Ephesians, cf. Sellin 2009.

[118] Echoes of 1 Cor 13.4 can be found in 4.2: compilation of constructive virtues and emotions (humility, gentleness, magnanimity: μακροθυμία).

[119] The textual tradition is unclear. Sellin supports "you." NA[28] reads "us."

[120] Here the notion of sacrifice is christologically written over insofar as Christ gives himself as an offering, i.e., is himself simultaneously priest and sacrifice.

[121] Sellin 2008, 424–71, esp. the introduction to the "form and function of the genre household code" on pp. 426–33.

[122] On love and marriage in Colossians and Ephesians, cf. Söding 2017a.

**5.21** Be subordinate to one another in the fear of Christ: **22** Wives to your own husbands as to the Lord, **23** for the husband is the head of the wife as also Christ (is) the head of the community (ἐκκλησία), he himself as savior of the body. **24** But just as the community is subordinate to Christ, so also the wives to the husbands in all (spheres).[123] **25** Husbands, *love* (ἀγαπᾶν) (your)[124] wives [],[125] just as Christ also loved the community and handed himself over for her, **26** in order to sanctify her by cleansing her through the bath of water by the word, **27** so that he might present the community to himself as a glorious community that has no spots, wrinkles or any such thing, but that she might be holy and blameless.[126] **28** In the same way husbands also should love their wives as their own bodies (σώματα). He who loves his wife, loves himself. **29** For no one has ever hated his own flesh (σάρξ), but he nourishes and cares for it, just as also Christ does to the community, **30** because we are members of his body (σῶμα). **31** "For this reason a man will leave his father and mother and will cleave to his wife, and the two will become one flesh."[127] **32** This mystery is great. But I am applying it to Christ and to the community. **33** (Thus) also each of you in any case: each should love his wife as himself, but the wife (for her it should apply) that she honors[128] the husband.

Conjugal love is only connected with the verb ἀγαπᾶν in the two household codes in Col 3.19 and Eph 5.[129] The author of Ephesians attaches the love of the husband for his wife[130] with the phrase "as his own body" additionally to the commandment of love for neighbor.[131] It is especially conspicuous that Paul himself, in his extensive comments on the question of marriage in 1 Cor 7, entirely avoids the verb ἀγαπᾶν, as well as other theological motifs of interpretation pertaining to marriage.[132] While Col 3.18–25 is restricted to a singular mention of "to love,"[133] though with this

---

[123] Underlining has been used to designate material that represents a surplus in relation to Col 3.18–19.

[124] Added according to F G it vg sy.

[125] [] designates additional text in Col 3.19b: "and do not be embittered against them."

[126] On the syntactic structure, cf. Sellin 2009, 447.

[127] Gen 2.24. Greek: ἔσονται οἱ δύο εἰς σάρκα μίαν.

[128] The Greek is φοβῆται: fear, treat with reverence.

[129] The author of Eph probably had Col 3.19 as a *Vorlage*. Cf. Sellin 2008, 432–33.

[130] Not reciprocally!

[131] In the sense of the "body" theology of chapter 5, however, he replaces "yourself" with "your own body."

[132] V. 10 concerns divorce. The Jesus tradition also does not know of the conception of conjugal *love*.

[133] Sellin 2008, 446.

it already brings a new tone into the marriage paraenesis, Eph 5.21–33
uses the term six times in the context of the marriage exhortations for the
*men*. Here, we thus find a quite distinctive conception of conjugal love that
is without parallel in the New Testament writings. In the comparison of
Colossians and Ephesians, Sellin speaks with reference to Eph 5.25–33
of a "metaphoric correspondence of marriage (relationship: husband-wife)
and the relationship of Christ and his church." He reaches the conclusion
that "this verse constitutes the center of gravity of the whole household
code."[134] This gives rise to the following question: What concept of conjugal love does the author of Ephesians set forth on the basis of the term
ἀγάπη?

The hierarchical gradation and thematic nesting of the paraenesis in Ephesians makes it necessary first to reexamine chapters 4–6 as a
whole. The opening sentence in 4.1–6,[135] which stands under the keyword
παρακαλῶ, evokes Pauline ethical modes of behavior, under which
ἀγάπη also functions. What leads the way here, however, is the theme of
unity—this too is already an ethical motif in the letters of Paul[136]—which
is invoked in a "verbless slogan"[137] in 4.5–6. In the following sections of
the fourth chapter, which partly have a theological-foundational character
and partly compile individual exhortations, love is found in vv. 15–16:

> **4.15** But being truthful, in *love* let us grow up in every way into him,
> who is the head, Christ, **16** from whom the whole body is fit and held
> together[138] through every supporting joint according to the power which
> is due to every member[139] and which makes the growth of the body for
> its building up in *love*.

This complicated and not very felicitous metaphoricism from the sphere of
medicine,[140] which involves the composition, cohesiveness, and management of the body, need not be analyzed in detail here. What is clear is that the
author constructs a *mutual movement of love*. The community, understood
as body of Christ, is to grow in love toward its head, Christ, and thus correspond to the great movement of love with which Christ accomplishes the
construction of the community. For Eph 5 it is especially important that four
entities are already set in relationship to one another in chapter 4—Christ,

---

[134] Sellin 2008, 433.
[135] Cf. the detailed interpretation in Sellin 2008, 306–28.
[136] Rom 12; 1 Cor 12; Gal 3.28; Phil 1.27; 2.2.
[137] Sellin 2008, 308.
[138] The translation does not retain the participial construction.
[139] Greek: "part."
[140] Cf., in detail, Sellin 2008, 349–51.

the community, σῶμα, and ἀγάπη. With this the basis for 5.21–33 is laid. Christ, the community, the body, and love also form the matrix into which the author's understanding of marriage is plotted in this central text.

As already mentioned, the text in Ephesians is an expansion of Col 3.18–4.1. The expansions pertain above all to Eph 5.23–24 and 5.25b–33.[141] These expansions lead to a double textual structure in Eph 5.21–33:[142]

> **5.21** Subordinate yourselves to one another in the fear of Christ: **22** Wives to your own husbands <u>as to the Lord,</u>[143] **23** for the husband is the head of the wife <u>as also Christ (is) the head of the community</u> (ἐκκλησία), he himself as savior of the body. **24** But just as the community subordinates itself to Christ, so also the wives to the husbands in all (spheres). **25** Husbands, *love* (ἀγαπᾶν) (your) wives, <u>just as Christ also loved the community and handed himself over for her, **26** in order to sanctify her by cleansing her through the bath of water by the word, **27** so that he might present the community to himself as a glorious community that has no spots, wrinkles or any such thing, but that she may be holy and blameless.</u> **28** In the same way husbands also should love their wives as their own bodies (σώματα). He who loves his wife, loves himself. **29** For no one has ever hated his own flesh (σάρξ), but he nourishes and cares for it, <u>just as also Christ does to the community, **30** because we are members of his body.</u> **31** "For this reason a man will leave his father and mother and will cleave to his wife, and the two will become one flesh." **32** This <u>mystery</u> is great. But I am applying (λέγω εἰς) it to Christ and to the community. **33** (Thus) also each of you in any case: each should love his wife as himself, but the wife (for her it should apply) that she honors[144] the husband.

This paraenetic text works with a christological foundation throughout, which is introduced in each case with "as." The relationship between husband and wife is described thereby in analogy to the relationship between Christ and the community.[145] The comparative structure (ὡς) already occurs in Col 3.18, though it has a significantly different form there from what we find in Ephesians:

> **3.18** Wives, be subordinate to your husbands, as is fitting in the Lord. **19** Husbands, love your wives and do not be embittered against them.

---

[141] Cf. the table in Sellin 2008, 432. See the underlined material in the translation.
[142] Cf. the table in Sellin 2008, 424.
[143] The comparisons are underlined, as well as the concluding interpretation in v. 32.
[144] The Greek is φοβῆται: fear, treat with reverence.
[145] On the "lower" and "upper" textual levels, cf., in detail, Ådna 1995.

In the Colossians text, the behavior of wives is compared with the general behavior of Christian communities. It is a case among other cases of correct behavior, not something special and not something related specifically to Christ himself. The author of Ephesians is no longer satisfied with these simple rules of Colossians. Rather, on the one hand, he develops a christological analogy, and, on the other hand, he employs an allegorical interpretation of Gen 2.24 as well as an implicit reference to the commandment of love for neighbor, i.e., two scriptural connections. He brings both lines together in a *christologically grounded conception of the love of the husband for his wife.*

Let us begin with the two references to "scripture": (1) 5.28 transfers—without explicit allusion and with a certain deviation—the specification of love for neighbor from Lev 19.18 to the love of the husband for his wife. This is not an intensification of love but a reduction of the intensity. The same love should apply to the wife—should we add "at least" here—as to the neighbor. (2) Gen 2.24 is used by Jesus in Mark 10.6 (par. Matt 19.5) as an argument *ex negativo* against the contemporary Jewish practice of divorce. Another variant of the *ex negativo* use occurs in 1 Cor 6.16: Paul refers to Gen 2 in his polemic against πορνεία. A positive reference to Gen 2 in the context of marriage[146] is restricted to Eph 5. Paul, however, already charges the quotation christologically in the context of the body of Christ theologoumenon in 1 Cor 6.13-20:

> **6.13** But the body (σῶμα) is not for sexuality outside of marriage (πορ-νεία)[147] but for the Lord, and the Lord for the body. **14** God raised the Lord and will raise us through his power. **15** Do you not know that our bodies are members of Christ? Shall I then take the members of Christ and make them members of a prostitute? May it never be! **16** Do you not know that the one who joins himself with a prostitute is one body (σῶμα) (with her)? For it says, "The two shall become one flesh (σάρξ)." **17** But the one who is joined to the Lord is one spirit (with him). **18** Flee sexuality outside of marriage (πορνεία). Every sin that a human being commits is outside of his body (σῶμα), but the one who engages in sexuality outside of marriage sins against his own body. **19** Or do you not know that your body is the temple of the Holy Spirit, which you have from God, and that you are not your own? **20** For you were dearly bought; therefore, glorify God with your body.

---

[146] Cf. Oepke 1959; Westbrook 2006 (GV = 1997); Urban 2005a. On marriage in primitive Christianity and on the contemporary pagan conceptions of marriage in connection with Eph 5 and its environment, cf. Zimmermann 2001, esp. 327–85.

[147] This perspective is male. The concern is precisely with every form of male sexuality outside of marriage.

In 1 Cor 5 and 6, Paul deals thematically mainly with sexual unfaithfulness and sexual transgressions[148] of men (inside and outside of marriage).[149] At no point does Paul mention "love," though he does speak, on the one hand, of the body (σῶμα) and, on the other hand, of "the Lord" or Christ. He understands the Christ-confessing Corinthians (12.3) as members of the new creation that has begun with the resurrection of Jesus Christ (chapter 15). They are connected with Christ in the σῶμα Χριστοῦ, the community. The individual members of the community are members of this body. This is why their body is of special importance: disordered sexuality defiles their body. The σῶμα thus becomes the central location of the new ethos.

The author of Ephesians takes up this theological interpretation of the community and its members and connects it with theological speculations on the σῶμα, which is, on the one hand, the body of Christ and—derived from this—precisely the body of the community, and, on the other hand, the body of the individual Christians. Material and spiritual aspects are inseparably joined together. This already applies to Paul, who draws on the quotation from Gen 2.24 (σάρξ) as an attestation for his understanding of σῶμα and juxtaposes both entities with πνεῦμα.[150] The interest of Ephesians lies then in a strengthening of the theological construction of the community as body of Christ.[151] In doing so, he incorporates more strongly than Paul not only the individuals but also the "Christian" houses into his construction. His concern is with a penetration of the model of the "Christian" house on the basis of Christ. He builds his model of order in individual steps. The "fear of Christ" stands over all. He is the head of all the groups who are addressed in the code (v. 21), i.e., all the remarks are tied to the model of hierarchical *subordination*, which takes its point of departure from Christ as the head of the body. The subordination of the women under the men—a component of early Christian paraenesis since 1 Cor 11[152] and Col 3—is initially tied back in detail to Christ (vv. 22–24). Here the soteriological

---

[148] Thus in chapter 5; on the unclear text, cf. Lindemann 2000, 124–25.

[149] The chapter contains a number of digressions.

[150] In 1 Cor 6.17 Paul is concerned with a "telling" point ("oneness" in πνεῦμα rather than in σάρξ). The statement as such is infelicitous, for in 6.1–20 Paul argues almost throughout with σῶμα and in v. 17 springs into the paradigm of πνεῦμα in a way that is not very convincing logically. V. 17 is at the same time an attestation for the fact that Paul understands πνεῦμα in a material way—in the sense of a somatic (but not fleshly) connection with Christ.

[151] Christ is its body. Thus already 1 Cor 11.2–16. On this strictly hierarchical text, cf. Lindemann 2000, 242–43. Cf. also the sketch in Sellin 2008, 430, in the context of his introduction to the ancient "*oikonomia-politeia* model."

[152] Cf. also 1 Cor 14.34.

motif of interpretation, which was likewise developed by Paul, comes alongside it: Christ has saved the community, i.e., his body (v. 23).[153] The same motif of interpretation is repeated and developed further in vv. 25–27[154] and now related to the *love* of the husbands for their wives. To be sure, subordination and love are not interchangeable, but they are indeed compatible. What is noteworthy is that the author emphasizes this aspect of the love of the husband for his wife in vv. 28–32 with the help of different traditional arguments: (1) Vv. 28–29 point implicitly, as already noted, to the commandment of love for neighbor.[155] (2) V. 31 quotes in detail Gen 2.24, though without taking into view the literal surface meaning.[156] Instead, this statement (3) is allegorically[157] related to Christ and the community. These interpretive moves fall within the circle of early Jewish interpretations.[158]

One could now ask the following question: Does the author have a special interest in the love of the husband, so that he seeks to develop and support this in a humanizing sense? Or is, on the contrary, the demand from Colossians—namely, that men are *to love* their wives—not plausible to him per se, so that he needs to support it with different arguments?[159] This question cannot be answered, but the fact that it can be posed in this way makes one thing clear. On the one hand, the author is concerned to give emphatic support to the recommendation of Colossians—which is new in comparison to Paul—and remind the husbands of their responsibility. On the other hand, the author does not succeed in *materially* filling the demand of Colossians beyond love for neighbor. Instead, he reaches for speculations about the σῶμα that show conjugal fellowship to be secondary vis-à-vis the fellowship with Christ and within the community. The material filling of the call for conjugal love in Ephesians falls far short of the emphasis with which the exhortation "Husbands, love your wives" is

---

[153] On the soteriological backgrounds and the head-body image, cf. Sellin 2008, 441–45. Here we encounter something like a preliminary stage to an ecclesial Christology of identification: Christ saves in a certain sense himself.

[154] The allusion to baptism in vv. 26b, 27 need not be elaborated on here.

[155] On this, cf. Zimmermann 2001, 361–62. Zimmermann follows Sampley 1971: "J. P. Sampley, who had first pointed out this designation in more recent research, was able to demonstrate that there was a Jewish tradition, according to which the 'neighbor' was related above all to the wife or beloved" (361).

[156] Gen 2.24 is related to the theme of divorce not only in Mark 10, but also in various early Jewish texts. Cf. Zimmermann 2001, 357–58.

[157] On this, see the very detailed discussion of Zimmermann 2001, 357–61, which provides substantiation of the allegorical understanding of Gen 2.24.

[158] Cf. Sellin 2008, 454–55.

[159] Sellin 2008, 446: "The text oscillates."

presented in Colossians.[160] Ephesians has created a materially new concept of conjugal love or perhaps only of the love of the husband for his wife insofar as, going beyond Paul, he has *theologically* interpreted the relationship of the marriage partner in the sense of a hierarchical Christology. From this standpoint, the path forward is not so much to conjugal love as the intention of the order of creation[161] as to an overarching theology of the Christ-confessing community into which marriage is also integrated. Conjugal love in the sense of mutual affection and attachment is not in focus in the text of Ephesians. On the whole the concern is more with the integration of the institution of marriage into the ἐκκλησία.

### 3. 1 Clement 49–50: Encomium on ἀγάπη

The author of 1 Clement is obligated to an integrative concept that has a different orientation. 1 Clement stands in the tradition of the Pauline epistolary literature[162] and reaches back at the same time to early Christian oral tradition. Chapter 49 is dedicated to the theme of ἀγάπη.

1 Clement interprets the different aspects of the lived reality of the community members theologically and concentrates it centripetally on Christ. In the process, the ethical component is reinforced. The extensive writing of the "church of God which sojourns in Rome to the church of God which sojourns in Corinth"[163] (1 Clem. 1.1) is not part of the New Testament canon but belongs to the so-called Apostolic Fathers, a group of early Christian writings that are close to the texts of the New Testament in time and in content, while also already looking back to the "apostolic" age.[164] Thus, the author of 1 Clement makes reference to 1 Corinthians (1 Clem. 47.1). In chapters 48.5–50.7 he plays with the New Testament ἀγάπη statements on the basis of 1 Cor 13, without explicitly mentioning the chapter. In the long text there is additionally only a single direct borrowing from 1 Cor 13.4 (ἡ ἀγάπη μακροθυμεῖ): πάντα μακροθυμεῖ (1 Clem. 49.5). A direct quotation is lacking. 1 Clement is an instructive example of the considerable development that the early Christian literature had already undergone. Pauline texts were not simply repeated but made the foundation of distinct extensive and literarily sophisticated

---

[160] This motif is also lacking in the corresponding texts in 1 Tim 2.8–15 and 1 Pet 3.1–7. Cf., by contrast, the remarks of Plutarch on conjugal love.

[161] The encyclical *Deus Caritas Est* draws out this line.

[162] On this, cf. Lindemann 1979, 72–82, 177–99.

[163] Trans. Holmes 2002, 29.

[164] On all introductory questions, cf. the commentaries of Lindemann 1992, 11–12; and Lona 1998, 13–110. For the current state of scholarship, see Lindemann 2010a (GV = 2009).

theological and ethical presentations. Chapter 49 is a successful example of the rhetorical device of *aemulatio/imitatio*. For 1 Clement Paul's first letter to the Corinthians is a literary model that the author aims to surpass.

According to A. Lindemann, the writing by the Roman community had a specific occasion. It "designates itself as an ἔντευξις ('*Eingabe*' or 'petition') περὶ εἰρήνης καὶ ὁμονοίας (63.2); The Roman community exhorts the hearers to restore peace and unity in the face of a Corinthian situation of conflict that is designated as στάσις multiple times."[165] The author repeatedly points to the occasion of his writing, thus also in chapter 47, where the clearest accusations against the Corinthian community are formulated. It is said to have rebelled against the presbyters. This is followed, as an introduction, by the exhortation to "pious and pure conduct of our love for brothers and sisters" (φιλαδεφία) in 48.1 and to justice (48.2–4). The text on ἀγάπη directly follows (1 Clem. 48.5–50.7, thematically concentrated in chapter 49):[166]

**48.5** Let a man be faithful (πιστός), let him be able to expound knowledge (γνῶσις), let him be wise (σοφός) in the interpretation of discourses, let him be energetic in deeds, let him be pure; **6** for the greater (μείζων) he seems to be, the more he ought to be humble, and the more he ought to seek (ζητεῖν) the common advantage of all, and not his own.[167]

**49.1** Let the one who has *love* in Christ fulfill the commandments of Christ. **2** Who can describe the bond of God's *love*? **3** Who is able to explain the majesty of its beauty? **4** The height to which *love* leads is indescribable. **5** *Love* unites us with God; "*love* covers a multitude of sins";[168] *love* endures all things, is patient (μακροθυμεῖ) in all things. There is nothing coarse, nothing arrogant in *love*. *Love* knows nothing of schisms, *love* leads no rebellions, *love* does everything in harmony. In *love* all the elect of God were made perfect; without *love* nothing is pleasing to God. **6** In *love* the Master received us. Because of the *love* he had for us, Jesus Christ our Lord, in accordance with God's will, gave his blood for us, and his flesh for our flesh, and his life for our lives.

---

[165] Lindemann/Paulsen 1992, 77. Cf. also Lindemann 2010a, 64: "1 Clement pursues an ecclesiological goal as ἔντευξις (63.2); the moral instructions, somewhat in the form of the catalogue of vices or even of the recounting of examples, without exception serve as argumentative support for the demand for 'peace and harmony' understood as ecclesiological, that is to say social, values."

[166] Trans. Holmes 2002, 84–85 (O.W.'s insertions and emphasis).

[167] This is a literary variation of 1 Cor 13.5.

[168] Prov 10.12; also cited in 1 Pet 4.8 and Jas 5.20.

**50.1** You see, dear friends, how great and wonderful *love* is; its perfection is beyond description. **2** Who is worthy to be found in it, except those whom God considers worthy? Let us therefore ask and petition his mercy, that we may be found blameless in love, standing apart from the factiousness of men. **3** All the generations from Adam to this day have passed away, but those who by God's grace were perfected in love have a place among the godly, who will be revealed when the kingdom of Christ visits us.[169]. . . **5** Blessed are we, dear friends, if we continue to keep God's commandments in the harmony of *love*, that our sins may be forgiven us through *love*. . . .[170] **7** This declaration of blessedness was pronounced upon those who have been chosen by God through Jesus Christ our Lord, to whom be the glory for ever and ever. Amen.

Unlike 1 Cor 13, 1 Clem. 49 is composed as an encomium:[171] a literarily and theologically sophisticated text that deploys the *praise of love* as the most important and highest argument against the Corinthian community's schismatic tendencies. *Ethos is mediated here through literature.*[172] To a much greater degree than Paul, the author of 1 Clement counts on the impact of artistic prose and rhetorical devices as well as the large argumentative arc,[173] whose impact is reinforced by the intentional recourse to religious forms of literature.[174] A literary high point is present in chapter 49, which is composed against the background of 1 Cor 13 and represents a quite distinct literary achievement. The argumentation is already prepared for in 48.5 following the "exhortation to repentance and humility,"[175] which is staged with religious topoi. The author varies motifs from 1 Cor 12 and 1 Cor 13.1–3: faith, knowledge, wisdom, the highest values, the striving for the highest.[176] These motifs can be related in a loose way to the current situation in Corinth and are known to the readers from 1 Corinthians. Chapter 49 then explains that all this is surpassed by ἀγάπη—this establishes a clear relationship to 1 Corinthians, a literary strategy that gives chapter 49 additional significance and authority. The statements in 49.1–3 stand under the motif of the "ineffability" of

---

[169] Quotation of Isa 26.20; Ezek 37.12.

[170] Quotation of Ps 31.1, 2. Cf. Rom 4.7–9.

[171] Cf. Lona 1998, 522. An important literary parallel is the encomium to hope in Philo, *Praem.* 11.

[172] This connects this text with Plutarch's *Amatorius.*

[173] On this, see Lona 1998, 20–41.

[174] Cf. the prayers in 59.2–61.3 and 64.

[175] Lindemann 1992, 140.

[176] Analysis in Lona 1998, 517 (on 1 Cor 12.8–10) and 519 (on 1 Cor 10.24). But attention must also be given to the connection to 1 Cor 13.1–3.

love.[177] V. 1 serves as a thematic opening to ἀγάπη and points at the same time to the commandment tradition and to Jesus.[178] Vv. 2–4 invoke the divine dimension of love. V. 5 contains the central statements about love. V. 6 adds the theological-christological deepening of ἀγάπη, which Paul had already set forth. Applicative are 50.1–7: v. 2 points to the concrete situation in Corinth, vv. 3 and 4 open the eschatological perspective, and in vv. 5–7 the whole text is ceremoniously concluded with a topical reference to forgiveness of sins[179] and a combination of formulas of religious language.[180]

What does the text say about *love*? And is a distinct concept of ἀγάπη present here? As we have already described, the author presents an integrative concept that draws basic motifs from 1 Cor 13 and supplements these through references to the Synoptic and Johannine Jesus tradition (49.1) and to traditional formulations.[181] The author stresses multiple times that love connects human beings with God and, in dependence on Paul, emphasizes the christological basis of love (v. 6). Here, already established early Christian theological knowledge is passed on. However, the distinctive character of the concept becomes clear especially in 49.5. The concern is with *harmony*. On the basis of 1 Cor 13.4–7, the author formulates his concept of ἀγάπη for the current situation of the community in Corinth: ἀγάπη σχίσμα οὐκ ἔχει, ἀγάπη πάντα ποιεῖ ἐν ὁμονοίᾳ.[182] The main idea is as follows: Love is a social entity; it is related to the community and operates in an integrative way. It is the attitude that holds the *community* together. Paul interprets love theologically by understanding it as an individual, personal act of proper knowledge of God (1 Cor 13.12). 1 Clement replaces this interpretation with a supra-individual concept of a community-related ethical attitude,[183] i.e., with a group ethos or a social

---

[177] On the motif, cf. Lona 1998, 523 (esp. Sir 18.4–5). On the structure of chapter 49, cf. Lona 1998, 520.

[178] Here the commandment line and the line of "love" are connected in a very harmonious way. The commandment line is not related to the Old Testament commandments but to the "instructions of Christ."

[179] Cf. Jas 5.19–20; 1 John 5.16–17.

[180] Beatitudes, quotation from Ps 31.1–2, doxology.

[181] Cf. Lona 1998, 525–26, on 49.5 "Love covers a multitude of sins." This saying is found in varied form in 1 Clem. 50.5; 1 Pet 4.8; Jas 5.20 (cf. Prov 10.12b according to the Hebrew text); 2 Clem. 16.4. The question of whether an agraphon stands in the background need not be pursued here. Cf. Lona 1998 on the expression "bond of love" and its possible motif-historical background (motif history since Plato, *Tim.* 41b).

[182] Cf. also 50.5.

[183] Here the concern is also not with love for neighbor but with harmony within the Christian community in Corinth.

culture. The combination of Pauline and Synoptic love traditions corresponds to this.

## 4. Johannine Literature

In the Gospel of John and in 1 John, love represents a central theologoumenon.[184] In the Johannine writings, ἀγάπη is neither only a general or group-related ethos[185] nor a comprehensive emotion but in the first place the universal structure of the divine world, which through Jesus Christ has also become the world of human beings. While the Gospel of John presents love in the story of Jesus narratively in personal relationships and in the composition of speeches, the author of 1 John strives for a definitional theological understanding of ἀγάπη in the framework of his theological criteriology and his perception of severe conflicts in the community. The two writings share the consistent relational metaphoricism, on the one hand, and the speculative extension of the term ἀγάπη to the entirety of the relationships between God, Jesus, the disciples, the believers, and their relationship to Jesus and to God, on the other hand. E. E. Popkes describes this relationship as 'reciprocal,'[186] so long as it is clear that the dynamic of the reciprocal process of love is a directed dynamic and that it proceeds exclusively from God.[187] The Johannine literature's concept of love has detached itself completely from the double commandment of love for God and love for neighbor. However, the commandment structure can still be recognized behind the texts. The author has Jesus teach *in the style* of the Synoptic tradition. This style is maintained in all the Johannine writings. Not only do the Gospel of John and 1 John use the language of commandment (ἐντολή) and not only does the first farewell speech of Jesus in the Gospel conclude with Jesus' reference to God's commandment, which he fulfills, but the large teaching on love in 1 John 4 also concludes with the powerful double statement:

**4.21** And we have this *commandment* from him, that the one who loves God must love his brother and sister also.

---

[184] Cf. Söding 1996, 306–57; Zumstein 2013; Moloney 2013.

[185] On the topic of Johannine ethics, cf. the thorough introduction of Labahn 2012 with its focus on the history of research. Special reference should be made to his introduction with the allusion to the quotation of Jerome and its subsequent history in Lessing (Labahn 2012, 3–4). Cf. now also Brown/Skinner 2017; Wischmeyer 2021.

[186] Thus E. E. Popkes 2005.

[187] Thyen 2005, 605, speaks of the "asymmetrical character of the relation of love." In this point the theology of the Johannine writings is not far from the Greco-Roman conviction that the gods must not be loved but honored (cf. Kany 2013, 661–62). See also Aristotle, *Metaph.* 12.7, love and God.

Linguistically and materially we find here a clear recourse to the double commandment of love, as it is expressed in Mark 12.28–31. However, in 1 John πλησίον is replaced by ἀδελφός.[188] This change necessarily attracts special attention.

Much work has been done on the theme of "love in Johannine literature" in the past generation of exegesis. In the process, the lines of questioning have changed multiple times in analogy to the different phases of Johannine exegesis. Every new interpretation must initially take into account this exegetical predecessor literature. In 1982 Fernando F. Segovia[189] looked back at the sometimes very extensive and demanding monographs of James Moffatt,[190] Victor Warnach, Ceslaus Spicq, Victor Paul Furnish,[191] André Feuillet,[192] and Michael Lattke,[193] which from Segovia's perspective were all devoted more or less to the material theme "love" in the Johannine writings and operate with the authorial model of two authors.[194] According to the state of Johannine exegesis in his time, Segovia himself sought a tradition-historical and redaction-critical differentiation by understanding the author of 1 John as one of the redactors of the Gospel. This gave rise to a certain depth of focus in relation to the term "love" in the Johannine writings. Moreover, Segovia took up the related question of the 'Johannine community,' in which the letters and the Gospel emerged and concerning whose history they could give information, a line of questioning that is especially associated with J. Louis Martyn, Wayne A. Meeks, R. Alan Culpepper, and Raymond Brown.[195] About ten years later the monographs of Sjef van Tilborg and Jörg Augenstein appeared.[196] While Augenstein investigated the special Johannine terminology of love in the Johannine writings, in which every reference to the "neighbor" (πλησίον) is lacking,[197] Sjef van Tilborg took up the narratological approach for the interpretation of the Gospel and presented the Johannine concept of love not on the basis of the semantics but on the basis of the different personal relationships that occur in the course of the narrative of the Gospel: family, Beloved Disciple, disciples and 'friends,' women, beloved

---

[188] In the Gospel of John only at the end: 20.17 and 21.23. "Brothers" as intensification of "friends": Thyen 2005, 764.

[189] Segovia 1982.

[190] Moffatt 1932.

[191] Furnish 1972.

[192] Feuillet 1972.

[193] Lattke 1975.

[194] In detail, of course, significant differentiations must be made here.

[195] See Martyn 2003 [1968]; Meeks 1972, 44–72; Culpepper 1975; Brown 1979.

[196] Van Tilborg 1993; Augenstein 1993.

[197] Augenstein 1993, 11.

human beings. Tilborg consequently understands the Gospel as a singular "love story."[198] In 2000, Jan Gabriel van der Watt integrated this approach into the framework of his study of Johannine metaphoricism.[199] Five years later the extensive dissertation of Enno E. Popkes on the theology of the love of God in the Johannine writings appeared.[200] Popkes combines the investigation of the semantics of love and the dualistic motifs in the Johannine writings in order to be able to provide a more exact specification of the relationship between "love" and "world." With this the topic of Johannine eschatology also comes into view, a topic that received a new, comprehensive presentation by Jörg Frey.[201] The quest for the Johannine community (or communities), the consideration of narratology and metaphoricism, and the expansion of the semantic basis—these research approaches have given new impulses to the exegetical interaction with the Johannine writings and can also be made fruitful for our line of questioning.

More difficult are the questions of how to determine the literary-historical and historical-theological location of the Gospel of John and the Johannine letters. It would be neither possible nor sensible to provide a brief presentation of the Johannine question.[202] For the Gospel of John, I follow the approach of the major commentary of Hartwig Thyen, who understands "the Gospel of John 1.1 to John 21.25 handed down to us in the canon as a coherent and highly poetic *literary* and *authorial* text."[203] Here, the accent lies on literary *and* authorial—both are important for the Gospel's theology of love. The question of the traditions and the phases of the possible history of emergence cannot be discussed here.

The relationship between Gospel and letters is contested among the exegetes.[204] I advocate the priority of the Gospel[205] and see a development that leads from the Gospel via 1 John to the two short letters. In what follows I forgo a discussion of the intertextual relationships between the Johannine writings and interpret the two large textual contexts that are devoted to the theme of "love" in the Gospel and in 1 John as respectively

---

[198] Van Tilborg 1993, 11.

[199] Van der Watt 2000. Chapter 4 deals with the theme "The family of the king." See pp. 161–393.

[200] E. E. Popkes 2005, 39–51, gives a very short history of research on the theme 'love' in the Johannine writings.

[201] Frey 1997–2000. Cf. also Frey 2018, 73–99.

[202] On this, see esp. Hengel 1993 (ET = 1989). By way of introduction, see Broer/Weidemann 2010, 245–50 (248–49 against the priority of 1 John vis-à-vis John).

[203] Thyen 2005, 1. Whether chapter 21 is not perhaps to be read as an addition is secondary for our question and need not be discussed here.

[204] Cf. Broer/Weidemann 2010, 245–50.

[205] For justification, see Wischmeyer 2009a, which also interacts critically with van der Watt 2006.

independent texts on the theme of "love." In doing so, it is important to call to mind once again that "love" and ethics or ethos are by no means coextensive in the Johannine writings and that a presentation of the Johannine concept of "love" is not a presentation of the ethics or ethos of this writing.[206]

## 4.1 John 13–17

The large narrative context of John 13–17[207] is exclusively devoted to the last gathering of Jesus with his disciples at the Passover meal. The narrative is dominated by the theme of Jesus' love for "his own." First, Jesus washes the disciples' feet during the meal (13.2–11) and attaches a teaching about discipleship (13.12–20). Right after this, in sharp narrative contrast, there follows the division of the disciples—Judas leaves the meal to betray Jesus to the authorities (13.21–30). To the remaining circle of the eleven, Jesus gives his last and most decisive instruction, which follows the commandment of love for neighbor in form, but expresses something entirely different and "new" in terms of content:

**13.34** I give you a new (καινός) commandment, that you love one another, just as I have loved you, that you also love one another. **35** By this all people will know that you are my disciples, if you have love (ἀγάπη) for one another.

In a second hard contrast, Peter seeks to reassure Jesus of his love by promising to lay down his life for him, but he is brusquely put in his place (13.35–38). Peter does not possess the love that dies for the friend. This love belongs solely to Jesus.[208] Two extensive farewell discourses of Jesus follow in chapter 14 and chapters 15–16.[209] The narrative context of the "last evening of Jesus with the disciples" comes to its end in chapter 17 in a long prayer-like speech of Jesus to God.[210] Jesus leaves the meal and

[206] On Johannine ethics, see esp. van der Watt 2006; and Watt/Zimmermann 2012. Cf. now also Brown/Skinner 2017; Wischmeyer 2021.

[207] On the Gospel of John as a whole, cf. the commentaries, esp. Schnelle 2016; Thyen 2005; Theobald 2009. On the topic of love and ethics in John with a focus on the history of research, see also Labahn 2012.

[208] The sharp answer to Peter makes clear that temporally and materially Jesus' death first creates the foundation for the disciples to practice love themselves. John 21.18–19 makes this clear: now Peter is prepared to do what he did not do for Jesus—namely, to give his life, in turn, for Jesus' sheep!

[209] The discourse is weakly structured. Several disciples pose questions (14.5, 8, 22; and 16.17–18, 29–30).

[210] The so-called high priestly prayer.

goes with his disciples into a garden beyond the Kidron brook, where he is arrested. The theme of love[211] opens and closes the narrative complex:

**13.1** Before the festival of the Passover, Jesus knew that his hour had come to pass over from this world to the Father and since he loved his own in the world, he loved them to the end (εἰς τέλος).

**17.26** I have made known your name to them and I will make it known, in order that the love (ἀγάπη) with which you loved me may be in them and I also in them.

In addition, the first farewell discourse in 14.31 also concludes with a reference to Jesus' love for the Father, so that the passion narrative that follows is already interpreted:

**14.31** . . . in order that the world may know that I love the Father and that I do just as the Father commanded (ἐνετείλατο) me.

Four theological aspects of love are decisive for chapters 13–17. First, there is the explication of Jesus' love for the disciples. Second, there is the love of God for Jesus and reciprocally of Jesus for God. The "new commandment" is, in turn, a consequence of Jesus' love for "his own." Third, Jesus' love is the model and example for the love of the disciples. This is the meaning of the symbolic action of the foot washing[212] and the ethical demand of the "new commandment," which stands at the center of the farewell discourses in terms of textual pragmatics. Fourth, these three aspects are brought together in the theme of unity.

In John 13–17, Jesus' love for the disciples or "his own"[213] is illuminated in different directions. First, in 13.23[214] the Gospel mentions the unnamed disciple "whom Jesus loved" (ἠγάπα) and "who was reclining on Jesus' bosom." Here, it is obvious that a personal, emotional relationship is in view, which is closer than the relationship to the other disciples.[215] To this corresponds *ex negativo* the emotional way Peter expresses his stormy love for God (13.6–10 and 13.36–38), though it is not steadfast

---

[211] The noun is used in 13.35; 15.9, 13; and 17.26. It occurs elsewhere only in 5.42.

[212] 13.5: ὑπόδειγμα.

[213] Only in 13.1 (anticipated in 10.3–4).

[214] Cf. 19.26; 20.2; 21.7, 20. On this, see Theobald 2009, 82–92; 2010. See there for additional literature on the "Beloved Disciple." Cf. also 11.5.

[215] Cf. the favorites of the gods in Greco-Roman mythology (Kany 2013). Cf. also Mark 10.21 (as personal affection).

and de facto reveals a lack of love.[216] This lack is first counterbalanced in 21.15: Peter now loves[217] Jesus "more" than "the rest" and will demonstrate this in martyrdom.[218] Jesus accuses the disciples of a lack of love in 14.28. That in the relationship between Jesus and the disciples the concern is with emotions is also evident from Jesus' references to the disciples' fear,[219] which the farewell discourses as a whole are devoted to overcoming. This becomes especially clear in 16.16–24 when Jesus himself explicates the motif of the pain of parting and the joy of reunion. The discourses are designed to oppose the fear of the disciples:

> **16.33** In the world you have tribulation, but take courage: I have conquered the world.

Behind this lies the Johannine writings' conviction that love drives out fear (1 John 4.18 φόβος).[220] To this is juxtaposed the joy that Jesus promises his own.[221] Following Sjef van Tilborg, Michael Theobald has drawn a line from the relationship of Jesus to the Beloved Disciple to Hellenistic friendship ethics: "In the case of the Beloved Disciple Jesus' relationship to him differs from his relationship to his remaining 'students' through its special quality of friendship, whose distinguishing characteristic is regarded, according to Greek-Hellenistic friendship ethics, as affectionate care and sharing in the knowledge of the friend."[222] To this can be added the motif of the equal status of friends.

Second, Jesus' love for the disciples is characterized by its consistency to the end: 13.1 and 14.31. To love "to the end" and "until completion" is a way of speaking of Jesus' sacrificial death in John 13–17. The notion of sacrifice is alluded to only in 15.13–14.[223] Here, however, the *religious* idea of sacrifice is avoided, and Jesus appears not as the one who is sacrificed (or handed over) *by God* but as the one who voluntarily sacrifices himself for his friends.[224] Jesus' sovereignty remains entirely preserved

---

[216] This applies, however, also to the Beloved Disciple. However, he stands with the women at the cross.

[217] Here with φιλεῖν. John uses φιλία synonymously with ἀγάπη multiple times.

[218] Here there is an underlying christological logic: The offering for the friends is already completed by Jesus. Only thereafter can Peter offer his life for Jesus!

[219] 14.1, 27: ταράσσω (be frightened), δειλιάω (to be despondent, to fear); 16.6: λύπη; 16.20–22: λύπη, λυπέω, κλαίω, θρηνέω.

[220] On this, cf. Theobald 1992.

[221] Χαρά 15.11; 16.20–24; 17.13.

[222] Theobald 2010, 518.

[223] The notion of sacrifice occurs explicitly only in 1 John 2.2 and 4.10.

[224] Cf. Thyen 1979; 2005, 647–48, in critical dialogue with Dibelius 1953. Thyen 2005, 648, rightly points out that v. 13 is not a foreign body in the Johannine concept of

through the fact that the paradigm of the *voluntary* sacrifice for friends is chosen. With the motif of death for friends a central keyword is mentioned that is used only here for the disciples and that indicates the closest connection between Jesus and "his own"—namely, friends.[225] In John 15.14 the change from μαθηταί to φίλοι takes place:

> **15.12** This is my commandment, that you love one another, as I have loved you. **13** Greater love has no one than this, that one lay down his life for his *friends*. **14** You are my friends if you do what I command you (ἐντέλλω). **15** I do not call you slaves, for the slave does not know what his master is doing; but I call you friends, for all the things which I have heard from my Father I have made known to you. . . . **17** These things I command to you, that you love one another.

In the process, Jesus' sovereignty remains so completely preserved that he can "command" love to the friends, without wounding their friendship status.

*God's love for Jesus and Jesus' love for God* in John 13–17 is defined through Jesus' sovereign giving of his life for the friends in a special way that adds another accent to the classic formulation of John 3.16:

> **16** For God so loved the world that he gave his only Son, so that everyone who believes in him may not perish but may have eternal life. **17** For God did not send the Son into the world to judge the world but in order that the world might be saved through him.

Here the religiously connoted notion of sacrifice is not far away. In any case, God is the sovereign,[226] while Jesus is the Son who is "given" for the human beings who believe in him. The relationship between Father and Son fluctuates between act of sacrifice and obedience and is obligated in its motifs to the Akedah conception. The dominance of the Father recedes in John 13–17, but the material filling of love as obedience remains (14.31). It is clear that Jesus' love for God is defined as keeping the *commandments* of God (15.9–12):

> **15.9** As the Father has loved me, so I have loved you. Remain in my love!
> **10** If you keep my commandments, you will remain in my love, just as

---

love that stems from the tradition. On parallel Greek-Hellenistic conceptions of friendship, cf. esp. Schnelle/Labahn/Lang 2001, 716–25 (the motif of dying for the friend). Cf. also Rom 5.7.

[225] Cf. also 11.11: "our friend Lazarus" (also 11.3, 36 in verb form), 11.5 ἀγαπᾶν.

[226] On the text, cf. Thyen 2005, 213–20.

I have kept *the commandments of my Father* and remain in his love.
**11** I have said these things to you so that my joy may be in you and your
joy may be complete. **12** This is my commandment, that you love one
another as I have loved you. . . . **17** These things I command you, that
you love one another.

What are "God's commandments"? The text makes clear that the concern
is with a single commandment—the commandment of love. This gives
rise to another question: What exactly is meant with the addition "as I love
you"? We find here the Johannine criteriology. "Love" must be measured
by specific criteria. The highest criterion is set by God himself—the *giving*
of the one who is most loved. For God it is the "only Son," for Jesus "his
own life," for "his own" likewise their own lives. Considered exactly, a
circle of giving is present here, out of which God is not exempted, since in
his Son he gives, after all, in a certain sense himself:

**1.18** No one has ever seen God; the only God,[227] who is in the bosom of
the Father—he has made him known.

Whether we read "the only God" with Papyrus 66, Papyrus 75, and Codex
Sinaiticus or "the only Son" with Codex Alexandrinus is of secondary
importance in relation to the fundamental statement that God gave in a
certain sense not only his Son but also himself. We find here the highest
theological-speculative intensification of the conception of the ἀγάπη of
God in the sense of the relationship between Father and only Son. The
whole economy of salvation of God, which in the Gospel is explicated
especially in the forms of sending Christology and revelation Christology,
is understood as a circle of a movement of love, which proceeds from God
and returns to God. It encompasses emotional traits of deep affection and
*attachment*[228] as well as unconditional *separation*, as it manifests itself in
the obedience of Jesus and "his own."[229]

*The love of the disciples for one another* makes the disciples true fol-
lowers of Jesus[230] and is their identifying mark in relation to the world
(13.35). In addition to John 13.34–35 and 15.12, 17; John 14.15–24 is

---

[227] On the text, cf. Thyen 2005, 105–7. Thyen argues with good reasons for the reading μονογενὴς θεός (like Nestle-Aland[27/28]) and for the understanding of God as apposi-
tion to "only-begotten." A literal translation would thus be, "No one has ever seen God.
The Only-begotten One, God, who is in the bosom of the Father, that one has reported."

[228] Cf. esp. the motif of εἰς τὸν κόλπον εἶναι from 1.18 and 13.23.

[229] For Peter in 21.15–19. For the disciples in 16.2.

[230] Cf. 13.36–37 in contrast to 21.19, 22.

devoted to this love of the disciples. Their love is like the love of Jesus for the Father in obedience and in fulfillment of the love commandment:

**14.15** "If you love me, you will keep my commandments. . . . **21** The one who has my commandments and keeps them—that one is the one who loves me; and the one who loves me will be loved by my Father, and I will love him and will reveal myself to him." . . . **23** Jesus answered and said to him, "If anyone loves me, he will keep my word, and my Father will love him, and we will come to him and will take up residence with him. **24** The one who does not love me does not keep my words, and the word that you hear is not mine but the Father's who sent me."

*Love brings about unity* between the lovers:[231]

**17.20** I do not ask for these only but also for those who believe in me through their word, **21** in order that all may be *one*, as you, Father, in me and I in you, that they may also be in us, in order that the world may believe that you have sent me. **22** And I have given them the glory that you have given to me in order that they may be *one*, as we are *one*— **23** I in them and you in me, in order that they may be perfected into *one*, in order that the world may know that you have sent me and have loved them as you love me.

Here, at the end of the high priestly prayer, Jesus looks beyond the narrative situation of that last shared meal with the disciples to the future history of the Jesus communities.[232] All believers—and not only the Beloved Disciple, the eleven, the 'friends'—will stand in the great context of love that proceeds from God, has manifested itself in Jesus in the world, and unifies all who believe in Jesus with God. Thus, the horizon expands at the end of the farewell discourses, and Jesus opens the perspective not for a small flock of 'his own' but *for all who believe in Jesus.* They all have a share in the love of God and are themselves bearers of this love, which Jesus has taught them.

From this standpoint it becomes clear in *retrospect* that the author of the Gospel, as a *historical narrator*, has adhered strictly to the situation of the last meal of Jesus with his disciples. *They*—and not "humanity," the "neighbor," or even only "the community"—are the addressees of the large speech of Jesus before his arrest. The question of whether the farewell discourses promulgate an internal community ethic or a general

---

[231] On the motif of unity or oneness, cf. Sprecher 1993. Cf. now also Byers 2017.
[232] Thus also in 16.1–4.

philanthropy or love for neighbor is falsely posed, for it leaves the narrative situation out of consideration.[233] The narrative imagines Jesus' last gathering with "his own" as the meal of the Son of God, the Revealer, the teacher with his "own" whom he loves, who are his friends, and from whom he separates himself for a short time in order to unite himself again with them definitively. It is a great love scene—to vary the diction of Sjef van Tilborg—that is staged literarily here. Jesus and his own, the disciple whom Jesus loves in a special way and who rests in his bosom, the speech of comfort of their Lord and master, which seeks to turn the disciples' grief over his parting into joy over an ultimate reunion and opens up a future with the Father.[234] All the more important is Jesus' forward glance into the future in 17.20–23. He himself makes clear that all human beings who believe in him are to belong to the community of love that he has established.

## 4.2 1 John 4.7–5.4

First John 4.7–5.4[235] presupposes a community situation that is characterized by divisions but then leads far beyond this situational radius and presents the most ambitious theological text on ἀγάπη in the New Testament.[236] First John 4–5 stands alongside 1 Cor 13[237] in its thematic concentration and theological claim, though not in its linguistic form:

---

[233] Cf. the vehement defense of the general application of the love in question in Thyen 2005, 607–13. From a material perspective Thyen is indeed correct when he polemicizes that against every attempt to find a sectarian ethic in the Gospel of John, it may be objected "that every unfolding of a Johannine ecclesiology must start from the *sending* of the disciples through the risen one" (610).

[234] John 16.29–33 makes clear, however, that the historical scene takes place before Jesus' resurrection, and the disciples, despite their affirmation in 16.29–30, do not yet have the strength of faith that will first be given to them after Jesus' "departure."

[235] On 1 John, cf. the very balanced introduction of Klauck 1991, 13–49. Klauck places the letter in Ephesus and dates it between 100 and 110 CE (49). A counter-position is advocated by Schnelle 2007, 494 (ET = 1998, 459), who, with G. Strecker, places the letter before the Gospel of John in time and dates it to "ca. 95 CE."

[236] The motif of love also occurs in 1 John 2 and 3. First John 4–5 takes up the already addressed aspects and draws them together into an extensive thematic text.

[237] To speak here, in analogy to 1 Cor 13, of a "Song of Songs of the Love" (of God) (cf. Klauck 1991, 244; E. E. Popkes 2005, 78 with n11), fundamentally misses the genre of 1 John, which alternates between efforts at definition, teaching, and exhortation. Klauck's reference to the Song of Songs of the Hebrew Bible is also inappropriate for 1 John 4–5. In contrast to what Paul does in some of his texts, the author of 1 John does not leave the epistolary situation or strive for "artistic prose." The characteristic of brevity is also lacking in 1 John.

**4.7** Beloved, let us love one another, because love is from God, and everyone who loves is born of God and knows (γινώσκει) God. **8** The one who does not love does not know God, for *God is love* (ἀγάπη). **9** In this the love of God has appeared among us, that God has sent his only Son into the world in order that we might live through him. **10** In this is love, not that we have loved God but that he has loved us and sent his Son as an atonement for our sins.

**11** Beloved, if God has so loved us, we also ought to love one another.

**12** No one has ever seen God. If we love one another, God remains in us and his love has perfected itself in us.

**13** By this we know that we remain in him and he in us, that he has given us of his Spirit. **14** And we have seen and testify that the Father has sent the Son as Savior of the world. **15** Whoever confesses that Jesus is the Son of God, God remains in him and he himself (remains) in God. **16** And we have come to know and to believe the love that God has for (in) us.

*God is love*, and the one who remains in love remains in God, and God remains in him. **17** In this love has come to perfection with us, that we have confidence on the day of judgment; for as that one is, so also are we in this world. **18** Fear is not in love, but perfect love drives out fear, for fear reckons with punishment, but the one who fears has not come to perfection in love. **19** Let us love, for he has first loved us. **20** If someone says, "I love God" and hates his brother or sister, he is a liar. For the one who does not love his brother and sister whom he sees cannot love God whom he does not see.[238] **21** And we have this commandment from him, that the one who loves God must loves his brother and sister also. **5.1** Everyone who believes that Jesus is the Christ is born of God, and everyone who loves the parent also loves the one born from him. **2** By this we know that we love God's children, when we love God and keep his commandments. **3** For this is the love of God, that we keep his commandments, and his commandments are not burdensome. **4** For everything that is born from God conquers the world; and this is the victory that has conquered the world: our faith (πίστις).

In a similar manner to Paul in 1 Cor 13 and to 1 Clement, 1 John also reacts to a situation of conflict within a community or more likely a group of communities[239] and regards love as the decisive argument in the struggle

---

[238] The Greek perfect forms are rendered here with the durative present.

[239] On the question of the addressees of 1 John, cf. Schnelle 2007, 473–75 and 494–95 (ET = 1998, 436–38 and 459–60). Schnelle's assessment—"Thus 1 John is not directed to a particular congregation of the Johannine school, but the whole [Johannine] church is

for the unity of the community. However, the situations to which the different epistolary writings react are very different in detail. Paul writes exhortatively to the Corinthian community, which he himself founded and whose inclination to esteem spiritual charisms and form groups he knows and corrects. The author of 1 Clement writes from the position of the—at least in its claim—unchallenged authority of the Roman community to the community in Corinth, whose members are in conflict with one another and in which factions have formed. By contrast, the relationship of the author of 1 John to his addressees is unclear and can only be envisioned in broad outlines through a historical reconstruction. Enno Edzard Popkes concisely expresses the dominant exegetical opinion on the situation between author and addressees as follows: "The problem of the intra-community love is, alongside the christological controversies, the main conflict of the Johannine schism."[240] Accordingly, "the remarks on the significance of the mutual love of believers in the Johannine letters" also stand "in a direct connection to the schism of the Johannine community."[241] This schism is addressed in 1 John 2.19. Who belonged to the secession from the Johannine community (or communities) and what religious profile this group had is subject to different historical reconstructions[242] and is not germane here. Two things are important. First, the author criticizes, from 2.2 onward, the incorrect understanding that the 'heretics' have of Jesus. Second, it is important that according to the assessment of the author, the 'heretics' claimed to have fellowship with God,[243] to be without sin,[244] to have come to know God,[245] to remain in

---

addressed" (Schnelle 1998, 495; GV = 2007, 494)—is plausible. First John thus stands, at least materially, in a line with the so-called Catholic Epistles.

[240] E. E. Popkes 2005, 75.

[241] E. E. Popkes 2005, 160.

[242] On the profile of the 'heretics,' cf. the excursus on "The false teachers in 1 John" in Strecker 1989, 131–39; Klauck 1991, 34–42; Schnelle 2007, 498–500 (ET = 1998, 463–66). The 'heretics' clearly advocate a docetic Christology. In connection with the question of the concept of love in 1 John, however, the specific religious-pneumatic self-understanding of the 'heretics,' which manifests itself in different statements of a high pneumatic self-awareness, is likewise unimportant. Note also 1 John 4.9: if someone says, "I love God." See further E. E. Popkes 2005, 136–43. Cf. already the pneumatic self-awareness of the Corinthians and the argumentation of Paul from the standpoint of love! (Cf. Klauck 1991, 35, with older literature).

[243] 1 John 1.6 (the first characterization of the 'heretics'). Cf. also 2.6. Here and in what follows, the author begins with the expression "when we *say*," continues with a description of the deficient *action* and reaches a negative *judgment*. In this way he can specify the principles of the heretics and at the same time correct them.

[244] 1 John 1.8, 10.

[245] 1 John 2.4.

God,[246] and to be in the light.[247] However, the author criticizes not the religious-pneumatic profile of the 'heretics' as such but their lack of love for brothers and sisters:

**9** The one who says that he is in the light and hates his brother or sister is still in the darkness until now. **10** The one who loves his brother and sister (by contrast) remains in the light and there is no fault in him.

Thus, false teaching about Christ and a lack of love for brothers and sisters are the two marks of the 'heretics' in the view of the author, who, for his part, derives love of God as God's love for human beings and love for brothers and sisters from each other and intertwines them with each other.

The work of the author, who does not name himself and also does not write under a pseudonym or official title[248] but was evidently simply known to his communities, can be assigned to a literary genre only with difficulty. The assignment to the so-called Catholic Epistles first takes place in late manuscripts[249] and is not a valid genre criterion. Still, it is a writing that establishes explicit written communication to a group of addressees in connection with a situation of conflict.[250] The author forgoes, however, a literarily configured address and a concluding greeting, so that the assignment to the genre of the symbouleutic letter, which Hans-Josef Klauck proposes,[251] can only represent an approximation.[252] It is ultimately an early Christian work that is without analogy, which was written in great material and linguistic proximity to the Gospel of John and yet at the same time develops its own linguistic and material profile.[253] The structure of the work can best be described as repeated

---

[246] 1 John 2.6.

[247] 1 John 2.9.

[248] We do find this in 2 and 3 John.

[249] On this, cf. Klauck 1991, 53n1.

[250] It is concerned with conflict management. The schism of the community has already occurred.

[251] Klauck 1991, 32.

[252] Schnelle 2007, 496 (ET = 1998, 460–61), lists different suggestions and decides for "*letter-like* homily" following Strecker 1989, 49. The connection to a homily cannot, however, be demonstrated. Rather, the text contains situationally focused didactic and exhortatory statements.

[253] Klauck 1991, 31. Following Brown 1982, 90–91, Klauck speaks of a "reading aid for the understanding of the Gospel of John." This, however, does not do justice to the concrete situation of the writing. Brown distances himself cautiously from the reading aid thesis and sets a somewhat different accent: "I John was written to preserve an interpretation . . . for insiders rather than to convince outsiders" (91).

alternation between didactic and exhortative textual sections,[254] which all circle around the double theme of love for brothers/sisters and proper Christology. Hans-Josef Klauck has uncovered this connection in the textual structure of 4.1–5.12:

> A portion of interpreters fails to recognize a connection between 4.1–6 and 4.7–21. It arises, however, without force if one observes the function of 3.23–24 as a transition to the last main section. The double commandment of faith and love needs explication in its two component parts. This occurs for faith in 4.1–6, for love in 4.7–21, and for both of them together again in 5.1–5.[255]

This double theme is in fact clear in chapter 4: 4.1–6 presents a doctrinal proposition about Christ:

> **4.2** By this you know the Spirit of God: every spirit that confesses that Jesus Christ has come in the flesh is from God, **3** and every spirit that does not confess Jesus is not from God.

What follows is a long exposition on love for brothers and sisters in 4.7–5.4. The definitional statement in 5.4 about faith transitions to the next textual unit in 5.5–12, which again has didactic-christological character.[256] Thus, the text on love for brothers and sisters is already prepared for in detail, and in 3.23 it is introduced thematically and joined with Christology. In 4.7–21 with the renewed christological perspective in 5.1–4, the author then creates a text that sets forth a distinct theology of love, which, on the one hand, is entirely in harmony with the preceding presentations and contains no new elements, and yet, on the other hand, in its didactic

---

[254] Cf. the thorough presentation in Klauck 1991, 24–29. Strecker 1989, 31, suggests a plausible structure in "dogmatic" and "paraenetic" presentations. He reads 4.7–5.4a as a third paraenetic presentation. However, this pragmatic suggestion neglects the fact that 1 John makes no real division between teaching and exhortation. Rather, paraenetic textual sections also have didactic character and are part of the *theology* of the author, as 4.7b already shows. 4.8b and 4.16b belong to the rare definitions of God in New Testament texts and represent theological pointed statements in paraenetic contexts.

[255] Klauck 1991, 244.

[256] Thus with Strecker 1989, 31. A different view is taken by Klauck 1991, 283, who no longer assigns 5.1–5 to the theme of love. However, the opposition between the two proposed outlines is only partial, for the new christological instruction does, in fact, already begin in 5.1. The closeness—indeed inseparability—of Christology and love for brothers and sisters for the author is demonstrated precisely by 5.1–4. 1 John works with flowing transitions, so that no distinct outline reflects back the textual structure in a completely adequate way.

and precise formulation, surpasses everything that is written about *love* in the Johannine literature.[257]

Hans-Josef Klauck has unpacked the ideational outline of the text in a felicitous structure as follows:[258]

(1) "The Origin of Love" (4.7–10)[259]
(2) "The Answer of Love" (4.11–12)[260]
(3) "The Experience of Love" (4.13–16)[261]
(4) "The Future of Love" (4.17–18)[262]
(5) "The Practice of Love" (4.19–21).[263]

The core of the text lies in vv. 7–12, which form a distinct, complete argument. V. 7 begins with a short paraenesis. In v. 8 the theological basic definition of love is given. V. 9 attaches to the basic definition our source of knowledge—the revelation of love. V. 10 makes the definition of v. 8 more precise on this foundation. Vv. 11 and 12 deepen the opening paraenesis.

Ad (1): The author has already mentioned in 2.5, 15; and 3.17—as something axiomatic, as it were—that love is from God or is simply "God's." In 4.7–10 he uses this idea to introduce a deepened instruction on love. At the front he places the commandment of love for brothers and sisters with which the text in v. 21 also concludes. There follows a theological instruction on the divine nature of love. Here, the author expresses a conviction that Paul already approached[264] and that implicitly reverses the direction of the commandment of love for God from Deut 5.4: God has loved human beings, not human beings have loved God. A second fundamental change is connected to this change of direction. A commandment becomes a specification of salvation, a state of mutual love that is pre-given by God. First John 4.9–10 grounds this reversal christologically, in v. 9 with implicit reference to sending Christology[265] and in v. 10 with reference to atonement Christology.[266] Thus, the love of God applies to human beings. It becomes efficacious not in the creation of human beings

---

[257] This also applies to the Gospel of John. See below.

[258] Here, it remains necessary always to take into account the fact that the author attempts to connect all the themes with one another.

[259] Klauck 1991, 245.

[260] Klauck 1991, 252.

[261] Klauck 1991, 255.

[262] Klauck 1991, 268.

[263] Klauck 1991, 273. Klauck understands 5.1–5 as a new start and summarizes the verses under the title "The Victory of Faith."

[264] 1 Cor 8.3: If someone loves God, he is known by him.

[265] Cf. John 3.16.

[266] This was already addressed in 2.2.

but in Jesus Christ's deed of redemption, which the author, like the evangelist, interprets not as handing over[267] but as sending.

Ad (2): 4.11–12 interprets the love commandment from 3.11, 23; 4.7 in the sense of the 'response' of human beings. More precisely, the concern is with the nature of the attachment to God. Astonishingly, it is not love for God but now specifically love for brothers and sisters that connects people to God,[268] for the direct vision of God and thus a direct love relationship is not possible. This presupposes the argument, love demands love in return. However, this reciprocating love is directed precisely not at God himself but at the brother and sister whom God has loved.

Ad (3): 4.13–16 deepens the theme of the vision of God. The author presents himself, taking up again 1.1–3, as a witness of the Son of God, who, for his part, according to John 1.18, "has brought tidings from God." Vv. 13–16 function as christological instruction and are part of the author's constant striving for a christological and theological criteriology.[269] The Spirit and the proper confession of Jesus function as criteria.

Ad (4): 4.17–18 directs our view to the future, and this means to the "day of judgment."[270] The idea that love drives out fear, which is without analogy in the Johannine writings, has special significance for eschatology. The future has lost its terrors for those who practice love for brothers and sisters. They already live *post iudicium*.

Ad (5): 4.19–21 returns, finally, once more to love for brothers and sisters. V. 21 takes up the commandment language of chapters 2 and 3 and at the same time leans on the double commandment of love (Mark 12.28–31 par.). In terms of textual pragmatics, love for brothers and sisters has the last word and presents the actual message of the text, as has been clear since 3.11:

**3.11** For this is the message that you have heard from the beginning, that we should love one another.

However, this ultimately simple and clear pragmatics does not alone constitute the character of the text on love in 1 John 4. The text also has a speculative dimension, whose purpose certainly lies in the reinforcement

---

[267] Cf. Rom 8.32 and elsewhere in Paul.

[268] On the motif of "remaining" in God, cf. the excursuses in Strecker 1989 and Klauck 1991.

[269] Cf. the close sequence of the expressions: "by this we know," "we have seen," "the one who confesses," "we have come to know." The reference to the Spirit also functions criteriologically in 1 John 4.1, 2, 3, 6.

[270] On the eschatology of the Johannine writings, cf. Frey 1997–2000. Cf. now also Frey 2018, 73–99.

of the action-related dimension but which leads, at the same time, beyond this dimension.

In retrospect, 1 John 4 gives rise to various questions that have attracted the attention of scholars in different ways and led to exegetical debates. These especially include (1) the concentration on love for brothers and sisters and (2) the interpretation of the statement "God is love."

Most contested is the theme of love for brothers and sisters, which constitutes the center of the most prominent and heated discussion about the nature of the ethics of 1 John. Are we dealing with a narrow-minded 'conventicle ethics'—thus Ernst Käsemann[271]—or with group ethics in connection with a schism of the community or community association, to which the author knows himself to be bound in theological and ethical respects? Does this alternative present an enduring dilemma? If we restrict ourselves, initially, to 1 John[272]—which is sensible in light of the fact that the relationship between 1 John and the Gospel of John has been and remains contested—and if, second, we refrain from speaking of the consciousness of the Johannine community[273]—since neither 'the community' nor its consciousness can be reconstructed historically—then the discussion loses its character as dilemma. The situation and the pragmatics of 1 John are clear to the extent that the author diagnoses a disturbing schism of the community or communities and calls for love for brothers and sisters in relation to this. His work is meant to give christological instruction, on the one hand, and ethical instruction, on the other, in this situation—which is perceived as an end-time[274] situation—and bring clarity in relation to the standpoints of the 'heretics.' This is why we find the lasting struggle

---

[271] Käsemann 1980c, 130. Cf. Käsemann 1968, 32, 39, 65, 73. On the discussion, cf. E. E. Popkes 2005, 3–5 and 131–36, which documents the most important participants in the discussion and the most important arguments. Schrage 1990, 317–18 (GV = 1989, 322) is especially sharp: "It is therefore quite possible for a situation of outward crisis and persecution to induce the community to close ranks, but this does not in itself legitimate a particularistic conventicle ethics—which is what 'loving one another' actually comes down to."

[272] That is, if we leave unconsidered the Gospel of John, on the one hand, and 2 and 3 John, on the other hand.

[273] Thus, e.g., though very cautiously, Meeks 1972, 71. Meeks appraises the situation of the community simply as one factor in "the symbolic universe suggested by the Johannine literature." Cf. the not unjustified—though exaggerated—polemics of Thyen 2005, 3, against this one-sided interpretation of the Gospel of John on the basis of the 'Johannine community': "Instead of reading it as a biography of the Jew Jesus our Gospel is now largely read as if it is the biography of this supposed 'Johannine community,' which is about to oust from his place the poet John as the one who 'has written' this Gospel according to John 21.24 and itself advance to the secret *author* of our Gospel." For a recent challenge to the existence of the 'Johannine Community,' cf. now also Mendez 2020.

[274] 1 John 2.18.

for criteria and for an extremely comprehensive criteriology for the orientation of the community. What is of interest to us here is the criterion of love for brothers and sisters, for it is also deployed as a criterion for proper theology and proper Christology. The community presents the framework. In this context, 4.20 represents the key pointed statement:

> **4.20** If someone says, "I love God" and hates his brother or sister, he is a liar. For the one who does not love his brother and sister whom he sees cannot love God whom he does not see.

Access to God leads exclusively by way of love for brothers and sisters. The whole letter is devoted to this connection. The community writing promulgates a community ethic, which is at the same time an expression of the nature of God and therefore to the highest and last degree normative. Thus, the focus on love for brothers and sisters results from the writing and from the endangered situation of the addressees. The author diagnoses hatred for the brother/sister, which for him is murder of the brother/sister.[275] How hatred for the brother/sister manifests itself remains unclear. However, 3.14–18 makes clear that love for brothers and sisters has a social component:

> **3.16** By this we have come to know love, that he laid down his life for us. Thus, we must also lay down our lives for the brothers and sisters. **17** But if someone has worldly possessions and sees his brother or sister in need and closes his heart to him, how does the love of God remain in him? **18** Little children, let us not love in word or in speech but in action and in truth.

One searches in vain for a consideration of the world outside of the community,[276] for in the view of the author, a fire has broken out *in* the community![277] The dilemma between 'conventicle ethics' and community ethics is an artificial one that stems from an exaggerated general-applicative ethic that seeks the timeless horizon of humanity in every New Testament text. If one reads the letter as what it is, a situational writing, the discussion of conventicle ethics becomes superfluous.

By contrast, *the definition "God is love"* does not exhaust itself in the situational pragmatics of the text. It is obtained from the soteriological conviction of early Christian theologians that God sent his Son to redeem

---

[275] 2.11 and 3.12, 15 (Cain).

[276] Cf., however, 2.2.

[277] Cf. the balanced presentation in E. E. Popkes 2005, 131–34.

human beings. Thus, love is here a relational and interpersonal event that arises from the most intensive form of participation and includes the sacrifice of one's own life as a sign of love. This very thing applies in total to God and to his Son. Thus, this definition is not one among others[278] but does, in fact, lead to the heart of what an early Christian theology with a christological and soteriological orientation can say about God. In the understanding of the author, the definition "God is love" must be read *first* as a definition of the nature of God. God is understood neither on the basis of his nature, singularity, or uniqueness, nor on the basis of his role as creator and preserver or his function as ruler and lawgiver, but on the basis of the event between God, his Son, and human beings with the cornerstones of love of God, sacrifice or sending of the Son, and salvation of human beings. This process is described as *love*. In this way, light also falls, second, on ἀγάπη. *Love* is not used simply for the feeling of affection or empathy or for the desire for another person but for an interpersonal saving event that can require the sacrifice of life. For this reason alone, the designation 'conventicle ethics' is already entirely inappropriate. In 1 John, with *love* the concern is not with a group ethic but with the description of the nature of God, whose basic lines the community members are to practice among one another. For it is therein and only therein that God can be experienced. Thus, love is not only a specification of the nature of God but also the form of the revelation of God that human beings can experience here and now in the relation to the brothers and sisters.

---

[278] Cf. also 1 John 1.5: God is light. With respect to the type of definition, 2 Cor 3.16 is comparable.

# 4

# The Concept of Love (ἀγάπη/ἀγαπᾶν) in the Writings of the New Testament

## 1. Introduction: Conceptualization as Interpretive Method for Historically and Thematically Related Writings

As I have shown in chapters 1–3, the first Christian authors take up statements about love for neighbor and ἀγάπη/ἀγαπᾶν that they knew from the normative tradition complex of the legal texts of Israel. In the Pauline and Deutero-Pauline epistolary literature and in the Catholic Epistles, love for neighbor and ἀγάπη/ἀγαπᾶν were thematized anew on this basis in different ways. Moreover, the Synoptic tradition handed down logia of Jesus on the double commandment of love and instructions on love for neighbor. Both strands of tradition found their literary configuration in the narratives of the Gospels. The Johannine writings present the theme of love / to love in a very distinctive way narratively, argumentatively, and paraenetically. Paul, John, and the author of 1 John developed distinct theological conceptions of ἀγάπη, which have the character of personal concepts. On the basis of these different traditions and individual concepts, I will inquire in what follows into the *New Testament concept* of love.

In this context, *concept* means neither idea[1] or plan[2] *prae textu* nor ethical or theological teaching *in textu*, but rather a "conception abstracted from perception,"[3] i.e., the *post textum* interpretive reconstruction in the sense of historical hermeneutics, as I practice it in my presentation. Such

---

[1] In what follows the concern is not with a history of ideas, nor even with a historical excerpt from a history of the idea of love.

[2] *Duden*: "skizzenhafter, stichwortartiger Entwurf . . . Plan, Program . . . Idee, Ideal" (roughly sketched, shorthand design . . . plan, program . . . idea, ideal).

[3] Likewise according to *Duden*.

concepts are neither already consciously written into the texts themselves[4] nor inherent in them. Rather, "concept" here has the heuristic character of an interpretive reading in the respective present and stands for the hypothesis that from the individual independent contributions of the New Testament writings to the theme of love we can put together something like a pattern of relationships, similarities, dependencies, new uses, and variations that can be opened up to structural understanding. This is not meant in the sense of a doctrine of love or a systematically developed value ethics. Instead, it refers to the early Christian concept of love that was conceptualized by different authors and different community situations around the lexemes ἀγάπη and ἀγαπᾶν.[5] The texts on ἀγάπη are just as different literarily as pragmatically. Developing a uniform thought structure or an early Christian theory of love would lead us far away from the texts and fail to recognize their non-doctrinal character. Paul, too, in no way sought to develop a theory of love. Instead, the exegetical task lies in tracing out how *we* can make the heterogenous statements on love accessible for our understanding in the present. This contemporary process of understanding and interpretation can be described as *conceptualization*. It is an investigative process that begins with the perception of semantics and ends with an inquiry into neighboring and opposing conceptions. We will carry out the process of conceptualization in this chapter by inquiring now—following the diachronic and analytical presentation of the individual strands of traditions and texts that we have made—into the overall concept that can be derived from the already presented texts and groups of texts on the basis of the current state of research.

The textual foundation is the writings of the New Testament canon where the foundational[6] writings of the first Christian generations are compiled.[7] The questions for these heterogeneous texts, which became part of an overall corpus only after the fact, run as follows: Which conceptions of love did the first Christian authors have, and which theological interpretations and ethical attitudes did they mediate to their communities?

In this chapter I will once again place distinct weight on the linguistic and literary aspects of the concept. This is important since too little consideration is often given to the fact that we are dealing with a concept that we know exclusively in linguistically mediated and literarily configured form. Neither the religious, social, and personal feelings, emotions,

---

[4] "Authorial intention." Cf. Utzschneider 2009.

[5] On φιλία and other lexemes, cf. below.

[6] In the double sense of community establishing and community guiding.

[7] On the topic, see Wischmeyer 2012a. It belongs to the foundations of reception history to read the writings gathered in the "New Testament" also in their impact as foundational texts of emerging Christianity.

inner attitudes, and modes of behavior and actions connected with ἀγάπη nor the social realities in the so-called *familia Dei* and the lived ethos of its members can be reliably reconstructed.[8] Rather, we have to interact with texts, their semantics,[9] their forms, and their literary situations and strategies. In what follows, I will time and again *interpret texts*. For only from texts—and not merely through the analysis of traditions, motifs, and terms—do we experience what the New Testament authors aimed to say about love, what was especially important to them with regard to this topic, what they sought to pass on to their addressees in didactic and exhortative pragmatics, and how they configured the theme linguistically and literarily.[10]

## 2. The Semantics of ἀγαπᾶν, ἀγάπη, and ἀγαπητός

Let us begin again with the linguistic level,[11] with semantics. As already presented in the introduction, ἀγάπη need not be specially defined in the writings of the New Testament, since the noun is already known from the language of the Septuagint, though ἀγάπη or ἀγάπησις belong to the Greek nouns that are used more rarely in the Septuagint.[12] The spectrum of meaning of the two nouns results from the very frequently used verb ἀγαπᾶν, which stands in the LXX for every kind of strong attachment between human beings and things, human beings and human beings, and God and human beings.[13] It stands for attraction and responsibility of every kind: for sexuality, eroticism, love in the family, friendship, recognition

---

[8] Emotion research, social history, and ethics research are extremely helpful for disclosing the New Testament concept of love. However, they constantly strike against the limits of the *literary configuration* of psychological, social, and ethical phenomena in the New Testament writings. Thus, the Johannine writings speak of love—but was love practiced in the Johannine communities? And in what way? The Johannine epistles set forth a theology of love, but its language is at certain points the language of hatred. We cannot know what emotions the authors had and what the social climate was like in the communities.

[9] On the language of ethics, cf. van der Watt/Zimmermann 2010; Luther 2015.

[10] The linguistic-literary aspect and its action dimension are often overlooked in favor of a classic history-of-ideas presentation. On the contemporary *Ideengeschichte*, which understands itself as a history of ideas or intellectual history, cf., by way of introduction, the articles "Neue Ideengeschichte" (G. Lottes) and "Neue Geistesgeschichte" in Eibach/Lottes 2002, 261–69 and 270–80.

[11] On this, cf. especially Dormeyer 1993, 51–66. On pp. 52–59, Dormeyer provides a lucid introduction to the New Testament compound metaphors (e.g., "gospel of Jesus Christ").

[12] Cf. Wischmeyer 1978. Cf. also the summary in Kany 2013, 667–69.

[13] Cf. Stauffer 1964 (GV = 1933). The most important Hebrew equivalent is אהב/אהבה; cf. Bergman/Haldar/Wallis 1977 (GV = 1973).

of the 'neighbor,' the love of God for Israel and for individual Israelites, and the love of Israel for God, which manifests itself in keeping the covenant and the covenantal commandments. Altogether, the range of meaning of ἀγαπ- in the Septuagint, on the basis of the Hebrew אהב/אהבה, comes close to the German semantics of *Liebe/lieben*, which is comparable, in turn, to the English semantics of love / to love.

The changes in the New Testament semantics of ἀγαπ- become even more clear. We find a strong reduction or concentration of meaning. The spheres of ἀγαπ-, and that means the fields of relations in which love occurs or for which ἀγαπ- is used, are restricted. Sexuality and eroticism are not thematized in connection with ἀγαπ- and thus fall away entirely in the New Testament semantics of love.[14] Attachment between the sexes is not dealt with under the keyword *love* but within the framework of the theme 'marriage versus πορνεία.'[15] Relationship, or attachment, is viewed rather under the theological-ethical perspective. Love is thus tied to a circle of relations that is simultaneously broad and exclusive. The different New Testament writings thematize the love of God for his Son and for human beings, Jesus' love for God and for his disciples, the love of the disciples for Jesus and their love for one another, and love as a social behavioral form of the members of the Christ-confessing communities in which the New Testament writings emerged. Here, the concern is respectively with love as a *fundamental personal bond*. Moreover, love concretizes itself in the community's life together as social behavior *and* as personal involvement.[16] Thus, love / to love can be explicitly assigned to ethics—as the *main virtue*, as a virtue among others, as spiritual gift/ charisma of the Christ-confessing communities, as commandment, and as general ethos that reaches beyond the members of the Christ-confessing communities. As we have seen, only two texts, 1 Cor 13 and 1 John 4, give—very different—individual *definitions* of ἀγάπη. The rest of the texts use the ἀγαπ- stem frequently and with different emphases, but often in central argumentative contexts,[17] without needing definitions. The concrete semantics emerges from the context and from the literary form.

Neighboring lexemes belong to the word "family," φιλ-: φιλεῖν, φίλος, φίλη, φιλία, φίλημα, φιλαδελφία, φιλάδελφος, φιλανθρω-πία, φιλανθρώπως, φιλάνδρος, φιλοξενία, φιλόξενος, φιλόστοργος,

---

[14] To this can be added the fact that ἐρᾶν, ἔρως and στέργειν, στοργή are completely lacking in the New Testament vocabulary. We do, however, find ἄστοργος in Rom 1.31 and 2 Tim 3.3

[15] Ephesians and Colossians constitute exceptions to this point.

[16] 1 Cor 16.24.

[17] E.g. Mark 12 par.

φιλότεκνος. They can designate both relationships of love and of friend-ship. As already demonstrated, especially in the Gospel of John, the rela-tionship between Jesus and the disciples can be interpreted as friendship.

## 3. Linguistic Forms of Love Ethics

The consideration of semantics has already made clear that love functions as a central relationship category in the New Testament texts. Themes cre-ate for themselves their linguistic realization. A short consideration of the metaphorical world in which the semantics of love are used will deepen this perspective.

### 3.1 Metaphorical Worlds

In the Johannine writings, the language of love is predominantly verbal and thus entirely oriented to interaction and relationships. Love lives in relationships—but in which ones? ἀγαπᾶν is an expression of the heart-felt and entirely personal *relationship* between God and his Son, the Son and the Father, God and the disciples, between the disciples and Jesus and the disciples among one another—in the Johannine epistles they are the "brothers/sisters." Jesus "loves" Martha, Mary, and Lazarus,[18] and his group of disciples includes the anonymous "disciple whom he loved."[19] The load-bearing metaphors are taken from the lifeworld of the family—Father and Son as well as brothers/sisters. It is a matter of personal relationships, which rest on the power of attraction of persons and can indeed establish exclusive relationships. In the Gospel of John, this becomes especially conspicuous in the comparison between Jesus' relationship to the so-called Beloved Disciple, on the one hand, and to Peter, on the other hand: Jesus loves the unnamed disciple, not Peter. The circle of human beings to whom the love of God and Jesus applies and who, for their part, are meant to return this love is restricted or, to express the matter better: Rather than being an impersonal, collective, or universal circle,[20] it is a *personal* and thus restricted circle, which is described through relational metaphors. Here, in the Johannine writings, the fundamentally metaphorical language of the early Christian concept of love can be perceived with particular clarity. God, Jesus, the disciples, the community members are consistently

---

[18] John 11.5. Cf. Mark 10.21: Jesus "loved" the rich man.

[19] John 13.23; 19.26; 21.7, 20. John 20.2 and 21.15–17 have φιλεῖν instead.

[20] John 3.16 represents an exception: according to it, God has loved the *cosmos*. On this, see Thyen 2005, 215, with reference to Wis 11.23–24 (ἀγαπᾷς γὰρ τὰ ὄντα πάντα). Both examples use creation terminology. Thyen points to the prologue of John.

designated as *Father*,[21] *Son*, and *brothers/sisters, children,* and *friends.* Jan
G. van der Watt has presented this metaphorical world in detail in his study
of Johannine family metaphors.[22] With this metaphorical world of familial assignments, the Johannine writings create a distinct relational sphere,
which is simultaneously determined in an everyday manner and exclusively, by superordination and subordination and by affection and attachment. The family[23] is the primary social entity of experience, order, and
relationships for all members of the early Christian communities, irrespective of whether they were influenced more by Jewish or Greek origin. The Johannine metaphoricism picks up this basic experience in
order to surpass and transform this experience—from the *familia* to the
*familia Dei*.[24]

The *Father* metaphor—God as Father of Jesus—which draws the Son
metaphor in its wake—Jesus as God's Son—is fundamental.[25] Here it is not
necessary to demonstrate that it belongs to the foundations of ancient life-
worlds and especially of religions and thus also forms a cultural connective
link between the culture of Israel and of early Judaism,[26] on the one hand,
and Greco-Roman religion, on the other hand.[27] According to the LXX,
"Father" is the epithet of God, the Father of the Jews. And this ascription
retains its significance, since the early Christians read the LXX.[28] At the
same time, they use the epithet for their own relation to God as Father
of the Christ-confessing community members.[29] Despite the address "our
Father" in the Lord's Prayer, the New Testament authors remain, however,
restrained in relation to the Father epithet in the general sense, for it is
reserved in the first instance for the relationship between God and Jesus

---

[21] In a double metaphorical refraction God is designated as the Father of his only Son
Jesus Christ and as the Father of the disciples of Jesus and of those who believe in Christ.

[22] Van der Watt 2000.

[23] Cf. the concise introduction in Urban 2005b (lit.).

[24] It is notable that the Gospel of John offers *little* insight into classical family structures, thus in 4.43–54. The sibling constellation of Lazarus, Mary, and Martha represents
the most important family. In a similar way as in the Synoptic tradition, Jesus' relationship to his mother and his family is presented as difficult (esp. 19.26–27: here the *familia
Dei* takes the place of the family of Jesus).

[25] Two central compound metaphors are present here. Cf. Schrenk/Quell 1967 (GV =
1954). Cf. now also Albrecht/Feldmeier 2014.

[26] Especially in Philo in his reception of Platonic cosmology in Timaeus. Cf. Schrenk/
Quell 1967, especially the attestations on p. 956n61 (GV = 1954, 956–57, esp. 956n61).

[27] What is important here is (1) the connection of ethical and unethical characteristics
of the patriarchally ruling pater familias Zeus, (2) the fatherhood of Zeus in the sense of the
mythological genealogy of the gods: Zeus has daughters and sons among the gods.

[28] Thus the Synoptics but also John 8.41–42.

[29] Thus the letters of Paul.

himself. It is the key metaphor of God as the Father of Jesus Christ,[30] to which corresponds the metaphor of the Son for Jesus.[31] The narrow and unique connection between Father and Son can also be expressed with the adjectives ἀγαπητός[32] and μονογενής.[33] This last epithet in particular is absolutely exclusive. By placing the Father-Son relationship fundamentally in the divine world, love is defined in the sense of the closest conceivable connection between two persons[34] as the basic constellation of the world in its entirety. The Gospel of John places the relationship between God and his "only Son," who is "in his bosom," in the 'time' before the creation and in Jesus' so-called high priestly prayer also opens up the time after Jesus' "return to the Father" for a comprehensive love between God, Jesus, and "his own" (17.20–26). The same applies for the only Son as for the beloved Son.[35] This attribute also expresses an equally unique, close, and exclusive relationship between God and Jesus, which goes beyond the intensity of all other conceivable relationships.

Alongside the *ex*clusive Father-Son relation stands the *in*clusive Father-child relation, which is freely used not only in the Johannine writings but also in the Pauline and Deutero-Pauline letters for the relation between God and the Christ-believing community members and for the equally strict and loving relationship of Paul to his coworkers and to

---

[30] Often in the Synoptics and very often in the Gospel of John. In the letters of Paul, by contrast, only Rom 15.6; 2 Cor 1.3; 11.31; as well as Eph 1.3 / Col 1.3.

[31] As "Son of God" often in the Synoptics, in the Gospel of John, in Paul (esp. Romans and Galatians), and in 1 John. As "Son" predominantly in the Johannine writings, but also Q 10.22 and Mark 13.32 / Matt 24.36. Cf. Wülfling et al. 1969.

[32] Only in Mark 1.11 par. and 9.7 par. (speech of God) [cf. 2 Pet 1.17: quotation]; 12.6 / Luke 2.13 (in the parable: speech of God). The quotation from Isa 42.1 in Matt 12.18 (without "Son") is also important.

[33] On this adjective, cf. Thyen 2007c. Only in prominent places in the Johannine writings: John 1.14, 18; 3.16, 18; 1 John 4.9. In Heb 11.17 the adjective refers to Isaac—the so-called Akedah. Cf. also the expressions in Rom 8.32: his "own" Son; John 1.18 "in the bosom of the Father" (used for the Beloved Disciple in 13.23). On the Akedah in the Johannine context, cf. Thyen 2005, 214–15. Thyen rightly remarks:

Every kind of human sacrifice is regarded as abhorrent to the whole Mediterranean world shaped by Hellenism. And as the Jewish history of interpretation of Gen 22 shows . . . Judaism is no exception there. By contrast, the "self-sacrifice" of a human being is not only conceivable but such cases are often emphatically invoked as noble examples and deeds that create atonement (cf. only 4 Macc 17.17ff). . . . As already the tradition before him (cf. Gal 2.20; Eph 5.2, 20 and elsewhere), our evangelist places the greatest of weight on this idea of the self-sacrifice of Jesus. (215)

[34] Father and only Son, not husband and wife!

[35] On this, cf. Bergman in Bergman/Haldar/Wallis 1977, 100 (GV = 1973, 106–7) concerning Egyptian language use.

the communities. Reidar Aasgard and Christine Gerber have presented[36] detailed studies on this theme and pointed out the significance of the family and the brother/sister metaphoricism. Gal 3 and 4 represent a theologically important example. Here Paul initially makes extensive use of the son metaphor in order to then transition to the child metaphor. After he demonstrated in Gal 3 that the addressees are "all sons of God through faith in Christ Jesus" (3.26) and thus can be regarded as "Abraham's descendants," he develops the son conception further in 4.1–7. As sons of God, the addressees are "free" and "heirs" (v. 7). Here, Paul uses the son metaphor in a legal sense. In 4.19, he then makes recourse to the child metaphor.

> **4.19** My children, to whom I am giving birth again, until Christ is formed in you.

As in Phlm 10, Paul describes himself here as a biological father. Unlike in Philemon, however, he does so here not with the begetting metaphor of the father but with the birth metaphor of the mother and seeks a rhetorical intensification with the blending of this surprising, because unexpected, metaphor.[37] The brother/sister metaphor[38] for community members is used especially in Acts and yet also in the Pauline correspondence and in 1 John. In Acts and Paul, it is often connected with ἀγαπητός and defined thereby as especially intense and as exclusive in relation to outsiders. Christine Gerber has investigated the whole complex of the family metaphor in Paul and reaches to the following conclusion:[39] "The sibling metaphor [is] for the Pauline letters an independent metaphor . . . , already lexicalized and rarely vitalized." Gerber recognizes three "independent sub-metaphors of the general family metaphor that are not correlated with one another";[40] namely, the God-Father metaphor, the sibling metaphor, and the Paul–father/mother of the community metaphor, and points to the respective independence of the metaphors.

   In summary, for the Pauline letters and for the Johannine writings the transfer of meaning achieved by the family metaphors is very important. Love relationships are imaginable in the Greco-Roman and in the early

---

[36] Aasgard 2004; Gerber 2005.

[37] This aspect is lightly passed over in the exegetical literature. Paul speaks precisely not of "mother Paul" (thus Gerber 2005, 274; Gaventa 2007). This resolution of the metaphor misses its metaphorical character. On the birth metaphor in Paul, cf. also Müller 2012, 110.

[38] On this, see below.

[39] Gerber 2005, 349.

[40] Gerber 2005, 349.

Jewish social and cultural world as relationships between the sexes, family relationships, or close friendship relationships. Unlike in the prophetic metaphoricism of the Old Testament, where love between the sexes plays a significant role,[41] the New Testament authors neither use love between the sexes nor marriage as source domains but refer exclusively[42] to the—for the most part male—family relationships: father[43] and son, brothers and—more rarely—sisters. Through the metaphorical transference a new social sphere is constituted beyond family relationships, which refers the close attachments of the family—though not the sexual/erotic attachment of married persons with each other—to the new conditions of the communities.

This transfer becomes clearest in the saying of Jesus in Mark 3.31–35:

> **31** And his mother and brothers came and standing outside they sent to him and called him. **32** And a crowd was sitting around him, and they said to him, "Your mother and your brothers[44] outside are asking for you." **33** And he answered them and says: "Who is my mother and my brothers?" **34** And he looked around at those who were sitting around him in a circle and says: "Behold, my mother and my brothers. **35** For whoever does the will of God, this one is my brother and sister and mother."

Taeseong Roh has investigated the metaphorical world of the *familia Dei* in the Synoptic Gospels[45] and reconstructed for Mark 3 a cogent line of development from a genuine saying of Jesus to the Markan final form. Roh is especially interested in the respectively altered social relational entities—the original hearers of Jesus, the itinerant charismatics, the place-bound sympathizers, and, finally, the communities whose

---

[41] Hos 1 and 3. Wallis (Berman/Haldar/Wallis 1977, 113; GV = 1973, 122) hypothesizes that "perhaps the concept of Yahweh's covenant with the people of Israel provided the impetus for the idea of a marital bond between Yahweh and his people." Marriage is said to have been understood less as an attachment of love than as a legal covenant.

[42] 2 Cor 11.1–4 constitutes an exception. On this, cf. Gerber 2005, 216–18.

[43] Τροφός, nurse, for Paul in 1 Thess 2.7. On this, see Gerber 2005, 274–94. Gerber argues for "mother" instead of "nurse," though wrongly in my judgment. However, both meanings are possible. In any case, Paul does use the lexeme "mother" in Rom 16.13 metaphorically: the mother of Rufus "and also mine." Cf. also the birth metaphor in Gal 4.19! On this, see Gerber 2005, 459–95. Mother and sisters: 1 Tim 5.2 ("An older man . . . I admonish as a father, the younger men as brothers, older women as mothers, younger women as sisters in all decency").

[44] Textual criticism: manuscripts A, D, and others also contain the phrase "and your sisters." This expression has presumably entered from v. 35.

[45] Roh 2001; on the text, see pp. 107–26.

brother/sister model of a *familia Dei* exhibits clear analogies to the Pauline communities—an important pointer, though it does not remove the tradition-historical dilemma that Paul, in his metaphorically supported new interpretation of the family structure, does not refer to Jesus and his new interpretation of the family.

## 3.2 Topoi

Themes and arguments aim to be understood. Linguistic repetitions and simplifications, in an extended sense the topical language that establishes recognition (pleasure of recognition)[46] and creates agreement, serve this end. Here, topos is not understood as a part of the "dialectical and rhetorical theory of argument, as systematized by Aristotle . . . in the *Topics*,"[47] but in the sense of the pre-shaped linguistic expression or figure of speech. However, the reference to rhetorical topics is not superfluous. For even though Paul did not work with the rules of ancient rhetorical handbooks, his letters nevertheless testify to considerable rhetorical abilities that he probably obtained during his activity as a public teacher rather than through rhetorical school instruction.[48] In line with this, Paul developed standard terms and established expressions, which occur especially in the beginning and concluding parts of his letters, though also as structuring elements in more extensive lines of argumentation. A short enumeration is sufficient here.

The use of topical speech is evident in the address "beloved" for whole communities and individual community members.[49] It occurs first in Paul, above all in Romans. It is formulated with special care as "beloved of God" in Rom 1.7 and in other places as "my beloved" or "chosen beloved" (Rom 11.28). The fact that we are dealing with the language of love here becomes clear in Phil 4.1:

**4.1** My *beloved and longed for* brothers and sisters, my joy and my crown, stand firm thus in the Lord, beloved.

The same address then occurs everywhere in the epistolary literature and is especially frequent in 1 and 3 John. The same applies to the address "brothers and sisters." With respect to Paul, Reidar Aasgard writes, "Paul

---

[46] Ostheeren et al. 2009, 695.

[47] Calboli Montefusco 2009, 781 (GV = 2002, 691).

[48] Cf. the balanced presentation of Lampe 2013.

[49] Thus Phlm 1 for Philemon and v. 16 for Onesimus. Cf. the reflections on "form and function of address" in Aasgard 2004, 263–68.

differs significantly from other authors in the frequency and virtually exclusive use of family address. . . . Thus, the frequency of sibling address in Paul emerges as extremely striking."[50] Christine Gerber makes this judgment more precise by pointing, on the one hand, to the occurrence of the metaphorical brother/sister address in religious environments,[51] while stressing, on the other hand, that the New Testament uses are independent from other texts.

Other topical addresses that are all closely related to the epithet "beloved" are κλητοί, ἐκλεκτοί, ἅγιοι. Paul uses the last of these addresses very frequently in Romans not only in address and greeting formulas but also in different lines of argumentation. These designations are, first, expressions of honor[52]—thus Paul grants to the Roman Christians the same epithet with which he introduces himself (1.1 and 1.7). Second, they are signs of the exclusivity of the community to which the addressees belong. Third, they are an expression of the religious character of their fellowship and of their end-time status. Together with the familial address "brothers and sisters" and the address topos "beloved" taken from the topic of love, there emerges a thick linguistic net for the constitution of a close elite fellowship, which oscillates between—new—family and bond of friendship or "brotherhood." How contrafactual and at the same time capable of creating new social, emotional, and religious facts this topical diction is becomes clear by way of example in Philemon 8–14. Here, Paul awards Onesimus a new status among the "saints" (Phlm 5, 7): οὐκέτι ὡς δοῦλον ἀλλ ὑπὲρ δοῦλον, ἀδελφὸν ἀγαπητόν (v. 16). At the same time, it is clear that this new form of the fellowship of love is arranged by Paul—namely, precisely when he, as in the letter to Philemon, uses the rhetoric of petition (vv. 8, 9).

## 3.3 Verb and Noun

It is sufficient in our context to look briefly at the different uses of verb and noun in the different New Testament writings. The *verbal* love semantics of the Johannine writings is the bearer of the networks of relationships that the Gospel in particular presents between God and Jesus, Jesus and "his own," and the disciples among one another. The verb stands for the love "of the Father" for the "Son":

**3.35** The Father loves the Son and has given all things into his hand.[53]

---

[50] Aasgard 2004, 267; cf. the statistics on p. 28.
[51] Gerber 2005, 348–49.
[52] See also Phil 4.1.
[53] Cf. 10.17.

As we have already shown, this love is understood as a perfect, exclusive, and most intimate attachment. It includes the aspects of the fatherly *potestas* and of obedience on the side of the Son. A statement such as 17.25 elevates this relationship into the transcendent and thereby places it in God's nature itself:[54]

**17.25** You have loved me before the foundation of the world.[55]

Jesus formulates the reciprocity of affection and the interplay of the *potestas* of the Father and the obedience of the Son only a single time, but at a prominent place at the conclusion of the first farewell discourse (John 14.31):

**14.31** . . . in order that the world may know that I love the Father and that
I do just as the Father commanded (ἐνετείλατο) me.

Eph 2.4–5 emphasizes the surpassing importance of the loving care of God for human beings through a *figura etymologica*, in which noun and verb are combined:

**2.4** But God, who is rich in mercy, because of his great love with which
he loved us, **5** even when we were dead in trespasses, made us alive
together with Christ . . .

While the verbal language points especially to the binding character of love, the substantival diction, which we have come to know especially in Paul and 1 John, also opens up the spheres of virtue and emotion.

### 4. Literary Forms of the ἀγάπη-Texts

Themes search for language that brings them to expression, and they also search for and create their literary forms. Language is used in the New Testament writings in the context of specific preliterary and literary forms and genres. The New Testament authors used not only the large literary genres of Gospel, historical narrative, letter, and apocalypse[56] but also, within these large forms, numerous smaller forms, whose format is varied. They vary from established forms of saying—such as commandments—and

---

[54] Despite the verbal diction, the concern here is with a statement of nature. First John 4.8, 16 is based on this.

[55] For this dimension of Jesus' existence with the Father, cf. John 1.1, 18.

[56] Cf. Wischmeyer 2004b, 29–46. See further Aune 1987; 1988.

their situational embedding in apophthegmata[57] via small narrative forms such as miracle stories, ethical paradigms, and parables, as well as small ethical forms, such as virtue and vice catalogs,[58] to larger forms such as paraeneses,[59] apocalyptical texts,[60] and passion narratives.[61] These large and small literary forms determine—and at the same time limit—the way in which the New Testament authors can speak of love, and the converse also applies: the authors choose specific forms in which they can present the theme love or, alternatively, only briefly address it.

While the New Testament does not contain *love literature* in the narrow sense, it does contain several love stories that can be recognized as such. Neither the Old Testament love songs of the Song of Songs[62] nor the Hellenistic love novel,[63] love poetry, or the philosophical dialogue 'on love'[64] have had any influence on the authors of the New Testament writings. This Hellenistic literature was probably not even known to them. Following the Septuagint and early Jewish ethical writings, they chose commandments, example stories, encomium, paraenesis in the form of short sentences, and argumentative texts for the theme ἀγάπη, ἀγαπᾶν. I have already described these questions regarding forms and genres in the detailed analyses. In what follows I will discuss two other texts on which particular light falls from the standpoint of their literary form. The concern is with two episodic narratives from the time of the public activity of Jesus, in which the theme of personal *love* stands at the center—in one case the love of a woman for Jesus and in the other case the love of Jesus for his friend. In short, these episodes are Jesus narratives that are

---

[57] Mark 12.28–34 par.

[58] See the note on vices in section 1 of chapter 5.

[59] E.g. Rom 12.

[60] E.g., Mark 13 par.

[61] The works of Klaus Berger remain fruitful for this theme: Berger 1984b; 1984a. See further Dormeyer 1993. Dormeyer distinguishes between oral (small) genres (separated respectively according to dominical and apostolic genres) and written large genres.

[62] On the allegorical history of interpretation of the Song of Songs, cf. Kuhn 1986; Köpf 1986. On the contemporary approaches of an allegorical reading, cf. Hagedorn 2015. See also M. W. Elliott 2000. This tradition is now cautiously taken up again in the encyclical of Benedict VXI, *Deus Caritas Est*.

[63] From the second century CE especially the *Metamorphoses* of Apuleius with the novella of Amor and Psyche. On the proximity of Esther, Judith, Tobit, and Joseph and Aseneth to the Hellenistic love novel, cf. Burchard 1983, 589–92; Wills 1995; Vogel 2009, 6–11; Wetz 2010; Bloch 2014. Bloch regards *Joseph and Aseneth* as a love novel, perhaps even as the oldest preserved example, and states, "As a love novel *Jos. Asen.* stands alone in ancient literature" (94). For Bloch the following statement of Aseneth is especially important: ἐγὼ ἀγαπῶ αὐτον ὑπὲρ τὴν ψυχήν μου (13.15).

[64] See above on Plutarch. See there also for love poetry.

also *love stories* and that shed new light on the concept of love in the New Testament.

## 4.1 Luke 7.36–50: A Love Story

Luke 7.36–50[65] is a short episodic narrative passage that addresses the theme of love exclusively in connection with the person of Jesus[66] and has no further ethical consequences. At the center of the narrative[67] stands a woman who in a special way meets Jesus with love and affection:

> **7.36** And one of the Pharisees asked Jesus to eat with him, and he went into the house of the Pharisee and reclined at the table. **37** And behold, in the city there was a woman, a sinner. When she heard that he was in the house of the Pharisee, she brought an alabaster vessel with ointment, **38** and standing behind him at his feet, weeping, she began to wet his feet with her tears and she dried them with the hair of her head and was kissing his feet and anointing them with the ointment. **39** When the Pharisee who had invited him saw it, he said to himself, "If this man were a prophet, he would know who and what sort of woman this is who is touching him, for she is a sinner."
>
> **40** And Jesus answered and said to him, "Simon, I have something to say to you." And he said, "Teacher, speak!" **41** "A certain creditor had two debtors. The one owed him five hundred denarii, the other fifty. **42** Because they did not have (the means) to pay it back, he remitted both (their debts). Which of them then will *love* him more?" **43** Simon answered and said, "I assume the one to whom he remitted more." And he said to him, "You have judged rightly."
>
> **44** And turning to the woman he said to Simon, "Do you see this woman? I came into your house, *you* gave me no water for my feet—but *she* wet my feet with tears and dried them with her hair. **45** You did not give me a kiss—but she, from the time I came in, has not ceased to kiss my feet. **46** *You* did not anoint my head with oil—but she has anointed my feet with ointment. **47** For this reason, I say to you, her many sins are forgiven, for she *loved* much; but the one who is forgiven little, *loves* little." **48** And he said to her, "Your sins are forgiven!" **49** And those who were

---

[65] For literature, see Wolter 2008, 289–90 (ET = 2016, 316–27).

[66] This applies on the literary level.

[67] On the Synoptic tradition and the side-stories in Mark 14.3–9 and John 12.1–8, cf. Wolter 2016, 317–18 (GV = 2008, 290–91). Cf. Wolter 2016, 316–27 (GV = 2008, 289–97) for the exegetical problems of the narrative (lit.). The side-stories have different *scopoi* (theme of the anointing of Jesus before his death and discussion of 'waste') and do not thematize the love of the woman; they are therefore not drawn upon here.

reclining at table with him began to say among themselves, "Who is this who even forgives sins?" **50** And he said to the woman, "Your faith has saved you. Go in peace."

In this three-part narrative, different theological themes and narrative interests are placed in relation to one another. (1) The thematic frame is presented by the polemic of the Pharisees, which in the mouth of Jesus runs as follows in Luke 7.34: "The Son of Man has come eating and drinking and you say, 'Behold, the man (is) a glutton and a drunkard, a friend of tax collectors and sinners.'" Thus, the concern is with the discussion of Jesus' proximity to human beings who are "sinners" in the understanding of the Pharisees. It belongs to the Lukan dramatic art to have Jesus' reaction to this attack take place in the house of a Pharisee.[68] (2) Jesus' power to forgive sins constitutes the theological center of the narrative. (3) On the *narrative level*, the text recounts Jesus' encounter with a woman known as a "sinner," who shows him her *love* in an extraordinary way. The encounter occurs in the house of the Pharisee Simon, who has invited Jesus to a meal and calls him "teacher," while at the same time doubting Jesus' prophetic knowledge concerning the woman. Within the narrative, Jesus presents, for his part, a short example story (vv. 41–42),[69] which concerns the seemingly scandalous behavior of the woman and fills her action with religious meaning. (4) The *narrative* center is formed by the actions with which the woman—she remains, as in the side-stories, anonymous—shows Jesus her love. That the concern is with demonstrations of love is made clear by Jesus himself with his comparison of the behavior of Simon, which is characterized by a lack of interest in Jesus, to that of the woman. But how can the meaning of her actions of love be determined?[70] The woman does not speak; it is Jesus himself who assigns a meaning to her actions.

Exegetes have always asked: Does the love Jesus shows the woman precede the forgiveness of sins? Or, conversely, is love an expression of thanksgiving for the forgiveness that has already taken place? The

---

[68] Wolter 2016, 317 (GV = 2008, 290).

[69] On this, see Wolter 2016, 320 (GV = 2008, 294), on the parable type of the "paradigmatic decisions."

[70] On this, see Wolter 2016, 325 (GV = 2008, 296). Wolter sees the logical contradiction between the parable and v. 47b (the one to whom much is given is very thankful: the woman is forgiven her sins, therefore she comes with thankful love to Jesus), on the one hand, and v. 47a (her love is the causal basis for the forgiveness of sins; cf. v. 50: her faith is the basis for the forgiveness), on the other hand, and explains it with reference to the tradition history. A different position is taken by Fitzmyer 1981, 686–87, who reads the ὅτι in v. 27 not causally but cognitively: not "why the fact *is* so, but whereby it is known to be so" (687).

significance of this line of questioning may be doubted, for the evangelist obviously did not feel this tension. Jesus' interpretation (ἠγάπησεν πολύ) determines the whole text. Her *love* enables the forgiveness of sins. The reverse conclusion, "the one to whom little is forgiven loves little," is to be understood as an implicit reproach of the Pharisee Simon and advocates the same logic as the Markan saying "It is not the healthy who need a doctor but the sick" (Mark 2.17). This means that there can be lasting help (only) where there is a strong lack. In the case of the woman, the lack lies in her "sins," which are not further exemplified. The help comes from her capacity for great love. This is the foundation for the forgiveness of her sins through Jesus. Behind the narrative stands the—here not quoted[71]—insight of Prov 10.12, as it is used as a "maxim"[72] in 1 Pet 4.8:

> **4.8** For love (ἀγάπη) covers a multitude of sins.

But what love? Only the personal love that the woman shows Jesus can be meant in Luke 7. The showing of her great agitation (her tears), her exaggerated manner, her thankfulness and posture of a slave (she stands by his feet and dries his feet with her hair!)—all this makes clear that she, in an act of great agitation, casts her whole existence upon Jesus. She "loves him with all her power" and hopes in *his* help.[73] At this point in the interpretation a consideration of the side-texts is illuminating. In Mark 14.3–9[74] the episode of the anointing of Jesus by an anonymous woman in the house of Simon—here, the leper—takes place in Bethany. In the Gospel of Mark, the passion narrative opens with this short narrative unit. The woman herself is not characterized in further detail.[75] She does not speak. Here too, Jesus is the one who fills the action of the woman with meaning. She anoints him in advance for his burial. In a unique way, Jesus connects this action with the proclamation of the gospel[76] and thereby shows high regard for her. As in Luke 7 the woman has a personal relationship with Jesus, which is emphasized by Jesus, whereas she provokes rejection in

---

[71] The sentence from Proverbs, which stands in the background here, is not quoted in the commentaries.

[72] Goppelt 1993, 297 (GV = 1978, 284). Cf. also Jas 5.20; 1 Clem. 49.5; 2 Clem. 16.4; Didascalia 2.3.3. First Peter and James follow the MT. The Septuagint translates the MT very freely: "Hatred stirs up strife, but friendship (φιλία) covers all who are not fond of strife" (trans. J. Cook in NETS). First Peter changes φιλία to ἀγάπη.

[73] From "the city" she could expect no help, no forgiveness.

[74] Matt 26.6–13 largely follows Mark.

[75] It is the lone deed of the woman that provokes offense. The characterization of her as 'sinner' and the framework with the theme "Jesus and the sinners" is, however, lacking. Accordingly, the disciples accuse her not of sin but of waste.

[76] Retained in Matt 26.13.

her environment. In John 12 the episode of the anointing of Jesus also takes place in Bethany, though there in the house of Martha and Mary and with Lazarus present, i.e., the persons whom Jesus "loved." As in the Gospel of Mark, the point in time is the beginning of the passion narrative.[77] Jesus is again the one who interprets the action of the woman and connects it with his death. In all three versions, however, the concern is with an exceptional action of a woman that applies personally to *Jesus*. This is made quite clear in the concise saying in John 12.8: "You do not always have *me* (with you)." *He* is washed, *he* is anointed, *he* is kissed.

The Lukan version of the anointing story is the one that makes this encounter of a woman with Jesus a *love story*. The keyword "love" occurs only in this version of the tradition about an anonymous woman who showed her love to Jesus in such personal and strong gestures that her action was perceived as offensive not only by Pharisees but even by the disciples of Jesus, but who is, by contrast, most highly praised by Jesus:

**7.47** . . . for she loved much.

The woman turns to Jesus with her whole love—and Jesus reacts with the highest good, the forgiveness of her sins,[78] with the opening of a new existence. Such love for Jesus is not reported about men, neither about Peter nor about the Beloved Disciple. Luke 7 is a great woman's story and love story, even and precisely when the theological emphasis lies on Jesus' ability to forgive sins.[79]

### 4.2 John 11.1–12.11: Another Love Story

The narrative of the raising of Lazarus is also a love story, this time the story of Jesus' love for Lazarus.[80] The length of the narrative clearly surpasses other episodic Jesus narratives. It would go beyond the framework of this study to discuss the text of the whole narrative here. Only the following

---

[77] See the very detailed analysis in Theobald 2009, 765–780. Cf. especially the splendid excursus "The Anointing Story and its Synoptic Relatives" (767–73), which discusses the overlaps in motifs and possible tradition-historical dependencies and developments.

[78] The evangelist evidently thinks of sexual "sin."

[79] The case is different with the pericope in John 7.53–8.11, which does not belong to the original Gospel of John. On the textual tradition, cf. U. Becker 1963. For an outstanding exegesis of the pericope, see Thyen 2007b. Cf. now also Knust/Wasserman 2019; Keith 2020. The pericope of the woman caught in adultery is not a 'love story' like Luke 7.36–50 but a biographical apophthegma that demonstrates Jesus' authority as a teacher of the law.

[80] On the text, cf. Thompson 2013.

need be said: (1) The narrative is composed of several episodes[81] and is advanced by changes of place and the appearance of different persons and person groups.[82] (2) The narrative functions as a narrative pivot or as κατα-στροφή (11.53). As Rudolf Schnackenburg correctly formulates, "To the supreme revelation of Jesus as life-giver corresponds the determination of unbelief to destroy him."[83] (3) Jesus' resurrection is anticipated and prepared for. Thus, the Lazarus narrative is the gateway to the passion narrative. (4) Theologically and christologically the concern is with the theme of the resurrection and its proper understanding according to the evangelist. The individual details of this unusually extensive narrative episode can just as little be commented on here as its emergence-historical backgrounds.[84]

Here the concern can only be to point out the dimension of *the personal love of Jesus* that runs through the narrative. For the Lazarus narrative is not only a or *the* New Testament miracle story that reports a miracle of the raising of someone from the dead, even though this dimension of the text is the decisive one in the structure of the Gospel (John 11.15–53 and 12.9–11), which has direct significance for the Christology of the Gospel. It is at the same time a narrative about a great love within the *familia Dei*, with Lazarus, his sisters, and Jesus and his disciples functioning as its members in a special way.[85] The motif of personal closeness and love is lacking in the two other resurrection miracles, i.e., the narratives of the daughter of Jairus and the young man of Nain.[86] By contrast, this motif is present throughout the Lazarus pericope: vv. 3, 5, 11c, 35, 36b.[87] In the Johannine version of the anointing narrative in 12.3–8, which is closely connected to the Johannine Lazarus narrative in terms of tradition history, the love motif is taken up again when Mary[88] anoints Jesus and dries his

---

[81] Cf. the arrangement of Theobald 2009, 712.

[82] On the source-critical and tradition-historical questions and on the relationship to the Synoptics, especially to Luke, cf. Thyen 2007b, and—with contrary results—Theobald 2009, 708–46.

[83] Schnackenburg 1985, 433 (ET = 1980, 345).

[84] Theobald 2009, 714–20, on the tensions in the text and possible models of resolution (against the synchronous reading of Thyen).

[85] Theobald 2009, 739: "The concern is thus with the *familia dei*, the friendship circle of believers, which gathers around Jesus' love." But it may be questioned whether the continuation of the sentence is accurate: ". . . and the friendship of Jesus to the three sisters already pictures the ecclesial fellowship understood in this way later." On the text, cf. also van der Watt 2000, 360–67. Van der Watt points out that the term friend does not stand in the foreground in John.

[86] In Luke 7.13 Jesus "has compassion" for the mother of the dead man.

[87] In the development of this motif, the evangelist can use φιλεῖν and ἀγαπᾶν alongside each other.

[88] In Luke 7.37 the woman remains nameless.

feet with her hair. However, unlike Luke, the evangelist has placed the motif of Jesus' burial in the foreground here.

In the Gospel of John, the motif of the personal love of Jesus for specific human beings occurs especially in the figure of the Beloved Disciple.[89] In John 13.23–26 and 19.26 this disciple, who stands personally closer than the other disciples and above all than Peter, is mentioned entirely as a matter of course as "the disciple whom Jesus loved." There is, however, no narrative devoted specifically to this disciple. Chapter 21 also does not present a narrative about the Beloved Disciple but is a *Peter narrative*. The disciple whom Jesus loved appears only as a figure of contrast. Jesus imploringly asks Peter whether Peter loves him—but he himself loves the unknown disciple! Peter becomes a tragic figure in chapter 21. Jesus entrusts the community to him and foretells his martyrdom, but he does not "love" him. This affectionate attention remains reserved for the anonymous disciple. Whether the figure of the Beloved Disciple is a literary figure, a historical entity, or a person from the Johannine school cannot be discussed here. In this context, only one thing is important for the theme of ἀγάπη: The author of the Gospel of John sets forth the figure of a Jesus who is himself the "only begotten Son" of the Father, who at the end of his life calls his disciples "friends,"[90] and who has among these friends one, "whom he loves," though he also loves Lazarus and his sisters. The concept of love in the Gospel of John also has emotional[91] and above all personal characteristics that clearly go beyond a general "ecclesial fellowship."[92]

Looking back at Luke 7 and John 11 it becomes clear that simple attributions such as mercy, love for neighbor, love for brothers and sisters, solidary structures of association or community, and metaphors such as *familia Dei* are not adequate to describe the different social and emotional dimensions of the language of love in the New Testament. The Gospel of Luke and the Johannine literature in particular open our eyes both to great *emotional*, individual, and elite images of the love between Jesus and individual men and women and to very different speculative-theological dimensions of the talk of God's eternal love for his Son. With respect to the question of what love in the New Testament can be, these texts prohibit a perspective that has been domesticated in a caritative or

---

[89] Cf. Mark 10.21 *ex negativo*.

[90] 15.14.

[91] On this point, the commentaries are mostly very—probably overly—reserved. Cf., however, Theobald 2009, 739, who emphasizes this aspect: Jesus' agitation, his weeping, and also his anger, which applies to those who do not believe in the resurrection of Lazarus and only see his death.

[92] Theobald 2009, 739.

communitarian way as well as one that is determined in a one-sidedly theological manner.

## 5. Literary Situations of the ἀγάπη-Texts

The writings of the New Testament do not speak everywhere of love. Rather, love is thematized in specific contexts and literary situations. These contexts will be sketched out in what follows. Where does the theme love occur in the texts of the New Testament?

### 5.1 Situations in the Letters of Paul

In what follows I will concentrate first on the letters of Paul as situational writings. Paul thematizes *love* in all his letters. The general literary situation is the—direct or current—situation of the epistolary communication and the—mediated or topical—situation of the epistolary community paraenesis.[93] Here, four areas can be distinguished. First, there is the theological-christological use in Romans.[94] The occasion is respectively a specific high point of the christological *argumentation*, a christological basic datum—namely, the reference to Christ's sacrificial death. The reference to Christ's love for human beings or to God's love, which proves itself in the giving of the Son, represents in Rom 5–8 a foundational argument for the *propositio generalis* of 1.16–17: The "justice of God," which Paul proclaims in his gospel, rests on Christ's vicarious death, through which justice is satisfied. *Love* is here a fundamental element of the christological argumentation.[95]

Second, there is, alongside this, the *ethical* use for a Christian basic virtue or mode of behavior, which carries the greatest material and argumentative weight. From 1 Thessalonians onward, Paul calls for ἀγάπη in the paraenetic sections of his letters.[96] Here, love is, however, more than one among many virtues. On multiple occasions, love appears together with faith.[97] While Michael Wolter seeks to find a closeness to the double virtue pair 'piety and justice' from Hellenistic ethics, we precisely do not

---

[93] The community paraenesis can of course also have characteristics of direct communication.

[94] See above. Cf. also Gal 2.20.

[95] This distinguishes love from πίστις and ἐλπίς. Christ is the bearer of the love of God but not of hope and faith. This is why love connects the believers with Christ and with God.

[96] Rom 12.9; 14.15; 1 Cor 8.1; 14.1; 16.14.

[97] Gal 5.6, 22; 1 Cor 13.13; 1 Thess 1.3; 3.6; 5.8; Phlm 5.

find love—whatever semantic form it might take—there.[98] If the literary and theological-ethical weight of 1 Cor 13 is taken into account, it becomes in any case clear that love is not simply a virtue among others[99] but a meta-virtue that establishes the conditions for Christian behavior as a whole, as 1 Cor 13 shows. Thus, the argumentation in 1 Cor 13 is located a step above the themes and argumentation of 1 Cor 12 and 14. This also applies to Gal 5.14 and Rom 13.8–10. There too Paul uses the reference to the love commandment in the sense of a higher ethical instruction that brings the normative and exclusive ethical validity of the Torah to its end.

Third, little attention has been given to *the personal use* in the context of the epistolary communication: 1 Cor 4.21; 16.24; 2 Cor 2.4;[100] 8.7–8, 24; Phlm 9. Phlm 8–14 is delivered in an especially personal tone:

> **8** Therefore, although I have much freedom in Christ to command you to do what is fitting, I prefer to ask because of *love*, I, Paul, an old man and now even a prisoner of Jesus Christ[101] **10**—I ask you for my child (τέκνον), whom I have begotten (ἐγέννησα) in chains, **11** who was formerly useless to you but now is very useful to you and to me, **12** whom I am sending to you, him, that is, my own heart.

In the further course of the letter, Paul calls the slave Onesimus his and Philemon's "beloved brother":

> **15** For perhaps he was for this reason separated (from you) for a time, so that you might have him back *forever*, **16** no longer as a slave but as

---

[98] Wolter 2013, 449: "With the joining of faith and love (Paul makes) the *interpretatio Christiana* of an older tradition of Hellenistic ethics." The combination of piety and justice precisely does not occur in Paul, though it does in Justin, *Dial.* 93.2. Wolter probably refers—without reference—to Berger 1972, 142–76. On p. 143, Berger advances the thesis that the double commandment of love goes back "to the combination of fear of God and love for neighbor attested in Greek-speaking Judaism" and to the "Greek combination" of εὐσέβεια and δίκαιον or δικαιοσύνη. Cf. Berger's excellent documentation on pp. 143–65. Especially important is the compilation of the New Testament attestations. These occur especially in Luke and in the Pastoral Epistles (p. 165). However, it is also important that while this Hellenistic topos is taken up by Josephus, Philo, and other early Jewish authors, it is precisely not taken up by the Jesus tradition and by Paul. For Paul in particular it is telling that he knows the formula "justice and piety" but does not use it theologically, since he engages critically with the interpretation of the law and not with the legacy of Jewish-Hellenistic virtue ethics.

[99] Paul can, however, indeed use it in this way.

[100] "The love that I have in excess for you." In 2 Cor 2.8 Paul demands this love from the Corinthians in relation to the 'sinner.'

[101] Müller 2012, 102, translates, "so wie ich bin: Paulus, ein alter Mann" (as I am: Paul, an old man). What is meant is probably "in my present condition."

someone who is more than a slave—a beloved brother, especially for me, but much more for you, both *in the flesh* and in the Lord. **17** If you regard me as a companion, receive him as me.

These may be the most personal statements of Paul on ἀγάπη. The expressions "forever"[102] and "brother in the flesh"[103] belong to the language of love as great emotion, which is very rare in the New Testament writings. Paul connects to individual community members not only an ethical and spiritual but also a deep personal relationship. Paul describes it, on the one hand, as an emotional relationship and at the same time uses the previously mentioned family metaphors to express its intensity. Paul, who is unmarried and without family and located in prison, understands Onesimus in this letter[104] as his physical son.

Fourth, love is placed multiple times in concluding formulas or similarly important positions in the text, such as Rom 15.30; 1 Cor 16.24; 2 Cor 13.11, 13. Whether it is epistolary communication or exhortation or blessing—the reference to love furnishes every one of these epistolary situations with the greatest emphasis. In the process a combination of the three aforementioned spheres takes place: theological/christological/pneumatological components stand alongside the personal affection of Paul (1 Cor 16.24) and alongside ethical exhortation. Phil 2.1–4 provides the best example of this concentration of meaning of love:

> **2.1** If there is any encouragement in Christ, any consolation of love, any fellowship of the Spirit, any compassionate heart (literally, "heart and compassion")[105]—**2** make my joy complete by thinking the same thing, having the same *love*, being united, thinking one thing. **3** Do nothing from strife or vainglory but in humility regard one another as superior to yourselves. **4** Let each of you look not to his own interests but to the interests of others. **5** Let the same mind be in you that (is) in Christ Jesus.

Paul portrays a dense picture of 'Christian' communal existence in love. In this respect, Phil 2.1–4 is a counterpart to 1 Cor 13. However, unlike what

---

[102] Müller 2012, 118–19, discusses various interpretive possibilities and decides for an "interpretation that gives duration to the new relationship between Onesimus and Philemon beyond the present life" (119).

[103] Müller 2012, 102, translates "in everyday life," thus also on p. 123. To me it seems more likely that the concern is with the opposition of spiritual ("brother/sister," who belongs to the house community) *versus* fleshly ("brother/sister" in the emotional sense).

[104] Here too, it applies that we cannot say how much personal feeling and how much goal-oriented rhetoric is contained in this statement.

[105] Bauer 1988, 1532.

we find in 1 Cor 13, Paul, in Phil 2, does not develop the virtue character of love, its modes of action and eschatological character, but focuses his exhortation entirely on the emotional and communitarian power of love and on its anchoring in the fate of Jesus. He interprets Jesus' incarnation as an expression and model of the love that he demands from the Philippians in 2.1–4. The main weight of the paraenesis of Phil 2.1–18 lies here. Love is here—in a way that is indeed comparable to the statements in the Johannine literature—a new way of being and existence that generates its own ethos. It has its *fundamentum in re* in Jesus' handing over of his life out of love, behind which stands God's love for human beings, and it becomes effective in the mutual appreciation for one another, the behavior of humility shaped through this, and the practical forms of life of the community members. Thus, ἀγάπη and ἀγαπᾶν present the basic structure of the new being in Christ or, put differently, of the eschatological existence of Christ-believers, as Paul invokes it in 2 Corinthians:[106]

**5.14** For the love of Christ drives us, who judge as follows: one died for all, therefore "all" died, **15** and he died for all in order that those who live no longer live for themselves but for the one who died for them and was raised.

The theological linking back of love to Christ is taken up by Colossians and Ephesians, and in Ephesians, as we have already demonstrated, related to the love of husbands for their wives (not vice versa!). The marriage paraenesis sets the situation, with the imbalance that exists in both letters between the love paraenesis and the subordination of the women to the correspondingly patriarchal love of the men being conspicuous. Here, love creates a one-sided attachment.

The Johannine letters are also written out of the situation of the community paraenesis. Paraenesis with a theology of love grounded in theology and Christology underlies 1 John.

## 5.2 Situations in the Gospels

The situations of the love texts in the Gospels are always literarily configured. We know nothing about possible original situations in the life of Jesus. The key situation of the Synoptic Gospels is Jesus' teaching before the people and before his disciples, especially in conflict with the Jewish religious authorities. Materially, the concern is with the authoritative interpretation of the law by Jesus. Mark and the Synoptics that follow

---

[106] The "universal power of the love of Christ."

him portray Jesus as the teacher of the Torah, whose interpretation of the Torah assigns a decisive role to the two love commandments and their interpretation. In the course of the subsequent history of reception and interpretation,[107] as the Torah became less important for Christian ethics, this picture of Jesus became separated from its original situation and developed into the picture of Jesus as the general teacher of *love* and of the *religion of love* to which I referred in the introduction.

There are, however, also quite rare literary situations or scenes outside the teaching on the two greatest commandments in which love plays a role. These may be mentioned again here briefly: the actions of love of the so-called sinful woman in Luke 7 and Jesus' love for the rich man in Mark 10.21. By contrast, the small scene in Mark 10.13–16, i.e., the blessing of the children, gets by without the keyword "love" or "to love." The verb ἐναγκαλίζομαι occurs only in Mark 9.36 and 10.16 in the context of Jesus' affection for children.[108] The verb stands for a loving gesture of physical closeness. However, the two scenes do not actually apply to the children but to the logic of the kingdom of God, which serves the low, the humble, the "last." Viewed with regard to the logic of the text, the blessing scene is an *exemplum*.[109] Nevertheless, it remains necessary to affirm that the Gospels ascribe to Jesus a special affection for human beings here and in other contexts. This behavior, however, is not part of the Synoptic literary concept of ἀγάπη.

The literary situations in the Gospel of John differ clearly from those of the Synoptic Gospels. In John Jesus also teaches on love and loving—especially in verbal language and above all within the circle of the disciples.[110] The love commandment in altered form is also given in the framework of the instruction of the disciples at the last meal with them. It has no general validity but is explicitly restricted to the disciples (13.35). The commandment is also not placed in the context of Jesus' Torah instruction. Instead, the personal behavior of Jesus is part of the literary concept of love in a special way, as the figure of the Beloved Disciple and the Lazarus narrative especially show. The detachment from the situation of Torah interpretation has progressed so far in the Johannine writings that the internal admonition of Jesus in John 13.34–35 is

---

[107] Nygren 1982.

[108] Lindemann 2010b.

[109] Thus Müller 1992, 220. I cannot share the consideration of Yarbro Collins 2007, 445, that a tradition directed against the exposure or killing of newborn children could stand behind the pericope.

[110] Exceptions: 3.16, 35 (meeting with Nicodemus); 3.35 (John the Baptist speaks here); 8.42 and 10.17 (Jesus speaks before some Pharisees and before the Jews).

introduced as a "new *commandment*."[111] The theme of the law is thus definitively left behind.[112]

Looking back, it becomes clear that a portion of the statements about love is situated in a theological-christological way, whereas another portion can be assigned to the paraenesis. The textual pragmatics is clearly divided. On the one hand, there is fundamental instruction about salvation; on the other hand, there is admonition and exhortation. The texts devoted to the personal aspect of love constitute a third textual pragmatic emphasis. Here, Jesus is presented to the hearers or readers of the Gospels as an authoritative, involved, and emotional person. Paul does the same with his own person. He presents himself as a person with great emotions, capacity for attachment, ethical responsibility, and authority—the components that make up the New Testament concept of love. Here, the textual pragmatics aim at the establishment of close mutual attachment, as Paul expresses it in 2 Cor 8.7.

> **8.7** But as you have excess in everything, in faith and in speech and in knowledge and in all zeal and in *the love, which* (comes) *from us* (and) (has taken hold) *in you*, (it should be) that you also have excess in this gift of grace (namely, the collection for Jerusalem).

## 6. Coordinates of the Concept of Love: Subjects, Recipients, Relations, Narrative

The New Testament concept of love is a relational concept, as it is natural for the theme of love. Therefore, the relevant questions are, Which relationships are understood as "love relationships"? and, Is there a hierarchy within these relationships? Our consideration of the different literary situations has made clear once again how heterogenous the components of the New Testament concept of love are. There are the two Old Testament love commandments, which are joined into the so-called double commandment in the New Testament, the virtue or spiritual gift of ἀγάπη, God's love for human beings, Christ's death as sacrifice for human beings and thus as the highest form of divine love, Jesus' emotionally grounded love for "his own," and the brotherly and sisterly love in the Pauline and Johannine communities. This heterogeneity applies both between the different New Testament groups of writings and individual writings as well as within

---

[111] First John 3.11 repeats this as "the message that you have heard from the beginning."

[112] Interestingly, the motif of the interpretation of the law occurs, however, in John 8.1–11: an indirect love story. But cf. what was said about John 8.1–11 and Luke 7.36–50 above.

these writings, especially in the Pauline letters, which contain almost all the aforementioned components, without Paul being interested himself in developing a consistent conceptual *structure*. He does not establish a relationship between a text such as 1 Cor 13 and a passage such as Rom 8.31–39. Thus, with a portrayal of the *New Testament* concept of love, which is developed from all the addressed texts, we consciously go beyond the texts and seek to discern in retrospect a pattern that was disclosed only in individual cases to the authors of the New Testament writings who worked in theological, ethical, and literary ways. The case in which this is developed most fully is 1 John 4.7–12. This late text is the key text for the whole New Testament concept of love and may be quoted here once again:

> **4.7** *Beloved*, let us *love* one another, because *love* is from God, and everyone who *loves* is born of God and knows (γινώσκει) God. **8** The one who does not *love* does not know God, for *God is love* (ἀγάπη). **9** In this the *love* of God has appeared among us, that God has sent his only Son into the world in order that we may live through him. **10** In this is *love*, not that we have *loved* God but that he has *loved* us and sent his Son as an atonement for our sins. **11** *Beloved*, if God has so *loved* us, we also ought to love one another. **12** No one has ever seen God. If we *love* one another, God remains in us and his *love* has perfected itself in us.

## 6.1 God Establishes the Relationships of Love

The starting point of love lies in and with God. To be sure, the definition "God *is* love" does not equate the two nouns and is not reversable,[113] for the predicate noun "love" cannot be exchanged with the subject God. Thus, the sentence can neither be read philosophically as "Love is God (or divine)" nor in the understanding of Greco-Roman religion as "*Eros* or *Agape* is a god." However, the Johannine definition is a fundamental and fully valid specification of essence (*Wesensbestimmung*), and in this meaning it is not replaceable. This means that other possible fundamental specifications of essence such as "God *is* justice," "God *is* peace," or "God *is* mercy"—we could also insert grace or goodness or perfection or holiness—do not occur in the New Testament texts. These and other essential characteristics of God are described adjectivally: "God is just" etc. They remain partial aspects of his nature and action.

The only *complete* definition is that of ἀγάπη. The only definitional material parallel to 1 John 4 is 2 Cor 3.17:

---

[113] We do not find the god "Love" or the sentence "Love is God" in the New Testament. However, 1 Cor 13.8 at least comes close to the divine quality of love.

**3.17** Now the Lord is the Spirit, and where the Spirit of the Lord is, (there is) freedom.[114]

Both definitions have, despite all differences, a commonality. They aim at the core of the nature (*Wesenskern*) of God and Christ. Only and exclusively the "Spirit" and "love" are understood by the early Christian theologians as complete expressions of the divine nature or essence. The close connection of the two entities is emphasized both in Paul and in the Johannine writings. Insofar as love makes up the nature of God, in the sphere of the community it always remains the gift of the Spirit.

God's nature discloses itself to the New Testament authors in Jesus Christ. The substantivized definition of nature "God is love" is expressed multiple times by the author of the Gospel of John in verbal form—paradigmatically in the laconic sentence: "The Father loves the Son" (John 3.35).[115] However, the metaphor "of the only-begotten or only (Son), who is in the bosom of the Father" (John 1.18) best brings to expression this singular closeness. The love of God as the only perfect description of his nature applies first to his Son. The *developed* notion of an inner-divine relationship of love before the creation, imagined as a Father-Son relationship, is Johannine.[116] However, it also occurs in linguistically altered form in Paul and in the Synoptics, for it is already given with the title Son and is intensified to the extreme through the sacrificial interpretation of this Son-Father relationship.[117] Through the connection of the love of God to the sacrifice of his Son for human beings— "God so loved *the world*"—the inner-divine sphere is then transcended. ἀγάπη applies not only to God and his only Son but also to the relationship between God and his Son, on the one hand, and to human beings, on the other hand. The New Testament writings make no further statements about "God per se" and "God and his Son per se"[118] but direct their interest to the love of God and Christ for human beings.

---

[114] Cf. the concluding expression "the Lord, who is the Spirit" (3.18). An interpretation of 2 Cor 3.12–18 cannot be carried out here.

[115] Cf. 10.17; 15.9; 17.23, 26.

[116] I have intentionally used an imprecise formulation at this point, since the concern here is not with a differentiating profile of individual writings. On the subject matter, cf. Thyen 2005, 97–98 and 213–16.

[117] On this, cf. now Karrer 2013. Karrer rightly points out that "all the aforementioned great traditions (atonement, redemption, reconciliation, handing over) are not connected with the title Son in Paul or elsewhere in the New Testament. This relativization does not, however, weaken our predicate but shows its breadth and ability to unify different soteriological approaches with personal Christology" (279).

[118] Cf. the conscious reserve of Paul in 1 Cor 2.10–16. Paul signals here that he indeed has a spiritual insight into "the depths of God." However, he immediately restricts this insight to the knowledge of "what is gifted to us by God" (2.12).

Cilliers Breytenbach points out that for Paul Christ's death means "the encompassing love of the Son of God (Gal 2.20 ['the Son of God who loved me and gave himself for me']) or of Christ (2 Cor 5.14)." However, beyond this, it can be said that Christ's death "is thus also the demonstration of the love of God to all (Rom 8.32), when they were still sinners (5.8), enemies of God (5.9)."[119] In the Gospel of Mark we find the phrase "beloved Son" for Jesus three times, twice as a speech of God (1.11; 9.7) and once in a parable (12.6). By contrast, the motifs of Jesus' sacrifice and his love for human beings are not joined in the Gospel of Mark.[120] Thus, the Gospel of Mark takes up the conception of God's love for his Son, though without extending it to Jesus' death and thus soteriologically expanding it, i.e., letting it come to human beings.[121]

If we ask about the (overall) New Testament concept of love, then the opening of the inner-divine relationship of love to human beings is decisive. First John 4.9 expresses this opening with the help of the vocabulary of revelation:

**4.9** In this the *love* of God has appeared (ἐφανερώθη) among us, that God has sent his only Son into the world in order that we may live through him.

Paul and the Johannine writings understand Jesus' death as equally an expression of the love of God and of Jesus for human beings. The concluding statement in Rom 8.39 connects both aspects as follows:

**8.39** Nothing will be able to separate us from the love of God, which is (or "becomes active") in Jesus Christ, our Lord.

For the Gospel of John, it is of great importance to clarify that Jesus dies for human beings voluntarily and is not, for example, compelled to do so by God. He is the master of his action, for only in this way can his sacrifice become effective:

**10.14** I am the good shepherd and I know my own and my own know me, **15** just as the Father knows me and I know the Father, and I lay down my life for the sheep. **16** And I have other sheep, which are not from this

---

[119] Breytenbach 2013, 331.

[120] The motif is lacking in the passion predictions and also in the Synoptic Last Supper texts. By contrast, John 13.1 places the last gathering of Jesus with the disciples under the motif of the love of Christ.

[121] The soteriology of the Gospel of Mark uses the δεῖ of suffering and death of the Son of Man as the presupposition of the resurrection.

fold; I must bring them also, and they will listen to my voice, and there will be one flock, one shepherd. **17** For this reason the Father *loves* me, because I lay down my life in order that I may take it up again. **18** No one takes it from me, but I lay it down on my own accord. I have the authority to lay it down, and I have authority to take it up again. **19** I have received this commandment from my Father.

Only a voluntary laying down of Jesus' life is a sacrifice that creates redemption for those for whom it is given. We have seen that the Gospel of John makes recourse to the conception of the place-taking death of the friend for the friend, which restricts the reach of the love and sacrifice to a specific group of human beings, whereas Paul—on this point closer to the Synoptic Gospels—emphasizes the obedience of the Son to the Father and does not in principle restrict the significance of the sacrifice.[122] Paul and John share the interpretation of the death of Jesus as the giving of life for others, understood as the highest form of love. The form of the giving of one's own life as the highest expression of love undoubtedly constitutes the theological-christological center of the overall New Testament concept of love. Here, in the inner-divine sphere, the basic form of love is pre-formed and pre-suffered. When John 1.1–3, 14, 18; and Phil 2.6–7 address the separation of the Son from the Father, which is expressed in another place as the "handing over (of the Son),"[123] and Jesus' fate of death is interpreted as the love of God and Jesus for human beings, then we are at the center of the concept of love—love and death mutually condition each other here but in such a way that love and thus life prevails.[124]

## 6.2 Relationships That Proceed from Human Beings

Love as constructive and helpful interpersonal relationship[125] is called for in the form of *love for neighbor* in the Gospels and letters with reference to the Torah and to Jesus' teaching. With this a course is set from the outset for the writings of the New Testament. Love is understood fundamentally as a *social relationship* within specific institutions. What is primarily in view is neither the erotically or sexually connoted love relationship between individual persons nor the likewise individually oriented close friendship.

---

[122] The motif is, however, also not lacking in the Gospel of John: John 10.19.
[123] Rom 4.25; 8.32; Gal 2.20; Eph 5.2.
[124] On the opposition of love and death, see below.
[125] Love for God, the first part of the double commandment, recedes in the New Testament writings.

Moreover, the loving relationships within the family—between spouses, parents and children, brothers and sisters—are also never employed literally but rather used exclusively in the image domain of metaphorical expressions such as "father," "son," and "brother/sister."

According to Leviticus, the radius of love for neighbor is restricted to the legal community of Israel. Thus, the commandment neither calls the hearers to a general humanity nor is concerned with a close internal ethics or group ethics. Rather, "the neighbor" points in the context of ancient Israel to a clear, ethnically, politically, and religiously defined group of people that is limited in principle and yet actually very extensive in scope. In the first century CE, the question of who is "the neighbor" then arises anew under the conditions of the Jewish diaspora and the *imperium Romanum*. We have seen that the commandment of love for neighbor from Leviticus becomes a foundation for the ethics of Jesus, as the Synoptic Gospels present it. In the process different reinterpretations of the social framework and of the group to which love for neighbor is meant to apply arise. The narrative of the merciful Samaritan shows by way of example how urgently the question of the "neighbor" required further precision under the political and religious conditions of the first century CE. Luke has a foreigner or member of a religious group that was perceived to be "different" practice mercy toward a Jew. Matt 5.43–48 explicitly expands love for neighbor to love for enemies, presents precisely this expansion as Jesus' own contribution, and criticizes at the same time mere love for neighbor as something that even the "gentiles" practice. While this interpretation has no parallel in the Synoptic Gospels, it is close to the recommendation of Paul: "Bless those who persecute you" (Rom 12.14).[126] In this way, the neighbors have become not only "others" or "foreigners" but precisely the dangerous "enemies," whereby the original sense of the commandment of love for neighbors is entirely changed. This change corresponds to the completely new social reality of the early Christian communities, who formed a distinct group (1 Cor 5.11: the "brothers/sisters"; 5.12: "those inside") and perceived "those outside" (1 Cor 5.12) as foreign and perhaps also as hostile.

In his study *Love without Pretense*, Walter T. Wilson rightly points to the rare treatment of this topic in Paul:

> It is noteworthy that besides the general statements in 1 Corinthians 4.12, Galatians 6.10, 1 Thessalonians 3.12, and 5.15 this [Rom 12.14] is the

---

[126] On the text, see Jewett 2007, 755. Against Nestle-Aland, Jewett argues that υμας should not be regarded as the more original reading. See his critical engagement with other interpretations on pp. 765–66. The question need not be decided here.

only place where Paul extends the discussion of love to those outside the Christian community. Moreover, Romans 12.14–21 is the only passage in which Paul calls on Christians to respond positively to enemies.[127]

However, statements like Rom 12.14 show that Paul always thinks not only of those "inside" but also of "those outside," whom he seeks to win or save (1 Cor 7.16; 14.23–25; Phil 2.15). Neither in the Gospels nor in Paul is the term "neighbor" further clarified. Rather, it is presupposed as an established Septuagint term. In Paul "the neighbor" occurs, outside the quotations in Rom 13.9–10 and Gal 5.14, only in Rom 15.2:

> **15.2** Let each of us please his *neighbor* for his good, to build him up.

Despite the aforementioned expansions of love for neighbor in the Synoptic Gospels and in Paul, ἀγάπη nevertheless predominantly designates the brotherly and sisterly love of the community members for one another. Expressed simply, into the place of the Israelite legal community steps the community of the Christ-confessors. The letters of Paul in particular are internal or group literature.[128] Its ethical portions give instruction for the behavior of early Christian communities in an environment that tends to be hostile.[129] The concern with internal ethics appears not only in the Gospel of John, which is often faulted for this, but also in the epistolary literature. However, love, precisely as love for neighbor or as ἀγάπη, is always also directed to the outside world, which is also to be led to Christ. Gal 6.10 is an eloquent example of this internal ethics, which is not closed to the outside:

> **6.10** Let us do good to all, but especially to the household of faith.

I have shown that Paul took the step from the commandment of love for neighbor to the *concept of love*. Love and loving as forms of behavior in the Christ-believing communities is especially thematized by him[130] in connection to the commandment of love for neighbor, on the one hand,

---

[127] Wilson 1991, 172.

[128] The extent to which this applies to the Synoptic Gospels is controversial.

[129] It is a great merit of the Romans commentary of Jewett to have interpreted Rom 12–14 from the internal situation of the Roman house communities, on the one hand, and from the (vis-à-vis the community) hostile political situation of the time of emergence of the letter, on the other hand.

[130] The motif of love for God is relatively rare in the New Testament. This motif, which alludes to Deut 6.5, occurs in Mark 12.30, 33 par. and, alongside this, a few times in Paul as a fixed expression: Rom 8.28; 1 Cor 2.9 (quotation); 8.3 (material correction of

and in the context of early Jewish / early Christian paraenesis, on the other hand:

**1 Thess 4.9** Now concerning love for brothers and sisters (φιλαδελφία) you have no need (for anyone) to write to you, for you yourselves are taught by God (θεοδίδακτοι) to "love one another," **10** for you are doing precisely this to all the brothers and sisters in all Macedonia.

Here it is quite clear to whom "love" refers. Paul equates love for brothers and sisters and ἀγάπη. He thinks explicitly only of the behavior of the community members among one another (4.17).[131] In terms of tradition history, v. 9 presents a synthesis between love for neighbor and love for brothers and sisters. The substantivized infinitive "to love one another" appears to make a connection to the love commandment from Lev 19.18.[132] The simple noun ἀγάπη can in the framework of the community paraenesis move into proximity to early Jewish ethics (Rom 12.9; 1 Cor 8.1; 13.4–7). Πίστις and ἀγάπη can jointly or together with ἐλπίς describe Christian existence toward God, the Kyrios, and human beings.

Love in the Pauline literature is not the only ethical mode of behavior, but it is the most decisive one. This means that Paul understands the behavior of the community members fundamentally from the standpoint of their *mutual relationships*. The συν-compounds,[133] the τὸ αὐτὸ φρονεῖν, the emphasis on unity, the high regard for the other person, the concern for the other, the retraction of the own person (Phil 2.1–5), the building up of the community[134]—all this makes up the love that the community members should express for one other. The concern is not with love for neighbor in the sense of the Leviticus commandment. The one to whom love is to apply is not in question. The neighbor is every member of the community. However, the concern is also not with a virtue, i.e., with self-perfecting, but with *love*, which is not a virtue but the most intensive form of relationship between human beings. Greek concepts of virtue always apply to the self and its formation,[135] i.e., they are conceptualized in terms of individual

---

Paul; cf. also 1 John 4.10); also James 1.12. In Eph 6.24 it is transferred to Christ; cf. also 1 Pet 1.8; 1 John 4.20. Cf. Wischmeyer 2004d.

[131] Cf. also 2 Cor 8.7, 24.

[132] Cf. the infinitive expression in Rom 13.8.

[133] Cf. the extremely numerous συν-compounds in the New Testament lexicon, which express closeness and fellowship.

[134] 1 Cor 8.1; cf. the detailed development of the metaphor in Eph 4.15–16.

[135] On the definition and function of virtue as "activity of the soul according to the rational element," cf. Aristotle, *Eth. nic.* 1.1098a (= ch. 6) and 1102a (= ch. 13). For Aristotle, virtues can be defined in a more strongly noetic way and more strongly in terms of

ethics. Love, as it is understood in the Pauline letters, is a relationship and not a character trait.[136] This love is deepened through the connection back to Christ and his fate, as Phil 2.1–11 demonstrates.

The Johannine writings understand love as interpersonal relationship completely within the framework of the community. On the narrative level of the Gospel, only the love of Jesus for the disciples and their love among one another can be thematized. The letters make possible a rich love paraenesis among the "brothers and sisters." The connecting back to the love of God is deepened, as 1 John in particular demonstrates. At the same time, love for the brothers is understood as practical relationship (1 John 3.18):

> **3.18** Little children, let us not love in word or in speech but in action and in truth.

The letters, however, are not only documents of this deepened conception of love but also documents of a new conflict. First John 2.18–29 makes clear that there are dissidents in the community of 1 John who have a false Christology. They are no longer designated as brothers and sisters: the correct Christology is decisive for whether someone belongs to the "brothers and sisters." A text like 1 John 4.19ff. shows the irresolvable conflict between the love of God, which makes itself concrete in the struggle for the truth of the contents of faith, and the absence (which the author of 1 John criticizes) of love for brothers and sisters. Both the cosmos and false theological conceptions restrict, in the view of the author, the territory of love. Love

---

ethics-character (6.1139a = ch. 2). See, by way of introduction, Horn/Rapp 2008; Stemmer et al. 1998, esp. 1544: "In the New Testament ἀρετή occurs only four times; of these twice incidentally in the sense of human virtue. . . . Where there is talk of virtues in the first centuries of Christian paraenesis and theory formation, an appropriation of Greek philosophy is always present."

[136] Time and again there are attempts to establish a closeness between New Testament ethics and Hellenistic virtue ethics. On this, cf. critically F. W. Horn 2013c. In his dispute with Guttenberger 2005, F. W. Horn comes to the clear conclusion that the cardinal virtues have *no* "fundamental significance" for the ethics of Paul (367). He argues similarly in F. W. Horn 2013d. Cf. the similar view of Löhr 2013. Löhr comes to three conclusions: (1) Parallels to Pauline ethics more likely occur in Jewish than pagan Hellenistic literature. (2) On the whole, Pauline ethics is more internally oriented. (3) Paul has "no systematic doctrine of virtue" (433). On love he writes, "Without doubt, however, ἀγάπη (love), understood as active co-humanity (including emotional components; cf. 1 Cor 13, esp. v. 6), stands out in Paul, who takes up Jewish-Hellenistic tradition here; it is, however, not understood as something that goes beyond the group or in a universal way" (443). Although Löhr's classification is to be affirmed on the whole, his definition of love as active co-humanity does not capture the core of the Pauline ἀγάπη concept. See, by contrast, the role of the cardinal virtues in Philo, Clement of Alexandria, and Origen, as presented in Classen 1979.

of enemies is not in view here, for the opponents are "apostate brothers and sisters"; the truth limits love (1 John 2.18–21).

On the other hand, the late New Testament letters—1–2 Peter and Jude as well as the Johannine epistles—intensify the address ἀγαπητός, ἀγαπητοί. Paul already uses the adjective for coworkers and community members. Such forms of address strengthen the early Christian community groups by using a highly intensive internal language.[137]

### 6.3 Love as New Culture

Love can be presented as a basic form of inner-divine relationships and divine relationships to human beings and as a basic form of interpersonal relationships: from this double basic pattern arise ethical instructions that are primarily action oriented as well as the development of behavioral forms that create a new kind of life conduct within the early Christian communities. While the Synoptic Gospels present Jesus as a teacher of love for neighbor, the Pauline and Johannine writings, in different ways, set forth the new *life form* of love for the members of the community. Here, Paul's thought was the most far reaching theologically.[138] The eschatological existence of the Christ-believing community members, which is shaped by the coordinates of Spirit and freedom, is not only a practical-ethical existence but already has a share in the new being in Christ (Phil 2; 2 Cor 5). Understood in this way, love is determined not simply ethically but in a theological-christological way as "letting the same mind be in you that [is] in Christ Jesus" and is described in its practical realization as "life in the Spirit":

**Gal 5.25** If we live in the Spirit, let us also walk in the Spirit.

With this Paul makes clear that for Christ-believing community members not only is the commandment structure of the law overcome but freedom is opened up, which transfers the inner-divine structure of love to the life in the communities. The ethos of love for neighbor becomes part of the larger concept of ἀγάπη. The basic structure of the responsible inter-human relationships is preserved, but the categories of commandment and good work[139] are replaced by the categories of the person and of freedom. The result is the *culture of love*, which Paul cultivates and promotes in

---

[137] Cf. the adjective in connection with Jesus as Son of God.

[138] On this, cf. Söding 2014.

[139] This does not mean that love does not also realize itself in the doing of good and in the form of good works. However, it is not identical with this.

his communities. This culture encompasses ethical, material, psychological, emotional, and social aspects. At the same time, Paul knows that the communities already participate in the new creation and that their culture of love is mediated and supported by the Spirit. In Paul and in 1 John, love creates a direct connection to God, to Jesus Christ, and to the future world. With this Paul and John have moved love far away from what the Leviticus commandment aimed for. From a commandment among others, whose goal was an ordered life together in Israel, there has arisen a life attitude and culture that fundamentally transcends the conditions of the contemporary *imperium Romanum*, including its society and social forms, as the Letter to Philemon shows in an exemplary way.

### 6.4 Love as Eschatological Narrative

Love as a relational concept has to do with persons and their history. The New Testament concept of love can therefore be reduced neither to ethical forms of behavior (designated as virtues in Greek), nor to mutual feelings (called 'emotions' in the present), nor to ontological definitions—"God *is* love"—even though all these aspects are part of the concept of love. However, what constitutes the special character of the New Testament conception is its theological-narrative character. In the continuation of the Old Testament narrative of God's love for his people Israel, the Gospels narrate the universal love story of God with all people, which is grounded in God himself and leads back again to God, in order that "God may be all in all" (1 Cor 15.28). By having the Son be with God before the creation of the world and letting him then come into the "cosmos," the theology of the Gospel of John starts the story of God's love for human beings in God himself. In the different models of soteriological Christology, the Synoptics, the Gospel of John, and Paul retell this story: the only Son who is loved by the Father dies for human beings and thereby redeems them from death. Here, different love motifs play into one another: God's love for his Son, the love of God and his Son for human beings, and the power of the "self-surrendering" or "sacrificial" love for the ransom of others. The Gospel of John in particular recounts the passion narrative as the love story of Jesus for "his own," after the interpretation of what follows was already given in John 3.16 in anticipation of the passion narrative:[140]

> **3.16** For God so loved the world that he gave his only Son, so that everyone who believes in him may not perish but may have eternal life.

---

[140] The passion predictions in the Synoptic Gospels have this same function.

From the Gospel of Mark onward, the passion narrative, in which all the motifs of love, self-surrender, and suffering are concentrated, stands at the center. Paul connected the passion narrative with his personal existence and expressed its soteriological and eschatological dimension as follows (Phil 3.8–11):

> **3.8** . . . that I may gain Christ **9** and be found in him . . . **10** in order to know him and the power of his resurrection and the fellowship in his suffering, being conformed to his death, **11** in order that I may somehow attain to the resurrection from the dead.

Paul also expresses the corporeal fellowship with Christ's fate of suffering, death, and resurrection in 2 Cor 4.10–11:

> **4.10** We always carry around with us the mortification of Jesus in our body in order that the life of Jesus may also appear in our body. **11** For we, the living ones, are always handed over into death through Jesus in order that the life of Jesus may also appear in our mortal flesh.

In 1 Cor 13 Paul expresses the eschatological dimension of the love story of God with the world and simultaneously describes this love as perfect mutual knowing between God and the human being:

> **13.8** Love never ends. . . . **12** Then I will know fully as I am fully known.

Only with this will the story of the love of God reach its end.

# 5

# Alternative and Counter-Conceptions in the Early Jewish and Early Christian World

In the ethical and religious literature of the first century CE neither the commandment of love for neighbor nor the concept of ἀγάπη were even remotely taken for granted, recognized, or even in the broadest sense known. Outside the distinctive worlds of the Greek-speaking Jewish diaspora and the infinitesimally small early Christian communities, an ethic of ἀγάπη must have remained unknown and irrelevant already for linguistic reasons alone. However, even within Greek-speaking Judaism and the emerging early Christian groups, this concept of ἀγάπη was only one concept among others and by no means the leading one in each case. The concept of love of the early Christian writings positioned itself in relation to the variety of adjacent alternative or opposing psychological, ethical, and religiously grounded concepts for the conduct of life. In order to better sketch the contours of the understanding of the concept of love as I have constructed it from the New Testament texts, I will, in what follows, sketch out early Jewish and early Christian counter- and alternative conceptions that were contemporaneous with and connected to the conceptions of ἀγάπη/ἀγαπᾶν in Paul, the Synoptic Gospels, and the Johannine literature in positive and negative ways, and yet, on the basis of their specific traditions and framework conditions, followed their own conceptions and had specific intentions.[1]

At the outset, it may be stressed that with these conceptions the concern is not only with ethical conceptualizations or virtues and vices but also with inner attitudes and their external manifestations, with the emotions

---

[1] Cf. the similar tendencies of the expansion of the classic terminological history through the incorporation of the semantic fields and counter-terms in the new history of ideas. It is not necessary to present specific methodological preliminary reflections for this chapter.

and affects as well as with "attitudes of long duration," which become enduring character traits and forms of behavior.[2]

## 1. Destructive Counter-Conceptions

From the perspective of a contemporary ethical culture of the Western world, which, as I addressed in the introduction, avoids all forms of open ethical destruction or at least does not prize it, the ancient destructive concepts that competed[3] with the concept of ἀγάπη or at least were openly opposed to it are especially instructive. While destructive attitudes and forms of behavior, such as hatred and violence, were also criticized in the different ethical conceptions of Greco-Roman philosophy, especially in the imperial period,[4] they were nevertheless at the same time recognized components of the emotional, social, and political reality and were thematized as such in the literature—it is sufficient to point to Dido's role in the *Aeneid*. Love, as a constructive emotional-relational and ethical-religious entity, constantly struck up against opposing emotional-ethical modes of behavior and contrary anthropological conditions.

The most important destructive concepts can be contrasted with love in classic oppositional pairs. I enumerate them in ascending order of their oppositional character: love as ἀγάπη versus sexuality, love for neighbor versus love for self, love versus fear, love versus violence, love versus enmity, love versus hatred and—perhaps the most significant antithesis—love versus death. These antithetical pairs make clear what was already addressed—namely, that love does not simply function as a virtue. The antithetical terms are not simply "vices"[5] but belong to very different spheres: ethical, emotional, existential. In some oppositional pairs, the social components of love—specifically, love for neighbor—come more to the fore, in others the emotional side, and, finally, in others the theological aspects of the concept of love. Thus, precisely the destructive counter-conceptions contribute to the task of tracing out the contours of the concept of love in primitive Christianity. For their part, the destructive powers form a field of related tendencies that mutually condition one another,

---

[2] Cf. Wischmeyer 1995, 214–18.

[3] That they are also present in our contemporary ethical discussion need not receive special emphasis.

[4] Cf. just Seneca and Plutarch. See below.

[5] Cf. the terms from the vice catalogs that are significant in our context: ὀργή, θυμός, ζῆλος (on anger, cf. esp. Eph 4.31; cf. also 1 Cor 13.4–5: οὐ ζηλοῖ and οὐ παροξύνεται). In the overall spectrum of possible vices, counter-terms to ἀγάπη are thus represented relatively rarely. On the vices from a present-day ethical perspective, see esp. Shklar 1984 (GV = 2014).

merge into one another, and often cannot be clearly distinguished from one another but rather are aspects of *one* great destructive basic attitude of self-preservation and destruction of the other. ἀγάπη stands against everything that involves self-love or anxiety for the self and mere self-assertion. It stands against fear, against every form of violence, against enmity in all its forms, and against hatred. And when we follow John and Paul, it stands not only against death but it alone conquers death.

## 1.1 Sexuality

The relationship of love in the sense of ἀγάπη to sexuality is not explicitly thematized in the writings of the New Testament. Love in the sense of *eros*, i.e., as the emotional and corporeal longing of two persons for one another does not occur at all. There is no neutral lexeme for sexuality as the corporeal union of two persons.[6] Thus, there is neither an explicit coordination of love and sexuality nor a clearly stated oppositional pair "love versus sexuality." Both spheres are only mentioned to the extent that they are touched on within the sphere of anthropology in the theme of the body.

The lack of reflection on sexuality in connection with "love" has implications for the conception of Christian ethics. Thus, there is no duality of "good" sexuality *in* marriage and "bad" sexuality *outside* of marriage. The interaction with sexuality is determined primarily in a legalistic and moralistic way. Sexual activity that breaks out of marriage is μοιχεία and prohibited by Exod 20.14 / Deut 5.18. Sexual activity outside the institution of marriage is πορνεία and this is regarded as bad per se, irrespective of whether homosexual or heterosexual relationships are in view. Both forms of behavior, μοιχεία and πορνεία, appear alongside each other in vice catalogs.[7] Within the institution of marriage, sexuality is, to be sure, legitimate and regulated as such (1 Cor 7.2–5[8]), but it is not designated as "good." It has no emotional or integrative value. Love is ultimately granted no independent place in the conjugal fellowship, neither in the sense of *eros* nor in the sense of positive valued sexuality. This picture is confirmed even and precisely by Eph 5.25–33. Here, ἀγάπη (cf. also Col 3.19) occurs as love of the husband for the wife (three times). However, what is in view is precisely not emotional and corporeal love but the *spiritual interaction* with each other (5.18) and mutual subordination in the Christian household order (5.21–24). For the husband this subordination means love—perhaps best described as selfless care—while for the wife

---

[6] Cf., however, 1 Cor 7.33–34.
[7] Cf. Matt 15.19; Heb 13.4.
[8] Cf. the references in Zeller 2010, 238–39.

it means subordination and obedience. At this point, community order is transposed into the order for households. It follows from this that while the household order offers a protected place for permitted sexuality between spouses, it does not offer a valued place for individual love between the sexes in the erotic sense. Instead, the same transindividual and non-erotic love ethos is to prevail in the houses and in the communities.

We find in the Deutero-Pauline texts an echo of the Pauline view of every form of corporeal love. In the Christ-confessing communities and their families, one ethos of ἀγάπη is meant to prevail, not individually related eroticism and its sexuality. In Ephesians the ethos must be worked out even more strongly than in Paul because the Pauline imminent expectation—which classified the institution of marriage as fundamentally provisional but whose significance basically resided in restraining corporeal desire for the sake of full eschatological concentration—had abated. The post-Pauline community leaders, by contrast, recognize that it is necessary to reinforce the institution of marriage and at the same time to define it programmatically as part of the community ethos. Through this an implicit criticism or at least correction of Paul is expressed, as we find it in 1 Tim 4.3: The "lying speakers," i.e., false teachers[9] prohibit marrying. This means in the countermove that in contrast to the fundamental Pauline preference for restraint in relation to marriage in light of the eschatological imminent expectation (1 Cor 7), marriage now belongs to the correct Christ-confessing community.[10] The Pauline pragmatics in the handling of sexuality and marriage is replaced here by an openly programmatic community ethics.

Paul's view of marriage, eroticism, and sexuality inside and outside of marriage is fundamental for the New Testament epistolary literature. The theme has often been addressed[11] and need not be taken up again as a

---

[9] On this, see Roloff 1989, 222–23 and 228–39 (profile of the opponents).

[10] Cf. also the Synoptic tradition: Mark 10.6–9 / Matt 19.3–6. However, in the Gospel of Matthew there is a clear tendency to prefer singleness: 19.10–12. On this, see the balanced analysis of Luz 2001, 496–503 (GV = 1997, 103–11), and on the problematization or complication of conjugal faithfulness (5.27–30).

[11] On the topic, cf., by way of introduction, Tiedemann 2005. See in detail the various works of W. R. G. Loader, e.g., Loader 2005; 2007; 2009; 2010; 2011a; 2011b; 2012; 2013; 2014. On 1 Cor 11, Rom 7, and Eph 5, see Watson 2000. See also the short summaries of Gaca 2014; and Zimmermann 2013b. I do not share the hermeneutical position that Zimmermann presents in his introduction. Zimmermann seeks a new appreciation of the Pauline position and defends it against exaggerated material criticism. So far so good. But his justification—"An 'objective,' neutral way between the Scylla of material criticism and the Charybdis of the justification of Pauline statements on the theme must exit hermeneutically and epistemologically" (378)—remains pure assertion. Why should this apply specifically to the theme of sexuality? In the framework of historical hermeneutics, the concern

whole in this context. Here, the concern is exclusively with the question of "ἀγάπη versus sexuality" in Paul. It also holds true for Paul that the opposition between the concept of love and sexuality is not explicitly thematized. On the other hand, precisely this opposition is constitutive for the Pauline concept of ἀγάπη, for Paul understands ἀγάπη in opposition to everything that sexuality is for him. The hypothesis that Paul thinks in the alternative "good" sexuality in marriage, which is understood as fellowship of love, versus "bad" sexuality outside of marriage is untenable.[12] As already stated, in Paul there is no connection between the theme of marriage and any form of love. For Paul, the institution of marriage—which was beyond all question for Paul as an implicit Decalogue commandment (Rom 13.9)[13] and was the predominant form of ordered living together between the sexes in the communities—served the avoidance of πορνεία (1 Cor 7.2; 1 Thess 4.3–4) and the restraining of corporeal desire and not, for example, living together in love. Paul understands marriage not as an emotional and corporeal bond of love[14] but as a purely corporeal fellowship of mutual obligation (1 Cor 7.3) within the framework of a legal institution. That he takes this very seriously is shown not only by his handling of the case of πορνεία in 1 Cor 5[15] but also by the whole seventh chapter of 1 Corinthians. He does not thematize the fact that marriages result in children.[16] He sets forth neither a positive ethics of marriage within the

---

is neither with rehabilitation nor with critical destruction but with fundamental material analysis. On the theme, see in detail F. W. Horn 2014, who points to additional literature.

[12] This must also be said against Zimmermann. Neither the "positive basic attitude toward marriage including its sexuality" nor the claim that "sexuality has a value of its own" (Zimmermann 2013b, 382) can be verified in Paul.

[13] On this, see Jewett 2007, 810. Paul appears to condemn adultery equally from both sides. Jewett speaks of the "egalitarian ethos of early Christianity." Cf. also Zimmermann 2013b, 380, who with due caution speaks of the "equal value of the sexes" in Paul. In any case, Paul is not concerned to devalue the woman. On the contrary, the frequent reciprocity points to the fact that Paul was not primarily interested in distinguishing between the sexes. However, Paul remains bound to the gender-hierarchical thought paradigm of Greco-Roman antiquity.

[14] When there is an echo of something like this in 1 Cor 7.33–34, it is precisely what Paul wants to avoid, since it diverts the powers of the marriage partner from the "things of the Lord." Paul is located with this understanding of marriage in the mainstream of not only Jewish but also Greco-Roman concepts of marriage. Plutarch, however, is an example of an author who takes a different view.

[15] On this, see Zeller 2010, 199–200. Zeller thinks that a marriage-like relationship of the man with his stepmother is in view. Against this, Paul appears to want the marriage of the father to be respected beyond his death.

[16] Instead, he makes recourse to metaphors of birth and children in his relation to specific community members and communities (see above). Zimmermann 2013b, 382, positively assesses the fact that Paul does not address the connection between marriage and children: "Sexuality has its own value and is not subordinated to other purposes. Thus,

framework of an ethics of creation in connection with Gen 1.27; 2.24,[17] nor does he relate it positively to the Decalogue commandment, which prohibits adultery and thus prizes marriage. Friedrich Wilhelm Horn has concisely expressed the relation of Paul to sexuality:

> Thus, sexuality appears to be understood neither as a moral-theological nor as an individual-ethical theme but pragmatically from the level of the portrayal of the Christian community and its holiness. It orients itself, here, on the one hand, through its double demarcation from the pagan and demonic world and, on the other hand, with a view to an apocalyptic basic orientation toward the world that is passing away. (1 Cor 7.29)[18]

However, thematically Paul is ultimately interested not in sexuality[19] but in ἀγάπη. And Paul does not speak of love in connection with marriage but in places where the concern is with the constructive behavior of community members. Thus, Paul campaigns not for marriage as a place for a possible fellowship of love but rather for ἀγάπη as the new structure of the Christ-confessing communities. Here ἀγάπη stands not against the Decalogue commandments—and thus not against marriage—but rather "fulfills" them (Rom 13.8–10). Paul makes clear what this means for marriage in 1 Cor 7. There he combines two opposing positions—on the one hand, careful advice on different questions about getting married and living as a married person and, on the other hand, the recommendation to

---

there is no reference to procreation, which is often viewed as a legitimation for sexuality and marriage in antiquity." While the reference to the fact that Paul does not support celibate or "spiritual" marriage is correct, I cannot recognize that sexuality is given a "value of its own" in either case. The power of sexuality is a fact; it must be restricted (1 Cor 7.5–6): no more and no less.

[17] Cf. Mark 10.6–8; Matt 19.4–6: both times with positive recourse to the Genesis text but only to establish a rigorous prohibition of divorce (cf. Matt 5.27–31). Paul quotes Gen 2.24 only once in the negative context of πορνεία. Eph 5.31 attempts to reinterpret the Genesis text to apply to the relation between Christ and the communities (σῶμα Χριστοῦ). This means that the creation aspect relating to the physical union between husband and wife is also reinterpreted in this text.

[18] F. W. Horn 2014, 293. Cf. also p. 299, where Horn explains "that Paul continues to orient himself to the Jewish norm structure that shapes him culturally, especially to purity conceptions." Cf. again 1 Thess 4.3–4 and especially the positions of Philo, *Opif.* 151–169. Philo constructs a chain of desires (πόθος), lust (ἡδονὴ τῶν σωμάτων), female sensuality (αἴσθησις), slavery of evil (πάθος), injustice, sin, and mortality. On this, see Loader 2011a; and on the Testaments of the Twelve Patriarchs, see further Konradt 2014. Konradt rightly points to the comparable radicalization and early Jewish position in the Testaments of the Twelve Patriarchs in which "the feeling of pleasure connected with sexual intercourse ultimately becomes a fundamental problem" (277). This also applies to Philo.

[19] Comments on ἡδονή are entirely lacking in his writings.

remain unmarried if at all possible and not to seek a new marriage.[20] However, what the community members ultimately "owe" one another under the conditions of the new life in the Spirit is not marriage but exclusively ἀγάπη (Rom 13.8).

For the sexes, Paul assumes as a matter of course that humans are created "as man and woman," i.e., that they have a biological sex and are mutually correlated to each other.[21] To this corresponds a "natural" sexual behavior[22] that excludes homoeroticism and homosexuality a priori.[23] By contrast, heterosexuality in marriage is a corporeal desideratum and necessary component of living together, from which neither of the two marriage partners may withdraw. The varieties of homosexuality that Paul enumerates in Rom 1.26–27 are for him πάθη ἀτιμίας and are oriented παρὰ φύσιν; they are driven by burning desire (ὄρεξις). The result of homosexuality is unrighteousness, and it belongs in the series of sins that Paul unpacks in the large vice catalog in Rom 1.29–31.[24] This means that for Paul homosexuality is destructive and leads, like all other forms of unrighteousness, to death.[25]

In summary, we can say the following. First, Paul himself lives "in self-control,"[26] i.e., unmarried and thus not sexually active (1 Cor 7.7–8).[27] He understands this way of life, however, not as a rule but as a charism and also respects the charism of marriage (1 Cor 7.7). Second, Paul respects the institution of lifelong single marriage, which can be ended only through

---

[20] In four lines of argument Paul presents being unmarried as "good" (καλόν): 7.1–7 (καλόν v. 1); 8–16 (καλόν v.8); 25–38 (καλόν v. 26; v. 28: good and better). Vv. 17–24 are a thematically deepening excursus. Paul mentions himself as an example in v. 7. On the predicate "good" in 1 Cor 7, cf. Zeller 2010, 235.

[21] The gender question need not be addressed here. It is significant that Paul strengthens the position of women in the communities and in the houses.

[22] Rom 1.26–27: φυσικὴ χρῆσις "natural intercourse with women." On this, cf. Jewett 2007, 175–76: the argument "according to nature" occurs not only in the Stoics but also in Plato, Philo, Plutarch, etc., i.e., it is a Greco-Roman and Jewish moral commonplace. Paul does not cite Gen 1.27.

[23] Here too Jewett 2007, 176, rightly points to the "striking egalitarian note" with which Paul deals with homosexuality in relation to both sexes.

[24] Lack of love (ἄστοργος) occurs here.

[25] A deepened and nuanced dispute with homosexuality is lacking in Paul. On this point, his argumentation is purely topical. The argumentation with "nature" is unsatisfactory since "nature" is equated here with "custom." Paul does not come to an argumentation of his own.

[26] Ἐγκράτεια, ἐγκρατεύεσθαι: Gal 5.23 and 1 Cor 7.9; 9.25.

[27] Whether he was married at the time of his Jewish mission against Christ-confessing groups is unknown. Zimmermann 2013b, 382, tones down the position of Paul when he writes, "To be sure, he shows a certain personal preference for being unmarried." It is correct, however, that Paul neither prescribes the unmarried and celibate life nor holds encratic positions. Cf. Chadwick 1962.

the death of the one partner,[28] as the only and exclusive possibility of regulated sexual life together between man and woman and thus also as the only possibility for active sexuality at all. Third, for him this establishment has, at the same time, something anachronistic. It actually belongs to the order "before Jesus Christ" (1 Cor 7.29–35). "Now" is the end time; not the concern for the husband or wife should predominate but the concern for the Lord. As in Rom 13.11–14, here too the imminent expectation is the basis for ethical behavior that corresponds to ἀγάπη (Rom 13.10). Not the institution of marriage but the life of self-control without marriage within the order of love of the community is in keeping with the time. Fourth, for Paul sexuality is per se powerful and dangerous (1 Cor 7.5):[29]

> **7.5** Do not deprive one another, except perhaps by agreement for a time in order that you may have opportunity for prayer and then come together again in order that Satan does not tempt you because of your lack of control. . . . **9** If (the unmarried) cannot practice self-control, it is better to marry than to burn.

Outside of marriage sexuality can be controlled only with difficulty. Thus, Paul is not concerned with a trivializing of sexuality but with a battle, as the Satan metaphor shows.

Fifth, the understanding of the body is the center of the whole theme. Paul is convinced that—unlike with the theme of food—sexuality always affects the person's own body (σῶμα) and thus the center of the person (1 Cor 6.13). Sexuality lives from the corporeal act:

> **6.13** But the body (σῶμα) is not for πορνεία but for the Lord, and the Lord for the body. . . . **15** Do you not know that our bodies are members of Christ? . . . **16** Do you not know that the one who joins himself with a prostitute is one body (σῶμα) (with her)? For it says, "The two are one flesh (σάρξ)." **17** But the one who is joined to the Lord is one spirit (with him). **18** Flee πορνεία. Every sin that a human being commits is outside his body (σῶμα), but the one who commits a sexual misdeed (ὁ πορνεύων) sins against his own body. **19** Or do you not know that your body is the temple of the Holy Spirit, which you have from God, and that you are not your own? **20** . . . Therefore, glorify God with your body.

---

[28] In 1 Cor 7, however, Paul also seems to envisage a voluntary separation (without remarriage).

[29] On this point he differs neither from the Jewish nor from the Greco-Roman view (which, for its part, is male dominated).

For Paul sexuality is tied to the σῶμα, i.e., to the person with their body. The body, however, is at the same time a part or "member" of the σῶμα of Jesus Christ. Thus, the body belongs to two world times and two modes of being.[30] Temporally, it is part of the old-world time and the dawning end-time. Spatially and materially, it is σῶμα ψυχικόν and σῶμα πνευματικόν (1 Cor 15.44). This is why for Paul the body can be a place for the avoidance of sin (adultery or πορνεία) but not a place for "good" sexuality, unless this sexuality has a spiritual quality. The spiritual quality of the body refers, however, not to a loving union with another person but rather to the union with Christ (1 Cor 6.17). By contrast, for Paul the corporeal union in marriage is characterized by mutual dependence and unrest (the motifs of burning and concern for the things of the world) from which times of prayer must be wrested, so to speak (1 Cor 7.1–7). Thus, Paul's own, eschatologically shaped understanding of the body has no place for good conjugal sexuality in the sense of loving emotional and corporeal intercourse with each other. On the other hand, Paul avoids a dualistic understanding of the body in which there would either be no place at all for conjugal sexuality or in which the members of the Christ-confessing community would have to live celibately. Marriage remains as an institution and with it (conjugally regulated) sexuality as corporeal necessity and mutual obligation or requirement (ὀφειλή, 1 Cor 7.3). This emergency solution is plausible only under the eschatological reserve of 1 Cor 7.29–31. Paul does not find a positive role for eroticism and sexuality. In the end, "the Lord" stands *against* marriage with its sexuality and *for* ἀγάπη as ethos of the new world time.

Sixth, no path leads from Paul to conceptions of love in marriage as an emotional and corporeal union of two individuals. From a social perspective, his coordinates are the community as place and sphere of ἀγάπη and, from an individual perspective, his self (σῶμα) in the love for the Lord.

Seventh, while there is no "good" sexuality for Paul in the sense of loving corporeal union, there is, nevertheless, definitely "bad" sexuality in the framework of adultery and extramarital homosexual and heterosexual relationships. The language of negative sexuality—πορνεία instead of ἀφροδίσια—as well as the different elements of the vice catalog in Rom 1.26 make this clear.[31] Bad sexuality is guided by transgression against

---

[30] Cf. Schnelle 2005a, 495–99 (GV = 2014, 536–40): "The σῶμα is the interface between the givenness of human existence in the world and the act of God for human beings. Precisely because a human being both is a body and has a body, God's saving act in Jesus Christ embraces and determines the body and thereby the person's concrete existence and history" (497; GV = 539–40).

[31] Cf. Zeller 2010, 224n179, with reference to Lindemann 2000, 146.

the natural law, by ruthlessness, lack of love, and self-assertion and thus stands against the concept of ἀγάπη.

## 1.2 Self-Love—Egoism—Self-Preservation

The concept of "self-love" is more likely to be expressed in our contemporary speech with the keyword "egoism."[32] It is based on the antithesis of "self" and "other"—or *Nächster* (neighbor) in Luther's language. The antinomy of self-love and love for neighbor finds a clear anchor point in 1 Cor 13.5, where it says of love:

**13.5** Οὐ ζητεῖ τὰ ἑαυτῆς.

This characteristic of love is indeed important to Paul. He also uses it in 1 Cor 10.24, 33; Phil 2.21; and in altered form in Rom 15.2–3 and in Phil 2.4—there explicitly in the sense of altruism.

**2.4** Μὴ τὰ ἑαυτῶν ἕκαστος σκοποῦντες, ἀλλὰ [καὶ] τὰ ἑτέρων ἕκαστοι.[33]

In Romans and Philippians, he simultaneously points to Christ as the model of the renunciation of self-preservation and self-assertion. Is renunciation of self-love and turning to the other the same as love for neighbor?

The opposition between self-love and love for neighbor ("love for the other") is not simply self-evident. Moreover, a difference is not easy to work out. The wording of the commandment of Lev 19.18 even contradicts it very clearly: "You shall love your neighbor *as yourself.*" The Leviticus commandment formulates a parallel and not an antinomy in the sense of "You shall love not yourself but your neighbor." Rather, in the logic of the Leviticus commandment, self-love is obviously not understood as a "weak," let alone false, norm but, on the contrary, as the strongest ethical formulation that was available. As much as one loves oneself, i.e., cares for oneself, so one should be available for the neighbor, not, for example, less (Eph 5.28–29). What this could mean is made clear by a sapiential-pedagogical writing such as Sirach.[34]

---

[32] Strictly speaking, ἀγάπη would thereby be defined as altruism. Here, however, the concern is only with the altruistic aspect of ἀγάπη and not with a definition. The term "altruism," which comes from Auguste Comte, is obligated to social-psychological thought. On the topic of love and altruism, cf. now Söding 2017b.

[33] For a discussion of the textual critical issues, see Reumann 2008, 315–17.

[34] On the topic of "care for oneself" in Sirach, cf. Wischmeyer 1995, 201–47.

If one reads Lev 19.18 in this light, then, first, the justification of the necessity of love for enemies in Matt 5.46–47 loses its plausibility, and it becomes evident how far removed love for enemies is from the love for neighbor that is called for in Lev 19. For, as already shown, the criticism of love for neighbor, i.e., that it is nothing special but is what everyone does, misses the core of love for neighbor. Love for neighbor in the sense of the Leviticus commandment is precisely not an easy task that even the "gentiles" could practice, for the "neighbor" is not only the "brother/sister" or "the one who loves you" but every member of the legal community of Israel. On the whole, in the case of love for neighbor, as it is expressed in Leviticus, the concern is not with friendship but with care for the other in the framework of the legal community of Israel. Here, the same standard is to be applied as in the "care for the self." It must be stressed once again that the neighbor is, however, also not the "foreigner," for whom there are specific rules in Leviticus.

How did the synthesis of self-love and love for neighbor come to be called into question and to be replaced by the antithetical pairing of love for neighbor versus self-love? Here, Paul plays a decisive role. Since the renunciation of self-love or "care for oneself" becomes so important to Paul that he can define ἀγάπη precisely by the renunciation of self-love, he positions himself in two directions. On the one hand, it is clear that he no longer understands the term πλησίον in the wording of the commandment of love for neighbor as an ethically strong term[35] but searches for new definitions for the absoluteness of ἀγάπη—here in a line with the concretion of love for neighbor as mercy in Luke 10.25–37 or with the radicalization of love for neighbor as love for enemies (Matt 5.43–48). Thus, the renunciation of self-love leads away from the commandment of love for neighbor and its logic materially. On the other hand, Paul also participates in another shift that becomes clearly visible in the Synoptic Gospels. The concept of "concern for oneself" is also criticized independently of the interpretation of love for neighbor. Sayings such as Matt 6.25–33 par. and Matt 10.39 par. juxtapose the concern for oneself and the concern for the kingdom of God or the giving of one's life for the sake of Jesus. In 1 Cor 7.32–34 Paul assesses the concern for "the things of the world" and for "the wife" negatively. Instead of this, he recommends "the concern for the things of the Lord."

As a result, neither self-love nor self-preservation or concern for oneself are still understood as ethical attitudes in the New Testament texts. Thus, ἀγάπη moves away from love for neighbor, which defines self-love as the standard of love for compatriots. Instead, seeking the kingdom

---

[35] In addition to Rom 13.9–10, it is found only in Rom 15.2.

of God and self-sacrifice become central values that also determine the understanding of ἀγάπη. There is just as little place for the sapiential recommendation of care for one's own person here as there is for a discussion with Hellenistic-Roman positions of "the care of the self," as Michel Foucault has presented them in profile.[36] Rather, we can speak of an anti-concept if we understand this term not historically but materially. The New Testament writings never make reference to the Hellenistic-Roman concept of ἐπιμέλεια ἑαυτοῦ, and they probably would scarcely have known about this concept. However, what they knew, without following it, was the educational program of Sirach and other early Jewish authors, which was materially very close to the Greco-Roman program of concern for oneself. On this point, the discontinuity between early Jewish wisdom and early Christian ethos is conspicuous. For the "concern for others" is de facto a counter-concept to the Old Testament commandment of love for neighbor. This will play a role in the question of the role of corporeal love. The fact that in 2 Tim 3.2 the attitude of self-love introduces a vice catalog that works with ἀφιλάγαθοι and φιλήδονοι μᾶλλον ἢ φιλόθεοι is a late echo of the course that Paul charted—the replacement of love for neighbor according to Lev 19.18 by the concept of ἀγάπη.

### 1.3 Fear

In 1 John fear and love are invoked as an oppositional pair. In 1 John 4.17–18 we read:

> **4.17** In this love has come to perfection with us, that we have confidence (παρρησία) on the day of judgment; for as that one[37] is, so also are we in this world (κόσμος). **18** *Fear* (φόβος) *is not in love*, but perfect love drives out fear, for fear reckons with punishment, but the one who fears has not come to perfection in love.

The argument is clear: Love acts out of love and not out of fear of punishment or with a view to the final judgment. Love is not something derivative but is entirely itself. Freedom, παρρησία, and not fear belongs to love. I already emphasized the idea of freedom from the commandment at the conclusion of the Pauline concept of ἀγάπη. First John 4 makes

---

[36] Foucault 1988. Cf., however, the important pointer of Ludwig 2002, 320–26: self-love was not a virtue in classical Greece, for *eros* always led beyond the person himself. Cf. Philo, *Det.* 32.

[37] The referent of ἐκεῖνος is not clear. It is most plausible to relate "that one" to Christ (v. 15). Cf. Strecker 1989, 250–51.

these thoughts even clearer. The keyword "fear" as a counter-entity to love also occurs in Paul. In Rom 8.14–15 he combines the idea of freedom (παρρησία[38]) with the absence of fear:

> **8.14** For all who are driven by the Spirit of God are sons of God. **15** For you have not received the spirit of slavery that you must fear again (εἰς φόβον), but you have received the spirit of sonship in which we cry out, "Abba, Father." **16** The Spirit itself confirms our spirit that we are children of God.

Freedom and love are connected because both entities are aspects of God's nature, which the Spirit gives to the "children of God." In Rom 13.3 Paul points to the connection between the absence of fear and the "good work": The one who does a "good work," i.e., does the good, does not need to be afraid. Love moves in the world of the good.[39] Hebrews follows a different trail: fear, lack of freedom, and death are connected (2.14–15):

> **2.14** Since the children are of flesh and blood,[40] he (Jesus) in like manner had a share in them, in order that through his death he might destroy the one who has power over death, that is, the devil, **15** and set free those who from fear of death (φόβος θανάτου) were subject to slavery for their whole lives.

We find here a "feeling of life," which earlier exegetes described as "ancient/late-antique existential understanding" of constant fear of death, which leads to inner lack of freedom.[41] Later, I will take up again the trail that leads from fear to death.

### 1.4 Violence

*Non vi, sed amore*: this modification of the Reformation antithetical motto *non vi, sed verbo* grants further insight into the conception of ἀγάπη. The contrast between violence and the renunciation of violence is concretized positively by replacing the renunciation of violence with love and simultaneously interpreting love also as renunciation of violence. Renunciation of violence is per se a theological theme in the New Testament. The communities experience violence primarily from outsiders

---

[38] On παρρησία in 1 John, cf. Strecker 1989, 247–48.
[39] Cf. Rom 15.2: "Let each of us please the neighbor for the good."
[40] Literally: have a share in blood and flesh.
[41] Cf. H.-F. Weiss 1991, 216–18 (lit.).

and not within their own new social world. Violence is not a tool within the communities. Pauline paraenesis always calls for the renunciation of violence.[42] Christ's renunciation of violence[43] is the theme of the so-called Philippians hymn, which Paul introduces with paraenetic sayings that can be described as a rhetorically elevated invocation of the inner-community love (Phil 2.1–8):[44]

> **2.1** If there is any encouragement in Christ, any consolation of love, any fellowship of the Spirit, any compassionate heart (literally, "heart and compassion")[45]—**2** make my joy complete by thinking the same thing, having the same *love*, being united, thinking one thing. **3** Do nothing from strife or vainglory but in humility regard one another as superior to yourselves. **4** Let each of you look not to his own interests but to the interests of others.
>
> **5** Let the same mind be in you that (is) in Christ Jesus, **6** who—being in the form of God—did not regard it as (welcome) plunder[46] to be equal to God, **7** but emptied himself—taking the form of a slave, becoming like human beings; and being found according to (his) appearance as a human being, **8** he lowered himself by becoming obedient until death . . .

The motif of the selflessness of ἀγάπη, which has already been discussed, is given a realistic accent here in a new way through the connection to the renunciation of violence. Paul aims at a community behavior that realizes the love of Jesus in the renunciation of self-preservation and self-assertion. Jesus is introduced by means of the violence metaphor[47] of the

---

[42] This holds true irrespective of the violent metaphors in Paul.

[43] On the topic of violence, see Enzmann 2013; Gudemann/Christ 2013 (here, theology is unfortunately absent from the disciplinary-related approaches). Cf. Wischmeyer 2004f.

[44] On the text, cf. E.-M. Becker 2015; 2020.

[45] Bauer 1988, 1532.

[46] ἁρπαγμός is a hapax legomenon in the New Testament. The verb is used multiple times by Paul and in Acts for "abductions" by the Spirit. Bauer 1988, 218, points out the double character of the metaphor. Plunder or booty can be understood from the perspective of the robbery or as a positive trove (as here), without the aspect of violence being lost. A detailed analysis of the exegetical attempts at explanation can be found in Reumann 2008, 333–83 (lit.). To me the comparison to Isa 53.12 appears materially central: here σκῦλα (plunder or booty) instead of ἁρπαγμός (robbery), i.e., the result instead of the (aggressive) event. The idea is the same: the servant of God or Christ Jesus *obtains* something.

[47] The term *Gewaltmetapher* (violence metaphor) appears appropriate to me here. In Paul an apocalyptic background is evident: cf. 2 Cor 12.2, 4; and 1 Thess 4.17; see further the attacker saying in Matt 11.12. Vollenweider 2002 speaks of the "expressive linguistic form" (277) and of the "negative semantics of the violent seizure of the 'being-equal-to-God'" (279). Vollenweider rightly emphasizes "the interactions of the semantic fields of

renunciation of *plunder* as the highest and most decisive ethical paradigm[48] of the renunciation of *violence*. Paul is not the only one to express
this variety of Christology. Renunciation of violence also belongs to the
picture that the Synoptic Gospels portray of Jesus, as Mark 8.34 par., the
saying about self-denial (ἀπαρνεῖσθαι ἑαυτόν), and Mark 10.42–45 /
Luke 22.25–27, the saying about violence and service,[49] especially show:

> **8.34** If anyone wishes to follow me, let him deny himself (ἀπαρνεῖ-
> σθαι[50]) and take up his cross and follow me. **35** For whoever wishes to
> save his life will lose it; but whoever will lose his life for my sake and
> the gospel's will save it.[51]

> **10.42** You know that those who are considered rulers forcefully exercise
> their rule[52] (κατακυριεύειν) and their great ones do violence to them
> (κατεξουσιάζειν).[53] **43** But it is not so among you. Whoever among you
> wishes to be great, must be your servant **44** and whoever among you wants
> to be first must be slave of all. **45** For even the Son of Man came not to be
> served but to serve and to give his life as a ransom for many.

Both sayings must be heard or read against the background of the reality of
violence and diverse experiences of violence in the world of Jesus and his
disciples and in light of the experience of Jesus' death. The first saying is
characterized by the violence metaphor of cross bearing[54] and follows the
first passion prediction; the second series of sayings thematizes the criticism of rulers[55] and refers to Jesus' giving of his life, which also occurs in
Phil 2.8 in the same context. Here too, a metaphor of violence stands at the

---

'rob' and 'rule'" (277). He argues with good reasons that we should understand the plunder
metaphor negatively: Jesus does not rob the equality with God; therefore (διό; v. 9), the
heavenly rule is given to him by God. The attacker saying (Q 16.16) presents the closest
semantic and motif parallels. It likewise points in the direction of early Jewish and early
Christian apocalyptic (mentioned briefly by Vollenweider [278n94]).

[48] Cf. E.-M. Becker 2015. Cf. also E.-M. Becker 2020.
[49] On the text, cf. Wischmeyer 2004e.
[50] Parallel to Mark: Matt 16.24.
[51] Cf. the parallel John 12.25. Here a psychologization in the sense of a distancing
from the own life has taken place. The attitude of φιλία for one's own life, which is correct
according to the paradigm of love for neighbor, leads, by contrast, to death.
[52] Cf. Bauer 1988, 838.
[53] New Testament hapax legomenon.
[54] On this, see Yarbro Collins 2007, 408. Collins argues for an interpretation that is
more literal than metaphorical: "The language reflects at least the expectation of persecution." While this is correct, we are still dealing with a metaphor. Cross stands pars pro toto
for violent punitive death.
[55] Cf. Wischmeyer 2004e, 202.

center—the slave. Thus, a motif ensemble is disclosed that reinforces the insights that already emerged from the analysis of the antinomy of love for neighbor and self-love. The tendency leads from the love for neighbor from Leviticus, which is understood in a synthesis with the concern for the self, to the defamation of the self.[56] In the background both here and there is Jesus' self-sacrifice in which his person is definitively revealed. To this corresponds the motif of the explicit renunciation of violence at Jesus' arrest in Matt 26.53–54[57] in the Synoptic passion narrative.

With this an outlying district or, alternatively, the final core of ἀγάπη is specified at the same time. The concern is no longer with a virtue or a constructive attitude or fruit of the Spirit, with the retraction of one's own person, or with altruism, but with self-destruction. Here, the hitherto consistently constructive attitude of love turns into destruction, though to the destruction of the self for the good of the other. The concern is with the fundamental paradox both of Christology and of love between two persons. The self fulfills itself through handing itself over. With this Jesus' sacrificial death comes into view again from a rather unexpected perspective as the foundation of the New Testament conception of ἀγάπη.

## 1.5 Enmity

The friend/enemy dichotomy presents the framework for the antinomy between love and enmity. Here, love stands for intensive friendship. In Galatians enmity (ἔχθρα) is a vice that is opposed to all forms of love:

> **5.19** But the works of the flesh are evident, which are: sexual immorality, moral depravity, debauchery, **20** idolatry, magic, *enmities*, strife, jealousy, passionate outbreaks of anger,[58] selfishness, dissensions, divisions.

In juxtaposition to the works of the flesh stand the fruits of the Spirit, with love at its head (Gal 5.22). The manifestations of enmity are presented with seven lexemes that have similar meanings. Enmity becomes operative in two directions—on the one hand, as negative or destructive emotion, characterized by jealousy and anger and, on the other hand, as social destabilization, as disunity. For the theme of anger, a differentiation must

---

[56] This does not mean the abandonment of one's own individuality but the renunciation of self-assertion.

[57] Not in Mark and Luke. Cf., however, John 18.36: the kingdom of Jesus is not "from this world."

[58] Θυμοί, translated according to Bauer 1988, 743.

be made. Anger as judicial and punitive anger (ὀργή) is reserved for God,[59] whereas for human beings what is said in Jas 1.19–20 applies:

> **1.19** Know this, my beloved brothers and sisters: Let every human being be quick to hear, slow to speak, slow to anger (ὀργή). **20** For the anger of a man does not produce the justice of God.

Instead, the author recommends πραΰτης (meekness, friendliness), an emotional virtue that is often mentioned together with love.[60] The rejection of anger as an instrument of behavior toward human beings falls in line with the educational maxim in Sirach[61] and in the Testaments of the Twelve Patriarchs[62] and yet also with Stoic educational ideas, as these are advocated by Seneca in *De ira*. In *De ira* 1.2.1–3, Seneca describes the destructive emotion of anger by means of negative ekphrasis.[63]

The New Testament authors understand enmity not so much as an individual attitude but rather view it instead from a social perspective, i.e., as a group phenomenon, and situate it in the context of divisions. Strife (ἔρις) occurs more frequently in the Pauline and Deutero-Pauline literature as a negative-destructive attitude within the communities, especially in connection with envy (φθόνος)[64] and jealousy (ζῆλος).[65] The consequence of envy and jealousy is the self-profile that leads to anger, destroys the unity of the community, and ends in αἱρέσεις.[66] With the theme of strife and enmity, the communitarian structure of the early Christian communities becomes especially clear. At the center stands not the cultivation of the individual and his proper attitude but the community members' relatedness to one another.

Alongside the inner-community manifestations of enmity, hostility from outsiders belongs to the most important experiences of ancient

---

[59] Matt 3.7par.; Rom 1.18; 2.5, and elsewhere.

[60] 1 Cor 4.21.

[61] Sir 1.22 (θυμός). On the strong negative affects in Sirach, cf. Wischmeyer 1995, 214–16.

[62] Cf. especially T. Dan 3–4; T. Gad 3–5 (with justice as the opposing term in 5.3 and with love as the opposing term in chapter 7).

[63] Rosenbach 1989, 100–101. Anger is the subject and doer and is described on the basis of its devastating actions. In terms of content, the section can be read as an expanded reply to 1 Cor 13. In the further course of book 1, Seneca time and again uses (anti-) ekphrastic descriptions of anger. Cf. Plutarch, *De cohibenda ira* (*Mor.* 6.452f–464d); Pohlenz 1929, 157–86. Cf. also the sharp rejection of anger in Matt 5.22 (the first antithesis of the Sermon on the Mount).

[64] Rom 1.29; Phil 1.15.

[65] Rom 13.13; 2 Cor 12.20; Gal 5.20; Jas 3.16.

[66] 1 Cor 11.19; Gal 5.20.

Judaism[67] and the early Christian communities.[68] I have already presented the concept of enmity. Both the Jesus tradition[69] and Paul[70] exhort one to respond to enmity with love. The relationship between love and enmity is processed in classic form in the fifth antithesis of the Sermon on the Mount—love for enemies is the ethical synthesis that reconciles the antinomy. It is also the case for this aspect of enmity that enmity is destructive. Anger and cruelty[71] accompany it.

## 1.6 Hatred

Hatred[72] and love or hating and loving could be understood as the fundamental binary structure of human behavior.[73] They appear as strong strivings and motions in the religious literature of Israel and in Greco-Roman literature and philosophy. Both here and there hatred is understood, on the one hand, as an emotion that can be juxtaposed only with love in its strength and absoluteness and, on the other hand, as a strong driving force of destructive action.[74] The evaluation of the two entities is not fixed one-sidedly on good and evil. They can complement each other or, alternatively, mutually exclude each other.[75] Hatred is thus not simply part of a negative ethical field and not necessarily per se bad or evil. John Procopé thus writes, "Hatred and anger were accepted in popular ethics as necessary for one's own survival in a world of rivalry."[76] However,

---

[67] With respect to Judaism, the situation was often turned on its head by the anti-Jewish pagan majority culture, which accused the Jews of "hatred of human beings" or "enmity toward human beings." But see also 1 Thess 2.15: The Jews are said to be ἐναντίος (opposed, hostile) to all human beings.

[68] The pagan accusation of *odium generis humani* was soon transferred to emerging Christianity.

[69] Matt 5.43–44 par.

[70] Rom 12.20.

[71] On these aspects, cf. esp. Seneca, *De ira*.

[72] For literature on hatred, see the *Journal of Hate Studies* (Gonzaga University Institute for Hate Studies). For antiquity, see Procopé 1986. Procopé points out that in antiquity hatred "usually did not need to be denied" (680). Hatred is a theme of current politics and justice: the 2006 Racial and Religious Hatred Act of the British Parliament incriminates certain aspects of the phenomenon of hatred (http://www.legislation.gov.uk/ukpga/2006/1/pdfs/ukpga_20060001_en.pdf).

[73] E.g. Deut 26.15; Eccl 3.8; Did 16.3 (love is transformed into hatred). Cf. also the famous saying of Tertullian (*Apol.* 39.7): "Vide, inquiunt, ut invicem se diligant; ipsi enim invicem oderunt."

[74] Thus esp. in Seneca, *De ira*.

[75] Thus in Ign. *Eph.* 14.2: "No one professing faith sins, nor does anyone possessing love hate" (trans. Holmes 2002, 147).

[76] Procopé 1986. Cf. e.g. Seneca, *De ira* 1 and 7.1.

he points at the same time to the closeness of envy, anger,[77] enmity, and hatred as destructive πάθοι in Greco-Roman literature and philosophical ethics,[78] so that a spectrum of negative emotions and forms of behavior that culminates in hatred is set over against a field of constructive emotions and forms of behavior that are placed under the umbrella terms of justice, friendship, renunciation of violence, and concern for the self.[79] Two famous examples may be selected here. When Sophocles has Antigone pointedly answer Creon's argument—Οὔτοι ποθ' οὐχθρός, οὐδ' ὅταν θάνῃ, φίλος—with the words Οὔτοι συνέχθειν, ἀλλὰ συμφιλεῖν ἔφυν (522–523), then this applies in the context of the question of the burial of beloved persons or relatives, but only here. It is not a general ethical maxim. This also applies to Catullus' *Carmina* 85:

Odi et amo. Quare id faciam, fortasse requiris.
Nescio, sed fieri sentio et excrucior.[80]

Catullus has pointedly summarized the simultaneity of love and hatred psychologically and thus justified hatred as an admittedly destructive but nevertheless necessary aspect of erotic-sexual love, though not as an ethical behavior. There were, accordingly, in the Greco-Roman world enough voices that warned against an excess of hatred.[81]

By contrast, in our literature[82]—unlike in the Greco-Roman world of values[83]—hatred, as a destructive emotion, is consistently and always the negative counterpart to love. Hatred is therefore not a personal and certainly not an ethical option.[84] Under the phrase "love of enemies," I have already

---

[77] On anger, cf. von Gemünden 2003.

[78] Procopé 1986. Cf. the compilation of hatred, envy, and lawlessness as well as anger, war, and haughtiness in T. Gad 4 and 5.

[79] Concern for one's own person is understood in a positive way in philosophical ethics. For examples, see Procopé 1986, 688. But cf. what was said above about "concern for one's self" in early Christianity.

[80] "I HATE and love. Why I do so, perhaps you ask. I know not, but I feel it, and I am in torment" (trans. F. W. Cornish, LCL, 163).

[81] Procopé 1986, 687–89.

[82] Cf. Procopé 1986. See also Michel 1967 (GV = 1942).

[83] In *Resp.* 1.334c, Plato writes, "It is natural . . . to love (φιλεῖν) those whom one regards as kind (χρηστούς) and to hate (μισεῖν) those whom one regards as evil (πονηρούς)."

[84] The saying in Luke 14.26 constitutes an exception. The Matthean form (Matt 10.37) is radically surpassed in the Lukan saying: "If anyone comes to me and does not *hate* his father and mother and wife . . . and his own life, he cannot be my disciple." Here, not only is the fourth commandment annulled (also the bond of marriage) but in opposition to Lev 19.18 self-hatred, i.e., the radical form of renunciation of self-preservation, is also demanded under a destructive banner. However, here "to hate" is understood formally as

explained that hatred of enemies cannot belong to the ethos of the disciples of Jesus but is explicitly excluded.[85] With this the Synoptic tradition also goes beyond the ethics of ancient Judaism, which incriminated hatred of the brother or sister in any case, but did not absolutely prohibit hatred of— i.e., hostility toward—the enemy of God or Israel.[86] Different modes of behavior were possible here. Alongside the explicit defense of hatred toward outsiders,[87] who were understood not only as personal enemies or as a threat to one's own group but also as enemies of God, there are the sapiential warnings against anger and hatred, as we find them in Sirach:

**5.15 (6.1)** καὶ ἀντὶ φίλου μὴ γένου ἐχθρός

and

**28.6** μνήσθητι τὰ ἔσχατα καὶ παῦσαι ἐχθραίνων.[88]

Of particular interest is the Testament of Gad,[89] which is devoted thematically to the πνεῦμα τοῦ μίσους[90] and condemns hatred by showing its destructive consequences. Several passages read almost as an anti-encomium to love[91] and are not far from 1 Cor 13.4–7. In 4.1–2 it says:

> **4.1** Beware, my children, of those who hate, because it leads to lawlessness against the Lord himself. **2** Hatred does not want to hear repeated his commands concerning love for neighbor (λόγων ἐντολῶν αὐτοῦ περὶ ἀγάπης τοῦ πλησίον), and thus it sins against God.[92]

Jürgen Becker rightly emphasizes that "the love commandment is meant to exercise a totalitarian claim on the whole of life also and precisely

---

separation and not materially as object of destruction. The same applies to the parallel formulation in John 12.25: "to love one's own life" versus "to hate one's own life."

[85] Cf., in addition to Matt 5.44, esp. Did. 1.3: φιλεῖτε τοὺς μισοῦντας ὑμᾶς. The notion of a general hatred of all against all as a sign of the end in Matt 10.21 par. and 24.10 is important.

[86] Cf. the nuanced presentation in Procopé 1986; see further Lipínski 1993; Michel 1967 (GV = 1942). Cf. now also Konradt 2018.

[87] On the Qumran texts, cf. Lipínski 1993, 838–39.

[88] "And do not become an enemy instead of a friend," and "Remember the end things, and cease to be at enmity" (trans. B. J. Wright in NETS). On this, cf. Wischmeyer 1995, 214–17. But cf. also Sir 50.25–26, which is indeed characterized by hatred.

[89] On the questions of dating, cf. J. Becker 1974, 17–31.

[90] T. Gad 1.9.

[91] T. Gad 3; 5.1–4.

[92] Translated by H. C. Kee in *OTP* 1:815.

when the one who is to be loved hates with enmity."[93] T. Gad is thus close to the commandment of love for enemies. However, the Testaments of the Twelve Patriarchs[94] refer—even though in the sense of an ethical paradigm—to Joseph and his brothers and not to enemies or opponents of Israel. They are an expression of an early Jewish paradigmatically conceptualized internal ethics.

First John leads into the reality of hatred for the "brother/sister" in the sense of the early Christian brother/sister metaphor.[95] Hatred instead of love among the brothers and sisters is one of its great themes. The author of the letter diagnoses hatred for the brother/sister in his communities.[96] In 3.15 the hatred for the brother/sister is characterized as murder.[97] The overly sharp polemic,[98] which 1 John shares with the antitheses of the Sermon on the Mount and with sections of James, is an expression not only of the familiar ethical rigorism but above all of the deep fear of the community leaders of the third generation[99] that they would not be able to hold their communities together. What Paul presented as lack of unity, factionalism, etc., the later community leaders diagnosed as ultimate destruction of the communities and incriminated deviating theological-christological positions as "hatred for the brother/sister." Hatred thus becomes an entity *within* the communities, and the community leaders are no longer occupied with calling for love toward the enemies who want to destroy the communities from the outside.[100] They must concentrate above all on excluding from the community the "brothers/sisters" who are not capable of love for brothers and sisters owing to destructive "hatred for the brother/sister" in order to oppose the destruction of the communities from within. The author of the Johannine letters considers the concept of love for brothers and sisters to be in danger and out of fear makes use of a new rhetoric of hatred himself. With this the concept of ἀγάπη comes to an end.

## 1.7 Death

The pair of terms "death and love" also presents a binary opposition. When Song 8.6 says κραταιὰ ὡς θάνατος ἀγάπη, "death and love," in

---

[93] J. Becker 1974, 27.

[94] For a recent discussion of the interpretation of Lev 19.17–18 in the Testaments of the Twelve Patriarchs, see Konradt 2018, 354–63.

[95] On this, see section 3.4 below.

[96] 1 John 2.9, 11; 3.15; 4.20 (love for God without love for brothers and sisters).

[97] Cf. the closeness to Matt 5.21–22.

[98] On this, cf., by way of introduction, E. E. Popkes 2011.

[99] On this, cf. E. E. Popkes 2011, 332–33.

[100] Thus passages in the Gospel of John and in the Synoptic Gospels.

modification of the opposition "death and life," are understood as the two vital fundamental powers that oppose one another. The natural opposing power to death, life, is defined entirely by love and its power, so that love takes the place of life.[101] Both entities are not connoted ethically here but specified as the two equally strong anthropological fundamental powers. In an evaluative context, the oppositional pair "death and life or love" is then presented when the ethical perspective is chosen. Death, which does not necessarily need to be connoted in a negative-destructive way in an ethical sense,[102] is understood in this context as a fundamentally destructive-evil power and can thus enter into a causal relationship with the two great destructive fundamental powers that are known in early Judaism and early Christianity—evil and sin, and sometimes also Satan.[103]

First, death is the last member in the series of catastrophic consequences of anger, violence, and hatred, which no one has described as impressively as Seneca. Anger merges into hatred and cruelty and leads to murder.[104] The chain of destructive emotions and actions leads to the highest form of destruction. Seneca, in *De ira*, uncovers the inner connection of emotions and actions. Anger can lead to unethical conduct. In this way, a light falls at the same time on love. Love as an ethical power[105] desires life. It will never kill—except in the form of self-sacrifice in order to save life.

From the religious perspective, death is then "the last enemy" (1 Cor 15.26). It is again the Testament of Gad that explicitly formulates this connection and simultaneously juxtaposes death and love (4.6–7):[106]

---

[101] The motto "omnia vincit Amor: et nos cedamus Amori" (Vergil, *Ecl.* 10), which personifies or deifies love, would be comparable.

[102] Cf. Bultmann 1965 (GV = 1938).

[103] On the history-of-religions context, cf. Wischmeyer 2016b.

[104] Cf. e.g., *De ira* 2 and 5.

[105] It looks different with *eros*, which can indeed be portrayed as destructive and also as a deadly power. Cf. just Sophocles, *Ant.* 781–99. On this, see the quotation in Graham 1895, 112:

> "See," said my friend . . . "how this strange thing, this love of ours, lives and shines out in the unlikeliest of places! You have been in the fields in early morning? Barren acres, all! But only stoop—catch the light thwartwise—and all is a silver network of gossamer! So the fairy filaments of this strange thing underrun and link together the whole world. Yet it is not the old imperious god of the fatal bow—ἔρως ἀνίκατε μάχαν—not that—nor even the placid respectable στοργή—but something still unnamed, perhaps more mysterious, more divine! Only one must stoop to see it, old fellow, one must stoop!"

On this, see Janka 2009, 79–82.

[106] On this, cf. Söding 1994/1995; Konradt 1997.

**4.6** Just as love wants to bring the dead back to life and to recall those under sentence of death, so hate wants to kill the living and does not wish to preserve alive those who have committed the slightest sin. **7** For among all men the spirit of hatred works by Satan through human frailty for the death of mankind; but the spirit of love works by the Law of God through forbearance for the salvation of mankind.[107]

This text shows most clearly the religious dimension that the opposition between death and love can include. I return here to the connection of fear and death, which is expressed in Heb 2. Love functions as an opposing power against the slavery of fear and death. The Testament of Gad reads like a commentary on the narrative of the raising of Lazarus, whom Jesus loved (John 11). To this corresponds the repeatedly quoted modification of the saying from Prov 10.12: Μῖσος ἐγείρει νεῖκος, πάντας δὲ τοὺς μὴ φιλονεικοῦντας καλύπτει φιλία.[108] In 1 Pet 4.8 the aphorism is taken up in the following modified form: "Above all have constant love (ἀγάπη) for one another, for love covers a multitude of sins." This version is repeated in 1 Clem. 49.5; 50.5 and in 2 Clem. 16.4.[109]

With this the explicitly religious perspective beyond the ethical is in play. Love displays soteriological-eschatological power, as 1 Cor 13.8–12 shows. Let us quote this text again here:

> **8** Love never ends; but if there are prophecies, they will pass away; if tongues, they will cease; if knowledge, it will pass away. **9** For we know in part and we prophecy in part. **10** But when the perfect/complete comes, the partial will pass away. **11** When I was a child, I spoke as a child, thought as a child. When I became an adult, I put away childish things. **12** For we see now indirectly,[110] enigmatically, but then face to face; now I know in part, but then I will know fully just as I am fully known.

In 1 Cor 13 love is the only one of the spiritual entities (χαρίσματα, πνευματικά) that overcomes death and remains in the eschaton. I have already explained how texts such as Rom 5 and Rom 8 anchor this soteriological dimension of ἀγάπη in Christ's act of love. Therefore, what is said in Rom 8.35–38 applies in conclusion to this ἀγάπη concept of Paul:

---

[107] Trans. H. C. Kee in OTP 1:815.

[108] "Hatred stirs up strife, but love covers all who do not love strife."

[109] It is modified in Jas 5.20. There it is the salvation of the sinner from his false way that "covers a multitude of sins."

[110] Literally: "(in a mediated way) through a mirror." What is meant is not directly but in a mediated way.

**8.35** Who will separate us from the love of Christ? Tribulation or distress or persecution or famine or nakedness or danger or the sword? **36** As it is written, "For your sake we are put to death all day long, we are reckoned as sheep to be slaughtered." **37** But in all these (situations) we gloriously conquer through the one who *loved* us. **38** For I am convinced that neither *death* nor life nor angels nor rulers nor present nor future nor powers nor height nor depth nor any other (form) of what has been created can separate us from the *love of God, which is in Christ Jesus, our Lord.*

## 2. Parallel Ethical Concepts

It is not only oppositions in the social, emotional, and theological sphere that give clearer contours to the concept of ἀγάπη. Something similar is accomplished by parallel concepts. In early Jewish and early Christian writings as well as in the Hellenistic-Roman philosophical-ethical literature, we find significant independent concepts or motifs[111] of constructive emotions, modes of behavior, and action that are not oriented against ἀγάπη but set *different accents* for constructive human interaction. A short sketch of these conceptions will clarify the concept of ἀγάπη from another side with respect to its distinct character.

### 2.1 Mercy

While Aristotle placed ἔλεος in a series with the destructive emotions of *eros*, fear, envy, and hatred,[112] the Old Testament Jewish tradition takes a positive stance toward the feeling and the behavioral form of mercy and its practical social manifestation of giving alms.[113] Here, mercy is not understood in an exclusively or primarily ethical way but anchored first in the nature of Yahweh: justice (אמת) *and* mercy (חסד) characterize his relation to human beings. In the Septuagint, δικαιοσύνη and ἔλεος are "interchangeable."[114] Yahweh's mercy is a model for the merciful behavior of human beings, which concretizes itself, on the one hand, in the giving of

---

[111] For our line of questioning, it is neither possible nor necessary to discuss whether we are dealing with motifs or developed concepts. It is clear, however, that these concepts or motifs are not comparable to ἀγάπη in significance. The discussed concepts all have a constructive-active orientation. Passive neighboring concepts such as humility will not be presented.

[112] *Eth. nic.* 2.1105b. He sets a different emphasis in *Rhet.* 2.1386a, b, 9ff. For the differentiation of the Greek term, see also Schwer 1950; Bultmann 1964b (GV = 1935).

[113] Cf. Witte 2014.

[114] Schwer 1950, 1202.

alms and, on the other hand, contains even stronger emotional aspects of interpersonal affection such as οἰκτιρμός, σπλάγνον, and the like.[115] The New Testament writings presuppose the giving of alms.[116] Mercy is, beyond this, an attitude of active, careful, and selfless love for neighbor that can indeed be an act of love to one who is most distant, i.e., a foreigner, as the story of the merciful Samaritan makes clear. The neighbor is "the one who does mercy (ἔλεος) to (the injured person)" (Luke 10.37). James expresses this in his own exaggerated rhetoric (2.13):

> **2.13** For judgment will be *without mercy* to the one who does not show *mercy*. *Mercy* triumphs over judgment.[117]

On the other hand, Paul and the later letters cultivate an emotional-social form of mercy or compassion as loving togetherness in the community, which—as in the Old Testament—refers directly to God's merciful care for human beings. In Rom 11.30–32 Paul grounds his whole discussion of "his brothers/sisters, his kindred according to the flesh" (9.3), the Israelites (9.4), upon God's mercy.

> **11.30** For just as you were once disobedient to God but now have (already) obtained mercy (ἐλεεῖν) because of their disobedience, **31** so those also are now (still) disobedient in order that you may experience mercy (ἔλεος) in order that they also may obtain mercy (ἐλεεῖν).

While the comparative argument can also lack clarity,[118] the conviction of Paul is nevertheless quite clear. God's mercy extends not only to the

---

[115] οἰκτιρμός as predicate of God in Rom 12.1 (introduction to the paraenesis). In Phil 2.1 σπλάγχνα καὶ οἰκτιρμοί as an introduction to the paraenesis. 2 Cor 1.3 (introductory predicate of God together with παράκλησις); Col 3.2. Limits of mercy: Heb 10.28. Almost classic is Jas 5.11: "The Lord is very compassionate and merciful." σπλαγχνίζεσθαι: Matt 9.36 and elsewhere as inner turning of Jesus to human beings who need his mercy. Cf. also Eph 4.32 and 1 Pet 3.8. On this, cf. Konstan 2014.

[116] Matt 6.2–4: instruction on the correct way to give alms as the first form of δικαιοσύνη.

[117] Viewed materially, the saying contains an oxymoron; rhetorically, the author seeks to formulate as concisely as possible.

[118] On the logical and rhetorical structure, cf. Jewett 2007, 709–12. With reference to U. Wilckens, Jewett stresses "the carefully contrived chiasm of vv. 30–31" (709). The logical structure is, however, only partially decisive, for the comparison is not convincing. The *tertium comparationis* of the comparison lies in the certainty of the salvation of the Jews analogously to the already enacted salvation of the Roman community members. The temporal structure is not, however, analogous. The earlier–now scheme of the Roman community members does not correspond to the now–now scheme of the Jews and their

members of the Christian community but also to the "Israelites" who do not "believe in the Lord" (10.9–11). Bultmann stresses the aspects of faithfulness, salvation, and general grace that characterize God's mercy in the New Testament.[119] This makes the difference between mercy and the concept of ἀγάπη very clear. On the one hand, mercy and love are closely related. Both terms designate positive relationships and emotions. Mercy with its practical variant of almsgiving can be understood and highly esteemed as a concretion of love for neighbor.[120] And both terms are used for God's care for human beings. However, in comparison to love, mercy has a rather one-sided direction, comparable to grace. This direction is — unlike with love — irreversible. Mercy lacks reciprocity. Love is therefore the much more comprehensive and significant New Testament concept, not only because of its tradition-historical anchoring in the commandments of the Tanakh and its history of reception but also owing to the possibility of a christological deepening of the conception of love, which personalizes the relationship between God and human beings far beyond the mercy of God and turns it into a with-each-other. Altogether, in comparison with mercy, love is a stronger form — in fact, the *strongest* form — of interhuman relationships, of relationships within God, and of the reciprocal relationships between God and human beings.[121]

## 2.2 *Philia, Philadelphia, Philanthropia, Philoxenia*

Unlike mercy and more clearly than love, friendship is *per definitionem* grounded in mutuality between equally ranking partners.[122] While Aristotle infers from this that there can be no friendship with the deity,[123] Philo can indeed designate the connection of God to the wise and pious human

---

salvation in the near future. Moreover, the temporal division itself is unclear. Vv. 30 and 31 say the same thing twice, once in the scheme once–now, then in the scheme now–now.

[119] Bultmann 1964, 480–81 (GV = 1935, 480–81).

[120] This is especially the case in the Lukan work. Cf. the discussion of the merciful Samaritan above.

[121] Rom 11.30–31 shows, however, how near mercy can come to love.

[122] On this theme, see in detail G. Stählin 1974 (GV = 1973); Treu 1972, especially on friendship in the Church Fathers; Fraisse 1974; Price 1989; Fitzgerald 1997. On the numerous tractates of Hellenistic-Roman ethics on the theme of "friendship," see G. Stählin 1974, 151 (GV = 1973, 149).

[123] Aristotle, *Eth. nic.* 8.1158b: "In friendship equality is primarily equality in quantity and secondarily equality in worth. This is made clear when a great disparity in virtue, vice, resources, or something else comes about, since then the parties are no longer friends and do not even claim that they deserve to be. This is most evident in the case of the gods, since they are the most superior to us in all good things" (trans. Reeve 2014).

beings and, conversely, of the wise to God as friendship. Moses, Abraham, and also the Therapeutai are all wise and friends of God:[124]

(Moses) had the courage to utter these thoughts to God. He reached this limit, I will not say of daring in general but of good daring, because all the wise are friends of God, and particularly so in the judgement of the most holy lawgiver. Frankness of speech is akin to friendship. For to whom should a man speak with frankness but to his friend? And so most excellent is it, that in the oracles Moses is proclaimed the friend of God (Exod. 32.11), to shew that all the audacities of his bold discourse were uttered in friendship, rather than in presumption. For the audacity of rashness belongs to the presumptuous, the audacity of courage or confidence to a friend.

The central role of friendship in Greek culture and philosophy since Plato and Aristotle, the Roman ideal of friendship as it is classically formulated in Cicero,[125] and the important role that being inculcated into wise friendship plays in early Jewish wisdom literature are well known and comprehensively discussed in the scholarly literature. The New Testament authors do not make φιλία into a theme of its own, for the communities are held together by the social concept of love and brotherliness (φιλαδελφία) and not by the individually conceptualized friendship between individual persons.[126] The Gospel of John constitutes an exception.[127] I have already shown that in the Gospel of John the verb φιλεῖν can take over the meaning of ἀγαπᾶν in all semantic aspects.[128] Correspondingly, individual persons

---

[124] *Her.* 21 (trans. F. H. Colson and G. H. Whitaker, LCL, 295). Cf. also *Ebr.* 94 and *Sobr.* 55–56: Moses as friend of God. Cf. also Jas 2.23: Abraham as "friend of God." See further in G. Stählin 1974, 168n182 (GV = 1973, 166n182).

[125] On the principle of equality as a basis of friendship, cf. *Eth. nic.* 8.158b. Alongside this, however, Aristotle also knows of the friendship that is based on the superiority of the one partner (8.158b). On the equality of interests, see Cicero, *Laelius de amicitia* 20.

[126] But cf. A. C. Mitchell 1997. Mitchell points out that especially Paul, Luke, and John can use the Greco-Roman topos of friendship to strengthen the relationships to their communities. Here, "friendship" is a practical instrument of communication and social cohesion.

[127] On friendship in the Gospel of John, see Culy 2010. Culy finds "ideal friendship" not only between Jesus and the disciples but also between God and Jesus (128 and 176–77). However, he evaluates the ἀγαπᾶν statements as attestations for ideal friendship without explaining why he does not distinguish—as John does—between friendship and love. On the Gospel of Luke, cf. G. Stählin 1974, 165–66 (GV = 1973, 162–63) on the closeness of the Lukan and Johannine concepts of friendship (personal friendship, joy, table fellowship).

[128] Paul exhibits this linguistic usage only once: 1 Cor 16.22, which is probably a liturgically shaped linguistic usage; see G. Stählin 1974, 136 (GV = 1973, 134). An echo of this semantics occurs in 2 Tim 3.4: φιλήδονοι μᾶλλον ἢ φιλόθεοι.

can be designated as friends of Jesus: Lazarus (John 11.11) and the disciples (15.14). In the farewell discourse, Jesus himself declares his love for the disciples in the mode of laying down one's life for one's friends (15.12–14).[129] Love (ἀγάπη) and friendship (φιλία) fuse in relation to the disciples:

> **15.12** This is my commandment, that you love one another, as I have loved you. **13** Greater love has no one than this, that one lay down his life for his *friends*. **14** You are my *friends* . . .

The Gospel of John integrates the Greco-Roman notion of friendship as the bond between few noble, likeminded, and equally ranked individuals[130] into the comprehensive ἀγάπη concept of the Johannine writings. This elevates the position of the disciples and emphasizes their personal relationship to Jesus.[131] In 3 John the metaphor of friendship is placed in the concluding greeting (v. 15)—probably as a sign of the "exclusiveness" of the Johannine communities,[132] whose members form a new elite grouping. On the whole, however, the New Testament authors follow the usage of the Septuagint in preferring to use ἀγαπᾶν/ἀγάπη over φιλεῖν/φιλία. Here too, we can say in summary: For the New Testament authors ἀγάπη is the comprehensive concept of mutual affection, whereas friendship is a subsector that especially designates the individual and prominent affection between equally ranked persons. On the other hand, the interchangeability of ἀγαπᾶν/ἀγάπη and φιλεῖν/φιλία also sheds light upon love. When the Gospel of John presents Jesus and the disciples in the last days in Jerusalem as a fellowship of friends, it elevates their status and paints a picture of a group of noble men facing the friendship-death of their "Lord and master," who is also their friend. The love concept of the New Testament does not exclude individual relationships.

A connection between friendship relationship and group relationship is presented by φιλαδελφία, which is called for on a few occasions in the paraenetic parts of the New Testament letters as a behavior that befits community members:[133]

---

[129] On this, cf. G. Stählin 1974, 153 (GV = 1973, 151).

[130] Few: Aristotle, *Eth. nic.* 8.1158a; noble: *Eth. nic.* 8.1155a, 1156b; likeminded: *Eth. nic.* 8.1155a; equally ranked: *Eth. nic.* 8.1156b.

[131] Cf. also John 20.2: "the disciple whom Jesus loved." Cf. also Luke 12.4.

[132] G. Stählin 1974, 166 (GV = 1973, 164).

[133] Here, it is also related to the female community members: Matt 12.50 par.; Rom 16.1; 1 Cor 7.15; 9.5; Phlm 2. In 2 John 13 it is used for a neighboring community. On φιλαδελφία, cf. Aasgard 2004, 261–84.

**Rom 12.10** Τῇ φιλαδελφίᾳ εἰς ἀλλήλους φιλόστοργοι.[134]

In Greek, φιλαδελφία designates loving affection among brothers and sisters.[135] In the New Testament, love for brothers and sisters is part of the family-related metaphoricism for the members of the early Christian communities,[136] which I have already presented. Peter Pilhofer has emphatically pointed out that a linguistic novum is present here.[137] The New Testament authors do not, however, have a distinctive profile of *philadelphia*, for the noun is used rarely and without special emphasis. What is important, by contrast, is the address with "brothers and sisters."

φιλοξενία occurs in Rom 12 in close connection with *philadelphia* and mercy (12.10–13) as one of the functions of ἀγάπη (12.9). This also applies to Heb 13.1–2. Here, *philoxenia* is a function of *philadelphia*. Rom 16.23 shines a bright light on the meaning of hospitality in the early communities:[138]

**16.23** Gaius, who houses (ξένος) me and the whole ἐκκλησία, greets you.

Robert Jewett hypothesizes that Gaius received Jewish Christian and Gentile Christian community members and thus de facto supported the mission that Paul pursued in Romans.[139]

By contrast, φιλανθρωπία plays no role at all in the New Testament, although it appears in the tradition of Greek and early Jewish semantics in Titus 3.4 at a prominent place as a predicate of God alongside χρηστότης. Here "the Christ event is portrayed as an epiphany of God's φιλανθρωπία."[140] Ulrich Luck points to the reserve vis-à-vis this term, which is coined in

---

[134] On this, cf. Jewett 2007, 760–61 (lit.). Jewett points out that the reinforcement with the New Testament hapax legomenon φιλόστοργος "augments this appeal [to include fellow believers] with a concept widely used in Hellenistic ethics" (761).

[135] On this, see Plutarch, *De fraterno amore* / Περὶ φιλαδελφίας (*Mor.* 6.478a–492d).

[136] Rom 12.10; 1 Thess 4.9; Heb 13.1; 1 Pet 1.22; 2 Pet 1.7 (together with ἀγάπη). On 1 Thess 4.9, cf. Pilhofer 2002.

[137] Pilhofer 2002, 146, speaks of "a Christian proprium" and an early Christian "special language." He basis this argument on two observations: (1) Outside early Christian lexis, *philadelphia* refers exclusively to physical brothers/sisters (thus also in Plutarch). (2) The brother/sister metaphor likewise occurs first in the New Testament, i.e., in Paul.

[138] Cf. also Matt 25.35: "I was a stranger (ξένος), and you received (συνηγάγετέ) me."

[139] Jewett 2007, 980. Cf. also G. Stählin 1967 (GV = 1954), with his discussion of additional aspects of hospitality in the early communities on pp. 20–23 (GV = 1954, 19–23). Cf. further the profound *RAC* article on hospitality (Hiltbrunner et al. 1972). See in detail Rusche 1958; Hiltbrunner 2005.

[140] Luck 1974, 111 (GV = 1973, 111).

the Greco-Hellenistic world and readily used in the late writings of the
Septuagint, in Josephus, and in Philo:[141] "In early writings apart from and
after the NT there is, as in the NT itself, a remarkable hesitation to describe
the conduct of Christians as φιλανθρωπία even though other terms for
virtues are now being used."[142] Alongside love and friendship, the very
generally oriented love for humanity found no place in the early Christian
paraenesis.

## 2.3 Virtues / "Fruits of the Spirit"

Finally, the virtues—here, as previously, understood again in an unspecific sense[143]—probably represent the closest neighboring parallel field
of themes.[144] Even though the virtues or fruits of the Spirit can be understood as a parallel—and that means independent—concept to love, a
sharp division between virtue and love is nevertheless impossible. This
is the case not only because in the very rare New Testament mentions of
ἀρετή, "virtue" stands *alongside* "love" and therefore should more likely
be translated with "capability" (*Tüchtigkeit*) rather than with "virtue"
(*Tugend*), but also because friendship is already a virtue in Aristotle.[145] In
the writings of the New Testament ἀρετή itself is, as already indicated,
not an independent ethical key term.[146] Such different texts as Phil 4.8
and 2 Pet 1.3, 5ff. show, however, that in the epistolary paraenesis "virtue" could indeed be used in ethical contexts, in Paul as a possible ethical umbrella term alongside others, in 2 Peter as a constructive attitude
alongside others, including love:

---

[141] Cf. e.g., the philanthropy of Abraham toward "the three men" (Philo, *Abr.* 107).
The most important text is *Virt.* 51–174. Moses is presented as a model of love for humanity: his legislation reflects his love for humanity. By contrast, the haughty are characterized
by their contempt for human beings (171–174).

[142] Luck 1974, 111 (GV = 1973, 111).

[143] Duden: "morally valuable characteristic of a human being." In this definition
"characteristic" (*Eigenschaft*) does not have a specifically philosophical connotation. The
designation "virtue catalog," which is often used in exegesis, also for the listing out of
the "fruits of the Spirit," is based on this same unspecific understanding of "virtue" (cf.
Stemmer et al. 1998).

[144] The relationship between hatred and vices stands over against the adjacent relationship between love and virtue(s) as a mirror image.

[145] Aristotle, *Eth. nic.* 8.1155a.

[146] On the definition and function of virtue as "activeness of the soul in the sense of
its essential capability," cf. Aristotle, *Eth. nic.* 1.1098a and 1102a. For Aristotle virtues can
be defined in a way that is more strongly noetic and in a way that is more strongly ethical-
characteristic (*Eth. nic.* 6.1139a). See, by way of introduction, Horn/Rapp 2008.

**1.5** For precisely this reason, make every effort to supplement your faith with virtue, virtue with knowledge, **6** knowledge with self-control, self-control with patience, patience with piety, **7** piety with love for brothers and sisters (φιλαδελφία), love for brothers and sisters with love (ἀγάπη).[147]

Second Peter 1 functions as a post-Pauline virtue catalog.[148] Here, virtue is part of a loose series[149] of ethical and religious behavioral forms with the help of which the author, at the beginning, seeks to establish an ethical basis for his coming remarks by specifying everything that God has given to the Christ-believers for "life and piety" (1.3). ἀρετή, love for brothers and sisters, and love appear alongside other constructive attitudes. The series is probably constructed climactically with respect to the forms of love, without it being possible to establish in detail a considered causal relationship between ἀρετή and the other items mentioned in vv. 5–7.[150] The actual theme of the letter is, however, not ethics but the correct knowledge of Jesus Christ and his return and the dispute with eschatological false teachers.[151]

More important is the concept of virtues or fruits of the Spirit in Paul. The concern is a priori with a multitude of ethical, emotional, and communitarian phenomena that mutually supplement one another and as such always remain fragmentary. I have already shown that ἀγάπη in the Pauline letters can occur as part of these virtue catalogs. It has also already become clear that Paul does not have an ethical system. He does not develop a doctrine of virtues[152] but rather sets forth an open[153] field of relationships and forms of emotion, behavior, and action that are compatible with love. Important is Gal 5.22–26; 2 Cor 6.6–7; and the statements that contain the so-called triad. The most important text is Gal 5.22–26:[154]

**22** But the fruit of the Spirit is: *love*, joy, peace, patience (μακροθυμία), kindness (χρηστότης), goodness (ἀγαθωσύνη), faithfulness,

---

[147] On ἀγάπη as a virtue, cf. Clement of Alexandria, *Quis dives salvetur* 18.1 (ed. O. Stählin 1909). See further Schrage 1999, 321 with note 248.

[148] See, fundamentally, Vögtle 1936. Cf. the excellent article of Fitzgerald 1992.

[149] Vögtle 1994, 149, speaks of a "virtue chain" following Fischel 1973. Cf. Rom 5.3–5, which likewise has ἀγάπη at the end, though here it is the love of God.

[150] A different view is advocated by Vögtle 1994, 150–51.

[151] 2 Pet 1.2–3, 5.

[152] Cf. the sketch in Löhr 2013.

[153] Open in reference to different constructive attitudes that can be specified but closed in relation to all destructive modes of behavior.

[154] On this, cf. Betz 1979, 286–95.

**23** gentleness (πραΰτης), self-control—the law is not against these (virtues). **24** But those who belong to Christ Jesus have crucified the flesh with the passions and desires. **25** If we live in the Spirit, let us also walk in the Spirit. **26** Let us not become vainglorious, provoking one another, envying one another.

Two different ethical approaches are placed next to each other here. (1) Verses 22–23 are formulated in the context of the topic of the law, which dominates the letter both situationally and theologically. In this first argument, Paul enumerates fruits of the Spirit that are "law-conforming." First, he mentions love, which is followed by other constructive modes of behavior. With this he takes up the argumentation of 5.13–14, which he will develop further in Rom 13.8–10. His positive main thesis—"Love is the fulfillment of the law" (5.14)—is repeated in 5.22–23 *ex negativo*: "The law is not against love" or the other gifts of the Spirit. Paul moves here within the "old" discourse about the interpretation of the law, i.e., about the question of how the continuity of the ethos of the Christ-believing communities to the fulfillment of the law is to be presented. (2) While the concern in the first argument is thus precisely with the question of the extent to which the Pauline love ethics fulfills the law, in Gal 5.24–26 Paul engages critically with the problem of "fleshly conduct" in a second line of argumentation. Here, Paul argues from his own, new ethical conception, which—amid enduring material continuity—has not the law but Christ and the Spirit as its foundation. How these two entities hang together is not discussed here. Rather, Paul starts from the double new reality in which the Christ-confessing Galatians live: they "are Christ's" and they "live in the Spirit." The Galatians are meant to fill these two realities[155] with existential meaning by reenacting the crucifixion of Christ on their own person[156] and "walking by the Spirit." Paul initially exemplifies walking by the Spirit through known forms of harmonious behavior and the retraction of the self. At the same time, this creates the basis for the positive new paraenesis of Paul, which he sketches in Gal 5.26–6.10 without any claim to systematization or completeness.

Here lies a distinct conception of constructive behavior and corresponding forms of behavior. In the context of the question of parallel conceptions to ἀγάπη, the metaphorical expression "fruit of the Spirit,"[157] which draws a chain of positive modes of behavior or virtues after it, is significant.

---

[155] On the reality of the reception of the Spirit, cf. Gal 3.1–5. On the reality of the "life in Christ," cf. Gal 1.4 and 2.19–20.

[156] Paul speaks of παθήματα and ἐπιθυμίαι, i.e., of destructive emotions.

[157] Κάρπος in Paul is often used for the positive result of ethical behavior.

Gal 5.22–26 is read by the commentators against the background of Greek-Hellenistic virtue lists and dualistically structured Jewish two-ways or two-spirits traditions.[158] Richard Longenecker documents the relevant texts in his Galatians commentary and concludes that it is not so much the Jewish two-ways traditions that stand behind Gal 5 as the Hellenistic catalog genre. The dualism is said to result from the Pauline juxtaposition of Spirit and flesh:

> Paul's own ethical dualism of "the flesh" versus the "spirit" provides a sufficient rationale for the dual lists of 5:19–23. Thus the dual nature of his catalogue here does not necessarily imply a Jewish "Two Ways" tradition as formative rather than a Hellenistic catalogue genre being followed.[159]

However, the Testaments of the Twelve Patriarchs not only use the two-ways scheme[160] but also speak of the 'spirits' of jealousy, envy, and anger or, alternatively, of the "knowledge of the Lord" (T. Jud. 20). However, it must be noted that in the Testaments of the Twelve Patriarchs, the "spirits" can be defined both positively and negatively, whereas Paul always speaks of the gifts of the Spirit of God, i.e., he uses this language only positively.[161]

More important than the controversial question of the derivation is Longenecker's pointer to the dualism of flesh and Spirit, which Paul employs argumentatively here.[162] With this a bridge is made to the Pauline lists of charisms,[163] which specify more clearly than Gal 5.22–26 that the Spirit itself is the *giver* and origin of the positive forms of behavior.

---

[158] There are, however, also catalogs of virtues. Cf. e.g., 2 En. 66.6; on this, cf. Böttrich 1995, 999–1000. Böttrich refers to Testaments of the Twelve Patriarchs. He disputes Christian influence (thus W. Bousset). Second Enoch 66.6 also contains the exhortation to love one another (cf. the Johannine linguistic usage).

[159] Longenecker 1990, 252.

[160] Especially T. Ash. 1.

[161] In the Testaments of the Twelve Patriarchs the spirits are repeatedly coordinated dualistically so that not only the constructive ("virtues") but also the destructive modes of behavior ("vices") are designated as "spirits" and assigned to negative powers—whether or not they are personified. The extent to which the talk about the "spirits" is a familiar speech pattern and where religious conceptions of (evil) spirits predominate must be tested in individual cases. In any case, Paul knows this diction, but rarely uses it: Rom 8.15 (spirit of slavery); 1 Cor 2.12 (spirit of the κόσμος); 2 Cor 11.4 ("another spirit": in a chain of rhetorical questions). In all other contexts, he always speaks of the Spirit of God, of the Holy Spirit, etc. Cf., in detail, Kleinknecht et al. 1971 (GV = 1959).

[162] On this, see the material in Schweizer 1971, 428–30 (GV = 1959, 425–28).

[163] On this, cf. F. W. Horn 2013a.

The charisms (1 Cor 12) can also be understood as a parallel concept to love. However, they remain entirely related to their function in the communities. In 1 Cor 12.31 and 14.1, Paul brings *love* into connection with the charisms or πνευματικά but in such a way that love is "greater" than the charisms. Thus, ἀγάπη is a distinct concept that is, however, closely connected to the gifts of the Spirit in the worship service and in the work of the community (πνευματικά and charisms) as well as to the psychological and ethical attitudes of the "fruit of the Spirit," with love itself also being able to function as a fruit of the Spirit. In Paul the concern is with the different aspects of the connection to the worship service, of the connection to the community, of ethical attitudes, and of the ethical behavior of the individual. By means of the virtues or fruits of the Spirit, Paul, in loose form and without definitional claim, stakes out the field of positive forms of behavior that characterize the new life of the Christ-confessing communities "in the Spirit."

Second Corinthians 6.1–7.4 adds another nuance to this concept. With the help of virtues, Paul sets forth here the image of the "coworker of God," i.e., he describes how he views himself and how he wants to be viewed by the Corinthians.[164] Alongside his tribulations (v. 4), he enumerates his virtues (v. 6), so that he can then come to his missionary task (v. 7) and portray his situation (vv. 8–10):

> **6.4** But in all things we prove ourselves as servants of God . . . **6** in holiness, in knowledge, in patience (μακροθυμία), in kindness (χρηστό-της), in the Holy Spirit, in *love* without hypocrisy, **7** in the word of truth, in the power of God.

This rather short virtue catalog is embedded in a peristasis catalog that reaches from v. 4 to v. 10 and concludes with a chain of oppositions that become polished oxymorons in v. 10. Here, important virtues—constructive forms of behavior—such as patience[165] and kindness[166] from Gal 5.22 stand *alongside*—not *under*—the entirely different entities of proclamation, the Holy Spirit, and the power of God.[167] Again, a field is opened up that binds together divine and human powers, here in order to sketch out the behavior and gifts of the apostle himself. The concept of virtues or fruits

---

[164] On the "self-recommendation of the servant of God," cf. Schmeller 2010, 340–61, here: 340.

[165] In Rom 2.4; 9.22 mode of behavior of God.

[166] In Rom 11.22 mode of behavior of God.

[167] In this series the renunciation of some sort of systematization is especially clear. On this, see Schmeller 2010, 353: "The listing out is meant to mediate the undifferentiated impression of a qualification through character-related and divinely given advantages."

of the Spirit is ethically integrative and at the same time transparent for the Spirit and the spiritual gifts. It is, however, more specifically tailored than the ἀγάπη concept and focused on the sphere of attitudes and actions of the community members.

On the whole we can say that mercy, friendship, and virtues or gifts of the Spirit never stand against love but are described either as concretions of love or come alongside love. Moreover, the opposite also applies: love can be understood as a gift of the Spirit. Instead of psychological, ethical, or social systematization, we find an open network of constructive entities in association with love. A circumstance, however, distinguishes the aforementioned entities from love. They have no—or only a little—reciprocal quality. Human beings cannot encounter God with mercy. The disciples can be designated as friends of Jesus in the Gospel of John, but they are not—unlike what is the case with Moses in Philo—designated as friends of God. While the virtues and gifts of the Spirit reach into the divine world with their origins, as effective powers they are entirely restricted to the interpersonal sphere.

### 3. Alternative Ethical-Religious Life Concepts

Mercy, φιλία, and other virtues are closely related to love. They are forms of relationships that stand alongside love or as aspects of love emphasize and strengthen the ethical side of the New Testament concept of love. However, the New Testament writings also know ethical-religious concepts that come from other traditions and privilege other ethical value conceptions. In what follows, the most important ethical-religious concepts that are independent of the concept of love in terms of tradition history or also compete with it at specific points will be sketched out in great brevity and with a single aim—namely, to illuminate again the distinctive character of the concept of love, so to speak, from the outside. Discipleship and imitation of Jesus Christ, goodness, perfection, holiness, and justice are themselves comprehensive life concepts that the New Testament authors work out in more or less detail for their communities. Sometimes these life concepts are set forth for specific addressee groups. At the same time, all these concepts are interested in the formation of the ethical-religious personality.[168] In comparison with the comprehensive concept of love, they are more clearly ethically focused, paraenetically formulated, and related to the life conduct of individuals and groups,[169] and in this respect they are close to virtues. What they lack—with the exception of the concept of discipleship—is the dimension of relationship as well as the concern for others. Both, however,

---

[168] Here, personality is understood merely in the sense of the individual person.
[169] Part of the epistolary exhortation or of the ethically focused logia of Jesus.

are decisive for love. On the other hand, goodness, perfection, holiness, and justice, just like love, belong to the central characteristics of God in the Old Testament, and the relationship between God and human beings is shaped by these characteristics of God. These concepts can also mutually connect with one another, come in contact with the concept of love, and enter into different constellations with this concept, while being independent in terms of tradition history and motif history. In this ensemble of related concepts, discipleship occupies a distinct place since this concept is related exclusively to Jesus. It is a pure concept of relationship, which, in addition, is not reciprocal. By contrast, goodness, perfection, and holiness are closely adjacent aspects. They are divine characteristics and at the same time forms of behavior in the framework of the existence of early Christian communities and their members. This also applies to justice, though its significance for the theology of the New Testament writings goes far beyond the role of the aspects just mentioned. Despite these differences, here too we find a field of closely related and sometimes almost identical modes of behavior and characteristics, whose individual aspects are all connected with love.

## 3.1 Discipleship/Imitation

The verb "to follow," ἀκολουθεῖν, is used especially in the Synoptic tradition for a specific behavior in relation to Jesus.[170] In 'sayings on discipleship,' Jesus, during his wanderings through Galilee, calls individual men to follow him on his peregrinations. Some 'discipleship stories' are configured as call stories of individual disciples.[171] Ferdinand Hahn states that discipleship means the

> unconditional readiness, on the basis of an authoritative word of Jesus, to give up the previous conditions of life and instead to enter into the life fellowship with Jesus. Among the life conditions that are to be given up, emphasis is placed on occupation and possessions and indirectly also on family.[172]

Discipleship implies a specific way of life, which Gerd Theissen has described as "itinerant radicalism." For the *concept* of discipleship in the Synoptic Gospels, the 'sayings on discipleship' in Mark 8.34–37 are important:[173]

---

[170] In monograph form, see Betz 1967. By way of introduction, see Hahn 2002, 1:74–91.

[171] Hahn 2002, 1:75–76. Mark 10.17–22 par. is important. Here Jesus' call to follow him fails because of the man's attachment to his possessions, although Jesus "loved him."

[172] Hahn 2002, 1:76. See there for the relevant logia.

[173] Cf. the short form of v. 25 in Luke 17.33 (there without reference to Jesus and discipleship); see further Mark 10.28–30 par., in Luke 18.28–30 with the expression "for the sake of the kingdom of God."

**8.34** And he called the crowd with his disciples and said to them, "If anyone wishes to follow me, let him deny himself (ἀπαρνείσθαι[174]) and take up his cross and follow me. **35** For whoever wishes to save his life will lose it; but whoever will lose his life for my sake and the gospel's will save it. **36** For what would it profit a person to gain the whole world and lose his life? **37** For what could a human being give in exchange for his life?"

The concept of discipleship is a relational concept. In distinction from what we find with ἀγάπη, here the relationship is established not only through positive forms of behavior and personal attachment but also through radical *renunciation*. Moreover, the disciple must renounce not only all forms of inner-worldly attachments but above all their own existence and, finally, their own life, as Mark 8 shows. In Mark's narrative, the concept of discipleship applies initially to the disciples.[175] In the three Synoptic Gospels, the concept is then expanded to all adherents of Jesus.[176] In distinction from the ἀγάπη concept, discipleship is focused strictly on a single person and therefore also limited—in Mark's narrative on the person of Jesus, in the other Synoptic Gospels on Jesus Christ. The concept of discipleship develops special stringency and is the bearer of an ethical rigorism that defines itself as exclusive in a double sense—exclusion of all inner-worldly attachments (to gain the κόσμος)[177] and at the same time exclusive attachment to Jesus.

The focus on the person of Jesus also fundamentally determines the parallel mimesis concept of Paul:[178] "Imitate me as I imitate Christ."[179] Johannes Weiss suggests that we fill this concise exhortation with Phil

---

[174] Parallel to Mark: Matt 16.24.

[175] Since Mark 1.17. The extent to which Jesus himself called for "following" and thus constituted his closer circle of disciples must remain open here.

[176] The addition "for the sake of the gospel" includes not only the hearers of the proclamation of Jesus but also the hearers or readers of the Gospel of Mark.

[177] This rigorous ethos is developed in the mission rules in Mark 6.7–13 par.

[178] Texts: 1 Thess 1.6; 2.14; 1 Cor 4.16; 11.1; (Eph 5.1); Phil 3.17. On the religious-historical perspective of the mimesis concept, cf. Betz 1967, with the definition on p. 4: "We designate as mimesis the contemporizing presentation of the mythical story of a deity through the believers, with this not being conceptualized as identical with the deity himself." E.-M. Becker 2015 is more convincing with respect to this point. Becker's literary-historical categorization in mimetic ethics captures the Pauline concept exactly. A further history-of-religions categorization remains fuzzy in comparison. What is clear is that Paul does not use the concept of discipleship; on this, see Betz 1967, 137–40. Paul's complete renunciation of the lexis of ἀκολουθείν and μαθητής indicates that Paul, who was not a disciple of Jesus, avoided this theme in favor of the themes of imitation and apostolate.

[179] 1 Cor 11.1.

2.5ff., i.e., not only with the renunciation of self-assertion (1 Cor 10.24, 33; Phil 2.6) but also with the giving of one's life (Phil 2.8).[180] With this the concept of imitation would become a parallel to discipleship. When Paul, in Phil 3.10–11, writes, "in order to know him and the power of his resurrection and the fellowship in his suffering, being conformed to his death, in order that I may somehow attain to the resurrection from the dead," then he does, in fact, pursue the same ideas as Mark 8.37–38: renunciation of the preservation of one's own person and life. However, Paul simultaneously promotes the opening up of the group of the disciples and the apostle to the members of the community in a more resolute way than the Synoptic Gospels and makes it explicit. In the subsequent course of the paraenesis in Philippians he makes the following exhortation in 3.17:

> **3.17** Become imitators of me, brothers and sisters, and have respect for those who walk just as you have us as a model (τύπος).

In this way, the concept of imitation, unlike discipleship, is not only freed from the limitation to the disciples of Jesus, but it can also forgo the relation to Jesus himself and become a distinct life form of the community. Hans Dieter Betz points out that in connection with the mimesis conception, the *imitatio Jesu* piety begins with 1 Peter. "It is fully developed in the Martyrdom of Polycarp (cf. 1.1, 2; 17.2, 3), where recourse is consciously made to the Gospel traditions as a pattern for the description of the martyrdom of Polycarp."[181]

The concept of discipleship and mimesis come into contact with the concept of love at two points that are as different as they are central—in the renunciation of the "concern for the self" and in the intensive person-oriented attachment. The difference lies *first* in the lack of "concern for others." In distinction from love, discipleship and mimesis are oriented to the perfecting of one's own person and not to the needs of others. Both concepts are focused on a person's own behavior and serve the perfecting of the self.[182] Second, the intensive relationality of discipleship or imitation does not apply to all human beings, and not even to all community members, but exclusively to Jesus or to the exalted Christ. Through Paul, however, this concept is also opened up into the history of the communities.

---

[180] J. Weiss 1970, 267.

[181] Betz 1967, 181–82.

[182] Here, it is necessary to take into account the fact that in both the Gospels and especially in Paul, the concept of love stands alongside or even over the concept of discipleship and imitation. There is no systematization but different situations, traditions, and aspects.

Finally, the concepts of discipleship and imitation lack the dimension of reciprocity, which is a feature of love.

## 3.2 The Good

In our context, the good need not be defined or broken down in detail into the good, goodness, and goods in the sense of a theory of goods. The good is *the* central self-explanatory positive ethical ordering term in all ancient Mediterranean cultures, in which early Judaism and early Christianity also participate.[183] The binary opposition of "good and evil"[184] makes clear that the concern is with an evaluative and possibly also norm-setting[185] term. It impresses one with its—apparent—simplicity, as shown in the opening question of the young man in the 'discipleship story' of Matt 19.16–22, which makes the theme of the good the starting point for a new definition:

> **19.16** And behold, someone came to him and said, "Teacher,[186] what *good* thing must I do to have eternal life?" **17** And he said to him, "Why do you ask me about the good?[187] There is only one who is good. But if you wish to enter into life, keep the commandments." **18** Then he said to him, "Which ones?" And Jesus said, "You shall not kill; you shall not commit adultery; you shall not steal; you shall not bear false witness; **19** honor your father and mother; and: *'You shall love your neighbor as yourself.'*" **20** Then the young man said, "I have kept these; what do I still lack?" **21** Jesus answered him, "If you wish to be perfect (τέλειος), then go, sell your possessions, and give to the poor and you will have treasure in heaven; and come and follow me!" **22** When the young man heard this word, he went away sorrowful; for he had many goods.

"The good" is in question here, i.e., as quintessence of an ethics of action[188] that is oriented in a way that is religiously successful in the sense of the Judaism of the time—namely, to "eternal life." Jesus wants to keep the attribute of the good reserved for God and thus criticizes the question, and yet

---

[183] On the latter, cf. the contributions in Horn et al. 2013, especially Zimmermann 2013a; C. Horn 2013; Röder 2013.

[184] On this, cf. de Bruin 2014.

[185] On the term ethical norm, cf. esp. Zimmermann 2013c.

[186] Mark 10.17 and Luke 18.18: "Good teacher."

[187] Mark 10.18 and Luke 18.19: "Why do you call me good?"

[188] Cf. the expression "do good" in Matt 19.16; John 5.29; Rom 2.10; 7.19; 13.3; Gal 6.10; Eph 6.8; 1 Pet 3.11. In nominal form: "good work / good works" in Acts 9.36; Rom 2.7; 13.3; 2 Cor 9.8; Eph 2.10; 2 Thess 2.17; 1 Tim 2.10; 5.10; 2 Tim 2.21; 3.17; Titus 1.16; 3.1.

nevertheless answers—namely, with the commandments of the Decalogue and the commandment of love for neighbor. To this point, the narrative moves exclusively in the framework of Judaism, even though the question about the good is posed in such a general way that it would be understood equally in the sphere of Greco-Roman ethics.[189] The fact that the narrative with the exhortation to follow Jesus is continued as the way to perfection makes two things clear. First, it shows how closely connected being good, being perfect, and following are. Second, it shows that in Matthew neither the Greek nor the Jewish conception of the good stands at the center of interest, but that the good is only thematized to the extent that it serves as a foil for the actual Jesus theme, the call to discipleship. The evangelist is not interested in "the good" and the "doing of the good" as such.

Paul and the author of the Deutero-Pauline letters follow the general linguistic usage when they speak of the good and of good works. Here, we find not so much a distinct concept as participation in an ethical discourse of the early imperial period.[190] This becomes especially clear in Rom 12 and 13:

> **12.1** I exhort you therefore, brothers and sisters, through the mercies of God to present your bodies as a sacrifice, which is living, holy, and well-pleasing to God, as your reasonable worship. **2** And do not conform yourselves to this age but transform yourselves through the renewing of your mind in order that you may test what is the will of God: the *good* and well-pleasing and perfect.

In this introduction to his extensive paraenesis, Paul connects cultic metaphoricism[191] with ethical basic vocabulary.[192] The exhortation is at the same time a statement regarding the situation and time that provides orientation. The members of the Roman house churches should understand that they belong not to the *old* aeon but rather to the *new* life that Paul has presented in chapters 3–8. The category of the good has here the character of a clasp. It creates continuity between the old and the new existence. The concern is always with the good, which is, however, newly interpreted as ἀγάπη. The good is the ethically positive and remains the fundamental formal concept of order, which as a characteristic of God, as an attribute

---

[189] On the good as central term of ethics since Socrates, cf., by way of introduction, Tornau 2008. see, in greater detail, Reiner et al. 1974.

[190] Cf. Grundmann 1964 (GV = 1933).

[191] Holiness, sacrifice, and worship service.

[192] Good, well pleasing, perfect, God's will.

of creation, and as an ethical norm describes the unified constructive structure of the fabric of God, creation, and human beings, while needing to be filled materially, i.e., with respect to the ethos, behavior, and conduct of human beings. The good is constructive—but how can the human being think and act constructively? The answers of the New Testament authors begin at this point. They are developed in different ways and encompass all the motifs and concepts discussed here, from mercy to holiness. Love also functions within this framework not as the material norm of the good but as a great concept—indeed, as the most significant concept—in connection with virtues, gifts of the Spirit, and other forms of interpersonal relations.

## 3.3 Perfection

Discipleship and imitation, on the one hand, and goodness or the doing of good, on the other, are not only closely connected with the concept of perfection but, viewed materially, also partial aspects of this concept. The notion of ethical perfection[193] in the sense of the highest intensification of good life conduct occurs twice at a prominent place in the Gospel of Matthew. In the narrative of the rich young man in Matt 19.16–22, a young man asks Jesus, "What good thing (ἀγαθόν) must I do to have eternal life"? When Jesus refers to the commandments from the Decalogue and to Lev 19.18,[194] the young man answers:

> **19.20** *"I have kept all these.* What do I still lack?" **21** Jesus said to him, "If you wish to be perfect (τέλειος),[195] go, sell your possessions, and give to the poor, and you will have treasure in heaven, and come, follow me."

Here, perfection is understood as the highest intensification of the good and at the same time tied to discipleship. The "good" is surpassed and must be surpassed. Perfection applies, first, exclusively to one's own person. Second, it is conceptualized quantitatively. Third, in the ethical context, it also has an eschatological perspective—the young man wants "to have eternal life," and Jesus promises him "treasure in heaven." Neither the keeping of the Ten Commandments nor the commandment of love for neighbor is enough. It is only the surrender of possessions and discipleship, i.e., entrance into Jesus' way of life that makes a person "perfect."

---

[193] On the traditions, cf. Delling 1972a (GV = 1969a); Kedar-Kopfstein 1995. The ritual side of perfection plays no role here; see also the section on "holiness" below.

[194] Lacking in Mark 10.19 and Luke 18.20.

[195] Lacking in Mark 10.21 and Luke 18.22.

The concept of discipleship as the highest form of a rigoristic way of life is placed here—as the concept of love is elsewhere—over the fulfillment of the law and specifically over the commandment of love for neighbor. And it is first this summons into discipleship that *over*taxes the young man. He cannot realize the perfection of a life conduct without possessions in the discipleship of Jesus. Ulrich Luz points out clearly that this episode is based on the conception of ethics as perfect life conduct, which encompasses different aspects—obedience to commandments, love for neighbor, and, finally, discipleship.[196] In this narrative, love for neighbor has lost its role as sufficient ethical mode of behavior.

This implicit criticism of love for neighbor and love for brothers and sisters as insufficient ethical instrument occurs in Matt 5.48:

> **5.46** For if you love those who love you, what reward do you have? Do not even the tax collectors do the same? **47** And if you greet only your brothers and sisters (ἀδελφοί), what do you do that is special? Do not even the gentiles do the same? **48** Therefore, you should be perfect (τέλειος), as your Father in heaven is perfect.

The theme of the antitheses is not discipleship but, as 5.48 makes clear, perfection as such. Here, it becomes an ethical concept itself. As already discussed, love for enemies is prized in the sixth antithesis. Only love for enemies makes "perfect." It leads to a behavior that is suited to God himself.[197] In Matthew it is not love for brothers and sisters (*philadelphia*) or love for neighbor but love for enemies that connects human beings in the character of their action with God. Ulrich Luz emphasizes that love for enemies in Matthew is "not one demand among others but the center and apex of all the commandments that lead to perfection."[198] And "there are two elements in this perfection: the unity of heart and totality of obedience as a subjective element and fulfilling of the law's demands as an objective element."[199] Here, we could indeed speak of an 'elitization' of ethics, which implies at the same time a strong individuation. Matthew's concept of perfection applies to the small elite flock of Jesus disciples. Even someone, such as the young man who does the good cannot follow this concept of perfection.

---

[196] Luz 2001, 513–14 (GV = 1997, 124–25).

[197] In the ἀγάπη concept, it is the ἀγάπη that is suited to God himself. Matthew clearly restricts God's love by completely expanding it! On the correspondence formula "to be perfect as God is perfect," cf. the section on holiness below.

[198] Luz 2007, 290 (GV = 2002, 410). Here too, Luz points to the quantitative aspect of perfection (289; GV = 409).

[199] Luz 2007, 289 (GV = 2002, 409).

In the letters of Paul, the eschatological meaning dynamizes the ethical conception of the perfection of the person, for example, in Phil 3.12–16:

> **3.12** Not that I have already obtained it[200] or am already perfected (τελειοῦν)—but I chase after it, in order to grasp it, because I also am grasped by Christ Jesus. **13** Brothers and sisters, I do not reckon that I have grasped it; but: I forget what lies behind me and stretch toward what lies ahead, **14** I rush after the goal to the victory prize of the upward call of God in Christ Jesus. **15** We all, who are perfect (τέλειος), should think in this way and if you think otherwise about something, God will also reveal this to you. **16** Only: to that which we have attained, to this let us hold fast.

Paul clearly interprets perfection differently than Matthew. Here, "perfection" lies not in a specific behavior but in the paradoxical state of perfection (v. 15) that realizes itself in the present existence of the apostle precisely as imperfection and as a "pursuit" of perfection (vv. 13–14). If it applies anywhere, then Bultmann's formulation of the "not-yet and yet already" of the eschatological reserve is accurate for this state. The fact that Paul also does not think systematically here but expresses his religious existential feeling in an ad hoc manner is clear from 1 Cor 13.9–10, where Paul places perfection wholly and exclusively in the future:

> **13.9** For we know in part and we prophecy in part. **10** But when the perfect/complete comes, the partial will pass away.

Here, Paul works with the part-whole scheme when he, at least between spiritual gifts and love, constructs a point of discontinuity in an eschatological sense and not a simultaneity of already and not yet. By contrast, in Rom 12.2 he uses the ethical meaning of the term "perfection" and at the same time highlights the theological anchoring of the term:

> **12.2** . . . in order that you may test what is the will of God, the good and well-pleasing and perfect.

Here, the proximity to Jas 1.7 is conspicuous. In James the notion that perfection is, on the one hand, a characteristic of God that belongs to the

---

[200] The accusative object is not specified. For concretion different objects can be supplied: resurrection (3.11), justice from faith (3.9–10), upward calling (3.14). All these aspects are intended in v. 12.

heavenly world and, on the other hand, something that is given to human beings is expressed in a carefully stylized religious speech:

> **1.17** Every good gift and every perfect gift is from above, coming down from the Father of lights, with whom there is no shifting or shadow of change.[201]

Moreover, the author of James can also choose a purely ethical perspective when he speaks with a view to proper speech of the "perfect man" (3.2) or of the patience "that is meant to carry out its complete work in order that you may be perfect (τέλειος) and blameless, and be lacking in nothing" (1.4).[202]

The author of 1 John has a distinct voice. In 4.16–21 he sketches out a picture of a perfect love that has παρρησία on the day of judgment. Ethically, this love is understood as love for brothers and sisters (*philadelphia*). First John 4.16–21 thus brings together the conceptions of perfection and love in an eschatological horizon.

One point, however, always applies: the concept of perfection is always related to one's own person[203] and not to "others" or to the neighbor. In a different way than the concepts of discipleship or imitation, however, the notion of perfection, like the notion of the good, reaches into the divine sphere and is in the first place a fundamental predicate of God.

## 3.4 Holiness

To a greater extent than the concepts that have been presented thus far, holiness is assigned to the religious sphere and is a fundamental part of both the ancient Near Eastern and the Greco-Roman religious conceptual world. קדשׁ is a central theological term in the Hebrew Bible[204] and is translated with ἅγιος.[205] It is correspondingly represented in the Septuagint, in the noncanonized Greek writings of early Judaism, and in the New Testament. Holiness, like perfection, has the character of a trait and belongs first to God but then equally to the people of God, the Israelites. At the same

---

[201] On the text and translation of v. 17, cf. Wischmeyer 2013b. Cf. now also Wischmeyer forthcoming, ad loc.

[202] The last two characteristics come close to ritual terminology.

[203] The closeness to early Jewish conceptions of perfection is clear.

[204] See Feldmeier/Spieckermann 2011, 17–50 (GV = 2010, 17–50). See, in detail, Kornfeld/Ringgren 2003 (GV = 1989).

[205] The LXX prefers ἅγιος as a translation of *qdš*. On this, cf. Dihle 1988. ἅγιος also predominates in the New Testament. The other Greek lexemes are hardly used. See further Procksch/Kuhn 1964 (GV = 1933).

time, the writings of the Old Testament are also familiar with the holiness of places, spaces, times, objects, and persons in the sense of separateness, purity, or taboo. The dichotomy of understanding holiness either as a characteristic of God or as a religious term falls short of the mark. This also applies to a description that concentrates *either* on the theological diction as "belonging to God"—here a certain tautology can be observed[206]—*or* on the religious studies perspective on the elements of the numinous, the taboo, and the sacred or pure.[207] In these alternatives, the important ethical dimension of the term is neglected. The writings of the Hebrew Bible construct holiness precisely at the intersection of *three* entities—conception of God, cult, and ethics. Here, the relationship of God to his people is determined by the demand that they correspond to divine holiness through the keeping of the law, which has purity as a consequence. This is the basic idea of the so-called holiness code in Lev 17–26. This relationship of correspondence is expressed exemplarily in Lev 19.1–2:[208]

> **19.1** The LORD spoke to Moses, saying: **2** Speak to all the congregation of the people of Israel and say to them: You shall be holy, for I the LORD your God am holy.[209]

Eckart Otto writes in a balanced manner: "YHWH's holiness . . . provides the basis for the possibility of obedience to the law, the covenant is the context in which it is established, and the exodus is the context in which it is recognized." What emerges is a "a post-exilic document of innerbiblical halakhah formed to demonstrate the unity of God's will despite differences in the torah."[210]

Here, the concern can only be with the concept of holiness in the New Testament in the comparison to the concepts of discipleship, goodness, and perfection, on the one hand, and to love, on the other hand. The eschatological and ritual aspects remain unconsidered here.[211] The ἅγιος concept develops its meaning, however, in clear connection to the Old Testament

---

[206] Cf. Hunsinger 2012, here, 370: "Strictly speaking holiness can be ascribed to God alone . . . Holiness is the perfection that distinguishes God from the world" (GV = 2000, 1535).

[207] Thus the perspective in the individual articles on the lemma "holy and profane" in Paden et al. 2012 (GV = 2000). The lemma "holiness" is lacking. Holy is constructed there from the opposition to profane and unclean, i.e., in a strongly cultic way.

[208] Cf. Exod 19.6; Lev 20.7, 26 (there the additional motif of the separation of the people of Israel); 22.31–33; Deut 7.6; Isa 6.3; 62.12; 63.18 and elsewhere. Cf. also Matt 5.48 (see above).

[209] Trans. NRSV.

[210] Otto 2009, 207–8 (GV = 2000, 1570).

[211] On holiness in Paul, cf. Schmidt 2010.

linking of theological, cultic, and ethical legal-theological aspects. First Peter 1.16 quotes Lev 19.2:

> **1.15** But as the one who called you is holy, you also be holy in all your conduct, **16** because it is written, "You shall be holy, for I am holy."

Through the addition "in all your conduct," the ethical components of the concept of holiness are made explicit. God's holiness[212] does not receive further emphasis in the New Testament writings. It is given in the pretext of the Septuagint. In the Synoptic Gospels God's holiness is transferred to Jesus, without this motif playing a distinct role in the development of New Testament Christology.[213] Rather, the whole emphasis is placed on the holiness of the community members, as the Pauline and Deutero-Pauline letters show.[214] The addressees are addressed as ἅγιοι in the proem of Romans, in 1–2 Corinthians, in Philippians, and also in Ephesians and Colossians. The motif has already been discussed in the context of the topoi.[215]

In the context of the concept of holiness, Rom 1.7 serves as a commentary in *two* respects: (1) Paul addresses the Roman Christians, who are unknown to him, with three expressions: "all who are in Rome," "beloved (ἀγαπητοί) of God," "called saints (ἅγιοι)." The compilation makes clear that the holiness of the Roman Christians is a result of the love of God and of his calling—and not a result of the ethical perfection of the Christians.[216] On the other hand, Paul calls precisely these Roman Christians to holiness and perfection in 12.1–2. (2) The fact that Paul addresses the community members as "saints" as a matter of course must also be emphasized. The extent to which an elaborated theology of the Spirit[217] and of baptism[218] is present in Paul, which has as its result the notion of the holiness of the baptized and realizes itself in a walking by the Spirit, can be left undiscussed here. What is clear is the connection between reception of the Spirit, walking by the Spirit (Gal 5.25), and the designation "saints." In the letters of Paul and in the Deutero-Paulines, οἱ ἅγιοι has become a

---

[212] Cf. the first petition of the Lord's Prayer.

[213] Cf. Dihle 1988, 39–40.

[214] Cf. Westerholm 2013.

[215] See there also for the calling terminology.

[216] This is pointed out especially by Jewett 2007, 113–14.

[217] Cf. e.g., Rom 8.27 where Paul imagines the closeness, indeed the exchange of identities between Spirit and saints, or 1 Cor 6.19: "Your body is the temple of the Holy Spirit, which lives in you" or Rom 12.1: "to present your bodies as living and holy sacrifice." Cf. what was said above on the virtues and spiritual gifts.

[218] On this, cf., by way of introduction, Schnelle 2013.

firm designation, a kind of technical term that designates the community members as a distinct group in relation to those ἔξω (1 Cor 5.12–13).[219] Robert Jewett hypothesizes that in Rom 15.25, 26, 31; 1 Cor 16.1; 2 Cor 8.4; 9.1, 12, we can clearly identify the group that Paul calls "the saints": "When the term 'saints' is used as a description of specific Christian groups in contrast to all Christians, it refers to Jewish Christians, loyal to or associated with Jerusalem."[220] The specified texts refer to the collection for the Christians in Jerusalem. On the other hand, Paul can speak in 1 Cor 14.33 also in a generalizing way of "all the communities of the saints."

In summary, we can say that the ethically focused concept of holiness leads in the Pauline and Deutero-Pauline letters to an internal group designation. It is exclusive and at this point functions in a similar way as the concepts of discipleship or imitation. Here too, the highest standards are set. The correspondence formula is used for both the concept of perfection and the concept of holiness.

### 3.5 Justice

Like goodness, perfection, and holiness, justice is a decisive predicate of God and thus at the same time also the decisive criterion for correct human action. The fact that justice played a corresponding role in the ancient Near East and in the legal and philosophical discourses of Greco-Roman antiquity can be presupposed here.[221] For the theology of the Old Testament, Hermann Spieckermann and Reinhard Feldmeier pointedly state that "righteousness has a place at the center of Old Testament theology."[222] It is also the basis of the New Testament understanding of God and at the same time an early Christian key category for the behavior of human beings. In the words of Spieckermann and Feldmeier once again, "Paul, like the whole New Testament, understands it to be self-evident that God is just in his judgment."[223] The different New Testament concepts of justice can just as little be presented here as the Pauline theology of justification.[224] It is uncontroversial that the theological-anthropological conception of justice represents the only *comprehensive* concept in the New Testament writings

---

[219] Woodward 1981 demonstrates the Jewish background of the expression.

[220] Jewett 2007, 114. In the group in Rom 16.5 Jewett postulates Jewish Christians who called themselves "saints."

[221] Cf., by way of introduction, Witte 2012.

[222] Feldmeier/Spieckermann 2011, 287 (GV = 2010, 287).

[223] Feldmeier/Spieckermann 2011, 298 (GV = 2010, 299).

[224] δικαιοσύνη is the main theme of Romans, an important theme in the other letters of Paul, and also in the Gospel of Matthew. Something similar can be said for the verb δικαιοῦν. For orientation, see Wolter/Niebuhr/Theobald 2013.

that is comparable in reach and significance to the concept of ἀγάπη.[225]
This distinguishes justice from the motifs of goodness, perfection, and
holiness, which represent only theological partial aspects. In our context,
the concern is therefore with the *single* question: *How do the two great
concepts of justice and love relate to each other?*[226] On the one hand, there
is a close relationship between love and justice. On the other hand, there is
a basic tension. Both, relatedness and tension, are thematized in the New
Testament in several classic texts.

Let us begin with the Gospels. Love, spelled out as mercy, goodness,
affection, and forgiveness, determines the behavior of the father toward the
"lost son" in the example story of Luke 15.11–32. The narrative obtains its
argumentative depth through the fact that alongside the father as the bearer
of goodness, two sons act as protagonists. First, the "lost son" is in focus,
who is portrayed as a sinner. The evangelist places the narrative under the
theme "one sinner who repents (μετανοεῖν)" (v. 10). In the narrative itself
this repentance is commented on metaphorically in the highest form of
intensification when the father says in conclusion, "Your brother was dead
and has come back to life." The other son then becomes the focal point. He
is portrayed as the prototype of the just human being, who demands, however, reward for his justice, which he experiences as a burden. He reacts
with anger to the forgiveness of the younger son and insists on distributive
justice in the apportionment of gifts. He has received nothing for his correct behavior as son, whereas the misconduct of the lost son meets with
love from the father instead of with the revocation of gifts.[227] With this
there is a juxtaposition of repentance and fatherly love and forgiveness,
on the one hand, and a materially justified demand for the prizing of good
behavior, on the other hand. The narrator makes clear that the demand for
just treatment is not wrong (v. 31), but it misses the situation.

> **15.32** It is necessary *to be happy* and *to rejoice*, for this brother of yours
> was dead and has come to life, and he was lost and has been found.

Justice is not annulled but exceeded through love in the form of forgiveness and mercy. The appropriate reaction is not the enduring demand for
the rewarding of justice, which is placed in the vicinity of the destructive emotion of envy in the story, but the positive emotion of joy, which
also plays a role in the virtue catalogs. Luke 15 is another love story, this

---

[225] By comparison, the other concepts—discipleship, goodness, perfection, and
holiness—represent partial concepts.

[226] Thematically, see Ricoeur 1996.

[227] On this, cf. Fitzmyer 1983, 1091–92; Wolter 2017, 256–59 (GV = 2008, 539–41).

time not related to the emotional relationship between Jesus and individual women and "friends" but in the literary framework of a parable to the relationship between father and son.

Matthew thematizes similar conflicts in the parable of the workers in the vineyard in 20.1–16. The landowner promises as a wage "ὅ δίκαιον" (v. 4). In the logic of the narrative, the promise of a just wage forms the basis for the work of the day laborers. But what is just? The workers who worked longer and receive the same—negotiated—wage as those who worked for a shorter time argue with reference to the absence of equality when they accuse the landowner: "You have made them equal (ἴσος) with us" (v. 12). The workers experience the equal payment for different work as a burden, as unequal treatment, and thus as injustice. The landowner assumes that justice is guaranteed, since he has not broken his wage promise. In his reply, however, he brings in goodness as an argument: "Is your eye evil (πονηρός), because I am good or benevolent (ἀγαθός)?" (v. 15). In this narrative, goodness occupies the place of mercy and fatherly love in Luke 15; the destructive emotion of envy as a result of a one-sided striving for justice is explicated clearly. Neither text calls justice into question. It is not only the landowner who emphasizes his justice by pointing to the just wage, but also the father when he says to the older son: "All that is mine is yours" (Luke 15.31). Only on the enduring foundation of just behavior in the sense of *iustitia distributiva* or ἰσότης is love possible as the exceeding of this justice in goodness or mercy or forgiveness. Justice forms the basic concept in both texts, without which relationships of every kind would not be possible. Love, however, is the expansion or also the exceeding of justice. Both stories establish the implicit double thesis: love stands over justice insofar as it transcends justice. In a conflict between justice and love, love has the last word. Love, however, is not opposed to justice and does not annul justice as the basic constellation of life together. Both narratives prize neither the abandonment of justice through mere love nor the establishment of justice in the sense of punishment and acknowledgment of achievement, but they prize forgiving love and goodness.

Justice is the theological theme of Romans.[228] Paul engages with this topic as he knows it as "old" interpretation from the Bible of Israel and sets forth a new, so to speak, "current" interpretation that corresponds to the νῦν καιρός (3.26). He shares the basic conviction of the Bible of Israel that God himself has established what is right[229] (δικαιοσύνη θεοῦ

---

[228] On the question of the central themes or central subject matter of Romans, cf. Wischmeyer 2012e, 286–90 (ET = 2012d, 250–53).

[229] The predicate of God "just" is used by Paul only in Rom 3.26. His theme is injustice (Rom 3.10) and the new justice of human beings.

as justice of God) and that human beings are obligated to keep what is right (δικαιοσύνη θεοῦ as justice of human beings before God).[230] This conviction is also the basis of Rom 13.1–7. Paul also shares the conviction and experience of the writers of Israel that human beings are time and again guilty in relation to what is right and that God is to be understood from the outset not only as the just one but also as the merciful one. The last idea opens up for Paul the possibility of presenting his own interpretation of God's justice "in Christ." He develops his interpretation against the double background of the "justice and mercy of God," which he shares with the religious writers of early Judaism and emerging Christianity. His own thesis on justice is that a new situation has come into being vis-à-vis the old covenant. God's justice (δικαιοσύνη θεοῦ) is revealed "now" *in the gospel* (Rom 1.17). This thesis entails different aspects. I mention only six points here.[231] First, the gospel takes the place of the law. It is not the Torah that offers justice[232] but the gospel as a communication of the new justice, "which counts before God." Second, Paul himself becomes part of the context of the justice of God, since he, the proclaimer of this gospel, is in the world of the *imperium Romanum*. Third, this new interpretation of justice entails at the same time a fundamental statement about time. The new justice, which is the subject matter of the Pauline gospel, is inaugurated since the redemption through Christ (Rom 3.26: ἐν τῷ νῦν καιρῷ), i.e., it is a message for the present of Paul and his addressees. Fourth, Paul interprets the death of Jesus as a sacrificial death "for all who believe" (3.22) and at the same time as proof of the love of God (5.6–8). This is the theological center of the new interpretation: God's *justice* finds its fulfillment in an extremely paradoxical deed of *love*: in handing over his only—beloved—Son as atonement for the injustice of human beings. Paul replaces, on the basis of earliest community tradition,[233] mercy through love. God's mercy could deal with the injustice of human beings without God—the just and merciful one—being touched himself. "Now," however, a new situation has arisen. Unlike what is the case with his mercy,

---

[230] This applies especially to Israel: The Israelites have the privilege of the law (Rom 9.4). In Rom 1 and 2, Paul makes clear, however, that "the law" as inner law also applies to non-Israelites—with the result that the "gentiles" are also guilty, since they do not fulfill the law.

[231] The earlier forms of the revelation of the justice of God are the "good" creation (Rom 1 and 2) and the law.

[232] Paul indicates in Rom 1.18–31 that this applies not merely "since Christ" but since creation. This also applies, however, since the gift of the law. This is the actual difficulty for Paul. He engages at multiple points with the law's inability to let justice come to humans, especially in Romans 2, 3, and 7.

[233] Wischmeyer 2012c.

God's love affects God himself at the core when he hands over his Son into death. God himself is now deeply affected. The decisive impulse for the development of the later Christology lies here. Fifth, in connection with the new interpretation of the justice of God, Paul sets forth a new hierarchy of values. God's power fulfills itself in love. The double character of the justice of demand and punishment—i.e., the aspect of power and violence that is indispensable for every conception of justice—is thus redefined as renunciation of the practice of violence. Sixth, the new justice, since it is connected to the fulfillment of the law and thus no longer an ethical-cultic quality, is also reenvisaged as a love that answers to God's deed of love, i.e., as a relationship that in formal terms sets aside a person's own interests, including the insistence on social and legal justice, to the benefit of the other. The new life in the Spirit is therefore described as the interplay of different spiritual gifts and loving attitudes and not as a new code of conduct.

In summary, the relationship between justice and love in Paul can be defined as follows: δικαιοσύνη is the linguistic sign for the good and ordered constitution of the creation, to which human beings are meant to correspond. Justice as good order is never up for renegotiation. It is grounded in God himself. Instead, it is the establishment and fulfillment of justice among human beings in general and in Israel in particular that has failed for Paul:

**Rom 3.10** No one is just, not even one.[234]

God cannot annul justice, but he also cannot establish it among human beings through the Torah. Instead, he fulfills it himself by sacrificing his Son. Through this there arises room for forgiveness, repentance, and new conduct in the Spirit. The divine act of love enables human beings to possess the status (not the reality: that remains reserved for the eschaton) of the just and even to live in accordance with love, through which God has bestowed life to them. Thus, justice is fulfilled in love and at the same time exceeded, though not abolished as the standard of the divine order.

Another tension between justice and love emerges at precisely this point. While the members of the Christ-confessing communities are to practice love in the form of the renunciation of the establishment of their own interests and rights,[235] this exceeding of justice is not practiced outside

---

[234] Eccl 7.20.

[235] See above. Paul gives an especially touching example in his letter to Philemon. In vv. 8–10 Paul renounces his right "to command" Philemon and instead "entreats" him διὰ τὴν ἀγάπην.

the community. There the demand for justice in the sense of a government legal system that works with the instruments of demand and punishment continues to be in force. How should the community members behave in relation to this intervention from the side of the imperium? Paul addresses this exact problem in Rom 13.1–7[236]—namely, from the quite specific perspective of the Christ-confessing missionary and his communities.

Under the line of questioning of love and justice, the text, which has already been discussed, obtains an additional dimension. Rom 13 reads like an *insertion into the argumentation of love*, which determines chapters 12–15.13. In his insertion Paul takes into account the fact that outside the communities, life together continues to take place according to the demanding and punitive justice—i.e., so to speak, in temporal delay *before* the revelation of the new justice of God—which he characterizes here, as often, as the avoidance of evil (13.3, 4). He does not question here how justice can still be produced at all outside of the order of love of the communities, for he is, after all, convinced that the demands of justice cannot in principle be fulfilled by anyone. Rather, the question is quite practically how the communities should relate to the demands and penal system of the state authority, since this reaches with its claims, norms, and demands into the social structure of the communities and into the lives of the community members. This occurs above all in two spheres—in the judicial system and in the form of taxation. Rom 13.1–7 is neither a contribution to the description of the "new justice from faith in Jesus Christ" nor a reflection on the Roman conception of government and law and its practical effects, let alone on the imperium as such. Instead, it functions as a practical rule of behavior and as a psychological support for the community members. The subject of Paul's inquiry is (only) how the community members are meant to behave toward the external governmental ordering structure that continues to form the large framework and general life reality within which the communities are located with their own ordering structures. Paul has the choice between a positive and a negative recommendation. The positive answer would call for or establish obedience, continuity, or even conformity. The negative recommendation, by contrast, would—correctly from a theological perspective—establish discontinuity between the governmental demand for justice and the gospel's new order of love and present disobedience or expatriation from society

---

[236] Cf., in general, Krauter 2009. On the one hand, Krauter reads Rom 13 "as, within contemporary political discourse, a largely conventional affirmation of rule and . . . subordination." On the other hand, he diagnoses "a distance toward political rule and a dedication to a way of life in the fellowship of the Christians that is shaped by the standard of love" (272–73). Important is Krauter's pointer that 12.14, 17–21 is the argumentative answer to 13.1–7. Cf. Wischmeyer 2004c.

as the solution. This, in turn, could lead via religious-literary dualistic apocalyptic scenarios[237] to armed struggle between state powers and the communities. Paul chooses the former possibility. He starts from God as the Lord of all state powers and authorities and describes the order of the state explicitly as a divinely legitimated legal order that pursues the goal of preserving what is right (13.1, 4)—to this extent Paul is in harmony with Greco-Roman theories of the state[238]—though it merely has the status of a servant, i.e., does not have its own significance and does not rule. In his argument, Paul conspicuously avoids the term "justice," which has, after all, new content for Christ-confessors, and instead makes recourse to the formal concept of the good. The one who does good—and this applies especially to the members of the Christ-confessing communities, as he has explained in detail in chapter 12—has, according to the legal order of God, which stands over the state[239] authorities, nothing to fear. This means that Paul regards the order of love and the order of the good or the just in the sphere of the state as compatible *from his perspective*.[240]

He thus argues *against* fear (13.3–4) and *for* freedom in doing good. At this point, the Roman community members receive insight into the self-understanding of the Christ-confessing Jew Paul, citizen from Tarsus, and possibly bearer of Roman citizenship.[241] Paul constructs neither a political or social nor a religious and specifically apocalyptically grounded opposition between the state authorities and the Christ-confessors. The latter act in a *good* way when they follow the laws, since both the penal law and the tax laws correspond to divine arrangements (13.2). The assurance that the governing authorities are instruments of God gives Paul the freedom and courage (παρρησία) that he repeatedly proves in his missionary activity in relation to the state and civic authorities. Should the presentation of Acts be historically accurate in conveying that Paul claimed the right of a Roman citizen for himself, then this appeal would be the best example for his own behavior in relation to the Roman authorities. Paul insists on equal status and on his right to be part of the legal order of the *imperium Romanum*.

---

[237] Mark 13; Revelation.

[238] Cf. Krauter 2009, 238–39.

[239] These are in reality usually civic authorities.

[240] It is clear that Paul argues from a different perspective in 1 Cor 5 and 6. There he argues for the active configuration of the order of love within the communities. The community members are to remain in the communities and maintain no false outside contacts, neither with persons who do not live in the order of love nor with the courts. By contrast, in Rom 13 the concern is with the question of how community members should behave when state authorities become active and intervene in the lives of the community members.

[241] Cf. the good discussion of the theme of "the Roman Paul" in Krauter 2009, 90–98.

Paul is the New Testament writer who fundamentally thought through the theme of justice and love from the perspective of the gospel of Jesus Christ and set forth the order of love as the *current form* of the revelation of God and the answer of human beings:

**Rom 13.8** Therefore, love is the fulfillment of the law.

How far does this perspective reach? In the adjoining text Rom 13.10–14, it becomes clear that Paul looked to the near future:

**Rom 13.11** And act in such a way, because you know the time: the hour has already come for you to rise from sleep, for our salvation is now nearer than when we came to faith.

For the short time that remained—according to Paul's understanding of time—until the return of the Lord, the tension between the order of love, as Paul wanted to establish it in the communities, and the order of the Roman state could be endured. In Rom 13 Paul recommends a reconciliatory solution between justice and love within the framework of his imminent expectation. The longer-term irreconcilability of the two orders already became evident, however, in his lifetime. The Neronian persecution and the execution of Paul showed very quickly the limits of this view of the state authorities. The communities, whose members did what was good, did not receive approval from the state (13.3). Paul, who did nothing illegal, was executed. The theological solution that Paul sought to find for the state authorities foundered. The conflict between justice in the sense of state legislation and the communities and their order of love was not resolved.

### 4. Love between Theology, Communitarian Ethos, Emotion, and Eschaton

The concept of love in the books of the New Testament is equally comprehensive and bold in its religious dimension and its theological basis. It is open in the formulation of its ethical claim and eschatological perspective and yet simultaneously limited in its societal reach. It is close to the texts of Israel and early Judaism, on the one hand, and not always far removed from texts of philosophical ethics and doctrine of emotions in the imperial period, on the other hand, and yet as an overall concept, it is indeed new and independent. In its combination of traditional and innovative elements, it represents a distinct hybrid concept type in the historical crosshairs of early Judaism and the Hellenistic-Roman urban world and its philosophical schools. In distinction from philosophical conceptions in the early imperial period, the early Christian concept is embedded in the new institution of the ἐκκλησίαι Χριστοῦ, as Paul conceptualized it and called it into life. The practical institutional side of the early Christian concept of love may not be neglected in favor of a theological or ethical accentuation. Part of the effective power and attraction of the early Christian concept lies in its programmatic and practical social-institutional dimension.

The comparison with the neighboring or opposing destructive and constructive entities has shown that love, in the understanding of the New Testament writers, is always *constructive*. It does no wrong to the neighbor (Rom 13.10);[242] it keeps no record of wrongs (1 Cor 13.5); it does not rejoice over evil (1 Cor 13.6). It is always operative in a way that preserves or promotes life. This applies in a special and at the same time paradoxical way in connection with the death of Jesus. It is an expression of the love of God and of the love of Christ for human beings and opens up life for them.

Love shares this constructive character with a series of other modes of behavior and ethical-emotional concepts. Love is not the only constructive form of life. It can be placed alongside virtues or appear as a virtue or emotion among others. In Paul it "fulfills" the law with its ethical demands. Love as an expression of the nature of God, as a cipher for his history of love with human beings, and as a description of the *reciprocity* of the relationship of God to human beings and of human beings to God is *singular* and the *greatest* among the virtues, charisms, and emotions. Here, love transcends the other constructive entities and has its own status

---

[242] This does not exclude the possibility that cruelty may be practiced in the name of love. May 2011, 114, points out that cruelty does not belong to the seven deadly sins. His sharp criticism of the examples of cruelty that the Christian church has practiced itself or tolerated is entirely justified. Cruelty is, however, not an immanent or latent element of the New Testament concept of love, as May suspects. It remains to be considered that New Testament anthropology does not know the ethical demand for the fundamental physical integrity of the body: see Jesus' fate of death and the Pauline peristasis catalogs. Bodily suffering on the basis of cruel treatment belonged to the unquestioned reality of Roman punishment by the police as well as to the treatment of slaves and children and was part of the contemporary lived realty and world of experience. The fact that cruelty was not ethically stigmatized in the way that it is in part of Western civilization and its judicial system is evident from the metaphorical language that runs through the New Testament writings from Jesus to the apocalypticist John. This comes to vivid expression in 1 Cor 13.3 ("and if I let my body be burned," used by Paul in the sense of a metaphor for the highest spiritual achievement but precisely in contrast to love). However, the fact that cruelty was suffered more than it was practiced by Jews (4 Maccabees) and Christ-confessors is also important. Fourth Maccabees makes clear that the answer to cruelty toward the body resided in the demonstration of courage and steadfastness. The cruelty itself was a reality, even though it is rhetorically exaggerated in 4 Maccabees. Not only Seneca, in *De ira*, opposes cruelty, but also Philo (e.g., in *Prov.* 2.15). On this topic, cf. now also Wischmeyer 2020, 193.

beyond ethics and charisms. It alone has an eschatological character: in the eschaton one no longer hopes and believes but sees and is "known" and *loved*. On this basis, love obtains its incomparable luminous power.

Love is *theological Grunddatum (fundamental basis)*, communitarian *ethos*, *emotion*, and bridge into the *eschaton*. Rather than standing in opposition to one another or alongside one another, these four aspects, *in the framework of the narrative of the love of God*, form the distinct concept of love in the New Testament.

# 6

# *The Concept of* Agape *and Current Conceptions of Love*

## 1. Introduction: Comparative Criticism as Metahistorical Interpretive Method

In this chapter I will juxtapose the results of the historical reconstruction of *agape* as an early Christian concept with some prominent conceptions of "love" in the present in order to sharpen the New Testament profile of love once more from the perspective of contemporary conditions of understanding. This procedure is rather uncommon in the sphere of historical hermeneutics and therefore must be justified in somewhat greater detail.

In chapters 1–4 I have reconstructed and interpreted the New Testament concept of love from the relevant texts. The *method* was textual exegesis[1] with the goal of textual explanation.[2] The *theoretical framework* was historical hermeneutics, whose goal is the understanding, description, and interpretation of texts from the past by considering as completely as possible the linguistic and ideational conditions of the time of the texts and their contexts. Finally, the heuristic conceptualization of the different New Testament texts and their contributions to the theme of "love" *gave shape to the structure* of these chapters. From the perspective of exegesis and historical hermeneutics, the understanding of the texts on love/loving in the New Testament has come to an end. Historical hermeneutics does not subject its texts to a critical material analysis (*Sachanalyse*) from the scholarly perspective of the *present*. It does not engage critically in terms of substance with the normative claim of the texts,[3] nor

---

[1] Cf. Pollmann et al. 2009.
[2] Cf. Erbele-Küster et al. 2009.
[3] The engagement with the normative components takes place in the history of reception and *Wirkungsgeschichte*. In the sense of reception history and *Wirkungsgeschichte*, it makes sense to understand the writings of the New Testament as a unity.

does it understand these texts to be at least potential dialogue partners in the present or interpret the texts in the context of a contemporary theoretical model.[4] Instead, historical hermeneutics seeks to understand the statement world (*Aussagenwelt*) of its texts in their contemporary historical contexts, *precisely without* setting it in relation to the present and its practical, moral, intellectual, and scholarly standards, i.e., the lifeworld and thought world of the exegetes. Categories of understanding are the historical gap, authorial intention, or—if the figure of authorial intention is rejected—the shaping group behind the texts, the distinct world of the texts, and above all "the foreign," the difference: all this must be respected if one does not only want to hear or read oneself at the end of the arduous exegesis. Here, the texts are consciously kept at a distance from the interpreter. But is everything that is necessary for understanding the concept of *agape* already done with this? Is the claim of this concept adequately presented? This question merits special consideration, which begins with a reflection on the reach of New Testament exegetically based textual interpretation.

The procedure of historical hermeneutics practiced in historical text-based research is the leading model of New Testament scholarship,[5] whose specific understanding of scholarship continues to be decisively shaped by the historical paradigm of the Tübingen school. Nevertheless, time and again, this model strikes up against limits in the case of canonized or so-called holy texts, especially when they form the basis of current large and influential religions, such as Judaism, Christianity, Islam, and Hinduism, to name only the most important. Instead of a clash of civilizations, one could speak here of a clash of various truth claims, namely, in a double sense. The canonical texts—here the Christian Bible—make moral claims and claims to explain the world that are regarded as obsolete in present-day scholarship and therefore are no longer thematized a priori.[6] At this

---

[4] A possible example would be the sociological system theory of Niklas Luhmann. Another would be the psychoanalytic interpretation of Julia Kristeva. On historical hermeneutics and criticism of this paradigm for dealing with texts, cf. Angehrn et al. 2009, which also includes literature on the criticism of historical hermeneutics.

[5] Cf. Wischmeyer 2003. This judgment and the underlying view of the discipline are certainly to be understood from a German exegetical perspective. The debate over the methods of the discipline in *JBL* 133, no. 2, June 2014 JBL Forum (on postmodern studies and New Testament scholarship) shows, by way of example, how differently, for example, the North American discussion proceeds, especially with respect to its historical references and its current dialogue partners.

[6] The dilemma of scholarly theology in the present community of scholarships and their institutions, especially of systematic theology, lies here. Theology can communicate in a scholarly way only with the fields of textual scholarship, historical scholarship, and ethics. The encyclicals of Pope Benedict XVI occupy a position that has received much

point, the post-Bultmann situation in New Testament studies differs fundamentally from the time of Bultmann and his school. Bultmann could refer to the existential analysis of Heidegger and had with this an instrument of general scholarly communication at his disposal, with the help of which he could present fundamental statements of the New Testament on anthropology in a scholarly accepted language and bring it into the academic anthropological discussion. This possibility of employing New Testament texts and themes on the material level in the scholarly discussion of "truth" or descriptions of reality and thus "to bring to language" their own claim has been lost in the course of post-existential philosophy and the succession of different postmodern turns. With this, however, a fundamental aspect of the statements of these texts for the scholarly discussion is also lost in the present—the part that makes a truth claim and provokes one to a material discussion.

A further dilemma in the scholarly context is presented by the different and ultimately mutually exclusive explanatory and normative claims of the different holy scriptures, which are taught and interpreted today alongside one another at academic educational institutions. Material discussions between the religions and their theoretical agents, however, do not get beyond—if they engage with one another at all—the mode of mutual respect. One thing applies equally, however, to Christian and Islamic scriptural theology, which is the main concern here. In today's scholarly world, the claim of the holy texts goes off into nothing. In the interreligious controversies over world explanation and the norming of life conduct since the Enlightenment, the instruments of polemic and apologetics have become just as blunt as in the controversies with philosophy and the theology.

In both spheres, the scholarly and the religious, there is at present no scholarly forum for material discussions of theological themes. New Testament scholars of the post-Bultmann period—to limit the radius of the circle of themes of the present study—have in general reacted pragmatically to this fact and largely withdraw themselves from these questions from the outset by concentrating on the historical paradigm of investigation described above and leaving possible material controversies to the systematic-ethical disciplines of theology.[7] Despite this, a perceptible hermeneutical lack remains in the case of the contemporary business of

---

attention. On a philosophical-dogmatic basis, they represent the claim to provide a scholarly and communicable explanation of the world, which includes the setting of ethical norms.

[7] This does not apply to the monograph of Landmesser 1999. Landmesser seeks such engagement here from the side of New Testament scholarship on the basis of the term "truth."

historical analysis and textual explanation—the lack of *material* engagement with the texts that have canonical status or are as so-called eminent texts part of our intellectual traditions. In this way, however, the most important dimension of the texts is removed from interpretation—namely, their claim to the "truth" of their world-interpretation. This means that precisely the eminent texts are made accessible neither to a methodologically guided material appreciation nor to a corresponding criticism.

It is above all male and female exegetes from the Anglophone and French-speaking lands and from the so-called Global South who have reacted to this lack. In the larger frame of reference of contextual hermeneutics[8] and new readings,[9] the hermeneutical biblical studies paradigm centered on historical reconstruction and authorial intention has been expanded and also changed. Contextual hermeneuts start from the questions, hardships, and experiences of their cultural, social, and material tradition world and lifeworld and *read* (not exegete) the biblical texts in these contexts. Their perspectives determine the agenda of the reading of the texts. Amid all criticism that meets the texts from power, gender, body, colonial, ethnicity, race, class, cultural, and regional perspectives, these readings nevertheless continue to refer to the Bible or to biblical texts as *normative* texts, which they either find helpful for their lines of questioning and bring into their ecclesial and societal discussions in new interpretation or criticize as kyriarchal texts (Schüssler Fiorenza). In particular, the models of critical reading in the sense of feminist, so-called third world, or postcolonial hermeneutics, to name especially successful new hermeneutics, only make sense in relation to texts that are understood to be normative, whose enduring power is meant to be destroyed or modernized. This criticism is not focused primarily on understanding the texts but on changing one's own lifeworld, and it uses the authority of the texts, which continues to be reclaimed in principle, for this goal.[10] A material critical engagement with the texts occurs here, but as an internal critical engagement within the framework of specific limited interests that are not subjected to further critical discussion, for which the texts are used—in short, in an instrumentalizing form that is far removed from the ethos of scholarship. However, all internal church, internal theological, or at least theologically interested contextual hermeneutics and applicative Bible cultures reach their limits at the point where the normative claim of religion, theology, and the Bible is viewed as obsolete, i.e., in the whole

---

[8] Cf. Körtner 2009.

[9] Cf. Runesson 2009.

[10] The fact that the categories of reception and readers are leading here does not require further discussion in this context.

sphere of contemporary cultural and social studies[11] as well as in post-religious (above all Western) or foreign religious contexts as a whole.

As we have shown, however, this is not only the problem of engaged versions of reading[12] but the great problem of *all* contemporary biblical exegesis and biblical hermeneutics. Precisely where these disciplines, for their part, open themselves to the discourse of poststructuralist and deconstructive scholarly perspectives, an answer is lacking from the side of other forms of scholarship. For the most part, there is no material exchange between the theological or religious studies[13] disciplines, on the one hand, and cultural, social, and political studies, on the other hand, since the latter are based without discussion on a decidedly post-Christian, post-religious—and sometimes also post-philosophical—worldview.[14]

This critical material engagement, however, *must* take place. But the forums at which theological concepts must ultimately be measured and prove themselves are not (or are no longer) held in the sphere of academic discussions but in the societal realm, in politics, in the media, and in the church. There, recourse can (and must) be made to the results of academic work.

Against the background of what has been said, it becomes clear why I do not follow the approach of contextual hermeneutics. I am bound in terms of scholarly approach to historical hermeneutics in textual analysis and textual explanation[15] with the limitation bound up with it, i.e., the obligation to understanding description without critical material engagement. Exegesis, as I practice it here, works neither applicatively nor normatively but analytically and explicatively. It has its place in the academic sphere. This does not mean, however, that the texts I explain must be read exclusively in the mode of the past, i.e., in the historical-hermeneutical coordinate system. The interpretation[16] of eminent texts of the past—whether Plato, the New Testament, Augustine, or Luther—can, as Gadamer stressed, be connected with a certain material sympathy. Instead of "sympathy," I would prefer to speak of "expectation" or "interest" and to start from the assumption that through the historical work of the reconstruction of past textual worlds, something can be disclosed

---

[11] This fact is not mentioned in the contributions in *JBL* 133, no. 2, June 2014.

[12] Here, the shift of meaning of *Leseart* is very characteristic—from a version of the text to a version of interpretation.

[13] On this, cf. the critical remarks in Schlögl 2013, 10.

[14] The *Lexikon der Bibelhermeneutik* (Wischmeyer 2013a) aims to bridge this gap. However, the lexicon is only a first step on the path to the attempt to bring theology in the form of biblical studies into the great contemporary discourses.

[15] Cf. Wischmeyer 2009c.

[16] Cf. Kreuzer et al. 2009.

that is indeed foreign and other and yet also important and connected with a great *Wirkungsgeschichte* — something with which it is worth-while or necessary to engage in a critical-interpretive way also under the intellectual conditions of the present.[17] The "expectation" is that the early Christian texts are not only cultural-historical *documents* but also *roots* of cultural identity, whose explanatory potential is not restricted to past constellations but indeed reaches into the present. What helps in getting to this insight is not only the history of ideas[18] but especially *the reception-historical perspective*,[19] which pursues the interpretation of the texts into the present and understands its own interpretation[20] as part of this reception. Reception is not concluded but is always subject, also as historical work, to the conditions of understanding of its time and thus already evokes the next interpretation. This model of interpreta-tion makes it possible in another step to confront the — usually implic-itly held — present-day presuppositions or scholarly frames in an explicit manner with the different aspects of historical contextualizing interpreta-tion in order to delineate more sharply the contours of the understanding of the exegetes or interpreters themselves. What is gained thereby is a kind of self-enlightenment of the exegesis and interpretation, which not only draws out the early Christian concept of love from the present-day perspective but also brings into consciousness the present-day coordi-nates of understanding of what love can be under present-day conditions of understanding.

Contemporary social studies, cultural studies, and post-historical his-torical studies[21] provide many interpretive models or theories[22] that address the theme of *love* and its texts and social forms and in doing so also draw historical lines. Here, we find adjoining structures that sharpen once more the contours of the early Christian concept of love under the conditions of understanding of the present and update the interpretation of the concept. I will therefore concisely sketch out important current approaches to the theme of love in the humanities and social sciences as I did previously

[17] Cf. Wischmeyer/Hiller 2009. See there Wischmeyer's criticism of the thesis that *Einverständnis* (agreement or consent) is a presupposition for understanding. The insight that criticism — and if need be rejection — is a form of understanding and thus a hermeneuti-cal procedure stands against this view. Cf. Behrens et al. 2009.

[18] This is shown for our theme above by works such as that of Simon May.

[19] On this, cf. now Becker/Scholz 2014.

[20] Cf. Wischmeyer 2009e.

[21] For an introduction, see Jordan 2009.

[22] Theory is not understood here in the sense of the natural sciences but in a sociologi-cal way as the interpretation of social phenomena with the help of experience and theoretical explanatory models.

with the counter- and parallel conceptions from the time of the New Testament texts. In doing so, my aim is to present the conceptual methods and interests with which *love* is currently interpreted and made culturally or sociopolitically relevant. The selection of authors must necessarily be very limited.[23] The sequence is determined to some extent by the publication date of the contributions, but, on the whole, the conceptions are simply placed alongside one another.[24] Finally, I attempt to confront the—predominantly post-Christian—contributions to the discourse on love once more with the early Christian concept of love. Here, it becomes evident that the early Christian conception of love is an eminent and—as Julia Kristeva in particular makes clear—a literarily and anthropologically successful narrative, which claims its own logic in relation to philosophical or sociological judgments.

## 2. Present-Day Concepts of Love

### 2.1 Love as Medium of Communication: Sociological System Theory (Niklas Luhmann)

Niklas Luhmann has written about the phenomenon of love from a system-sociological perspective at least since 1969. In the framework of his theory of social systems,[25] Luhmann describes love as a central means of communication. In this way he places the phenomenon of love rigorously in the social context and interprets it on the basis of its functions in society.[26] Luhmann deepens the consistently sociological perspective historically. He assumes that "during the course of the social system's evolution, there is an increase in the complexity of society, and of the world it is able to sustain internally"[27] and that in the course of differentiation "greater use

---

[23] Important contributions from the past thirty years that cannot be discussed here are Barthes 2010 (French = 1977); Alberoni 1983 (Italian = 1979); Ariès/Béjin 1986 (GV = 1984); Foucault 1988 (French = 1984); Irigaray 2002. This also applies to recent contributions such as Singer 2009; Nussbaum 2013; Tömmel 2013; May 2019. See also the bibliography in Helm 2017. For the seminal work of Nygren 1982, see Wischmeyer 2015a.

[24] Certain temporal differences are present. Thus, Luhmann's texts are already modern "classics," Beck's stocktaking mirrors the time of the 1980s, and Nussbaum's societal plea is already overhauled by new developments, though these do go in the direction of her demands.

[25] Luhmann 1967.

[26] Luhmann 1984. For his preparatory work, see Luhmann 2010 (GV = 2008). In what follows, I refer above all to Luhmann 2010 (GV = 2008).

[27] Luhmann 2010, 19 (GV = 2008, 25).

is made of communication media."[28] The notions of love react "to their respective society."[29]

Luhmann's historical sketch need not be reproduced here. Certain aspects, however, merit special mention. Luhmann finds two opposing societal concepts of love in the European tradition. He takes the first concept from Greek antiquity. There, *philia* is said to have been a "constituting feature of society itself" in the sense of solidarity and *amicitia*.[30] Luhmann does not discuss the early Christian ἀγάπη concept, which has shaped European culture in such a lasting way.[31] His appraisal of the second, opposing conception of love, which prevailed at the latest since the invention of *amour passion* is interesting:

> Evolutionary success lay in the opposite direction, not in universalization, but rather in the constraining and mobilization of the medium; not in loving everyone, but in loving a random, chosen other person. The conception of love that does this is created from the end of the Middle Ages onwards and becomes dominant in modernity.[32]

For the early Christian concept of love Luhmann's historical judgment means that it is compatible with the Greek concept insofar as it is a concept of fellowship. Modernity has distanced itself from such concepts in favor of "reflexivity."[33]

According to Luhmann, the modern concept also has effects on the role of sexuality—another aspect that is of interest for the early Christian ἀγάπη concept. "Along with the impassioning of love, the sexual relationship between lovers also acquires an altered status."[34] According to Luhmann's diagnoses, in the modern concept sexuality is integrated into the communicative medium of love, which "thus takes over a social function that goes far beyond the function of bearing offspring." "Sexuality acquires a basic function in the case of love,"[35] which is based on its bodily

---

[28] Luhmann 2010, 19 (GV = 2008, 26).

[29] Luhmann 2008, 27; cf. 2010, 21.

[30] Luhmann 2010, 23 (GV = 2008, 29). Luhmann refers to the historical study of Dirlmeier 1931.

[31] He also does not mention *eros*.

[32] Luhmann 2010, 24 (GV = 2008, 30–31).

[33] Luhmann 2010, 32 (GV = 2008, 38). Cf. the definition on p. 34 (GV = 40): "What it involves is a corresponding feeling being affirmed and sought in the realm of feelings. It involves loving oneself as the one who loves and is loved—in other words, it involves directing one's feelings toward this co-incidence of feelings." Cf. Luhmann 1986, 138.

[34] Luhmann 2010, 36 (GV = 2008, 42).

[35] Luhmann 2010, 37 (GV = 2008, 43).

dimension.[36] Or as Luhmann also formulates the matter: "Sexuality forces one into a non-dissociable mode of involvement"[37] and thus supports the conception of love as passion. Finally, Luhmann points out that the "autonomization and functional specification of communication media," described by him, cannot "be institutionalized at the level of processes alone (by creating order in the *sequence* of events)."[38] Thus, "passionate love leading to sexual relationships finds in the founding of a family a system that is capable of lasting. This means, specifically, a family based on monogamous marriage."[39]

On the whole, Luhmann's study can be described best with his own words from the introduction to his work *Love as Passion: The Codification of Intimacy*: in accordance with "an overall theory of generalized symbolic media of communication," love is not "treated here as a feeling (or at least only secondarily so), but rather in terms of its constituting a symbolic code, which shows how to communicate effectively in situations where this would otherwise appear improbable."[40] Luhmann is concerned to show that love (*amour passion*) is "a quite normal improbability," whose function in modern society he seeks to specify.[41] He finds this function in the task of "facilitating, cultivating and promoting the communicative treatment of individuality."[42] Thus, for Luhmann, "love as a medium is not itself a feeling, but rather a code of communication, according to the rules of which one can express . . . feelings."[43]

Luhmann's social theory of love makes clear how the modern conception of love differs from premodern conceptions—in his work the focus is primarily on the ancient Greek conception of *philia*. Modern love, understood as passion, serves, in a society that is constantly differentiating and reflecting, as a medium of communication of individuals who actually cannot communicate at all: "Love transmits specific selections by means of orientation towards the individual's own understanding of themselves and the special world-view of another person or several other people."[44] Thus, love as passion has a central role in modern society. By contrast, ancient societies, to which the early Christian

---

[36] Paraphrased as "the organic sphere" in Luhmann 2010, 38 (GV = 2008, 44).

[37] Luhmann 2010, 59 (GV = 2008, 64: "Sexualität zwingt zu unabspaltbar Selbstbeteilung").

[38] Luhmann 2010, 48 (GV = 2008, 54).

[39] Luhmann 2010, 50 (GV = 2008, 55).

[40] Luhmann 1986, 8–9 (GV = 1984, 9).

[41] Luhmann 1986, 9 (GV = 1984, 9).

[42] Luhmann 1986, 14 (GV = 1984, 15).

[43] Luhmann 1986, 20 (GV = 1984, 23).

[44] Luhmann 2010, 14 (GV = 2008, 21).

communities also belonged, were much less differentiated and used love to "make interaction easier," which benefited the members of society in the form of "knowing and feeling comfortable with one another" and of "belonging and mutual support."[45]

Luhmann's theory is itself historically contextualized and therefore compatible with other historical conceptions of love. Although he does not analyze the Jewish–early Christian concept of love, some of the results of his presentation of the Greek *philia* conception can nevertheless be adopted. Like Luhmann's presentation of *philia*, the ἀγάπη conception is community based and functions in different ways as a factor of the stabilization of the Jewish legal community and of the early Christian communities. The lack of the individual dimension of ἀγάπη, which became clear in Paul, can be explained from the pre-complex structure of ancient society.[46] The fact that sexuality receives its own societal function in the modern communication medium of love only with the "impassioning of love"[47] is extremely revealing. With this sociological thesis, the exegetes' defense strategy of wanting to find "good" sexuality in the New Testament texts becomes pointless.

Luhmann's concept of love includes the complete renunciation of a community-based or social function of love, which beyond the stabilization of the all-dominant individuality has even further-reaching social dimensions by means of marriage (*caritas*).

### 2.2 Love as Entirely Normal Chaos: Empirical Sociology (Ulrich Beck and Elisabeth Beck-Gernsheim)

The sociologists Ulrich Beck and Elisabeth Beck-Gernsheim[48] have placed their sociological analysis of the present,[49] which was first published in 1990, under a title that varies and dramatizes Luhmann's statement about the "quite normal improbability"[50] of love—namely, *The Normal Chaos of Love*.[51] Beck and Beck-Gernsheim analyze the change in the understanding of marriage and family as the fundamental societal institutions by

---

[45] Luhmann 2010, 23 (GV = 2008, 30).

[46] Related to "the social differentiation of intimate relationships" (Luhmann 2010, 26; GV = 2008, 32).

[47] Luhmann 2010, 36 (GV = 2008, 42).

[48] Beck/Beck-Gernsheim 1995 (GV = 2012).

[49] While this analysis is focused on the Federal Republic of Germany (cf. the statistical material from the Federal Office of Statistics in the notes), it applies in principle to Western societies, which they define as post-religious.

[50] Luhmann 1986, 9 (GV = 1984, 9).

[51] See Beck/Beck-Gernsheim 1995 (GV = 2012).

interpreting the processes of differentiation, individuation, and emancipation between the sexes as "the historically emerging opposition between love, freedom, and family."[52] Their lead thesis is that the life together of human beings based on love can only "emerge from individual biographies, from discussing and questioning each step, finding new arrangements, meeting new demands, justifying one's decisions, and would have to be protected from the centrifugal forces, the transience which threatens the order of our lives."[53] For the authors, the category that decisively describes the societal change is not (or no longer) the emancipation of women but "individualization."[54] It applies to both sexes and *per definitionem* goes beyond the difference between the sexes. Not only women but also men live first their individual biographies and search only in a second line for partners, partners who, as far as possible, do not change them.

In five chapters there emerges a panorama of contemporary processes of erosions and new formations around the themes of gender roles, relationship questions, attachment and separation, children, marriage, and family after the end of the normative images of marriage and family. Constitutive for the changes in the past sixty years are material and labor-political factors, in connection with the process of the economic, political, and societal emancipation of women, the increasing significance of occupations, and the fragmentation of large families. This massive process of radical change, which Beck and Beck-Gernsheim capture with rhetoric, statistics, and historical nuance, cannot be reproduced here. What is important for our theme is how they specify the role of love in the new paradigm of individuality, of I-ness and authenticity.[55]

The sixth and final chapter is devoted to this theme: "love, our secular religion."[56] At the end of the large sociological presentation, Ulrich Beck attempts to define "the significance of the theme for the post-traditional,

---

[52] Beck/Beck-Gernsheim 2012, 7. Cf. 1995, 1–2.

[53] Beck/Beck-Gernsheim 1995, 4 (GV = 2012, 12).

[54] Beck/Beck-Gernsheim 1995, 4 (GV = 2012, 12). What is important is the indication that individuality as such is not a result of modernity but the democratization of individuality: "In the olden days it was small groups, elite minorities which could afford the luxury of concentrating on their own interests, nowadays the 'risky opportunities' (Heiner Keupp) associated with individualization are being democratized or, putting it more tersely, being brought about by the way we live—in the interplay between prosperity, education, mobility and the like" (ET = 8; GV = 17).

[55] On this, cf. the remarks of Beck-Gernsheim in Beck/Beck-Gernsheim 1995, 53–54 (GV = 2012, 75–76): "The magic formula is known as authenticity" (53/76). And "The motto is 'How To Be Your Own Best Friend'" (54/77). Love for neighbor is not provided for in this model (ET = 180; GV = 238).

[56] Beck/Beck-Gernsheim 1995, 168–201 (GV = 2012, 222–66: "Die irdische Religion der Liebe").

non-religious, individualized lifeworld" of Western societies, especially of German society.[57] Here, Beck's analysis of religion is an important factor. The book reckons with societal relations in which religion in the form of Christian churches is driven out of or withdraws from public life. Beck speaks without further ado of the "post-Christian inner-modern meaning" of love, which he seeks to define,[58] and in this way condemns de facto to nonexistence not only the churches but also the Christianity of Catholic and Protestant Christians as well as its reflective instrument, theology. The growth of Islam, in which distinct conceptions of families, marriage, and love predominate, in the West is not yet in view for the author. Nor does he engage with the phenomenon that Friedrich Wilhelm Graf describes as "the return of the gods."[59] Against the background of Benn's decision for existential nihilism ("the void and the designed self"),[60] Beck asks in a paradoxical manner about "meaning," though now about inner-modern meaning, i.e., immanent meaning. If one does not stumble upon the paradox, one is led into the new role that Beck intends for love: it is "secular religion."[61] Love is the answer to the post-religious quest for meaning. This thesis increases in plausibility when Beck points to the "totalitarian" claim of modern love: *De-traditionalized love is everything in I-form: truth, justice, morality, redemption, transcendence, authenticity."*[62] Alongside its totalitarian character, Beck invokes the utopian side of love, its boundary experience (Robert Musil) and propensity to cross boundaries, its revolutionary potential[63] in support of its character as "'religion' *without tradition."*[64] Important is Beck's pointer that the death of love remains "empty of meaning or meaningless for the post-religious religion."[65] Here Beck rightly finds the limits of the comparison between religion and love as religion according to religion. The modern form of love is wholly this-worldly. The transcendent dimension, which love has not only in Plato and in the New Testament but also in many European conceptions,[66] falls away here.

[57] Beck/Beck-Gernsheim 2012, 222; cf. Beck/Beck-Gernsheim 1995, 168.

[58] Beck/Beck-Gernsheim 2012, 223; cf. 1995, 169.

[59] F. W. Graf 2005; 2014.

[60] Beck/Beck-Gernsheim 2012, 222; cf. 1995, 169.

[61] Beck/Beck-Gernsheim 1995, 169 (GV = 2012, 222: "irdische Religion").

[62] Beck/Beck-Gernsheim 2012, 225 (emphasis original); cf. Beck/Beck-Gernsheim 1995, 170–71: "In this world where no one demands obedience or respect for old habits, love is exclusively in the first person singular, and so are truth, morality, salvation, transcendence and authenticity."

[63] Cf. Alberoni 1983.

[64] Beck/Beck-Gernsheim 2012, 233 (emphasis original); cf. 1995, 177.

[65] Beck/Beck-Gernsheim 2012, 237; cf. 1995, 180.

[66] See the essays in Düsing/Klein 2009, esp. Leinkauf 2009. On this, see further Leitgeb 2010. On Duns Scotus, see Boulnois 2014.

When Beck, in conclusion, understands modern love as the "embodiment of societal individualization and at the same time . . . (as) promise of saving the isolated individuals from its anomic other side,"[67] he takes up, in a certain way, Luhmann's description of 'love as passion' in modern society. As an analysis of the prevailing societal mental states and attitudes toward love in the Federal Republic of Germany around 1990[68]—i.e., in the "old" Federal Republic—*The Normal Chaos of Love* is indispensable and has lost nothing of its relevance. The analysis had great future potential.[69] What remains difficult, however, is the frequently appearing combination of societal analysis or empiricism and essentialist interpretation. Not only Germany but Western societies as a whole are less homogenous than Beck/ Beck-Gernsheim suggest. And the normatively operating gesture of "that's no longer an option today" obscures the fact that the tendencies of societal behavior that guide the analysis do not represent normative conceptions of value. It also does not become clear that there is great societal debate over the aforementioned themes and that with their book Beck/Beck-Gernsheim are part of this debate and fight for the prerogative of interpretation and of norm-setting.[70] At this point at the latest, the timebound character—which is necessarily bound up with the method—of the analysis becomes clear, which, at least for the sphere of religion in Germany, has already become outdated.

### 2.3 Love as Great Feeling: Psychoanalysis (Julia Kristeva)

The *Histoires d'amour* of Julia Kristeva was published in 1983 in Paris, with translations in English and German appearing shortly thereafter.[71] In six chapters Kristeva follows

> through time, but also immoderation, and under the hold of personal predilection as love demands, some of the major *ideas* about love that have made up our culture; some of the major *myths* that have fascinated it; some of the *manners of speech* that have twisted even into language signs the spellbinding power of that necessary madness.[72]

---

[67] Beck/Beck-Gernsheim 2012, 253; cf. 1995, 196.

[68] Beck and Beck-Gernsheim greatly expanded the perspective later. See Beck/ Beck-Gernsheim 2014 (GV = 2011).

[69] Cf. the EKD orientation guide *Zwischen Autonomie und Angewiesenheit: Familie als verlässliche Gemeinschaft* (EKD 2013), which in labored form seeks to sketch the results of Beck/Beck-Gernsheim's study into the Protestant family image, without even mentioning their study.

[70] This same phenomenon appears with M. Nussbaum.

[71] Kristeva 1983; 1987; 1989.

[72] Kristeva 1987, 17 (emphasis original).

Here, we encounter the writing of a woman scholar of linguistics and literature who is at the same time a psychoanalyst and places her review of the Western intellectual history of love under the banner of the Freudian thesis of narcissism. Chapter 1, which is devoted to the theme "Freud and love: treatment and its discontents," is the hermeneutical key to all that follows.

This is not the place for a detailed critical engagement with Freud's theories and their adaptation by Julia Kristeva.[73] I will focus on the first part of chapter 4, in which Kristeva addresses in three passes the New Testament *agape* conception ("God Is *Agape*"), Bernard of Clairvaux, and Thomas Aquinas. There is scarcely another text that expresses the New Testament concept of love in a way that is so close to the text, concise, fundamental, and radical, and yet at the same time interprets it in such an alienating way on the basis of an almost hermetically intensified perspective as the subchapter "God Is Love."[74] The strong attachment of her textual perception to psychoanalytic theorems makes it necessary to quote the text in detail, especially as Kristeva linguistically and materially—i.e., conceptually—takes the gloves off with the Pauline and Johannine love texts by specifying the revolutionary significance of the early Christian theology of love and thereafter poses a key question that is related to my own line of questioning:

> Is it [sc. the dynamic of Paul's thought] still, for us, scandal or insanity, as Christ's Passion was, according to Paul, in the eyes of Jews and Greeks? Do we still remain Jews and Greeks? *Is there a post-Christian actuality?*[75]

First, she sketches the "true revolution" of the early Christian conception of love, which was

> doubtless dependent on the waning Hellenistic world, but above all on a new, unprecedented, scandalous, insane attitude, which transformed Greek *Eros* and biblical *Ahav* into *Agape*—Christian love. . . . Paul is responsible for the most precise and most specifically new expression of this unprecedented attitude. . . . Such a concept of theocentric love, as opposed to human deserved love as it is to an eros aiming at happiness. . . . Paul, to whom we owe the new definition of God as God of

---

[73] I lack the subject expertise to provide a material-critical presentation of the psychoanalytic side of Kristeva's interpretation.

[74] Kristeva 1987, 139–50.

[75] Kristeva 1987, 140 (emphasis mine).

love . . . reveals . . . that the disinterested gift the Father's love consists of is, all things considered, the sacrifice of the Son—the *agape* is the agape of the Cross.[76]

This thick perception of the text makes it possible for Kristeva to specify the center of the Pauline construction of *agape*, *agape* as gift, more precisely as gift of God:

> In the love relationship we are dealing with, the stress is thus placed on its source, God, and not man, who loves his creator. . . . The essential moment of this theocentrism is the inversion of Eros' dynamics, which *rose* toward the desired object or supreme Wisdom. Agape, to the contrary, inasmuch as it is identified with God, *comes down*; it is gift, welcome, and favor.[77]

With this, however, the New Testament concept of love is not yet adequately described for Kristeva. At the center of her interpretation stands the "sacrifice of a body . . . the body of Christ, of the son."[78] It is illuminating to quote her again, for she is probably the one philosopher who, after Nietzsche, has chosen the most radical language with which to describe the Christology of sacrifice:

> Love is accomplished by means of a death that is temporary, to be sure, and yet scandalous, insane, inadmissible. Such a love does not aim at eternity but resurrection, shouldering in its trajectory the low point of the annihilation of the loved one. Is this masochistic madness, sacrilege, the end of the divine in the sense of the untouchable? The end of strictly forbidden things and for that very reason the end of the Almighty?[79]

Kristeva grapples further with the interpretation of the notion of sacrifice, basing her thought primarily on Rom 5–6 and Paul's teaching on baptism with its reconciling effect. Her interpretation circles around the bodily side of the sacrifice of Christ and around the material side of the Eucharist, with which humans have a share in the sacrifice. In contrast to ancient sacrifice, which is "obliterated" on the basis of a contract, the sacrifice of Christ establishes an "*identification*" between God and baptized

---

[76] Kristeva 1987, 139–40 (emphasis original).
[77] Kristeva 1987, 140–41.
[78] Kristeva 1987, 141. May 2011, 265, criticizes precisely this subject matter.
[79] Kristeva 1987, 141.

Christians.[80] Here, Kristeva works with the not very felicitous category of homology—a substantiated analogy is probably intended: "The passion of Christ and, by homology, any passion that ends up in death, is thus only evidence of love and not a sacrifice stemming out of the law of social contract."[81] "Homologizing," becoming the same, "identification"—this is what Kristeva sees in the Pauline Christology, and she explains Christ's sacrifice in a paradox:

> There is no idealizing identification without the murder of the loved object, which, in this homo-logical situation, is also a killing of oneself: that is what the agape of the cross has come to lay down. This internalization of murder is its consummation, its consumption, too.[82]

Baptism is something like an act of "the killing of his own body":[83]

> Inhabited by Christ, "adopted" by the Father, the believer puts to death only his sinful body, on the path that leads him to agape. Putting one's body to death is thus an episode of adoption.[84]

Kristeva appeals to the meaning of the name formula at baptism and comes to the following conclusion:

> The killing of the body is the path through which the body-Self has access to the Name of the Other who loves me and makes of me a Subject who is immersed (baptized) in the Name of the Other. A triumph of idealization through a sublimatory elaboration of suffering and of the destruction of the body proper, agape marks, for that very reason, the end of sacrifice. Or rather, it neutralizes it by means of subjective internalization: by a working-through in the Gospel's narrative.[85]

Kristeva likewise interprets love for neighbor in the same psychoanalytical context:

> Depending on the logic we have just skimmed over, the love of one's neighbor contains an additional element that completes the ideal relief of narcissism.[86]. . . The absorption of narcissism within the image of a Oneself

---

[80] Kristeva 1987, 143.
[81] Kristeva 1987, 142.
[82] Kristeva 1987, 143.
[83] Kristeva 1987, 144.
[84] Kristeva 1987, 144.
[85] Kristeva 1987, 146.
[86] Kristeva 1987, 146.

stretched to include neighbors, foreigners, and sinners will have been the final touch brought to this structure where the dynamics of internal life may henceforth be played out: construction-deconstruction, life-death . . .[87]

Finally, Kristeva very fittingly points to the "cosmic dimensions" that the *agape* idea takes in the Johannine writings.[88] At the same time, her concluding statement on John opens up the view to the mysticism of the Middle Ages:

> Possibly what is outlined here is a sublime Platonic Eros, a celestial Eros lacking his burden of carnal lust, exclusively opening up idealizing perspectives for an important trend in Christendom.[89]

At the end of this very incomplete sketch the question arises again: Does the early Christian idea of *agape* still have relevance in a post-Christian world? How does Kristeva answer this question? At the end of her long path through the stages of the European idea of love stands the following reflection:

> The fact that today we have no love discourse reveals our inability to respond to narcissism. Indeed, amatory relationship is based on narcissistic satisfaction on the one hand, on idealization on the other. If the "crisis" of psychic space sinks its roots into the "death of God" let us remember that for the West, "God is love." Paul's agape of the cross, John's "God is love" doubtless leave us cold, but empty too.[90]

For psychoanalysis there is after Freud no path that leads back to the *agape* of the New Testament or to further stages of the processing of narcissism in Christianity. Rather, what she tends to imagine at the end is the liberation from "narcissistic wounds"[91] through psychoanalytical conversation: language-imagination-fantasy as new possibilities *after* the great Christian story of love.

## 2.4 Love as Construction from the Perspective of the Two: Philosophy (Alain Badiou)

The French philosopher and author Alain Badiou makes clear from the outset—already through his choice of literary genre—that he will make a

---

[87] Kristeva 1987, 147.
[88] Kristeva 1987, 148, with reference to Anders Nygren.
[89] Kristeva 1987, 148.
[90] Kristeva 1987, 381.
[91] Kristeva 1987, 382.

case on the basis of a societal analysis, a case for the passionate love that Luhmann and Beck/Beck-Gernsheim thematize, which has come to an end for Kristeva and which Badiou regards as endangered. Unlike Kristeva, Badiou, however, opposes this possible loss. In his *Éloge de l'amour*,[92] Badiou makes recourse to the classic form of the encomium, though it is realized in the form of an interview with Nicolas Truong. Badiou takes as his starting point the following thesis:

> Love confronts two enemies, essentially: safety guaranteed by an insurance policy and the comfort zone limited by regulated pleasures.[93]

His analysis concerns a situation *after* the one that Beck/Beck-Gernsheim described. Badiou believes that "it is the task of philosophy, as well as other fields, to rally to its [love's] defense" and that "it also needs reinventing."[94] Thus, the literary hybrid form of an apologetic encomium as dialogue arises—a literary form that allows for thetic, polemic, personal, and roughly sketched material, without surrendering the philosophical gesture. For Badiou

> love isn't simply about two people meeting and their inward-looking relationship: it is a construction, a life that is being made, no longer from the perspective of the One but from the perspective of the Two.[95]

Badiou's statement that "love begins when something impossible is overcome,"[96] which is again reminiscent of Luhmann, makes clear how dramatically he appraises this possibility. Here, Badiou places great value on the fact that this construction endures over time and coins for this the felicitous formulation "love is a tenacious adventure."[97] To this corresponds his notion that love is a "truth procedure"[98] and thus far more than mere sexuality or an arrangement for procreation.[99]

---

[92] Badiou/Truong 2009 (ET = 2012).
[93] Badiou/Truong 2012, 10.
[94] Badiou/Truong 2012, 10.
[95] Badiou/Truong 2012, 29.
[96] Badiou/Truong 2012, 68.
[97] Badiou/Truong 2012, 32.
[98] Badiou/Truong 2012, 38.
[99] Badiou/Truong 2012, 60, therefore views selfishness as love's "main enemy" and means by this also interpretations that want to reduce love to sexuality. Philosophical skepticism regards love only as "merely something the imagination constructs to give a veneer to sexual desire" (34).

As a communist philosopher Badiou acknowledges, to be sure, the contribution of Judaism and Christianity to the concept and the reality of love and can designate Christianity as "a religion of love."[100] At the same time, however, he criticizes the binding of love to transcendence, which Christianity—though by taking up Plato—is said to have carried out.[101] In his polemical analysis, Badiou strikes upon a core of the New Testament *agape* construction when he writes, "Christianity grasped perfectly that there is an element in the apparent contingency of love that can't be reduced to that contingency."[102] Badiou, however, immediately argues with passion that this "universal element" must be viewed not as transcendent but rather as immanent.[103] For him, the Christian form of love is a "devout, passive, deferential love," which is contrasted with his own conception of love as "combative love . . . that earthly creation of the differentiated birth of a new world and happiness won point by point."[104]

Badiou's *Praise of Love* obtains its strength from the way that he connects three things: his struggle against a shallow postmodernism that suffers from exaggerated individuation and a strong need for safety and promises partnership without risk and responsibility; his struggle against what he criticizes as transcendence, which he connects with the rule of the Christian church;[105] and his passionately supported invocation of an immanent love, whose sphere he seeks to secure with paradoxical formulations such as "a declaration of eternity to be fulfilled or unfurled as best it can within time."[106] The philosophical contribution can perhaps most likely be located in the clear-sighted criticism of the combination of safety and comfort with the promise of the "absence of risks" in love[107] and, also, in the attempt, under the conditions of the present, to express the fundamental anthropological significance of love. With a view to the early Christian concept of love, Badiou's polemic against the transcendent dimension of love is decisive. Here, opposing world-interpretations stand over against each other as mirror images. Badiou invokes the immanence of love with the same rigor and enthusiasm with which Paul locates ἀγάπη in transcendence.

---

[100] Badiou/Truong 2012, 15.

[101] Badiou's differentiation between the Judaism of the Song of Songs and the transcendental conception in Christianity (64ff.) is an example of the selective and tendentious perception of historical texts. Badiou passes over the central theological love texts of the Old Testament as well as the social construction of ἀγάπη in the New Testament.

[102] Badiou/Truong 2012, 65.

[103] Badiou/Truong 2012, 65.

[104] Badiou/Truong 2012, 66–67.

[105] What is meant is probably the Catholic Church.

[106] Badiou/Truong 2012, 47.

[107] Badiou/Truong 2012, 9.

## 2.5 Love as Societal-Cultural Construction: Humanistic Feminism
## (Martha C. Nussbaum)

With Martha Craven Nussbaum, professor of law and ethics at the University of Chicago, we enter the realm of philosophical ethics, which gains a hearing for itself in the public sphere. Nussbaum has written various publications on the topic of love.[108] In her essays in *Sex and Social Justice*,[109] she understands herself as a sociopolitically engaged humanistic feminist. Her view of the phenomenon of love combines moral-philosophical, judicial, and sociopolitical reflections with feminist intentions. In doing so, she is indeed guided by an awareness not only of cultural differences but also of historical depth dimensions and changes. Her major essay "Constructing Love, Desire, and Care"[110] from 1999[111] circles around the classic question of feminism since Simone de Beauvoir[112] of whether and to what extent love and justice are shaped more by "nature" or by "culture." Its starting-point assumption is conveyed by the statement, "Maybe there is more custom and law in nature than we usually think."[113] This is a rather careful and not very surprising formulation, which takes account not only of social-constructivist gender research but at least indirectly also its critically trans-formative updating by Judith Butler.[114] Martha Nussbaum, however, does not so much take a side in the well-known contemporary discourse for and against the differentiation of *sex* and *gender*[115] but rather seeks her own argumentation in the combination of lines of questioning from the history of philosophy, cultural studies, and cognitive science. She does not simply accept the constructivist thesis that "human love, desire, and sexuality are 'socially constructed'"[116] as a given but investigates it independently from a philosophical perspective in relation to three themes—the emotion of love, sexual aspects of the body, and family.

Her general thesis is that "in many central respects, the sexual domain of human life, and its close relative, the domain of the family, are domains of symbolic cultural interpretation, shaped by historical and institutional

---

[108] See especially Nussbaum 1992; 2013.

[109] Nusbaum 1999a.

[110] Nusbaum 1999b.

[111] This essay appeared before Judith Butler's second major book, *Undoing Gender* (Butler 2004).

[112] De Beauvoir 1949 (ET = 1974).

[113] Nussbaum 1999b, 255.

[114] Butler 1990; 2004.

[115] There are no references to S. de Beauvoir or J. Butler. Cf., however, Martha Nussbaum's sharp critique of Butler in Nussbaum 1999c (quoted below).

[116] Nussbaum 1999b, 255.

forces, though within constraints imposed by biology."[117] Here, she points especially to the "depth of social conditioning,"[118] which shapes the emotions of human beings precisely in this sphere. Nussbaum develops her own mission from this subject matter. This insight "opens up a space for normative argument, political criticism, and reasoned change."[119] As a legal scholar she is concerned not only with social-scientific analyses, with the mapping of the present, whether emotions, social constructions, or institutions, but also with the formation of norms that she, as a societally engaged ethicist, wishes to establish. In this double mission, she also demarcates herself relatively sharply from the cultural studies literature, to which she imputes a double deficit. She misses the incorporation of philosophical arguments and the connection of studies of the "constructedness of desire and sexuality to a study of the cultural construction of emotion,"[120] i.e., the very topic that has been investigated from every angle in German-language cultural studies of the past thirty years.[121] The extent to which this deficit actually existed in the American discussion around 2000 cannot be discussed here. In any case, with this critical analysis, Martha Nussbaum makes clear her own approach. She seeks to get beyond the perspective of cultural studies and provoke effects that change the whole society. What are her own contributions and to what results do they lead?

Martha Nussbaum works first with "a cognitive view of emotion."[122] She forges a connection to Aristotle's *Rhetoric*, that repository of ancient teaching on emotions.[123] She attempts to demonstrate in this area a balance

---

[117] Nussbaum 1999b, 256.

[118] Nussbaum 1999b, 256.

[119] Nussbaum 1999b, 256.

[120] Nussbaum 1999b, 256.

[121] Cf. just the works of Ute Frevert, e.g., Frevert 2013; 2014b 2020. See also Frevert et al. 2014.

[122] Nussbaum 1999b, 256. The analysis remains, however, very general. Here, an approach such as that of Breithaupt 2012 would advance the discussion, though empathy research has itself become an unwieldy and controversial area of research between psychology, neuroscience, behavioral research, and philosophy. On this topic, cf. Slaby 2014. Slaby himself speaks of a "hype around empathy as change of perspective," which underestimates "people's capacity for action" (p. 9). See, in detail, Breyer 2013. What holds true for empathy research can also be applied analogously to research on emotions. The theme of the emotions or affects is worked on from the standpoint of very different academic lines of questioning. Alongside cultural studies, which Nussbaum regards as deficient, there are also important sociological conceptions such as Gerhards 1988. Historical emotion research is especially active. See the internet portal of www.history-of-emotions.mpg .de. Further perspectives include clinical psychology, ethnology, and anthropology.

[123] On Aristotle, see Nussbaum 1999b, 257–58, 264–65, 273–74. With Aristotle, Nussbaum investigates the question of what human flourishing actually is. See pp. 264, 272, 274.

between biologically constrained conditions for human regulations of emotion and "social shaping and variation."[124] Here, what is interesting is the notion that not only valuations of emotions in different cultures but also *"individual histories vary, and emotions bear traces of their history."*[125] With this the model of the cultural construction of emotions is differentiated in a significant way, and the term "culture" is restricted in its holistic or leveling sense. Nussbaum develops her thesis in relation to the example of erotic love and makes plausible how different the normal understanding and the taxonomy of emotions are in different cultures. Two important pointers occur in this context. First, she points to a fundamental attitude of the Greco-Roman world to sexuality, which is not discussed in the exegetical discussions about the absence of erotic love and "good" sexuality in the early Christian writings: "The ancient Greeks seem, on the whole, to have considered *erôs* a fearful and terrible sort of bondage and constraint. . . . The ancient Greek feels bound and made passive by *erôs*."[126] Second, she emphasizes the lack of mutuality in Plato's *eros*: Plato defines eros as "possession of an object one views as good."[127] Here, Nussbaum can be thought further in the context of our theme, though this is far from her mind. Both observations let the absolute reserve of the early Christian authors toward *eros* appear in a very different light from the accusation that the early Christian concept of love knows nothing about eroticism and sexuality, which is rather naive from a historical point of view. If *eros* is not necessarily something good in an ethical sense—thus, it can be thought further here—then there was also not an absolute necessity for the early Christian authors to take up *eros* into their *agape* concept. Moreover, with this the unconditional interest of some exegetes in finding "good" *eros* or "good" sexuality—which we have already touched on at multiple points—also falls away.

Let us return, however, to Martha Nussbaum. Her observations support "cultural variation" in questions of the emotion of erotic love.[128] Nussbaum, however, insists that within a certain framework[129] a normative analysis and "ethical arguments" are nevertheless possible.[130] With this she has marked out a moderate-normative framework within which

---

[124] Nussbaum 1999b, 259.

[125] Nussbaum 1999b, 261 (emphasis original).

[126] Nussbaum 1999b, 262. Sappho's poems show, however, that women could have the same emotion.

[127] Nussbaum 1999b, 262.

[128] Nussbaum 1999b, 264.

[129] Nussbaum 1999b, 264. In this context, Nussbaum speaks of "metaphysical beliefs we can no longer accept" and "forms of life we can never replicate."

[130] Nussbaum 1999b, 264.

we may pose the question of "what forms of erotic love are and are not compatible with our other commitments, to justice, to equality, to productive work, to other loves and friendships."[131] From here the path leads to societal changes, which also find expression in legal and institutional spheres or from there have an impact on society. With these consequences, Martha Nussbaum has reached her goal—to have a positive influence on the institutional and legal structure of society with her argumentation in order to improve morality by having "emotions become part of the domain of moral effort, so construed."[132]

In what follows, Nussbaum applies the insights she has gained to sexual desire and demonstrates its cultural-constructive components.[133] Here she provides an excellent sketch of the question of possible homosexuality in Athens in the fifth century BCE. Her conclusion that "ancient Greece, in short, does not divide its sexual actors according to the concept of a stable inner 'preference' for objects of a particular gender" so that "in that sense, it lacks the very experience of homosexuality in its modern sense"[134] appears to me to be valid for archaic and classical Greece but, interestingly, is no longer valid for Plutarch. What Nussbaum does not address is the anchoring of the concept of what she calls the stable inner "preference" for objects of a certain kind in the Israelite-Jewish culture, in which Paul participates with his understanding of 'homosexuality.' Instead, Nussbaum refers exclusively to the classical Greek concept of eroticism and uses this as a contrast to present-day values that are—in her view—out of date. Is she thinking of a revival of classical Greek cultural influences? Surely not. Rather, she uses the Greek example to demonstrate the variety of cultural constructions of love and desire. From the viewpoint of historical hermeneutics, her argument would have increased in its significance with respect to the current question of the construction of sexual desire if she had also presented the Israelite-Jewish–early Christian position, which forms, after all, the basis for the version of the argument from nature that she critically examines and rejects.[135]

Nussbaum's discussion of the understanding of the female and male body from a constructive-social perspective fits as a distinct voice into the already mentioned tendency to call into question the distinction between the biological category of sex and the societal category of gender and also understand the biological aspects of the body as "objects of cultural

---

[131] Nussbaum 1999b, 264.

[132] Nussbaum 1999b, 265.

[133] Nussbaum 1999b, 265–69.

[134] Nussbaum 1999b, 269.

[135] At the beginning of this essay, Nussbaum refers to Philo, who uses the well-known φύσις argument, which is also used by Paul. See Nussbaum 1999b, 253–55.

interpretation and representation."[136] In this respect, the discussion in the past fifteen years has advanced very quickly, and we need no longer provide a separate presentation of Nussbaum's insights. This also applies to her discussion of family, which she describes as "an artifact of human arrangements," which have the goal of being "homes for love and care."[137]

What does Martha Nussbaum contribute to the understanding of love in the present? First, the contexts in which love appears are clear: sexuality, desire, emotion, sex and gender, body, society and its institutions (marriage, family). The perspective from which these aspects are viewed is the striving to improve life on the basis of convictions that are partly liberal and partly feminist. With respect to this point, Nussbaum speaks of care. The goal is societal change, which is sought through enlightenment, freedom from traditions, and insight into the social construction of love. However, this perspective does not only affect *love*. Socially related constructivism is used in many contexts, and engagement with the goal of change occurs precisely in the sphere of love, but it also applies to other themes. With respect to the theme of *love*, we learn, upon closer examination, nothing new from Martha Nussbaum. She appears to presuppose that *love* is adequately described with the coordinates mentioned above. Love is here a societal construction whose sociological development and philosophical-political correction can contribute to the humanizing of society. She draws her arguments for change from her own political-societal convictions on the basis of care for human beings — in philosophical terms, the good, as she recognizes it herself in critical engagement with the tradition. In a word, love becomes an element or tool of social life, among others, and must be "optimized" in a humanistic-feminist way.[138]

## 2.6 Love as Divine Program: The Catholic Magisterium (Benedict XVI)

The encyclical *Deus Caritas Est*[139] of Benedict XVI from 2005/2006 leads into a conceptual and linguistic counter-world. The pope speaks not as a systematic theologian but as a teacher of the church, i.e., he *teaches* and *announces*, while arguing in detail with the help of the tradition of Israel

---

[136] Nussbaum 1999b, 270.

[137] Nussbaum 1999b, 272.

[138] In her more recent book *Political Emotions: Why Love Matters for Justice* (Nussbaum 2013), Nussbaum develops her political-ethical-emotional understanding of love further (cf. the review of Frevert 2014a).

[139] Pope Benedict XVI signed off on the encyclical on December 25, 2005. It was published one month later on January 25, 2006, in Latin, and translated into multiple languages, including English and German. Quotations in what follows will be taken from Benedict XVI 2006.

and the Christian tradition. He starts from the love of God as the highest reality and on the basis of this conception presents the double picture of love as divine power (part 1) and of the *caritas* that human beings practice in the form of love for neighbor, as well as the caritative activity of the Catholic Church (part 2). What idea of love guides the pope, and on what does he base his view?[140] At the outset, the basic instruments of his world-interpretation may be specified: Benedict connects a synthesizing biblical theology with classic philosophical lines of questioning and argues from both testaments of the Bible and from the writings of the church fathers and certain philosophers. In his argumentation, biblical theology has priority. The pope takes special care to understand the Old Testament—and that means the religious heritage of Israel as foundation of Christian theology. Alongside the synthesis as a figure of thought, we find the figure of unity. From the Old Testament via the New Testament, the church fathers, and the papal encyclicals, the one truth is unfolded through time. It is the task of the papal encyclicals to discover and write forward this unity again and again in the course of church history—thus also in this encyclical, especially in its second part.

The programmatic introduction to the encyclical is of special interest for our purposes. The pope chooses—in accord with the title of the encyclical—the most theologically demanding New Testament love text as his entry point to the theme of *caritas*, i.e., 1 John 4.16. With 1 John 4.16 and John 3.16, these foundational texts of Johannine love theology, the pope marks out the framework for "the Christian image of God and the resulting image of mankind" (§1). Moreover, he finds in 1 John 4.16 "a kind of summary of the Christian life" (§1). The encyclical therefore speaks of the "centrality of love," which is meant to be understood not as an idea but as "the encounter with an event, a person" (§1). Here, at the beginning, Benedict has reached a central formulation that can also be regarded as a foundation of the New Testament concept of love. He explains love as a message and grounds the selection of the theme of love for his first encyclical[141] as follows: "In a world where the name of God is sometimes associated with vengeance or even a duty of hatred and violence, this message is both timely and significant" (§1).[142]

---

[140] The encyclical cannot be interpreted here in all its details. I will limit myself to the question of the theological approach and the linkage to Old and New Testament texts.

[141] There follows *Spe Salvi* (on hope) and *Caritas in Veritate* (encyclical on Catholic social teaching on the relationship between justice and love. Here, the theme of the second half of the first encyclical is treated in a deepened way under the impression of the financial crisis). The encyclical *Lumen Fidei* as the third of Benedict's texts on the triad "love, hope, faith" appeared under the name of Francis I.

[142] Benedict could have deepened this central idea.

After this New Testament / Johannine groundwork, the encyclical, in
its first part, presents the "unity of love in creation and in salvation history."
With this, the key conception of his theological thinking, the synthesis, is
already expressed. Synthesis, not antithesis, defines this theology. What
is Benedict's concern? The entire argumentation of this part is an implicit
critical engagement with the antithesis of *eros* and *agape*[143] formulated
by Anders Nygren,[144] which Benedict reads under Nietzsche's accusation
that Christianity destroyed *eros* or under the key phrase of Christianity's
hostility to the body. He seeks to neutralize this accusation. The pope sets
the ancient insight into the destructive elements of *eros* against the glorification of *eros* by Nietzsche.[145] This critically limits a one-sided glorification of *eros* and sex, without *eros* itself being removed from the game.
Rather, Benedict recommends a purified *eros*. For unlike the New Testament authors, the pope neither wants to renounce nor can renounce *eros*,
for he wants to integrate the categories of creation, bodiliness, biological
sex, and love between man and woman[146] into his concept of love.[147] Thus,
he sets forth his synthesis of *eros* and *agape* in this way. According to his
concept of love, "far from rejecting or 'poisoning'[148] *eros*," purification
and growth in maturity "heal and restore its true grandeur" (§5). Thus, it is
not a matter of *agape* instead of *eros* but *agape* and a tamed *eros*. To this
corresponds another idea, which is clearly Platonic:[149] love as *eros* is an
ascent;[150] indeed, it is also "ecstasy," but "not in the sense of a moment of
intoxication, but rather as a journey, an ongoing exodus out of the closed
inward-looking self toward its liberation" (§6), whose archetype is Jesus'
loving self-sacrifice. Thus, here too, it is a matter of the correction rather
than the abrogation of *eros*.

In §7 the pope pursues the line of the synthesis between *eros* and
*agape* further and makes clear why this synthesis is necessary for him:

---

[143] Nygren is not mentioned. It is interesting that Benedict explicitly "fights" with
Nietzsche but not with the Swedish Lutheran bishop and professor Nygren.

[144] On Nygren and the encyclical, cf. Düsing 2009, 30–40.

[145] On this, see also Nussbaum.

[146] Note the almost effusive language in §2: "love between man and woman, where
body and soul are inseparably joined and human beings glimpse an apparently irresistible
promise of happiness. This would seem to be the very epitome of love; all other kinds of
love immediately seem to fade in comparison" (Benedict XIV 2006, 5).

[147] Cf. Eph 5.

[148] Thus the nasty dictum of Nietzsche.

[149] Benedict refers not to Plato but to Pseudo-Dionysius the Areopagite, *Divine Names*
VI 12–14. See Benedict XIV 2006, 53.

[150] Here the pope refers to the Song of Songs: אהבה / ἀγάπη is said to mean "the
discovery of the other, moving beyond the selfish character" that *eros* initially had (§6).
See Benedict XIV 2006, 9.

Were this antithesis [sc. between *eros* and *agape*] to be taken to extremes, the essence of Christianity would be detached from the vital relations fundamental to human existence, and would become a world apart, admirable perhaps, but decisively cut off from the complex fabric of human life.

To avoid this—the pope argues—the early church authors would have already had to present the connection of *eros* and *agape* as ascent and descent to and from heaven. Thus, Benedict formulates an initial interim conclusion: "Fundamentally, 'love' is a single reality, but with different dimensions" (§8). This conclusion is based not only on Benedict's insistence on the reality and necessity of *eros*, but it also simultaneously helps him to understand *agape* as a necessary component of what we call love. What is characteristic for paragraphs 1–8 is not only the synthetic thinking but also the unwavering insistence on love between man and woman as the starting point of all further statements on love. Thus, the pope—after the introduction—begins *dogmatically* with creation and not with redemption; *biblically* with the Old and not the New Testament, with special reference to the creation account and the Song of Songs, i.e., the very texts that thematize *eros*; and, finally, *ethically* with marriage between man and woman. In this way, he supports not only the continuity between *eros* and *agape* but also the continuity between the structures, which are understood in a deeply synthetical way—namely, creation and redemption, Old and New Testament, Israel and the church.

This insistence on continuity makes it possible for him, in paragraphs 9–11, to emphasize "the newness of biblical faith" in comparison with the cultures of the ancient world (§8). Here, Benedict once again argues synthetically by understanding the relationship between Old and New Testament images of God and human beings as the relationship of a gradual progression. Again, the accent lies first on the Old Testament. Benedict rightly stresses the completely gratuitous character of God's love for Israel. For him, as a philosophically educated theologian, it is of special significance that the God of Israel, who, viewed philosophically, is active as Logos, as the "ultimate source of all being," is "a lover with all the passion of a true love" (§10).[151] To this corresponds the newness in the image of human beings. Once again, Benedict returns to the creation: the human being—Adam—first becomes "whole" through

---

[151] Here Benedict again invokes the Song of Songs, this time with explicit reference to the Jewish and Christian allegorical interpretation, especially in Christian mysticism. The difference that he sees between the Old Testament and Aristotle (*Metaph.* 12.7) in §9 is important. See Benedict XIV 2006, 53.

Eve:[152] "Only in communion with the opposite sex can he become 'complete'" (§11). The pope sees—in accordance with the New, not the Old, Testament—monogamous marriage grounded in Adam and Eve: "Corresponding to the image of a monotheistic God is monogamous marriage.... This close connection between *eros* and marriage in the Bible has practically no equivalent in extra-biblical literature" (§11).[153]

Paragraphs 12–15 are then devoted to what is new in the New Testament. Here, Benedict expresses himself in a pointed manner in the vein of his synthetic thinking: "The real novelty of the New Testament lies not so much in new ideas as in the figure of Christ himself, who gives flesh and blood to those concepts—an unprecedented realism"[154] (§12), namely, by dying for human beings. In §§13 and 14, Benedict interprets the Eucharist as bodily union of love with Christ. In doing so, he presents not only the mystical-individual but also the caritative-social dimension of the Eucharist and points out that "*agape* also became a term for the Eucharist" (§14). From the Eucharist emerges love for neighbor and once again Benedict expresses the great synthesis: "Faith, worship, and ethos are interwoven as a single reality which takes shape in our encounter with God's love" (§14).

In paragraphs 16–21, which are devoted to love for God and love for neighbor, Benedict engages critically with two classic questions: "Can we love God without seeing him? And can love be commanded?" (§16). Both questions are resolved and answer themselves when one looks at Jesus who has made God visible and has courted us human beings (§17). Again, the pope refers to central passages of Johannine theology. In doing so, he uses the felicitous language of the "love-story between God and man" (§17). Both aspects—love for God and love for neighbor—"are ... inseparable.... But both live from the love of God who has loved us first" (§18).

If one asks from a New Testament perspective where the encyclical places 1 Cor 13, then one must go far into the second part, which is devoted to the practical and operational side of ecclesial *caritas*, before one reads the following statement in §34:

> Saint Paul, in his hymn to charity (cf. *1 Cor* 13), teaches us that it is always more than activity alone. . . . This hymn must be the *Magna*

---

[152] Eve is not mentioned.

[153] The pope does not discuss the polygamy in the Old Testament, nor does he address the fact that *eros* and marriage are not connected in the New Testament (see above). On the theme, cf. also what was said about Plutarch above. Plutarch is concerned with the connection between love and marriage, though without entirely wanting to take leave of the love for boys.

[154] Benedict does not discuss the category of the new in Paul, for example, in its significance for the Torah.

*Carta* of all ecclesial service; it sums up all the reflections on love which I have offered throughout this Encyclical Letter. Practical activity will always be insufficient, unless it visibly expresses a love for man, a love nourished by an encounter with Christ.[155]

Here, *caritas*, which as *caritas* is part of the activity of the Catholic Church, is interpreted from the perspective of *agape*. The encyclical concludes in this sense with a call to prayer and with reference to the loving activity of the saints, especially Mary.

The encyclical as a contemporary authoritative Catholic theological-ecclesial text on love, which has no counterpart in Protestantism, deserves our close attention in two directions—in criticism and in sympathy. The undertaking as such must be met with sympathy. The theme is central, and Benedict has wrestled with the available resources of Catholic theology to present anew *love* as the decisive center of Christian theology and ecclesial action. His intention was not to *repeat* the New Testament concept of *agape* but to *interpret* this concept in connection with the rich Old Testament love texts and the interpretations of the church fathers for the contemporary situation of the worldwide Catholic Church. This explains the strong shifts of emphasis to the interpretation of marriage as a fellowship of love that integrates *eros* and leads to caritative action in society, which crosses over the boundaries of communities or the Church. Neither belongs to the New Testament concept of *agape*. Rather, they are expressions of the ethical guidance of the worldwide Catholic Church. The so-called accommodation or the *aggiornamento*, to speak with Pope John XXIII, is a necessary form of interpretation of the Bible and as such only to be welcomed.

However, against the background of my own analysis of the early Christian conception of love, the criticism will, nevertheless, be predominant in detail—namely, not with respect to the fact of interpretation as such but with regard to the kind of theological interpretation that cultivates the dialogue with the past but does not take up the argumentative dialogue with the present. The world-perception of the encyclical and its argumentation are *one-sidedly* conservative in the sense of being tied to tradition

---

[155] I cannot present here the remarks on the ecclesial *caritas*, on its history since Acts 2 and its relation to the state, which the pope discusses under the classic line of questioning of "justice and love." What is important is the perception of the social NGOs, whose work the pope acknowledges again under the perspective of the synthesis. The increase of NGOs "is ultimately due to the fact that the command of love of neighbor is inscribed by the Creator in man's very nature" (§31).

without critically engaging with concepts that are understood as progressive. This one-sidedness applies not only to the horizon of interpretation, which the pope finds in the Old and New Testaments and in dialogue with the great theologians of the early church, the encyclicals of his predecessors, and certain great Western philosophers but beyond this also to the public and scholarly spheres, to which his argumentation applies—the state and state theory, the Catholic Church, classical philosophy. These are the traditional fields with which the Catholic Church interacts. The present-day scholarly fields of perception—psychology, sociology, cognitive science, cultural studies, political science—are just as little addressed as the very influential perspectives—also in the Catholic Church[156] and theology and among Jewish men and women scholars,[157] especially in the United States—of deconstruction, feminism, gender studies, and queer theory[158] and the concomitant societal changes.[159] This retreat of the encyclical to certain "classic" areas and scholarly disciplines is serious, for it contradicts

---

[156] Above all Mary Daly, Rosemary Radford Ruether, Mary E. Hunt, and Elisabeth Schüssler Fiorenza.

[157] E.g., Susan Bordo and Judith Butler. Precisely in this very lively sphere of questions, positions, and polemic, there are controversial debates into which theologians can intervene. Cf., e.g., the heated polemic of Nussbaum 1999c against J. Butler. Nussbaum writes:

> The great tragedy in the new feminist theory in America is the loss of a sense of public commitment. In this sense, Butler's self-involved feminism is extremely American, and it is not surprising that it has caught on here, where successful middle-class people prefer to focus on cultivating the self rather than thinking in a way that helps the material condition of others. Even in America, however, it is possible for theorists to be dedicated to the public good and to achieve something through that effort. . . . Finally there is despair at the heart of the cheerful Butlerian enterprise. The big hope, the hope for a world of real justice, where laws and institutions protect the equality and the dignity of all citizens, has been banished, even perhaps mocked as sexually tedious. Judith Butler's hip quietism is a comprehensible response to the difficulty of realizing justice in America. But it is a bad response. It collaborates with evil. Feminism demands more and women deserve better.

If one reads the entire anti-Butler text of M. Nussbaum, then one will, however, find many of the accusations that Nussbaum makes against J. Butler also in Nussbaum. What distinguishes the two is, in fact, most likely the individual core of Butler's understanding of love.

[158] Sedgwick 2000.

[159] On this, cf. *Zwischen Autonomie und Angewiesenheit: Familie als verlässliche Gemeinschaft stärken; Eine Orientierungshilfe der Evangelische Kirche in Deutschland* (= EKD 2013). This study tends to step back from the theme of love and also from theological argumentation (54–71) and instead enters into discussion with the present-day conditions of life and living together. The EKD publication represents almost a counter-picture of the encyclical and must itself face the criticism of being one sided and of merely belatedly reproducing the societal discourse, without making a theological contribution of its own.

the synthetic claim and thinking that the pope himself advocates, whose fundamental conviction he expresses, among other ways, as follows (§8):

> And we have also seen, synthetically, that biblical faith does not set up a parallel universe, or one opposed to that primordial human phenomenon which is love, but rather accepts the whole man; it intervenes in his search for love in order to purify it and to reveal new dimensions of it.

Through his limited perception of the world and the texts, however, Benedict gives precisely the impression of speaking from a parallel or counter-world. Benedict would have needed to conduct a *dialogue*—perhaps one that was indeed polemical—with Catholic women representatives and, corresponding to his conviction that the scriptures of Israel are also the foundation of Christian theology, also with Jewish women philosophers. For the concern of all those involved is also with *eros*—from whatever perspective that may take. And, as the pope himself writes, one can speak of *agape-caritas* only in critical engagement with *eros* and *sexus* in their contemporary construction. This polemical dialogue—not with Nietzsche or with Nygren but with contemporary women theologians and philosophers—would have been all the more necessary since women philosophers[160] such as Judith Butler and Martha Nussbaum themselves live in heated controversies and vehemently, normatively, and frequently advocate their own theories as counter-positions to Christian conceptions. It is not only something to be feared but is entirely self-evident that the encyclical is a purely *insider* text, not only in the sense of the address—which as an encyclical, i.e., a papal teaching document, is ordinarily not addressed to non-Christians[161]—but also in the extremely selective perception of reality and humanity, which appears to prohibit the pope from entering into critical engagement with the theological movements of the past two generations, which he knows well. From a Christian and theological perspective, one must say that a great opportunity was missed here. With this teaching claim and this diction, the pope excludes himself a priori from the present-day debate on love to the extent that it is conducted outside the inner circle of the governing body of the Catholic Church.

With respect to the New Testament and the theme of love, I am also critical of the encyclical's perception of the texts. I undoubtedly find some of the basic lines that Benedict sketches in the texts. One can, as the pope

---

[160] I intentionally specify women here, since the feminist initiatives have proceeded from women, some of whom have been decidedly Christian.

[161] In 1963, however, Pope John XXIII did address the encyclical *Pacem in Terris* also "to all men of good will."

does, prefer the Johannine theology of love to the *agape* concept of Paul. By contrast, the strong fixation on the *eros-agape* relationship, which Benedict has taken over from Nygren in order to correct it, is difficult. As I have presented the matter, *eros* does not occur in the New Testament, either as a lexeme or as a theme. The connection of *eros* and marriage is not present. Instead, an *agape* ethic for the communities is set forth in the New Testament. The communities and not the married couple are the bearers of the new *agape* culture. Precisely at this point, however, every contemporary theology of love must think further. How can the New Testament *agape* culture live under the conditions of the individualization and particularization of our societies? Could the declining acceptance of marriage and of the restriction to heterosexual attachments be healed or overcome in a new community thinking? In any case, the rigorous combination of love theology and marriage theology does not come from the New Testament. It is a given that every present-day theology, whether Catholic or Protestant, can and must critically question, develop further, and change the emphases of New Testament concepts. The encyclical legitimately pursues an entirely different purpose than the present investigation, and neither desires nor is able to come to similar results as a New Testament study but can use its perception of the New Testament concept of love only as a foundation for its own conception. However, if it also aims to be perceived *extra muros*, the encyclical must lay bare and reflect upon this necessary process of interpretation. This also applies to the strong emphasis that the encyclical places on *caritas* in its second part. *Caritas* in the sense of the encyclical is not primitive Christian but from the early church. It must and can be made plausible in the present also as a 'modern' interpretation of Christian love in a post-community societal world. ἀγάπη, by contrast, is not *caritas*, i.e., help or aid, but the culture of the life together of Christ-confessing community members, who await the Lord, and thus also the form of life of the Catholic communities. This concept is not satisfactorily covered by *caritas*. The encyclical could explicate the shifts toward current societal conceptions and the role of the Catholic Church in these new contexts. Here, however, it is not possible to postulate a simple continuity from Acts to the present. In truth, history is replaced by a pious story here.

The leading German-language Protestant[162] systematic theologian Eberhard Jüngel has read the encyclical with more sympathy than criticism. Let me briefly highlight a few of his important thoughts and observations. By way of introduction, Jüngel speaks of an "authentic beginning" of the papal

---

[162] Jüngel 2009 shows himself to be very Lutheran here. I will not comment on the documentation of the agreement of the pope with Luther or Lutheran theology, which seems somewhat forced at times. Jüngel speaks of a "deep and far-reaching ecumenical agreement" (481).

teaching and agrees with the pope that 1 John 4.16 "can be regarded as the shortest and most precise expression of the nature of Christianity."[163] Jüngel describes the way the pope perceives his teaching office as "meditating."[164] As a systematic theologian, Jüngel also affirms the papal plea for the belonging together of faith and reason—the basic synthesis of the theology of Joseph Ratzinger.

What does the Lutheran systematic theologian perceive in the Catholic teaching document? I will simply provide a list: the primacy of the indicative of the divine love before the commandment;[165] the interpretation of purified *eros* as *agape*,[166] which Jüngel understands as *caritas fide formata*;[167] the unity of *eros* and *agape* as different dimensions of love;[168] and the permeability of the Johannine interpretation of love to the Trinity.[169] Jüngel can with a certain justification strike Lutheran fire out of the comments on the Eucharist,[170] but he is more successful with the theme "justice and love" from the second part of the encyclical. The Lutheran Jüngel reads here "with lively agreement . . . and theological profit" "something like the summary of a papal 'doctrine of two kingdoms.'"[171]

We do not find a critical approach to the theme of the encyclical, love, in Jüngel. More than this theme Jüngel appears to have been impressed with the theological diction of the pope, the appeal back to the New Testament (whose one-sidedness escapes him), the caution, the cultivated theological-philosophical manner of argumentation. This is all comprehensible and yet also a sign of the powerlessness and intellectual weakness of a present-day polemical theology that presents itself as interconfessional theology, which finds its greatest joy in being able to impute to the pope an implicit closeness to Luther, which he certainly does not have. Jüngel's sympathy does not make the encyclical better but shows rather that he too lives far away from the contemporary discourses on love. Jüngel contributes nothing of his own to the theme.

In conclusion, the encyclical is a decisive text for Catholic and Protestant men and women theologians. For this is *the* current Christian theological text

---

[163] Jüngel 2009, 482.

[164] I do not find meditation in the encyclical but announcement, tidings of the love of God.

[165] Jüngel 2009, 486.

[166] Jüngel 2009, 488. Jüngel comments on this interpretation of the pope with reference to 1 Cor 13. Cf., however, what was said above on §34.

[167] Jüngel 2009, 488–89. For Jüngel this is the most important ecumenical component of the encyclical.

[168] Jüngel 2009, 492 (after a long excurse on Nygren).

[169] Jüngel 2009, 492–93 (Jüngel reinforces and clarifies this perspective).

[170] Jüngel 2009, 494–95.

[171] Jüngel 2009, 500.

at the highest level on the theme of love, which theologically—and church politically—deserves all respect *and* all criticism. For precisely this reason it must also be said that the theme is squandered insofar as the pope did not perceive the task of placing the Christian concept of love and its grounding in the New Testament concept of ἀγάπη in the current discourse and actively arguing in these discourses and—if necessary—also against them.

Alongside the criticism of certain of Benedict's basic theological decisions, criticism must, finally, be made of the linguistic and argumentative gesturing of the document.[172] The encyclical claims a high intellectual niveau for itself, interprets and quotes decisive texts from the Western cultural sphere, while at the same time lacking every current linguistic form, connection to the theme, and conceptual engagement with contemporary positions. Theology, however, has, since the time of the earliest theologians, always arisen in critical engagement with the time and has spoken in adoption and difference the language of its respective time. An encyclical must also achieve this communication if it aims to reach this world into which it has been written. The fact that the Catholic world is—fortunately—a global world with many regional variations makes this communication more differentiated but not impossible.

## 2.7 Love as Ontological Rootedness: The Philosophical History of Ideas (Simon May)

A completely different path is taken by the English philosopher and historian of philosophy Simon May. He presents the main stations of the European idea of love in fifteen chapters,[173] beginning with the Old Testament and ending with Freud and Proust. While he calls his book a *history* of love in an understated manner, in reality he is the only one, next to Benedict, who develops a distinct *doctrine* of love that indeed possesses a normative claim and ontological foundation. At the outset, he describes his own position with great precision:[174]

> This work has three principle aims. First, to show how love came to play God—and just to be deprived, in key respects, of its humanity. (And, of course, like all gods, to be abused and misappropriated by its worshippers.) Second, to trace some of the debilitating illusions of this hubris:

---

[172] This criticism applies to an even greater extent to the text of Jüngel, who is not, after all, pope and does not need to compose a second encyclical.

[173] As far as I can see, May does not represent the concept of the history of ideas of the Cambridge school.

[174] For May's understanding of love, see now also May 2019.

above all the belief that genuine love is unconditional. And third, to propose a way of love that is truer to its fundamental nature—and so doesn't burden it with misconceived expectations. Here I will develop the idea . . . that love is the intense desire for someone whom—or something which—we experience as grounding and affirming our own existence. And that this desire seeks two forms of intimacy . . . the intimacy of possessing another and the intimacy of making ourselves unreservedly available to them. It will present a picture of love as a harbinger of the sacred without pretending that it is an all-powerful solution for the problem of finding meaning, security and happiness in life.[175]

It would be tempting to pursue the individual stations of the Western idea of love with May and to compare his analysis with that of Julia Kristeva or at least to comment on chapters 6, "Love as the Supreme Virtue: Christianity,"[176] and 7, "Why Christian Love Isn't Unconditional."[177] To understand May's own position, however, the concluding chapter is the most suitable: "Love Reconsidered."[178] Here, he engages again materially—this distinguishes his from the other conceptions discussed here, with the exception of the encyclical—with the Christian concept of love. In distinction from Martha Nussbaum, for example, he assumes that the Christian concept of love has deeply influenced the Western world of values and that this influence is still increasing in the midst of the general weakening of the Christian religion in the Western world, with the Christian-religious founding framework fading away but the great claim of love preserved. Alain Badiou would be the best example of this hypothesis. May evaluates this development critically since he finds three fundamental illusions in the Christian idea—first that love is "unconditional,"[179] second that it is "eternal,"[180] and third that it is "selfless."[181] In his view, these modes of behavior could be meaningful as predicates of God but not as human modes of behavior. In the course of secularization, they are said to have been falsely ascribed to human beings and to have led to exaggerated and false notions of love as a consequence:

---

[175] May 2011, 13.
[176] May 2011, 81–94.
[177] May 2011, 95–118.
[178] May 2011, 235–56. Cf. now also May 2019.
[179] May 2011, 236.
[180] May 2011, 237.
[181] May 2011, 238. The three predicates that May specifies occur in 1 Cor 13: Love believes all, love never stops, love does not seek its own. May rejects precisely this Pauline construction of *agape*.

As that decline [sc. the Enlightenment] has progressed, so men and
women have increasingly expected their love to take over where God's
left off.[182]

Simon May sees this danger both in the societal and in the individual
sphere. Let us turn first to the *societal* aspect. Here, May places the "idola-
trous and sometimes horrific attempts to impute this divine role [of love] to
a community or nation or state or ethnic group" in the vicinity of National
Socialism.[183] May does not believe that there is "unconditional"[184] love
and invokes as an example of this the failure of the politics of the Vatican
in relation to the persecution of the Jews. The Christian concept of love
understands itself to be limitless, but it is in reality limited and therefore
untrue and dangerous. Other religions are excluded from love and thus
also from the obligation to care for them.

This argumentation is not only historically extremely imprecise but
above all does not capture the New Testament conception. "Other religions"
in the sense of opposing entities were not in view for the first Christians.
The Christ-confessing communities were not only, in relation to "Jews" and
"gentiles," infinitesimally small groups who had to fight lasting persecution.
Much more importantly, they wanted to bring "Jews" and "gentiles" the
gospel of their salvation. All the weightier, on the other hand, are the accusations against the later Christian churches that they practiced love only within
their boundaries. However, this argumentation is equally imprecise and
historically inaccurate, for here the historical reality is much worse, and the
criticism must be much more fundamental: the Christian leaders raged in a
terrible way not only against Jews and Muslims but also against Christians,
both inside and outside their own churches. Correct doctrine consistently
stood over love for brothers and sisters. However, May's mercilessly critical
view of the fundamental lack of love in the history of the Christian church
directs one's gaze not only to the fact that the New Testament conception
of love was betrayed in the history of the church again and again but also
uncovers a weakness that I pointed out already in the later New Testament
writings—the beginning of parties or schisms in the communities,[185] which
the early Christian community leaders could not deal with.

Let us turn then to the *individual* aspect. May diagnoses a tendency
since Rousseau to interpret love as the epitome of individualism—a

---

[182] May 2011, 238.

[183] May 2011, 111–14.

[184] May 2011, 95.

[185] Especially in the Johannine Epistles and in the other Catholic Epistles and in the
community letters of Revelation.

perception that Luhmann had already worked out. His diagnosis for both developments, the societal and the individual is as follows:

> Love is being overloaded.[186]

Here, May's judgment goes in a completely different direction from Luhmann's analysis and Badiou's perception. He warns against every form of excessive, unconditional love and understands love as a human rather than as a divine possibility and as a human need, as "ontological rootedness."[187] In distinction from Paul and John, he comes to the following conclusion:

> Instead of the hubris of modelling human love on how God is, questionably, said to love us, we are better off looking at how we are to love him. The command to love God is a way of saying that our flourishing is founded upon a lifelong search for a powerful relationship to the ground of our being—and that, whether it take religious or secular form, such a search is the ultimate purpose of a well-lived life.[188]

At this point May's otherwise very clear remarks become unclear and lose historical and material plausibility. It is clear that he makes recourse here to the Old Testament or Jewish form of the commandment of love for God, which appears human to him. By contrast, the early Christian life-form of love and its grounding in Christology (gift or grace) appear to him to be inhuman, unreal, and a form of *hubris*. Here, however, the theological counterquestion must be, Why is the love for God more human and, so to speak, more normal than God's love for human beings? There is no justification for this view in the Old Testament.[189] Moreover, May, if he wants to speak substantially and not metaphorically of ontological rootedness, does not avoid the "religious trap" of early Christian *agape*. For this is precisely what Paul seeks to designate with the "love of Christ"—the redemption of human beings and their access to God or ontological rootedness.

May's concept of love is especially interesting for the present study. On the one hand, he presents the only conception that is conceptualized not exclusively in a descriptive-analytical or prescriptive manner but presents, with the help of a hybrid language that is to be read in a philosophical-theological way, an ontological definition of love. On the other hand, he engages not only interpretively (as Julia Kristeva does) but

---

[186] May 2011, 239.

[187] May 2011, 240.

[188] May 2011, 265. Here the closeness to Augustine is obvious.

[189] See above on the theology of the love of God for Israel in the prophets.

in a material-critical way with the New Testament conception of love. His option for love for God instead of the love of God, to express his view in compressed form, represents a clear and conscious critical counter-conception to New Testament love. The charge that the New Testament concept of love exceeds the possibilities of love is weighty and calls into question the significance of the concept.

# Looking Forward

## The New Testament Concept of Love

The early Christian conception of love in the form of love for God and love for neighbor or of ἀγάπη has fundamentally shaped what love is to this day. This is confirmed not only by theological contributions such as the study of Werner G. Jeanrond[1] or especially historically oriented conceptions such as those of Julia Kristeva and Simon May, but also by presentations that are post-religious from the outset, such as those of Ulrich Beck and Elisabeth Beck-Gernsheim and Alain Badiou, to name only the works discussed here.[2] By contrast, completely forgoing any engagement with the shaping power of the Christian conception of love is one of the weaknesses of the theories of love of Niklas Luhmann and Martha Nussbaum. For the global Catholic Church, the encyclical of Benedict XVI newly updates the early Christian conception of love in altered form.

However, the examination of some important present-day concepts of love has made clear how far and how fundamentally the current discourse on love has moved away from the conceptions of the Christ-confessing community writers of the first century CE. Postmodern discourse on the topic excludes a simple adoption or even only a modified recourse to the early Christian concept. The religious and social-institutional framework conditions of the concept are present neither in Western societies as a whole nor in the Christian churches. This applies not only to the ἀγάπη concept as a whole but also to love for neighbor. Love for neighbor is the concept of ancient Israel. Hellenistic Judaism and emerging Christianity already had to adjust the Leviticus commandment to their political and social realities. They reached for the ethical forms of behavior of mercy and love

---

[1] Jeanrond 2010.
[2] Cf. also the very knowledgeable afterword of Schmölders 1996, 279–305.

for enemies in order to update love for neighbor for their time. A mere return to the commandment of love for neighbor may appear natural in this context.[3] It is prohibited, however, in light of the need for *new* concepts, which early Judaism and emerging Christianity already recognized. Thus, new interpretations, which go far beyond the encyclical, are also indispensable for the present.

This gives rise to the concluding question of the profile, limits, and impulses of the ἀγάπη concept for the present. The answer follows in a retrospective conversation with ancient Greek and Jewish concepts of love and with contemporary concepts of love in the tension between the enduring claim of the concept and its historical limitations.

## Profile

I have shown that the profile of the New Testament *agape* concept lies in the connection of theological, communitarian, ethical, emotional, and eschatological aspects and that it has a comprehensive relational structure between God and human beings, and human beings with one another as its theme, which is based on the great story of the love of God for human beings and on the love and self-sacrifice of Christ. The concept can be reduced neither to the purely theological-speculative and possibly also mystical aspect nor to an individual or communitarian ethical aspect. The double structure is given in the double commandment of love for God and love for neighbor and is worked out both by Paul and by the Johannine writings. It is not sufficient to love God if one does not love one's brother/sister. And the love for enemies of the individual does not make love for brothers and sisters in the fellowship of the Christ-confessing communities superfluous.

By contrast, the profile of the *agape* concept encompasses neither the intellectual, psychic, physical, and sexual eroticism between two persons as in Plato or Plutarch nor its institutional location in marriage as the encyclical *Deus Caritas Est* suggests. The concept is pre-individualistic and conceptualized entirely from the perspective of the fellowship with God and human beings. Individualization, eroticism, and sexuality are not aspects of the concept. By contrast, the encyclical shows—though without making this explicit—how the Catholic Church has expanded the concept by adjusting the New Testament concept of love to what has been recognized by the church as anthropological constants and desideratum—such as the connection of marriage and love or love and sexuality—and thus both developed and changed the original conception.

---

[3] Cf. the sympathy that S. May has toward love for neighbor.

## Claim

"Love" is a fundamental element of the proclamation and life practice of the contemporary global Christian churches and their theologians.[4] As such the requirement of love for God and love for neighbor and for enemies always makes a public political-ethical-religious *claim*, which is asserted beyond the cultural, religious, and ecclesial boundaries and also applies to the sphere that understands itself and sometimes normatively defines itself as secular or post-religious. This claim corresponds to certain universal tendencies of the New Testament texts themselves and is the basis of their *Wirkungsgeschichte*. It thus belongs to the horizon of the understanding of the New Testament texts just as much as the prehistory and historical contextualization of these texts do and may as such be briefly illuminated again here.

Already in the Gospel of Mark, the double commandment of love for God and love for neighbor is more than only one of many ethical statements of Jesus. It can appear as a summary of his teaching in general and aims at enduring significance beyond the inner-Jewish discourse on the law during Jesus' lifetime (Mark 12). Since the author of the Gospel of Mark has connected Jesus' teaching so strongly with the double commandment of love, Jesus' activity has been viewed time and again from the perspective of the motif of love. Thus, the author of the Gospel of John reacts to the Markan picture of Jesus by placing Jesus' whole activity, indeed his whole life under the principle of love in the farewell discourses: "Greater love has no one than this, that one lay down his life for his friends" (John 15.13). Likewise, texts such as the Sermon on the Mount (Matt 5–7), the so-called Song of Songs of Love (1 Cor 13), and the parable of the merciful Samaritan are paradigmatic texts whose significance reaches beyond situational community paraenesis and beyond the contemporary contexts. The claim of the parable of the merciful Samaritan explicitly applies beyond religious boundaries. The pericope of love for enemies is in its paradoxical radicality an impulse for critical debate for every other ethical conception. And the bold definition of love in 1 John: "God is love" (1 John 4.8, 16), which underlies the encyclical, is an interpretation of the concept of God that need not necessarily be restricted to the Christian religion but also presents a general contribution to the mysticism of the great religions.

---

[4] Cf., by way of example, the third international conference of the Lutheran World Federation in Chicago 2014: "Lutheran Hermeneutics and the Gospel of Matthew" with very different contributions on the topic "love in the Gospel of Matthew and in the contemporary Lutheran churches and communities," especially in African, Asian, and Latin American political and social contexts.

I have said above that the early Christian concept of *agape* had its historical context and cannot simply be placed in the present-day discourse, even though nothing has changed with regard to its fundamental claim. The fundamental reach of the claim of the New Testament conception of love in Western culture and the great influence that this claim still exerts is, however, made clear by the following reflection *ex negativo*, which is not often made. Positions that *materially reject* the commandment of love for neighbor or the demand to love one's enemies can hardly be advocated with success. Sharply contoured counter-positions such as "kill your enemies," "hate your enemies," "show neither understanding nor pity toward your enemies," and "rejoice at the defeat of your enemies" are ostracized not only in the global Christianities but also at least in the overall contemporary discourse of Western culture. Less contoured recommendations such as "don't care for your enemies" or "don't care for your neighbor," "show disinterest for human beings," and "empathy is senseless," also have no place in contemporary Western discourse, which is not characterized by self-assertion and enmity but precisely by the call for empathy, solidarity, acceptance, and appreciation for otherness as well as for social and pedagogical inclusion. It is not necessary to point to opposing concepts of non-Christian cultural circles and religions.

The same applies to positions that regard love as the closest relationship between two persons in principle as an error, as nonexistent, irrelevant, or harmful. This is made clear by Simon May's definition of love as the feeling of ontological rootedness. Who would call into question this feeling or the longing for this feeling? Thus, the continuing impact of the Christian concept of love is clear in both spheres, i.e., in the communitarian (usually called "social" today) and in the individual (usually called "personal" or "private" today). By contrast, explicit social and individual anti-love concepts are not successful in the public discussion of the Western world.

## Limits

Thus, in the comparison with present-day concepts of love, the determinants, distinctive characteristics, and effects of the early Christian concept of love emerge just as clearly as its *limits*. The historical attachment to the prescriptive Torah of Israel with its commandment structure, which mandates love for God and for neighbor; the religious anchoring in the faith of the early Christians, which connects love with faith in God, with the relationship to Jesus Christ, and with the Spirit of God; and the communitarian ethical focus on the Christ-confessing communities present the conditions within which this concept was developed and is carried forward in modified form in the churches. I have characterized the New Testament concept in the field of theology, communitarian ethos, emotion, and eschaton. With this, the material limits of the concept from the perspective of the present are also already specified. It can be lived only within ecclesial-community structures and within the framework of eschatological hope. We are dealing with a concept of the early Christ-confessing communities. The integration of marriage and family into the concept was already difficult, as Ephesians shows. The encyclical strives to integrate *eros*, sexuality, and emotional love in marriage and in the family into the concept and thereby changes the ἀγάπη concept fundamentally. The approach to the modernizing interpretation of the original concept is understandable but falls short of the mark and must be called into question as a whole in its intention. For this modern Catholic adaption also lacks almost everything that makes up the term "love" today in the Western world—relatedness to the body, sexuality, and eroticism and emotion beyond marriage, family, and offspring.

However, even more decisive than this change in the coordinates of the term is the question of what happens when the religious framework conditions as a whole fall away or only experience a decline in their general plausibility—a circumstance that Simon May has especially thematized repeatedly. Here lies the actual limit of the New Testament *agape* concept, and this fundamental limit is very clearly perceived by the present-day theories of love.

For in the contemporary post-Christian conceptions of love, the concern—with the exception of May—is less with detailed criticism of the New Testament concept. Rather, on the whole the concern is with the negation of these framework conditions—the foundations of the Christian interpretation of the world and of life. The threshold that divides all modern conceptions from the encyclical of Benedict XVI is the intellectual interaction with the phenomenon of "Western" secularization. All the authors essentialize the phenomenon—Martha Nussbaum expresses it in a normative way. They start from the general validity and irreversibility of secularization and write *from* and *for* a "Western" world that is not only non-Christian but also post-religious, which they regard as the exclusive sphere of life, interpretation, and influence. Religion in general and the Christian religion in particular—with respect to this point Niklas Luhmann, Ulrich Beck and Elisabeth Beck-Gernsheim, Alain Badiou, and Martha Nussbaum, despite all the differences in their positions, are in agreement—are irrelevant for the theme of "love." For Beck/Beck-Gernsheim and Badiou, love replaces religion. Therefore, the individual differences between the Christian and the "post-Christian" concept of love no longer need to be discussed.

In this theoretical framework, the embedding of "earthly" love into "heavenly" love[5] has lost its foundation and its significance. What is left is, first, love as the most intensive connection between two persons and, second, the social action of the individual and of the societal and government institutions. The individual love between two partners stands at the center. It is sometimes falsely overloaded with the inherited religious claim. According to the perception of some theorists of modern love, love between two human beings becomes the new religion or pseudo-religion. While Luhmann still emphasizes the positive social binding function of individual love in the form of marriage, Beck/Beck-Gernsheim and May place the impossibility of such an elevation of individual relationships in the foreground. While Beck/Beck-Gernsheim remain on the whole in the realm of the descriptive ("love as religion after religion"), Simon May writes from a decidedly normative and at the same time trans-religious standpoint, in which he rejects Christian love, in the form in which he interprets it, as excessive and instead gives a moderate essentialist definition ("ontological rootedness"),[6] while at the same time leaving open "whether [love] takes religious or secular form" — when it takes place only in the search for a "powerful relationship to the ground of our being," without this metaphor being filled out. For Simon May secularization itself has already experienced a decline in significance. His understanding of love applies in the religious and in the nonreligious context, i.e., it is, so to speak, post-post-religious. Alain Badiou and Julia Kristeva also write from a post-religious position, though without wanting to give up the deep dimension of love, which has been defined in a religious manner up to now. Julia Kristeva seeks new post-Christian linguistic forms, while Alan Badiou defends passionate love as an impossible possibility, as an existential paradox. The ethical and communitarian or overall societal implications of love are emphatically thematized by Martha Nussbaum. In doing so, she does not build on love for neighbor since she, *a limine*, does not take religiously based traditions into consideration.

It is clear that, amid all the differences between these contemporary interpretations, there is an unbridgeable opposition here between all the described positions, on the one hand, and the encyclical of the pope, on the other: In a so-called Western world-explanation that is defined in general as post-Christian, Christian *agape* can no longer develop its theological meaning and also can no longer be understood as a communitarian form of life or as *caritas*. Every conception of love is wholly de-theologized and

---

[5] Cf. the title (added after the fact) of a painting by Titian in the Galleria Borghese: *Earthly and Heavenly Love*.
[6] May 2011, 256.

refers exclusively to the psychic, sexual, and social relationship between two human beings. *Caritas*, however, is carried over in empathy and social programs.

## Inspiration

A historical-hermeneutical study will take note of this situation—not, however, in order to understand it either as a fait accompli or as a dead end but rather in order to get beyond the situation of speechlessness and lack of relationship between the two worlds—namely, the New Testament concept of love and the historically developed and newly articulated or newly to be articulated "teachings of the church,"[7] on the one hand, and the current Western post-religious discourse on love between sexuality, emotion, and empathy, on the other. However, the contemporary fragmentation of the world into religious and post-religious discourses does justice neither to the theme of love nor to the reality of a global world in which religions and post- or nonreligious world-interpretations do not exist *after* one another but rather *alongside, with*, and *against* one another.

I have traced out the New Testament concept of love and presented its Old Testament foundations, its historical contexts, and its contours in the contemporary academic discourse on love. The strengths and limits of the concept have become clear in the different comparisons. However, precisely the confrontation with the post-Christian contemporary conceptions of love makes clear not only the limits of the concept but also reveals which *inspiration* proceeds from this New Testament concept—irrespective of whether its theological premises and religious and communitarian experiences are shared. The question of the extent to which current cultural and societal discourses could gain inspiration from the New Testament concept of love shall stand at the end of this study and make the way free for new, contemporary interpretations.

It is not a theological voice but Julia Kristeva who invokes this inspiration most powerfully. No one has more clearly traced out the Old and New Testament love story of God with human beings "after the death of God" and in the process uncovered the way in which psychological and erotic aspects are contained in this story: God's love for his Son, the bodily suffering and violent death of the Son of God, interpreted as loving

---

[7] The Protestant churches appear not to have a position of their own on the theme of "love." Unlike Pope Benedict, the EKD orientation guide *Zwischen Autonomie und Angewiesenheit* (EKD 2013) does not even recognize the significance of this theme. The writing campaigns for the political support of families with different compositions. The Christian concept of love does not come into view.

self-sacrifice for "the friends" or "for many," pathos, passion, total commitment, and participation—all this is part of this story. Julia Kristeva has attempted, with the linguistic and conceptual resources of psychoanalysis and with recourse to Christian mystical linguistic tradition, to express the unfathomable conception of the death of God out of love for human beings and the somatic mystical participation of human beings in Christ's body. With this she has captured fundamental features of the New Testament conception of love linguistically better than the exegetical analysis. In summary it is the bodiliness and emotionality of this love story that has been told, since the Gospel of Mark, as a story of suffering and death, specifically as the "passion," and has been presented especially in the Western passion music. Bodiliness, eroticism,[8] visibility, enthusiasm, attraction, emotion, passion, pathos, pain, longing, fulfillment, loss, breaking through norms, presence and absence—all these aspects, which are reserved for two human beings in "modern" post-religious love, are also part of the New Testament love story of God with his Son, of God with human beings, of Jesus with human beings, of the Christ-confessing human beings with one another.

## Once Again Limits

Julia Kristeva's interpretation, however, also points to the *limits* of the early Christian concept of love. For two aspects are consciously lacking in this great concept of love and thus also in the early Christian *agape* culture—beauty[9] and sexuality as an integral component of love.[10] It is those "Greek" aspects of love about whose suppression Nietzsche accused Christianity with just as much one-sidedness as implacable sharpness. Nietzsche incisively uncovered the deficiencies of the original *agape* concept, which at the latest the medieval and modern Christian mysticism wanted to counterbalance in spiritual form. As I have shown, the early Christian conception itself has very consciously not assigned the bodily aspects of beauty and sexuality to love since sexuality and sexual attraction

---

[8] Cf. what was said above on the Gospel of John and on Luke 7.36–50.

[9] Cf. Phil 2.7 and the frequent reference of Paul to his bodily weaknesses (esp. Gal 4.12–14). Since the servant songs of Isaiah, bodily beauty does not belong to the theologically and ethically positively connoted attributes. Exceptions include Joseph and Aseneth and texts in the Testaments of the Twelve Patriarchs. The concern is especially with the beauty of women, which is always understood as dangerous. A different view is represented by Philo on Adam in *Opif.* 136. There the first human being is καλὸς καὶ ἀγαθός.

[10] Sexuality is not lacking as such, but it is not connected with ἀγάπη and is not part of the New Testament concept of love.

were experienced and understood as potentially destructive.[11] By contrast, one of the most important concerns of the encyclical *Deus Caritas Est* is to understand sexuality as constructive and to integrate it into the institution of marriage.[12] The encyclical distances itself in this topic from the early Christian *agape* concept and sets forth a different concept, that of Christian marriage as ordering structure for sexuality *and* as bodily and emotional relationship of love. On the other hand, the encyclical does not find a connection to the high estimation of free eroticism and sexuality that Western society has carved out[13] and whose boundaries have not yet been reached.

However, the high esteem for sexuality in all its manifestations must, in turn, let itself be called into question. The caution toward the destructive traits of sexuality—which is not only early Christian but also Greek and Jewish—experiences new relevance in light of current debates about pornography, child molestation, and criminal prostitution. In light of the connection of sexuality with voyeurism, power, violence, money, and murder, mere confessions of "good sexuality" that prize every form of sexuality—in whichever theoretical frameworks they may occur—must be regarded as well-meant but nevertheless problematic ideological constructions rather than helpful concepts. Sexuality and eroticism also cannot get by without an ethos of responsibility.

## History of Liberation and Loss

The development of the "Western" concept of love is rightly described in general as a history of liberation in the course of which love finally comes "to itself," becomes "human," and liberates itself from every religious ballast, which Simon May understands as hubris. At the same time, it can also be written as a story of loss. For against the background of the *agape* concept, it becomes equally clear what the Western concepts of post-Christian, individually, emotionally, and sexually grounded love lack and what as inspiration could enter into the post-Christian talk of love or

[11] For the Greek understanding of *eros* as destructive power, cf. the discussion of Nussbaum above. In his work *De Amore*, Andreas Capellanus expressed the matter in a classic and ambiguous way: "Love is a certain inborn suffering derived from the sight of and excessive meditation upon the beauty of the opposite sex" (trans. J. J. Parry in Capellanus 1960, 28).

[12] Here, it would have been important to point to positive concepts of marriage such as that of Plutarch.

[13] A fundamental disparity or nonsimultaneity is present here between liberal Western cultural conceptions, on the one hand, and the rejection of homosexuality and other sexual perspectives in other cultural circles.

lead to a new conversation. It lacks the conception of a transcendent origin and eschatological reach of love, which is nevertheless sought in the contemporary conceptions time and again and invoked in paradoxes—love as religion or as ontological rootedness. The concentration of this love in the life and death of the human being Jesus, and this means in the sacrifice for the beloved person, has been lost—a motif that is not understood at present in the well-ordered Western world, which cannot fill suffering, sacrifice, and death with meaning. It thus lacks the great foundational story of love that furnishes the human love stories with the emotional significance that the post-Christian conceptions cannot present and make plausible. Love is obviously still experienced as greater than the limited post-religious interpretive possibilities. Finally, it lacks in particular the theological dimension in the narrower sense—God conceptualized from the inner-divine *love relationship* between "Father" and "Son." Likewise, the conception of divine love that comes to human beings is completely lacking in the current discourses on love.

However, it also lacks the obligating dimension of love in the form of charity (*caritas*) and personal mercy, which in contemporary Western ethical discourses does not have as secure a place as pallid empathy. This was rightly pointed out by Pope Benedict XVI in the second part of his encyclical. Here too, the New Testament concept has an inspiring effect.

## Perspectives

An interpretation that takes place in the vein of historical hermeneutics and sketches its results into the present-day discourse forgoes the formulation of metaphysical, essentialist, normative-positional, or appellative answers or the presentation of position statements. Out of the description arise questions that the texts pose to the present and that the present answers with its questions in return. The significance of the texts that have been interpreted can be tested only in the discussion of the questions that were posed. On the one hand, in the horizon of these very questions, the early Christian conception of love is one among other ethical and religious layers of tradition in the archaeology of our Western culture shaped by Judaism and Christianity. It is a facet of our religious-cultural memory as well as a worthy voice in the round dance of historical concepts of love. It has its own historical and material place in antiquity and its own limits. On the other hand, it is a relevant and inspiring question to the present-day ethical, religious, and post-religious love discourse of our time and part of the ethical teaching of the Christian churches around the world.

Accordingly, the concluding question must be the following: Where does the New Testament concept of love find its place here apart from

Christian communities and their internal ethos or their interpretation of the *agape* culture? As a religiously grounded concept, the early Christian interpretation of ἀγάπη can become efficacious above all in contemporary discussions about religion. It will decisively inspire current debates about monotheism and the so-called monotheistic religions with their questions and stimulate new discussion about the theological and ethical potential of the monotheistic religions:

Does it make a difference whether a religion that is called monotheistic places the element of personal love in God himself?

Does it make a difference whether a monotheistic religion regards the love of God for human beings to be so great that God sacrifices his beloved Son for human beings?[14]

Does it make a difference whether God in the form of his Son dies for human beings?

Does it make a difference whether Jesus *loves* his disciples?[15]

Does it make a difference whether God is imagined as one who shows mercy or as one who loves? As one who in good paternalism inclines with mercy to human beings or as one who loves them and sacrifices himself for them?

Finally, does it make a difference whether a social and religious culture places love as *agape* and *caritas* at the center?

From the perspective of these questions, the early Christian concept of love is not an out-of-date form of life and thought from which we must — if it is still necessary — liberate ourselves but a highly intellectual and courageous attempt to think God and to live according to God and a religious, intellectual, and ethical challenge both to other religions on a global scale and to a Western culture that defines itself as post-religious. The concept is a special challenge to Christian churches and communities in their global diversity. They too cannot simply repeat the concept of love but must interpret it — from caritative, social, individual-ethical, and theological perspectives.

---

[14] The so-called Akedah goes precisely in the opposite direction.

[15] As far as I can see, this dimension of the Christian religion plays no role in the current debate about monotheistic religions and violence! A discussion of the theses of Jan Assmann must begin here.

# Bibliography

## Finding a Work in the Bibliography

In the English translation, works have been referenced in two different ways. First, a small number of works have been referenced using abbreviations, which are explained below. Second, most literature has been referenced by author and date (e.g., Becker 2020). If necessary, works from the same year have been distinguished through the addition of a letter (e.g., Wischmeyer 2016a and 2016b). While the bibliography sometimes includes earlier publication dates in square brackets (e.g., Schnelle 2016 [1998]), this information is often not included in the body of the translation.

## (1) Abbreviations

The abbreviations used in this work are based on the list of abbreviations in volume 8 of the fourth edition of *Religion in Geschichte und Gegenwart* (Tübingen, 2007), i.e., *RGG*[4], and on the second edition of *The SBL Handbook of Style* (Atlanta: SBL, 2014).

For the text and bibliography, special note should be made of the following abbreviations, some of which differ from the conventions adopted in the aforementioned works.

*AB*   *Anchor Bible*
*ABD*  *Anchor Bible Dictionary*. Edited by D. N. Freedman. 6 vols. New York: Doubleday, 1992.
BDR    Blass, F., and A. Debrunner. *Grammatik des neutestamentliche Griechisch*. Bearbeitet von F. Rehkopf. 17th ed. Göttingen: Vandenhoeck & Ruprecht, 1991.
*BNP*  *Brill's New Pauly, Antiquity*. Edited by H. Cancik and H. Schneider. Leiden: Brill, 2002–2010.
*DNP*  *Der neue Pauly*. Edited by H. Cancik, H. Schneider, and M. Landfester. Stuttgart: Metzler, 1996ff.

*EDEJ*    *The Eerdmans Dictionary of Ancient Judaism*. Edited by J. J. Collins and D. C. Harlow. Grand Rapids: Eerdmans, 2010.

FV    French Version

GV    German Version

*HWP*    *Historisches Wörterbuch der Philosophie*. Edited by J. Ritter and K. Gründer. 13 vols. Basel: Schabe, 1971–2007.

*LBH*    *Lexicon der Bibelhermeneutik*. Edited by O. Wischmeyer. Berlin: Walter de Gruyter, 2009.

LSJ    Liddell, H. G., R. Scott, and H. S. Jones. 1996. *A Greek-English Lexicon*. 9th ed. Oxford: Clarendon Press.

*OTP*    *The Old Testament Pseudepigrapha*. Edited by J. H. Charlesworth. 2 vols. Garden City, N.Y.: Doubleday.

*RNT*    Regensburger Neues Testament. Regensburg: Pustet Verlag.

*PW*    *Paulys Real-Encyclopädie der classischen Alterthumswissenschaft.* New ed. G. Wissowa. Stuttgart: Metzler, 1894–1980.

*RAC*    *Reallexikon für Antike und Christentum*. Stuttgart: Anton Hiersemann Verlag.

*RGG4*    *Religion in Geschichte und Gegenwart*. 4th edition. Edited by H. D. Betz, D. S. Browning, B. Janowski, and E. Jüngel. Tübingen: Mohr, 1988–2007.

*RPP*    *Religion Past and Present*. Edited by H. D. Betz, D. S. Browning, B. Janowski, and E. Jüngel. Leiden: Brill, 2006–2013.

*SKPAW*    *Sitzberichte der Königlich Preussischen Akademie der Wissenschaften zu Berlin*. Berlin: Verlag der Akademie der Wissenschaften.

*TDOT*    *Theological Dictionary of the Old Testament*. Edited by G. J. Botterweck and H. Ringgren. Grand Rapids: Eerdmans, 1974–2006.

*TDNT*    *Theological Dictionary of the New Testament*. Edited by G. Kittel and G. Friedrich. Translated by G. W. Bromiley. 10 vols. Grand Rapids: Eerdmans, 1964–1976.

*ThHK*    *Theologischer Handkommentar zum Neuen Testament*. Edited by J. Herzer and U. Schnelle. Leipzig: Evangelische Verlagsanstalt.

*ThWAT*    *Theologisches Wörterbuch zum Alten Testament*. Edited by G. J. Botterweck and H. Ringgren. Stuttgart: Kohlhammer, 1973–2001.

*ThWNT*    *Theologisches Wörterbuch zum Neuen Testament*. Edited by G. Kittel and G. Friedrich. Stuttgart: Kohlhammer, 1932–1979.

*ThWQ*    *Theologisches Wörterbuch zu den Qumrantexten*. Edited by H.-J. Fabry and U. Dahmen, Stuttgart: Kohlhammer, 2011ff.

*TRE*    *Theologische Realenzyklopädie*. Edited by G. Krause and G. Müller. Berlin: Walter de Gruyter.

WaPh    *Wörterbuch der antiken Philosophie.* Edited by C. Horn and
        C. Rapp. 2nd edition. Munich: Beck, 2008.
WBC     *Word Biblical Commentary.* Dallas, Tex.: Word Books.

## (2) Literature

Aasgard, R. 2004. *"My Beloved Brothers and Sisters!" Christian Siblingship in Paul.* JSNTSS 265. London: T&T Clark International.

Achenbach, R. 1991. *Israel zwischen Verheißung und Gebot: Literarkritische Untersuchungen zu Deuteronomium 5–11.* EHS.T 422. Frankfurt am Main: Lang.

Ådna, J. 1995. "Die eheliche liebesbeziehung als Analogie zu Christi Beziehung zur Kirche." *ZThK* 92: 434–65.

Alberoni, F. 1979. *Innamoramento e amore.* Milan: Garzanti.

———. 1983. *Falling in Love.* Translated by L. Venuti. New York: Random House.

Albrecht, F., and R. Feldmeier, eds. 2014. *The Divine Father: Religious and Philosophical Concepts of Divine Parenthood in Antiquity.* Themes in Biblical Narrative 14. Leiden: Brill.

Allison, D. C. 2010. *Constructing Jesus: Memory, Imagination, and History.* Grand Rapids: Baker Academic.

Angehrn, E., et al. 2009. "Hermeneutik." Pages 245–54 in *LBH.*

Ariès, P., and A. Béjin. 1984. *Die Masken des Begehrens und die Metamorphosen der Sinnlichkeit: Zur Geschichte der Sexualität im Abendland.* Frankfurt am Main: Fischer Taschenbuch Verlag.

———. 1986. *Western Sexuality: Practice and Precept in Past and Present Times.* Translated by A. Forster. Oxford: Blackwell.

Augenstein, J. 1993. *Das Liebesgebot im Johannesevangelium und in den Johannesbriefen.* BWANT NF 14. Stuttgart: Kohlhammer.

Aune, D. E. 1987. *The New Testament in Its Literary Environment.* Philadelphia: Westminster.

———. 1988. *Greco-Roman Literature and the New Testament.* Atlanta: Scholars Press.

Badiou, A., with N. Truong. 2009. *Eloge de l'amour.* Paris: Flammarion.

———. 2012. *In Praise of Love.* Translated by P. Bush. London: Serpent's Tail.

Barthes, R. 1977. *Fragments d'un discours amoureux.* Paris: Éditions du Seuil.

———. 2010. *A Lover's Discourse: Fragments.* Translated by R. Howard. New York: Hill and Wang.

Bauer, W. 1988. *Griechisch-deutsches Wörterbuch zu den Schriften des Neuen Testaments und der frühchristlichen Literatur.* Edited by K. Aland and B. Aland. 6th ed. Berlin: Walter de Gruyter.

Beauvoir, S. de. 1949. *Le deuxième sexe.* Paris: Gallimard.

———. 1974. *The Second Sex.* Translated and edited by H. M. Parshley. New York: Vintage Books.

Beck, U., and E. Beck-Gernsheim. 1995. *The Normal Chaos of Love.* Translated by M. Ritter and J. Wiebel. Cambridge: Polity.

———. 2011. *Fernliebe: Lebensformen im globalen Zeitalter*. Frankfurt am Main: Suhrkamp.

———. 2012 [¹1990]. *Das ganz normale Chaos der Liebe*. 12th ed. st 1725. Frankfurt am Main: Suhrkamp.

———. 2014. *Distant Love: Personal Life in the Global Age*. Translated by R. Livingstone. Cambridge: Polity.

Becker, E.-M. 2015. "Mimetische Ethik im Philipperbrief: Zu Form und Funktion paulinischer exempla." Pages 219–34 in *Metapher—Narratio —Mimesis—Doxologie: Begründungsformen frühchristlicher und antiker Ethik*. Edited by U. Volp, F. W. Horn and R. Zimmermann. Tübingen: Mohr (= E.-M. Becker 2019, 245–62).

———. 2019. *Der Philipperbrief des Paulus: Vorarbeiten zu einem Kommentar*. NET 29. Tübingen: Francke. https://elibrary.narr.digital/book/99.125005/9783772056888.

———. 2020. *Paul on Humility*. Translated by W. Coppins. Edited by W. Coppins and S. Gathercole. BMSEC 8. Waco, Tex.: Baylor University Press.

Becker, E.-M., and H. Scholz. 2014. *Auf dem Weg zur neutestamentlichen Hermeneutik: Oda Wischmeyer zum 70. Geburtstag*. Tübingen: Mohr.

Becker, J., ed. 1974. *Die Testamente der zwölf Patriarchen*. JSHRZ III 1. Gütersloh: Mohn.

———. 1991. *Das Evangelium nach Johannes: Kapitel 11–21*. 3rd ed. ÖTK 4/2. Gütersloh: Mohn.

Becker, U. 1963. *Jesus und die Ehebrecherin: Untersuchung zur Text- und Überlieferungsgeschichte von Joh 7,53–8,11*. BZNW 28. Berlin: Walter de Gruyter.

Behrens, A., et al. 2009. "Kritik." Pages 347–50 in *LBH*.

Bendlin, A., and H. A. Shapiro. 2000. "Personifikation." Pages 639–47 in *DNP 9*.

———. 2007. "Personification." Pages 842–50 in *BNP 10*.

Benedict XVI. 2006. *God Is Love: Deus Caritas Est; Encyclical Letter*. Vatican City: Libreria Editrice Vaticana.

Berger, K. 1972. *Die Gesetzesauslegung Jesu: Ihr historischer Hintergrund im Judentum und im Alten Testament*. Part I: *Markus und Parallelen*. WMANT 40. Neukirchen-Vluyn: Neukirchener Verlag.

———. 1984a. *Formgeschichte des Neuen Testaments*. Heidelberg: Quelle & Meyer.

———. 1984b. "Hellenistische Gattungen im Neuen Testament." Pages 1031–432 and 1831–85 in *ANRW* II 25/2.

Bergman, A., A. O. Haldar, and G. Wallis. 1973. "ahab." Pages 105–28 in *ThWAT* 1.

———. 1977. "ʾāhabh." Pages 99–118 in *TDOT* 1.

Bertschmann, D. H. 2014. "The Good, the Bad and the State in Rom 13.1–7 and the Dynamics of Love." *NTS* 60: 232–49.

Betz, H. D. 1967. *Nachfolge und Nachahmung Jesu Christi im Neuen Testament*. BhTh. Tübingen: Mohr.

———. 1975. *Plutarch's Theological Writings and Early Christian Literature*. SCH III. Leiden: Brill.

——. 1978. *Plutarch's Ethical Writings and Early Christian Literature*. SCH IV. Leiden: Brill.

——. 1979. *Galatians: A Commentary on Paul's Letter to the Churches in Galatia*. Hermeneia. Philadelphia: Fortress.

Bilde, P. 2013. *The Originality of Jesus: A Critical Discussion and a Comparative Attempt*. SANt 1. Göttingen: Vandenhoeck & Ruprecht.

Bloch, R. 2014. "Take Your Time. Conversation, Confidence and Tranquility in Joseph and Aseneth." Pages 77–96 in *Anthropologie und Ethik im Frühjudentum und im Neuen Testament: Wechselseitige Wahrnehmungen*. Edited by M. Konradt and E. Schläper. WUNT 322. Tübingen: Mohr.

Bornkamm, G. 1957. "Das Doppelgebot der Liebe." Pages 85–93 in *Neutestamentliche Studien für Rudolf Bultmann zu seinen 70. Geburtstag*. Edited by E. Eltester. BZNW 21. Berlin: Walter de Gruyter.

——. 1968. "Das Doppelgebot der Liebe." Pages 37–45 in *Geschichte und Glaube*. Vol. 1. BEvTh 48. Munich: Kaiser.

Bornscheuer, L. 1984. "Topik." Pages 454–75 in vol. 4 of *Reallexicon der deutschen Literaturgeschichte*. 2nd ed. Edited by W. Kohlschmidt. Berlin: Walter de Gruyter.

Böttrich, G., ed. 1995. *Das Slavische Henochbuch*. JSHRZ V 7. Gütersloh: Mohn.

Boulnois, O. 2014. *Duns Scotus: Die Logik der Liebe*. Stuttgart: Kohlhammer.

Bovon, F. 1989. *Das Evangelium nach Lukas (Lk 1,1–9,50)*. EKKNT III/1. Zürich: Benziger.

——. 1992. *Luke 1: A Commentary on the Gospel of Luke 1:1–9:50*. Translated by C. M. Thomas. Hermeneia. Minneapolis: Fortress Press.

——. 1996. *Das Evangelium nach Lukas (Lk 9,51–14,35)*. EKK III/2. Zürich: Benzinger.

——. 2013. *Luke 2: A Commentary on the Gospel of Luke 9:51–19:27*. Translated by D. S. Deer. Edited by H. Koester. Minneapolis: Fortress.

Boyce Gibson, W. R., et al. 1974 [1914]. "Love." Pages 151–83 in *ERE* 8.

Braulik, G. 1986. *Deuteronomium 1–16,17*. Das Neue Echter Bibel 15. Würzburg: Echter.

Breithaupt, F. 2012. *Kulturen der Empathie*. 3rd ed. stw 1906. Frankfurt am Main: Suhrkamp.

Bremer, D. 2009. "Erkenntnis und Eros bei Platon." Pages 41–62 in *Geist, Eros und Agape: Untersuchungen zu Liebesdarstellungen in Philosophie, Religion und Kunst*. Edited by E. Düsing and H.-D. Klein. Würzburg: Königshausen & Neumann.

Brenk, F. E. 2012. "Most Beautiful and Divine: Greco-Romans (and especially Plutarch), and Paul, on Love and Marriage." Pages 87–111 in *Graeco Roman Culture and the New Testament: Studies Commemorating the Centennial of the Pontifical Biblical Institute 2012*. Edited by D. E. Aune and F. E. Brenk. Leiden: Brill.

Breyer, T., ed. 2013. *Grenzen der Empathie: Philosophische, psychologische und anthropologische Perspektiven*. Munich: Fink.

Breytenbach, C. 2013. "Interpretationen des Todes Jesu." Pages 321–31 in *Paulus Handbuch*. Edited by F. W. Horn. Tübingen: Mohr.

Broer, I., in collaboration with H.-U. Weidemann. 2010. *Einleitung in das Neue Testament*. 3rd ed. Würzburg: Echter Verlag.

Brown, R. E. 1979. *The Community of the Beloved Disciple: The Life, Loves, and Hates of an Individual Church in New Testament Times*. London: Geoffrey Chapman.

———. 1982. *The Epistles of John*. AcB 30. Garden City, N.Y.: Garden Day.

Brown, S., and C. W. Skinner, eds. 2017. *Johannine Ethics: The Moral World of the Gospel and Epistles of John*. Minneapolis: Fortress.

Bruin, T. de. 2014. *The Great Controversy: The Individual's Struggle between Good and Evil in the Testaments of the Twelve Patriarchs and in Their Jewish and Christian Contexts*. NTOA/StUNT 160. Göttingen: Vandenhoeck & Ruprecht.

Buchheim, T. 2008. "Erôs." Pages 153–54 in *WaPh*.

Bultmann, R. 1935. "ἔλεος κτλ." Pages 474–83 in *ThWNT* 2.

———. 1938. "θάνατος κτλ." Pages 7–25 in *ThWNT* 3.

———. 1964a. *Das Evangelium des Johannes*. 18th ed. KEK. Göttingen: Vandenhoeck & Ruprecht.

———. 1964b. "ἔλεος κτλ." Pages 477–87 in *TDNT* 2.

———. 1965. "θάνατος κτλ." Pages 7–25 in *TDNT* 3.

———. 1971. *The Gospel according to John*. Translated by G. R. Beasley-Murray. New York: Doubleday.

Burchard, C. 1974. "Das doppelte Liebesgebot in der frühen christlichen Überlieferung." Pages 39–62 in *Der Ruf Jesu und die Antwort der Gemeinde: Exegetische Untersuchungen Joachim Jeremias zum 70. Geburtstag*. Edited by E. Lohse. Göttingen: Vandenhoeck & Ruprecht.

———. 1983. *Joseph und Aseneth*. JSHRZ II 4. Gütersloh: Mohn.

———. 2000. *Der Jakobusbrief*. HNT 15/I. Tübingen: Mohr Siebeck.

Butler, J. 1990. *Gender Trouble*. New York: Routledge.

———. 2004. *Undoing Gender*. New York: Routledge.

Byers, A. 2017. *Ecclesiology and Theosis in the Gospel of John*. MSSNTS. Cambridge: Cambridge University Press.

Bywater, I., ed. 1894. *Aristotelis ethica Nicomachea*. Oxford: Clarendon.

Calboli Montefusco, L. 2002. "Topik." Pages 691–93 in *DNP* 12/1.

———. 2009. "Topics." Pages 782–84 in *BNP* 14.

Capellanus, A. 1960. *The Art of Courtly Love*. Translated by J. J. Parry. New York: Columbia University Press.

Chadwick, H. 1962. "Enkrateia." Pages 343–65 in *RAC* 5.

Christensen, D. L. 1991. *Deuteronomy 1–11*. WBC 6A. Dallas, Tex.: Word.

Classen, C. J. 1979. "Der platonisch-stoische Kanon der Kardinaltugenden bei Philon, Clemens Alexandrinus und Origenes." Pages 68–88 in *Kergygma und Logos: Festschrift für C. Andresen*. Edited by A. M. Ritter. Göttingen: Vandenhoeck & Ruprecht.

Cohn, L., ed. 1896. *Philonis De opificio mundi*. Pages 1–60 in vol. 1 of *Philonis Alexandrini opera quae supersunt*. Edited by L. Cohn. Berlin: Walter de Gruyter.

Culpepper, R. A. 1975. *The Johannine School*. SBLDS 26. Missoula, Mont.: Scholars Press.

Culy, M. 2010. *Echoes of Friendship in the Gospel of John*. NTM 30. Sheffield: Sheffield Phoenix Press.

Dahmen, U. 2011. "'ojeb." Pages 87–91 in *ThWQ* 1.

de Jonge, M. 1970. *Testamenta XII Patriarchum*. 2nd ed. PsVTGr. Leiden: Brill.

Delling, G. 1969a. "τέλος κτλ." Pages 50–88 in *ThWNT* 8.

———. 1969b. "τρεῖς, τρίς, τρίτος." Pages 215–25 in *ThWNT* 8.

———. 1972a. "τέλος κτλ." Pages 49–87 in *TDNT* 8.

———. 1972b. "τρεῖς, τρίς, τρίτος." Pages 216–25 in *TDNT* 8.

Dibelius, M. 1953. "Joh 15,13: Eine Studie zum Traditionsproblem des Johannes-Evangelium." Pages 204–20 in *Botschaft und Geschichte: Gessamelte Aufsätze*. Vol. 1. Edited by G. Bornkamm. Tübingen: Mohr.

Dihle, A. 1962. *Die Goldene Regel*. SAW 7. Göttingen: Vandenhoeck & Ruprecht.

———. 1966. "Ethik." Pages 646–796 in *RAC* 6.

———. 1988. "Heilig." Pages 1–63 in *RAC* 14.

Dirlmeier, F. 1931. "ΦΙΛΟΣ und ΦΙΛΙΑ im vorhellenischen Griechentum." Diss. Munich.

Dormeyer, D. 1993. *Das Neue Testament im Rahmen der antiken Literaturgeschichte: Eine Einführung*. Darmstadt: Wissenschaftliche Buchgesellschaft.

Draper, J. A. 2009. "Die Didache." Pages 17–38 in *Die Apostolischen Väter: Eine Einführung*. Edited by W. Pratcher. Göttingen: Vandenhoeck & Ruprecht.

———. 2010. "The Didache." Pages 7–26 in *The Apostolic Fathers: An Introduction*. Edited by W. Pratcher. Waco, Tex.: Baylor University Press.

Dunn, J. D. G. 2003. *Jesus Remembered*. CM 1. Grand Rapids, Mich.: Eerdmans.

Düsing, E. 2009. "Geist, Eros und Agape—eine historisch-systematische Problemskizze." Pages 7–40 in *Geist, Eros und Agape: Untersuchungen zu Liebesdarstellungen in Philosophie, Religion und Kunst*. Edited by E. Düsing and H.-D. Klein. Würzburg: Königshausen & Neumann.

Düsing, E., and H.-D. Klein, eds. 2009. *Geist, Eros und Agape: Untersuchungen zu Liebesdarstellungen in Philosophie, Religion und Kunst*. Würzburg: Königshausen & Neumann.

Ebersohn, M. 1993. *Das Nächstenliebegebot in der synoptischen Überlieferung*. MThSt 37. Marburg: Elwert.

Eckermann, J. P. 2011. *Gespräche mit Goethe in den letzten Jahren seines Lebens*. Edited by C. Michel. Deutscher Klassikerverlag im Taschenbuch 50. Berlin: Deutscher Klassiker Verlag.

Eibach, J., and G. Lottes, eds. 2002. *Kompass der Geschichtswissenschaft*. UTB 2271. Göttingen: Vandenhoeck & Ruprecht.

EKD 2013. *Zwischen Autonomie und Angewiesenheit: Familie als verlässliche Gemeinschaft stärken; Eine Orientierungshilfe der Evangelische Kirche in Deutschland (EKD)*. Gütersloh: Gütersloher Verlagshaus.

Elliott, M. W. 2000. *The Song of Songs and Christology in the Early Church*. STAC 7. Tübingen: Mohr.

Elliott, N. 2008. *The Arrogance of Nations: Reading Romans in the Shadow of Empire*. Minneapolis: Fortress.

Enzmann, B., ed. 2013. *Handbuch Politische Gewalt*. Wiesbaden: Springer.

Erbele-Küster, D., et al. 2009. "Erklärungen/Erklären." Pages 147–52 in *LBH*.

Fabry, H.-J. 2011. "ahab." Pages 65–72 in *ThWQ* 1.

Falls, T. B., T. P. Halton, and M. Slusser. 2003. *Justin Martyr, Dialogue with Trypho*. Translated by T. B. Falls; revised and with a new introduction by T. B. Halton. Edited by M. Slusser. Washington, D.C.: Catholic University of America Press.

Falter, M., and H. Färber, eds. 1961. *Marcus Tullius Cicero, Laelius de amicitia*. Latin-German. Edited and translated by M. Falter and H. Färber. Munich: Heimeran.

Fantuzzi, M., C. Reitz, and U. Egelhaaf-Gaiser. 2004. "Ekphrasis." Pages 871–80 in *BNP* 4.

Feldmeier, R., and H. Spieckermann. 2010. *Der Gott der Lebendigen: Eine biblische Gotteslehre*. Tobith 1. Tübingen: Mohr.

———. 2011. *The God of the Living: A Biblical Theology*. Translated by M. E. Biddle. Waco, Tex.: Baylor University Press.

Feuillet, A. 1972. *Le mystère de l'amour divin dans la théologie johannique*. Paris: Gabalda.

Fischel, H. A. 1973. "The Uses of Sorites (Climax, Gradatio) in the Tannaitic Period." *HUCA* 44: 119–51.

Fitzgerald, J. T. 1992. "Virtue/Vice Lists." Pages 857–59 in *ABD* 6.

———. 1997. *Greco-Roman Perspectives on Friendship*. SBL Resources for Biblical Study 34. Atlanta: Scholars Press.

Fitzmyer, J. A. 1981. *The Gospel according to Luke I–IX*. AB 28. New York: Doubleday.

———. 1983. *The Gospel according to Luke X–XXIV*. Garden City: Doubleday.

Foerster, W. 1935. "ἐχθρός, ἔχθρα." Pages 810–15 in *ThWNT* 2.

———. 1964. "ἐχθρός, ἔχθρα." Pages 811–15 in *TDNT* 2.

Foucault, M. 1984. *Le souci de soi*. Paris: Gallimard.

———. 1988. *The History of Sexuality*. Vol. 3: *The Care of the Self*. Translated by R. Hurley. New York: Vintage Books.

Fraisse, J.-C. 1974. *Philia: La notion d'amitié dans la philosophie antique*. Paris: Vrin.

Frevert, U. 2013. *Vergängliche Gefühle*. Göttingen: Wallstein.

———. 2014a. "Die Soziale Macht der Liebe [Review of Political Emotions: Why Love Matters for Justice, by Martha Nussbaum]." *Neue Zurcher Zeitung (NZZ)*, October 4, 2014, Neue Sachbücher 15. https://www.nzz.ch/feuilleton/buecherherbst/die-soziale-macht-der-liebe-1.18395149.

———. 2014b. *The Moral Economy of Trust: Modern Trajectories*. London: German Historical Institute.

———. 2020. *The Politics of Humiliation: A Modern History*. Translated by A. Bresnahan. Oxford: Oxford University Press.

Frevert, U., M. Scheer, A. Schmidt, P. Eitler, B. Hitzer, N. Verheyen, B. Gammerl, C. Bailey, and M. Pernau. 2014. *Emotional Lexicons: Continuity and Change in the Vocabulary of Feeling 1700–2000.* Oxford: Oxford University Press.

Frey, J. 1997–2000. *Die johanneische Eschatologie.* 3 vols. WUNT 96, 110, 117. Tübingen: Mohr.

———. 2018. *The Glory of the Crucified One.* Translated by W. Coppins and C. Heilig. Edited by W. Coppins and S. Gathercole. BMSEC 6. Waco, Tex.: Baylor University Press.

Fuller, R. H. 1978. "The Double Commandment of Love: A Test Case for the Criteria of Authenticity." Pages 41–56 in *Essays on the Love Commandment.* Edited by L. Schottroff. Philadelphia: Fortress.

Furnish, V. P. 1972. *The Love Commandment in the New Testament.* London: SCM.

Gaca, K. L. 2014. "Early Christian Sexuality." Pages 549–64 in *A Companion to Greek and Roman Sexualities.* Edited by T. K. Hubbard. Oxford: Blackwell.

Gärtner, H. A. 2007. "Priamel." Pages 816–17 in *BNP* 11.

Gaventa, B. 2007. *Our Mother Saint Paul.* Louisville: Westminster John Knox.

Gemünden, P. v. 2003. "Die Wertung des Zorns im Jakobusbrief auf dem Hintergrund des antiken Kontexts und seine Einordnung." Pages 97–119 in *Der Jakobusbrief: Beiträge zur Rehabilitierung der "strohernen Epistel."* Edited by P. v. Gemünden, M. Konradt, and G. Theissen. Beiträge zum Verstehen der Bibel 3. Münster: LIT.

Gerber, C. 2005. *Paulus und seine 'Kinder': Studien zur Beziehungsmetaphorik der paulinischen Briefe.* BZNW 136. Berlin: Walter de Gruyter.

Gerhards, J. 1988. *Soziologie der Emotionen.* Weinheim: Juventa.

Gerlitz, P., et al. 1991. "Liebe." Pages 121–91 in *TRE* 21.

Gerstenberger, E. S. 1993. *Das 3. Buch Mose: Leviticus.* ATD 6. Göttingen: Vandenhoeck & Ruprecht.

———. 1996. *Leviticus: A Commentary.* Translated by D. W. Scott. Louisville: Westminster John Knox.

Gertz, J. C., ed. 2010. *Grundinformation Altes Testament.* 4th ed. Göttingen: Vandenhoeck & Ruprecht.

Goppelt, L. 1978. *Der Erste Petrusbrief.* Göttingen: Vandenhoeck & Ruprecht.

———. 1993. *A Commentary on 1 Peter.* Translated and augmented by J. E. Alsup. Edited by F. Hahn. Grand Rapids: Eerdmans.

Görgemanns, H. 2005. "Eros als Gott in Plutarchs 'Amatorius.'" Pages 169–95 in *Gott und die Götter bei Plutarch: Götterbilder—Gottesbilder—Weltbilder.* Edited by R. Hirsch-Luipold. Berlin: Walter de Gruyter.

———. 2006. "Einführung." Pages 3–38 in *Plutarch, Dialog über die Liebe: Amatorious.* Eingeleitet, übersetzt und mit interpretierende Essays versehen von H. Görgemanns, B. Feichtinger, F. Graf, W. Jeanrond, und J. Opsomer. Sapere 10. Tübingen: Mohr.

———. 2013. "Eros als Gott in Plutarchs 'Amatorius.'" Pages 339–64 in *Philologos Kosmos.* Edited by H. Görgemanns. STACh 73. Tübingen: Mohr.

Görgemanns, H., B. Feichtinger, F. Graf, W. Jeanrond, and J. Opsomer, eds. 2006. *Plutarch, Dialog über die Liebe: Amatorious.* Eingeleitet, übersetzt und mit interpretierende Essays versehen von H. Görgemanns. Sapere 10. Tübingen: Mohr.

Graf, F. 2006. "Der Kult des Eros in Thespiai." Pages 191–207 in *Plutarch, Dialog über die Liebe: Amatorius*. Eingeleitet, übersetzt und mit interpretierende Essays versehen von H. Görgemanns, B. Feichtinger, F. Graf, W. Jeanrond, und J. Opsomer. Sapere 10. Tübingen: Mohr.

Graf, F. W. 2005. *Die Wiederkehr der Götter: Religion in der modernen Kultur*. 3rd ed. Munich: Beck.

———. 2014. *Götter global: Wie die Welt zum Supermarkt der Religionen wird*. Stuttgart: Beck.

Graham, K. 1895. *The Golden Age*. London: John Lane.

Greschat, K., and M. Tilly, eds. 2005. *Justinus, Dialog mit dem Juden Tryphon*. Translated by P. Häuser. Wiesbaden: Marix.

Grundmann, W. 1933. "ἀγαθός κτλ." Pages 10–18 in *ThWNT* 1.

———. 1964. "ἀγαθός κτλ." Pages 10–18 in *TDNT* 1.

Gudemann, C., and M. Christ, eds. 2013. *Gewalt: Ein interdisziplinäres Handbuch*. Stuttgart: Metzler.

Gurney, E. 2011. "Thomas More and the Problem of Charity." *Renaissance Studies* 26: 197–217.

Guttenberger, G. 2005. "Klugheit, Besonnenheit, Gerechtigkeit und Tapferkeit: Zum Hintergrund der Vorwürfe gegen Paulus nach 2Kor 10–13." *ZNW* 96: 78–98.

Hagedorn, A. C. 2015. "Erotische und theologische Aspekte der Liebe im Hohelied." *JBTh* 29: 23–41.

Hahn, F. 2002. *Theologie des Neuen Testament*. Vol. 1. Tübingen: Mohr.

Harnack, A. v. 1911. *Das Hohe Lied des Apostels Paulus von der Liebe (I. Kor. 13) und seine religionsgeschichtliche Bedeutung*. SKPAW 1911, 1:132–63. Berlin: Walter de Gruyter.

Hauck, F. 1942. "ὑπομένω κτλ." Pages 585–93 in *ThWNT* 4.

———. 1967. "ὑπομένω κτλ." Pages 581–88 in *TDNT* 4.

Hauschild, W.-D. 1977. "Agapen I. In der alten Kirche." Pages 748–53 in *TRE* 1.

Heilig, C. 2015. *Hidden Criticism? The Methodology and Plausibility of the Search for a Counter-imperial Subtext in Paul*. WUNT II/392. Tübingen: Mohr. https://www.mohrsiebeck.com/en/book/hidden-criticism-9783161537967.

Helm, B. 2017. "Love." In *The Stanford Encyclopedia of Philosophy*. Edited by E. N. Zalta. Fall 2017 edition. https://plato.stanford.edu/archives/fall2017/entries/love/.

Hembold, W. C. 1961. "Plutarch, The Dialogue on Love." Pages 303–441 in *Plutarch's Moralia*. Vol. 9. With an English translation by E. L. Minar Jr., F. H. Sandbach, and W. C. Hembold. LCL 425. Cambridge, Mass.: Harvard University Press.

Hengel, M. 1989. *The Johannine Question*. Translated by J. Bowden. London: SCM.

———. 1993. *Die johanneische Frage: Ein Lösungsversuch; Mit einem Beitrag zur Apokalypse von J. Frey*. WUNT 67. Tübingen: Mohr.

Hentschel, A. 2007. *Diakonia im Neuen Testament.* WUNT 2/226. Tübingen: Mohr.

———. 2010. "Paul's Apostleship and the Concept of DIAKONIA in 2 Corinthians." Pages 15–28 in *Diakonia, diaconiae, diaconato: Semantica e storia nei Padri della Chiesa.* Rome: Institutum Patristicum Augustinianum.

———. 2013. *Gemeinde, Ämter, Dienste: Perspektiven zur neutestamentlichen Ekklesiologie.* BThST 136. Neukirchen-Vluyn: Neukirchener Verlag.

Hillmann, K.-H., and G. Hartfiel, eds. 2007. *Wörterbuch der Soziologie.* Stuttgart: Kröner.

Hiltbrunner, O. 2005. *Gastfreundschaft in der Antike und im frühen Christentum.* Darmstadt: Wissenschaftliche Buchgesellschaft.

Hiltbrunner, O., et al. 1972. "Gastfreundschaft." Pages 1062–123 in *RAC* 8.

Hirsch-Luipold, R. 2000. "Plutarch." Pages 11–30 in *Plutarch, ist "Lebe im Verborgen" eine gute Lebensregel?* Edited by U. Berner. Sapere 1. Darmstadt: Wissenschaftliche Buchgesellschaft.

Hirzel, R. 1895. *Der Dialog: Ein literaturhistorischer Versuch.* 2 vols. Leipzig: Hirzel.

Hoffmann, P., and C. Heil, eds. 2002. *Die Logienquelle Q: Studienausgabe Griechisch und Deutsch.* Darmstadt: Wissenschaftliche Buchgesellschaft.

Holmes, M. W. 2002. *Apostolic Fathers: Greek Texts and English Translations.* 2nd ed. Grand Rapids: Baker Books.

Horn, C. 2013. "Der Güterbegriff der antiken Moralphilosophie." Pages 61–72 in *Ethische Normen des frühen Christentums. Gut—Leben—Leib—Tugend.* Edited by F. W. Horn, U. Volp, R. Zimmermann, and E. Verwold. WUNT 313. Tübingen: Mohr.

Horn, C., and C. Rapp. 2008. "aretê." Pages 59–64 in *WaPh.*

Horn, F. W. 2001. *Das Ende des Paulus: Historische, theologische und literaturgeschichtliche Aspekte.* BZNW 106. Berlin: Walter de Gruyter.

———. 2013a. "Die Gabe des Geistes." Pages 420–22 in *Paulus Handbuch.* Edited by F. W. Horn. Tübingen: Mohr.

———, ed. 2013b. *Paulus Handbuch.* Tübingen: Mohr.

———. 2013c. "Paulus und die Kardinaltugenden." Pages 351–69 in *Paulus—Werk und Wirkung: Festschrift für A. Lindemann zum 70. Geburtstag.* Edited by P.-G. Klumbies and D. S. Du Toit. Tübingen: Mohr.

———. 2013d. "Tugendlehre im Neuen Testament? Eine Problemanzeige." Pages 417–31 in *Ethische Normen des frühen Christentums: Gut—Leben—Leib—Tugend.* Edited by F. W. Horn, U. Volp, R. Zimmermann and E. Verwold. WUNT 313. Tübingen: Mohr.

———. 2014. "Nicht wie die Heiden! Sexualethische Tabuzone und ihre Bewertung durch Paulus." Pages 283–307 in *Anthropologie und Ethik im Frühjudentum und im Neuen Testament.* Edited by M. Konrad and E. Schläper. Tübingen: Mohr.

Horn, F. W., U. Volp, R. Zimmermann, and E. Verwold, eds. 2013. *Ethische Normen des frühen Christentums: Gut—Leben—Leib—Tugend.* WUNT 313. Tübingen: Mohr.

Hubert, C. 1971 [1938]. *Plutarchi Moralia.* Vol. 4. Leipzig: Teubner.

Hunsinger, G. 2000. "Heilig und profan: V. Dogmatisch." Pages 1534–37 in *RGG4* 3.

———. 2012. "Sacred and Profane: V. Dogmatics." Pages 370–71 in *RPP* 11.

Irigaray, L. 2002. *The Way of Love.* Translated by H. Bostic and S. Pluháček. London: Continuum.

Jacobi, C. 2015. *Jesusüberlieferung bei Paulus? Analogien zwischen den echten Paulusbriefen und den synoptischen Evangelien.* Berlin: Walter de Gruyter.

Janka, M. 2009. "Der sophokleische Eros und sein Dialog mit Euripides." Pages 63–96 in *Geist, Eros und Agape: Untersuchungen zu Liebesdarstellungen in Philosophie, Religion und Kunst.* Edited by E. Düsing and H.-D. Klein. Würzburg: Königshausen & Neumann.

Jeanrond, W. G. 2010. *A Theology of Love.* London: T&T Clark.

Jervell, J. 1998. *Die Apostelgeschichte.* KEK 3. Göttingen: Vandenhoeck & Ruprecht.

Jewett, R. 2007. *Romans: A Commentary.* Hermeneia. Minneapolis: Fortress.

Jordan, S. 2009. *Theorien und Methoden der Geschichtswissenschaft.* UTB 3104. Paderborn: Schörningh.

Jüngel, E. 2009. "Durch Glaube geformte Liebe (Caritas fide formata). Die erste Enzyklika Benedikt XVI.: *Deus Caritas est*—gelesen mit den Augen eines evangelischen Christenmenschen." Pages 481–500 in *Geist, Eros und Agape.* Edited by E. Düsing and H.-D. Klein. Würzburg: Königshausen & Neumann.

Kany, R. 2013. "Nächstenliebe u. Gottesliebe." Pages 652–720 in *RAC* 25.

Kapl-Blume, E. 2005. "Liebe im Lexikon: Zum Bedeutungswandel des Begriffes 'Liebe' in ausgewählten Lexika des 18. und 19. Jahrhunderts." Pages 107–29 in *"Liebe" im Wandel der Zeiten: Kulturwissenschaftliche Perspektiven.* Edited by K. Tanner. Theologie—Kultur—Hermeneutik 3. Leipzig: Evangelische Verlagsanstalt.

Karrer, M. 2013. "'Sohn Gottes' bei Paulus." Pages 265–88 in *Paulus—Werk und Wirkung: Festschrift für Andreas Lindemann.* Edited by P.-G. Klumbies and D. S. Du Toit. Tübingen: Mohr.

Karrer, M., and W. Kraus, eds. 2011. *Septuaginta Deutsch—Erläuterungen und Kommentare.* Vol. 2: *Psalmen bis Danielschriften.* Stuttgart: Deutsche Bibelgesellschaft.

Käsemann, E. 1968. *The Testament of Jesus: A Study of the Gospel of John in the Light of Chapter 17.* Translated by G. Krodel. Philadelphia: Fortress Press.

———. 1980a [1973]. *An die Römer.* 4th ed. HNT 8a. Tübingen: Mohr.

———. 1980b [1973]. *Commentary on Romans.* Translated by G. W. Bromiley. London: SCM.

———. 1980c. *Jesu letzter Wille nach Johannes 17.* 4th ed. Tübingen: Mohr.

Kedar-Kopfstein, B. 1995. "tāmam." Pages 688–701 in *ThWAT* 8.

Keith, C. 2020. "Pericope Adulterae (John 7:53–8:11)." Pages 197–208 in *The Reception of Jesus in the First Three Centuries.* Vol. 1: *From Paul to Josephus: Literary Receptions of Jesus in the First Centuries.* Edited by C. Keith, H. K. Bond, C. Jacobi, and J. Schröter. Volume 1 edited by H. K. Bond. London: T&T Clark.

Klauck, H.-J. 1991. *Der erste Johannesbrief.* EKK 23/1. Zürich: Benziger.

Klein, H. 2006. *Das Lukasevangelium.* KEK I/3. Göttingen: Vandenhoeck & Ruprecht.

Kleinknecht, H., F. Baumgärtel, W. Bieder, E. Sjöberg, and E. Schweizer. 1959. "πνεῦμα κτλ." Pages 330–453 in *ThWNT* 6.

——. 1971. "πνεῦμα κτλ." Pages 332–455 in *TDNT* 6.

Klostermann, A. 1877. "Ezechiel und das Heiligkeitsgesetz." *Zeitschrift für die lutherische Theologie und Kirche* 38: 401–45.

Knust, J., and T. Wasserman. 2019. *To Cast the First Stone: The Transmission of a Gospel Story.* Princeton, N.J.: Princeton University Press.

Konradt, M. 1997. "Menschen- und Bruderliebe? Beobachtungen zum Liebesgebot in den Testamenten der Zwölf Patriarchen." *ZNW* 88: 296–310.

——. 2014. "'Fliehet die Unzucht!' (TestRub 5,5). Sexualethische Perspektiven in den Testamenten der zwölf Patriarchen." Pages 249–81 in *Anthropologie und Ethik im Frühjudentum und im Neuen Testament.* Edited by M. Konradt and E. Schläper. WUNT 322. Tübingen: Mohr.

——. 2016. *Studien zum Mattäusevangelium.* Edited by A. Euler. WUNT 358. Tübingen: Mohr.

——. 2018. "Das Gebot der Feindesliebe in Mt 5.43–48 und sein frühjüdischer Kontext." Pages 349–89 in *Ahavah: Die Liebe Gottes im Alten Testament.* Edited by M. Oeming. Leipzig: Evangelische Verlagsanstalt.

Konstan, D. 2014. "The Varieties of Pity." *JBL* 137: 869–72.

Köpf, U. 1986. "Hoheslied III. Auslegungsgeschichte im Christentum. III/1. Alte Kirche bis Herder." Pages 508–13 in *TRE* 16.

Kornfeld, W. 1983. *Levitikus.* Die Neue Echter Bibel 6. Würzburg: Echter Verlag.

Kornfeld, W., and H. Ringgren. 1989. "qdš." Pages 1179–204 in *ThWAT* 6.

——. 2003. "qdš." Pages 521–45 in *TDOT* 12.

Körtner, U. H. J. 2009. "Kontextuelle Bibelhermeneutiken." Pages 344–45 in *LBH.*

Krauter, S. 2009. *Studien zu Röm 13,1–7: Paulus und der politische Diskurs der neronischen Zeit.* WUNT 243. Tübingen: Mohr.

Kreuzer, S., et al. 2009. "Interpretation/Interpretieren/Interpret." Pages 289–96 in *LBH.*

Krispenz, J., et al. 2009. "Zitat." Pages 689–95 in *LBH.*

Kristeva, J. 1983. *Histoires d'amour.* Paris: Denoel.

——. 1987. *Tales of Love.* Translated by L. S. Roudiez. New York: Columbia University Press.

——. 1989. *Geschichten von der Liebe.* Translated by D. Hornig. Frankfurt am Main: Suhrkamp.

Kugler, R. A. 2010. "Testaments." Pages 1295–97 in *EDEJ.*

Kuhn, H., and A. Schöpf. 1980. "Liebe." Pages 290–328 in *HWP* 5.

Kuhn, P. 1986. "Hoheslied II. Auslegungsgeschichte im Judentum." Pages 503–8 in *TRE* 16.

Kümmel, W. G., and H. Lichtenberger, eds. 1973ff. *Jüdische Schriften aus hellenistisch-römischer Zeit (JSHRZ).* 6 vols. Gütersloh: Mohn.

Labahn, M. 2012. "'It's Only Love'—Is that All? Limits and Potentials of Johannine 'Ethic'—a Critical Evaluation of Research." Pages 3–43 in *Rethinking the Ethics of John: "Implicit Ethics" in the Johannine Writings*. Edited by J. G. van der Watt and R. Zimmermann. WUNT 291. Tübingen: Mohr.

Lampe, P. 2013. "Rhetorik und Argumentation." Pages 149–58 in *Paulus Handbuch*. Edited by F. W. Horn. Tübingen: Mohr.

Landmesser, C. 1999. *Wahrheit als Grundbegriff neutestamentler Wissenschaft*. WUNT 113. Tübingen: Mohr.

Lange, A., and M. Weigold. 2011. *Biblical Quotations and Allusions in Second Temple Jewish Literature*. JAJ Suppl 5. Göttingen: Vandenhoeck & Ruprecht.

Lattke, M. 1975. *Einheit im Wort: Die spezifische Bedeutung von ἀγάπη, ἀγαπᾶν und φιλεῖν im Johannesevangelium*. StANT 41. Munich: Kösel.

Leinkauf, T. 2009. "Liebe als universales Prinzip: Zur Auseinandersetzung mit Platons Symposion im Denken der Renaissance; Marsilio Ficino und ein Ausblick auf die Liebes-Traktate des 16. Jahrhunderts." Pages 205–29 in *Geist, Eros und Agape: Untersuchungen zu Liebesdarstellungen in Philosophie, Religion und Kunst*. Edited by E. Düsing and H.-D. Klein. Würzburg: Königshausen & Neumann.

Leitgeb, M. C. 2010. *Concordia Mundi: Platons Symposium und Marisilio Ficinos Philosophie der Liebe*. Vienna: Holzhausen.

Lewandowski, T. 1994. *Linguistisches Wörterbuch*. Vol. 1. 6th ed. Heidelberg: Quelle & Meyer.

Lewis, C. S. 1960. *The Four Loves*. New York: Harcourt.

Lindemann, A. 1979. *Paulus im ältesten Christentum: Das Bild des Apostels und die Rezeption der paulinischen Theologie in der frühchristlichen Literatur bis Marcion*. BHTh 58. Tübingen: Mohr.

———. 1992. *Die Clemensbriefe*. HNT 17. Tübingen: Mohr.

———. 2000. *Der Erste Korintherbrief*. HNT 9/1. Tübingen: Mohr.

———. 2009. "Der erste Clemensbrief." Pages 59–82 in *Die Apostolischen Väter: Eine Einleitung*. Edited by W. Pratscher. UTB 3272. Göttingen: Vandenhoeck & Ruprecht.

———. 2010a. "The First Epistle of Clement." Pages 47–70 in *The Apostolic Fathers: An Introduction*. Edited by W. Pratscher. Translated by E. Wolfe. Waco, Tex.: Baylor University Press.

———. 2010b. "... ἐκτρέψετε αὐτὰ ἐν παιδείᾳ καὶ νουθεσίᾳ κυρίου (Eph 6.4). Kinder in der Welt des frühen Christentums." *NTS* 56: 169–90.

Lindemann, A., and H. Paulsen, eds. 1992. *Die apostolischen Väter: Griechisch-deutsche Parallelausgabe*. Tübingen: Mohr Siebeck.

Lipínski, E. 1993. "שָׂנֵא śanēʾ." Pages 828–39 in *ThWAT* 7.

Loader, W. R. G. 2004. *The Septuagint, Sexuality, and the New Testament*. Grand Rapids: Eerdmans.

———. 2005. *Sexuality and the Jesus Tradition*. Grand Rapids: Eerdmans.

———. 2007. *Enoch, Levi, and Jubilees on Sexuality: Attitudes toward Sexuality in the Early Enoch Literature, the Aramaic Levi Document, and the Book of Jubilees*. Grand Rapids: Eerdmans.

———. 2009. *The Dead Sea Scrolls on Sexuality: Attitudes toward Sexuality in Sectarian and Related Literature at Qumran.* Grand Rapids: Eerdmans.
———. 2010. *Sexuality in the New Testament: Understanding the Key Texts.* London: SPCK.
———. 2011a. *Philo, Josephus, and the Testaments on Sexuality: Attitudes towards Sexuality in the Writings of Philo, Josephus, and the Testaments of the Twelve Patriarchs.* Grand Rapids: Eerdmans.
———. 2011b. *The Pseudepigrapha on Sexuality: Attitudes toward Sexuality in Apocalypses, Testaments, Legends, Wisdom, and Related Literature.* Grand Rapids: Eerdmans.
———. 2012. *The New Testament on Sexuality.* Grand Rapids: Eerdmans.
———. 2013. *Making Sense of Sex: Attitudes towards Sexuality in Early Jewish and Christian Literature.* Grand Rapids: Eerdmans.
———. 2014. "Marriage and Sexual Relations in the New Testament World." Pages 189–205 in *The Oxford Handbook of Theology, Sexuality, and Gender.* Edited by A. Thatcher. Oxford: Oxford University Press.
Lohfink, G. 1963. *Das Hauptgebot: Eine Untersuchung literarischer Einleitungsfragen zu Dtn 5–11.* Analecta Biblica 20. Rome: Pontifical Biblical Institute.
Löhr, H. 2013. "Zur Eigenart paulinischer Ethik." Pages 440–44 in *Paulus Handbuch.* Edited by F. W. Horn. Tübingen: Mohr.
Lona, H. E. 1998. *Der erste Clemensbrief.* Translated and commented on by H. E. Lona. KAV II. Göttingen: Vandenhoeck & Ruprecht.
Longenecker, R. N. 1990. *Galatians.* WBC 41. Dallas, Tex.: Word Books.
Luck, U. 1973. "φιλανθρωπία κτλ." Pages 107–11 in *ThWNT* 9.
———. 1974. "φιλανθρωπία κτλ." Pages 107–12 in *TDNT* 9.
Ludwig, P. W. 2002. *Eros and Polis: Desire and Community in Greek Political Thought.* Cambridge: Cambridge University Press.
Luhmann, N. 1967. "Soziologie als Theorie sozialer Systeme." *Kölner Zeitschrift für Soziologie und Sozialpsychologie* 19: 615–44.
———. 1984. *Liebe als Passion: Zur Codierung von Intimität.* 5th ed. Frankfurt am Main: Suhrkamp.
———. 1986. *Love as Passion: The Codification of Intimacy.* Translated by J. Gaines and D. L. Jones. Cambridge, Mass.: Harvard University Press.
———. 2008. *Liebe als Passion [Typoskript Übung SS 1969] = Liebe: Eine Übung.*
———. 2010. *Love: A Sketch.* Translated by K. Cross. Edited by A. Kieserling. Cambridge: Polity.
Luther, S. 2015. *Sprachethik im Neuen Testament: Analyse des frühchristlichen Diskurses im Matthäusevangelium, im Jakobusbrief und im 1. Petrusbrief.* WUNT 2/394. Tübingen: Mohr.
Luz, U. 1997. *Das Evangelium nach Matthäus (Mt 18–25).* EKK I/3. Zürich: Benzinger Verlag.
———. 2001. *Matthew 8–20.* Translated by J. E. Crouch. Edited by H. Koester. Hermeneia. Minneapolis: Fortress.
———. 2002. *Das Evangelium nach Matthäus (Mt 1–7).* 5th ed. EKK I/1. Zürich: Benzinger Verlag.

————. 2005. *Matthew 21–28: A Commentary*. Translated by J. E. Crouch. Edited by H. Koester. Hermeneia. Minneapolis: Fortress.

————. 2007. *Matthew 1–7: A Commentary*. Translated by J. E. Crouch. Edited by H. Koester. Hermeneia. Minneapolis: Fortress.

Marcovich, M., ed. 1997. *Iustini Martyris Dialogus cum Tryphone*. PTS 47. Berlin: Walter de Gruyter.

Martin, H. J. 1978. "Amatorius (Moralia 748 E–612B)." Pages 442–537 in *Plutarch's Ethical Writings and Early Christian Literature*. Edited by H. D. Betz. SCH 4. Leiden: Brill.

Martyn, J. L. 2003 [1968]. *History and Theology in the Fourth Gospel*. 3rd ed. Louisville: Westminster John Knox.

Mathys, H.-P. 1990. *Liebe deinen Nächsten wie dich selbst: Untersuchungen zum alttestamentlichen Gebot der Nächstenliebe (Lev 19,18)*. 2nd ed. OBO 71. Göttingen: Vandenhoeck & Ruprecht.

May, S. 2011. *Love: A History*. New Haven, Conn.: Yale University Press.

————. 2019. *Love: A New Understanding of an Ancient Emotion*. Oxford: Oxford University Press.

Meeks, W. A. 1972. "The Man from Heaven in Johannine Sectarianism." *JBL* 91: 44–72.

Mell, U. 1999. "Die Entstehungsgeschichte der Trias 'Glaube Hoffnung Liebe' (1 Kor. 13,13)." Pages 197–226 in *Das Urchristentum in seiner literarischen Geschichte: Festschrift für J. Becker*. Edited by U. Mell and U. B. Müller. BZNW 100. Berlin: Walter de Gruyter.

Mendez, H. 2020. "Did the Johannine Community Exist?" *JSNT* 42: 350–74. https://doi.org/10.1177/0142064X19890490.

Merk, O. 1969. "Der Beginn der Paränese im Galaterbrief." *ZNW* 60: 83–104.

Michel, O. 1942. "μίσεω." Pages 687–98 in *ThWNT* 4.

————. 1967. "μίσεω." Pages 683–94 in *TDNT* 4.

Milgrom, J. 2000. *Leviticus 17–22*. AB 3 A. New York: Doubleday.

Mitchell, A. C. 1997. "'Greet the Friends by Name': New Testament Evidence for the Greco-Roman Topos on Friendship." Pages 225–62 in *Greco-Roman Perspectives on Friendship*. Edited by J. T. Fitzgerald. SBL Resources for Biblical Study 34. Atlanta: Scholars Press.

Moffatt, J. 1932. *Love in the New Testament*. London: Hodder and Stoughton.

Moloney, F. J. 2013. *Love in the Gospel of John: An Exegetical, Theological, and Literary Study*. Grand Rapids: Baker Academic.

Moran, W. L. 1963. "The Ancient Near Eastern Background of the Love of God in Deuteronomy." *CBQ* 25: 77–87.

Most, G. W. 2005. "Six Remarks on Platonic Eros." Pages 33–57 in *Errotikon: Essays on Eros, Ancient and Modern*. Edited by S. Bartsch and T. Bartscherer. Chicago: University of Chicago Press.

Müller, P. 1992. *In der Mitte der Gemeinde: Kinder im Neuen Testament*. Neukirchen-Vluyn: Neukirchener Verlag.

————. 2012. *Der Brief an Philemon*. KEK 9/3. Göttingen: Vandenhoeck & Ruprecht.

Nanos, M. N., ed. 2002. *The Galatians Debate: Contemporary Issues in Rhetorical and Historical Interpretation*. Peabody, Mass.: Hendrickson.

Neudecker, R. 1992. "'And You Shall Love Your Neighbor as Yourself—I Am the Lord' (Lev 19.18) in Jewish Interpretation." *Biblica* 73: 496–517.

Niederwimmer, K. 1989. *Die Didache.* KAV I. Göttingen Vandenhoeck & Ruprecht.

Nielsen, E. 1995. *Deuteronomium.* HAT I/6. Tübingen: Mohr.

Noth, M. 1962. *Das dritte Buch Mose: Leviticus.* ATD 6. Göttingen: Vandenhoeck & Ruprecht.

———. 1965. *Leviticus: A Commentary.* Translated by J. S. Anderson. Philadelphia, Penn.: Westminster.

Nussbaum, M. C. 1992. *Love's Knowledge: Essays on Philosophy and Literature.* Oxford: Oxford University Press.

———. 1999a. *Sex and Social Justice.* Oxford: Oxford University Press.

———. 1999b. "Constructing Love, Desire, and Care." Pages 253–75 in M. C. Nussbaum, *Sex and Social Justice.* New York: Oxford University Press.

———. 1999c. "The Professor of Parody: The Hip Defeatism of Judith Butler." *New Republic*, February 22, 1999. https://newrepublic.com/article/150687/professor-parody.

———. 2002a. *Konstruktion der Liebe, des Begehrens und der Fürsorge: Drei philosophische Aufsätze.* Translated by J. Schulte. Stuttgart: Reclam.

———. 2002b. "Konstruktion der Liebe, des Begehrens und der Fürsofge." Pages 163–233 in M. C. Nussbaum, *Konstruktion der Liebe, des Begehrens und der Fürsorge: Drei philosophische Aufsätze.* Translated by J. Schulte. Stuttgart: Reclam.

———. 2013. *Political Emotions: Why Love Matters for Justice.* Cambridge, Mass.: Belknap Press of Harvard University Press.

Nygren, A. 1930/1936. *Den kristna kärlekstanken genom tiderna: Eros och Agape.* Stockholm: SKD.

———. 1982. *Agape and Eros.* Translated by P. S. Watson. Chicago: University of Chicago Press.

Oeming, M., ed. 2018. *Ahavah: Die Liebe Gottes im Alten Testament.* Leipzig: Evangelisches Verlagsanstalt.

Oepke, A. 1959. "Ehe." Pages 650–66 in *RAC* 4.

Ostheeren, K., et al. 2009. "Topos I." Pages 630–724 in vol. 9 of *Historisches Wörterbuch der Rhetorik.* Edited by G. Uedling. Tübingen: Mohr.

Otto, E. 2000. "Heiligkeitsgesetz." Pages 1570–71 in *RGG4* 3.

———. 2009. "Holiness Code." Pages 207–08 in *RPP* 6.

Paden, W. E., et al. 2000. "Heilig und profan." Pages 1570–71 in *RGG4* 3.

———. 2012. "Sacred and Profane." Pages 366–72 in *RPP* 11.

Pechriggl, A. 2009. *Eros.* Vienna: UTB GmbH.

Philippi, P. 1981. "Geschichte der Diakonie." Pages 621–44 in *TRE* 8.

Pilhofer, P. 2002. "Περὶ δὲ τῆς φιλαδελφίας . . . (1 Thess 4,9). Ekklesiologische Überlegungen zu einem Proprium früher christlicher Gemeinden." Pages 139–53 in *Die frühen Christen und ihre Welt: Greifswalder Aufsätze 1996–2001.* WUNT 145. Tübingen: Mohr.

Piper, J. 1979. *"Love Your Enemies": Jesus' Love Command in the Synoptic Gospels and in the Early Christian Paraenesis; A History of the Tradition and Interpretation of Its Uses.* MSSNTS 38. Cambridge: Cambridge University Press.

Pohlenz, M. 1929. *Plutarchi Moralia.* Vol. 3. Leipzig: Teubner.

Pollmann, K., et al. 2009. "Exegese." Pages 166–74 in *LBH.*

Popkes, E. E. 2005. *Die Theologie der Liebe Gottes in den johanneischen Schriften: Zur Semantik der Liebe und zum Motivkreis des Dualismus.* WUNT 2/197. Tübingen: Mohr.

——. 2011. "Die Polemik um die Christologie im Ersten Johannesbrief und ihr Verhältnis zu den polemischen Zügen des Johannesevangelium." Pages 331–55 in *Polemik in der frühchristlichen Literatur: Texte und Kontexte.* Edited by O. Wischmeyer and L. Scornaienchi. BZNW 170. Berlin: Walter de Gruyter.

Popkes, W. 2001. *Der Brief des Jakobus.* ThHK 14. Leipzig: Evangelische Verlagsanstalt.

Pratscher, W., ed. 2009. *Die Apostolischen Väter: Eine Einleitung.* Göttingen: Vandenhoeck & Ruprecht.

——, ed. 2010. *The Apostolic Fathers.* Waco, Tex.: Baylor University Press.

Price, A. W. 1989. *Love and Friendship in Plato and Aristotle.* Oxford: Clarendon.

Procksch, O., and K.-G. Kuhn. 1933. "ἅγιος κτλ." Pages 87–116 in *ThWNT* 1.

——. 1964. "ἅγιος κτλ." Pages 88–115 in *TDNT* 1.

Procopé, J. 1986. "Haß." Pages 677–714 in *RAC* 13.

Prostmeier, F.-R. 1999. *Der Barnabasbrief.* KAV 8. Göttingen: Vandenhoeck & Ruprecht.

——. 2009. "Der Barnabasbrief." Pages 39–56 in *Die Apostolischen Väter: Eine Einleitung.* Edited by W. Pratscher. Göttingen: Vandenhoeck & Ruprecht.

——. 2010. "The Epistle of Barnabas." Pages 27–45 in *The Apostolic Fathers: An Introduction.* Edited by W. Pratscher. Waco, Tex.: Baylor University Press.

Race, W. H. 1982. *The Classical Priamel from Homer to Boethius.* Leiden: Brill.

Rapp, C. 2012. "Aristoteles: Bausteine für eine Theorie der Emotionen." Pages 45–68 in *Handbuch Klassische Emotionstheorien.* Edited by H. Landweer and U. Renz. Berlin: Walter de Gruyter.

Reeve, C. D. C., ed. 2014. *Aristotle: Nicomachean Ethics.* Translated with introduction and notes by C. D. C. Reeve. Indianapolis, Ind.: Hackett.

Reiner, H., et al. 1974. "Gut, das Gute, das Gut." Pages 937–72 in *HWP* 3.

Reinmuth, E., ed. 2009. *Joseph und Aseneth.* Sapere XV. Tübingen: Mohr.

Reiser, M. 2001. "Love of Enemies in the Context of Antiquity." *NTS* 47: 411–27.

Reumann, J. 2008. *Philippians: A New Translation with Introduction and Commentary.* New Haven, Conn.: Yale University Press.

Ricoeur, P. 1990. *Liebe und Gerechtigkeit.* Tübingen: Mohr.

——. 1996. "Love and Justice." Pages 23–39 in *P. Ricoeur: The Hermeneutics of Action.* Edited by R. Kearney. Translated by D. Pellauer. London: Sage.

Ringgren, H. 1973. "'ajab." Pages 228–35 in *ThWAT* 1.

———. 1977. "'āyabh." Pages 212–18 in *TDOT* 1.

Rist, J. M. 2001. "Plutarch's Amatorius: A Commentary on Plato's Theories of Love?" *Classical Quarterly* 51: 557–75.

Robinson, J. M., P. Hoffmann, and J. S. Kloppenborg, eds. 2000. *The Critical Edition of Q.* Minneapolis: Fortress.

Röder, J. 2013. "Was ist 'gut' im Neuen Testament? Funktionale Bedeutungsmöglichkeiten des ἀγαθός-Begriffs in der ethischen Argumentation." Pages 93–130 in *Ethische Normen des frühen Christentums: Gut—Leben—Leib—Tugend.* Edited by F. W. Horn. Tübingen: Mohr.

Roh, T. 2001. *Die familia dei in den synoptischen Evangelien: Eine redaktions- und sozialgeschichtliche Untersuchung zu einem urchristlichen Bildfeld.* NTOA 37. Göttingen: Vandenhoeck & Ruprecht.

Roloff, J. 1989. *Der erste Brief an Timotheus.* EKK XV. Zürich: Benzinger Verlag.

Rosenbach, M. 1989. *L. Annaeus Seneca, Philosophische Schriften: Lateinisch und Deutsch.* Vol. 1. 4th ed. Darmstadt: Wissenschaftliche Buchgesellschaft.

Ross, W. D., ed. 1959. *Aristotelis ars rhetorica.* Oxford: Clarendon.

———, ed. 1970 [1924]. *Aristotle's Metaphysics.* 2 vols. Oxford: Clarendon.

Runesson, A. 2009. "Reading." Page 481 in *LBH.*

Rusche, H. 1958. *Gastfreundschaft in der Verkündigung des Neuen Testaments und ihr Verhältnis zur Mission.* Munster: Aschendorff.

Sampley, J. P. 1971. *"And the Two Shall Become One Flesh": A Study of Traditions in Ephesians 5:21–33.* SNTSMS 16. Cambridge: Cambridge University Press.

Sanders, E. 2013. *Erôs and the Polis: Love in Context.* BICS Suppl. 119. London: Institute of Classical Studies, University of London.

Sauer, J. 1985. "Traditionsgeschichtliche Erwägungen zu den synoptischen und paulinischen Aussagen über Feindesliebe und Wiedervergeltungsverzicht." *ZNW* 76: 1–28.

Schilling, H. 2013. *Martin Luther: Rebell in einer Zeit des Umbruchs.* 2nd ed. Munich: Beck.

Schlögl, R. 2013. *Alter Glaube und moderne Welt: Europäisches Christentum im Umbruch 1750–1850.* Frankfurt am Main: Fischer.

Schmeller, T. 2010. *Der Zweite Brief an die Korinther (2 Kor 1,1–7,4).* EKK VIII/1. Neukirchen-Vluyn: Neukirchener Verlag.

Schmidt, E. D. 2010. *Heilig ins Eschaton: Heiligung und Heiligkeit als eschatologische Konzeption im 1. Thessalonicherbrief.* BZNW 167. Berlin: Walter de Gruyter.

Schmölders, C. 1996. *Die Erfindung der Liebe: Berühmte Zeugnisse aus drei Jahrtausenden.* Munich: Beck.

Schnackenburg, R. 1980. *The Gospel according to St. John.* Vol. 2: *Commentary on Chapters 5–12.* Translated by K. Smyth. New York: Seabury Press.

———. 1982. *The Gospel according to St. John.* Vol. 3: *Commentary on Chapters 13–21.* Translated by K. Smyth. New York: Crossroad.

——. 1985. *Das Johannesevangelium: Kommentar zu Kap. 5–12.* Vol. 2. 4th ed. HTh IV/2. Freiburg: Herder.

——. 1986. *Das Johannesevangelium: Kommentar zu Kap. 13–21.* Vol. 3. HThK IV/3. Freiburg: Herder.

Schneider, C. 1966. "Eros." Pages 306–12 in *RAC* 6.

Schnelle, U. 1998. *The History and Theology of the New Testament Writings.* Translated by M. E. Boring. Minneapolis: Fortress.

——. 2003. *Paulus. Leben und Denken.* Berlin: Walter de Gruyter.

——. 2004. *Das Evangelium nach Johannes.* 3rd ed. ThHK 4. Leipzig: Evangelische Verlagsanstalt.

——. 2005a. *Apostle Paul: His Life and Theology.* Translated by M. E. Boring. Grand Rapids: Baker Academic.

——. 2005b. "Das Liebesgebot im Neuen Testament: Jesus, Paulus und Johannes." Pages 21–30 in *"Liebe" im Wandel der Zeiten: Kulturwissenschaftliche Perspektiven.* Edited by K. Tanner. Theologie—Kultur—Hermeneutik 3. Leipzig: Evangelische Verlagsanstalt.

——. 2007. *Einleitung in das Neue Testament.* 6th ed. Göttingen: Vandenhoeck & Ruprecht.

——. 2013. "Die Taufe als Teilhabe an Christus." Pages 332–37 in *Paulus Handbuch.* Edited by F. W. Horn. Tübingen: Mohr.

——. 2014. *Paulus: Leben und Denken.* 2nd ed. De Gruyter Studium. Berlin: Walter de Gruyter.

——. 2016 [1998]. *Das Evangelium nach Johannes.* 5th ed. ThHK 4. Leipzig: Evangelische Verlagsanstalt.

Schnelle, U., M. Labahn, and M. Lang, eds. 2001. *Neuer Wettstein: Texte zum Neuen Testament aus Griechentum und Hellenismus.* Parts 1/2: *Texte zum Johannesevangelium.* Berlin: Walter de Gruyter.

Scholz, H. 2009. "Begriff/Begriffsgeschichte." Pages 73–74 in *LBH.*

Schottroff, L. 1975. "Gewaltverzicht und Feindesliebe in der urchristlichen Jesustradition." Pages 197–221 in *Jesus Christus in Historie und Theologie: Festschrift Hans Conzelmann.* Edited by G. Strecker. Tübingen: Mohr.

——. 1978. *Essays on the Love Commandment.* Philadelphia: Fortress.

Schrage, W. 1989. *Ethik des Neuen Testament.* 5th revised and expanded ed. NTD Eränzungsreihe 4. Göttingen: Vandenhoeck & Ruprecht.

——. 1990. *Ethics of New Testament.* Translated by D. E. Green. Edinburgh: T&T Clark.

——. 1999. *Der Erste Brief an die Korinther: 1 Kor 11,17—14,40.* Vol. 3. Neukirchen-Vluyn: Neukirchener.

Schrenk, G., and G. Quell. 1954. "πατήρ κτλ." Pages 946–1024 in *ThWNT* 5.

——. 1967. "πατήρ κτλ." Pages 945–1022 in *TDNT* 5.

Schürmann, H. 1994. *Das Lukasevangelium: Kommentar zu Kapitel 9.51–11.56.* Vol. 2/1. HThK III. Freiburg: Herder.

Schweizer, E. 1959. "πνεῦμα κτλ. E. III. Paulus." Pages 413–35 in *ThWNT* 6.

——. 1971. "πνεῦμα κτλ. E. III. Paul." Pages 415–37 in *TDNT* 6.

Schwer, W. 1950. "Barmherzigkeit." Pages 1200–1207 in *RAC* 1.

Scornaienchi, L. 2016. *Der umstrittene Jesus und seine Apologie—die Streitgespräche im Markusevangelium.* Göttingen: Vandenhoeck & Ruprecht.

Sedgwick, E. K. 2000. *A Dialogue on Love*. Boston: Beacon.

Segovia, F. F. 1982. *Love Relationships in the Johannine Tradition: Agape/ Agapan in 1 John and the Fourth Gospel*. SBL.DS 58. Chico, Calif.: Scholars Press.

Sellin, G. 2008. *Der Brief an die Epheser*. KEK 8. Göttingen: Vandenhoeck & Ruprecht.

———. 2009. "Die Paränese des Epheserbriefes." Pages 180–98 in *Studien zu Paulus und zum Epheserbrief*. Edited by D. Sänger. Göttingen.

Shklar, J. N. 1984. *Ordinary Vices*. Cambridge, Mass.: Belknap Press.

———. 2014. *Ganz normale Laster*. Translated by H. Bajohr. Berlin: Walter de Gruyter.

Singer, I. 2009. *Philosophy of Love: A Partial Summing-Up*. Cambridge, Mass.: MIT Press.

Slaby, J. 2014. "Gemeinsam handeln, nicht einfühlen: Warum Empathie überschätzt ist." *philanthropie und stiftung* 2014/1: 8–9. https://www .hochschulverband.de/fileadmin/redaktion/download/pdf/stiftung/ beilage_philanthropie-und-stiftung_1_2014.pdf.

Smith, J. Z. 1990. *Drudgery Divine: On the Comparison of Early Christianities and the Religions of Late Antiquity*. Chicago: University of Chicago Press.

Söding, T. 1992a. *Die Trias Glaube, Hoffnung, Liebe bei Paulus*. SBS 150. Stuttgart: Katholisches Bibelwerk.

———. 1992b. "Das Wortfeld der Liebe im paganen und biblischen Griechisch." *EThL* 68: 284–330.

———. 1993. "Agape: I. Der ntl. Sprachgebrauch." Pages 220–22 in *LThK3* 1.

———. 1994/1995. "Solidarität in der Diaspora: Das Liebesgebot nach den Testamenten der Twölf Patriarchen im Vergleich mit dem Neuen Testament." *Kairos* 36/37: 1–19.

———. 1995. *Das Liebegbot bei Paulus*. NTA 26. Münster: Aschendorff.

———. 1996. "'Gott ist Liebe': 1 Joh 4,8.16 als Spitzensatz Biblischer Theologie." Pages 306–57 in *Der Lebendige Gott: Festschrift für W. Thüsing*. Edited by T. Söding. Münster: Aschendorff.

———. 2011. *Die Verkündigung Jesu—Ereignis und Erinnerung*. Freiburg: Herder.

———. 2014. "Das Liebesgebot bei Paulus und Markus." Pages 465–503 in *Paul and Mark: Comparative Essays*. Part I: *Two Authors at the Beginnings of Christianity*. Edited by O. Wischmeyer. BZNW 198. Berlin: Walter de Gruyter.

———. 2015. *Nächstenliebe: Gottes Gebot als Verheißung und Anspruch*. Freiburg im Breslau: Herder.

———. 2017a. "Ehe aus Liebe: Der Ansatz des Kolosser- und Epheserbriefes." *Communio* 46: 80–93.

———. 2017b. "Wie weit reicht die Nächstenliebe? Das biblische Konzept in der Diskussion über den Altruismus." *Evangelische Theologie* 77: 258–67.

Spicq, C. 1955a. *Agapè: Prolégomènes à une ètude de Théologie néotestamentaire*. StHell 10. Louvain: E. Nauwelaerts.

———. 1955b. "Φιλοστοργος (À propos de Rom. IXX,10)." *RB* 62: 497–510.

———. 1958–1959. *Agapè dans le Nouveau Testament*. 3 vols. Paris: Gabalda.

——. 2007. *Agape in the New Testament*. Translated by M. A. McNamara and M. H. Richter. 3 vols. Eugene, Or: Wipf & Stock.

Spieckermann, H. 2000. "Mit der Liebe im Wort: Ein Beitrag zur Theologie des Deuteronomiums." Pages 190–205 in *Liebe und Gebot: Studien zum Deuteronomium*. Edited by R. Kratz and H. Spieckermann. FRLANT 190. Göttingen: Vandenhoeck & Ruprecht.

——. 2001a. "'Barmherzig und gnädig ist der Herr. . . .'" Pages 3–19 in *Gottes Liebe zu Israel: Studien zur Theologie des Alten Testaments*. Edited by H. Spieckermann. FAT 33. Tübingen: Mohr.

——. 2001b. "Die Liebeserklärung Gottes: Entwurf einer Theologie des Alten Testaments." Pages 197–223 in *Gottes Liebe zu Israel: Studien zur Theologie des Alten Testaments*. Edited by H. Spieckermann. FAT 33. Tübingen: Mohr.

Sprecher, M.-T. 1993. *Einheitsdenken aus der Perspektive von Joh 17: Eine exegetische und bibeltheologische Untersuchung zu Joh 17.20–26*. EHS.T 495. Bern: Lang.

Stählin, G. 1954. "ξένος κτλ." Pages 1–36 in *ThWNT* 5.

——. 1967. "ξένος κτλ." Pages 1–36 in *TDNT* 5.

——. 1973. "φιλέω κτλ." Pages 112–69 in *ThWNT* 9.

——. 1974. "φιλέω κτλ." Pages 113–71 in *TDNT* 9.

Stählin, O., ed. 1909. *Clemens Alexandrinus, Quis dives salvetur*. In *Clemens Alexandrinus*. Vol. 3. GCS. Berlin: Akademie.

Stauffer, E. 1933. "ἀγαπάω, ἀγάπη, ἀγαπητός." Pages 20–55 in *ThWNT* 1.

——. 1964. "ἀγαπάω, ἀγάπη, ἀγαπητός." Pages 21–55 in *TDNT* 1.

Stemberger, G. 2009. "Zitat: V. Judaistisch." Pages 692–93 in *LBH*.

Stemmer, P., et al. 1998. "Tugend." Pages 1532–70 in *HWP* 10.

Strecker, G. 1989. *Die Johannesbriefe*. KEK 14. Göttingen: Vandenhoeck & Ruprecht.

Strobel, A. 1956. "Zum Verständnis von Röm. 13." *ZNW* 47: 67–93.

Tanner, K. 2005. *"Liebe" im Wandel der Zeiten: Kulturwissenschaftliche Perspektiven*. Theologie—Kultur—Hermeneutik 3. Leipzig: Evangelische Verlagsanstalt.

Theissen, G. 2014. "Gemeindestrukturen und Hilfsmotivation: Wie haben urchristliche Gemeinden zum Helfen motiviert?" Pages 413–40 in *Anthropologie und Ethik im Frühjudentum und im Neuen Testament*. Edited by M. Konradt and E. Schläpfer. WUNT 322. Tübingen: Mohr.

Theissen, G., and A. Merz. 1998. *The Historical Jesus: A Comprehensive Guide*. Translated by J. Bowden. Minneapolis: Fortress.

——. 2001 [1996]. *Der historische Jesus: Ein Lehr- und Arbeitsbuch*. 3rd ed. Göttingen: Vandenhoeck & Ruprecht.

Theobald, M. 1992. "Angstfreie Religiosität: Röm 8,15 und 1Joh 4,17 im Licht der Schrift Plutarchs über den Aberglauben." Pages 321–43 in *Lebendige Überlieferung: Prozesse der Annäherung und Auslegung; Festschrift für H.-J. Vogt*. Edited by N. el-Khoury, H. Crouzel, and R. Reinhardt. Beirut: Friedrich-Rückert-Verlag.

——. 2009. *Das Evangelium nach Johannes: Kapitel 1–12*. RNT 4/1. Regensburg: Pustet.

———. 2010. "Der Jünger, den Jesus liebte: Beobachtungen zum narrativen Konzept der johanneischen Redaktion." Pages 493–533 in M. Theobald, *Studien zum Corpus Iohanneum*. WUNT 267. Tübingen: Mohr.

Thompson, M. M. 2013. "Lazarus: 'Behold a Man Raised Up by Christ!'" Pages 460–86 in *Character Studies in the Fourth Gospel: Narrative Approaches to Seventy Figures in John*. Edited by S. A. Hunt, F. D. Tolmie and R. Zimmermann. Tübingen: Mohr.

Thür, G. 2004. "Gnome." Pages 884–92 in *BNP* 5.

Thyen, H. 1979. "'Niemand hat größere Liebe als die, daß er sein Leben für seine Freunde hingibt' (Joh 15,13)." Pages 467–81 in *Theologia Crucis—Signum Crucis. Festschrift für E. Dinkler*. Edited by C. Andresen and G. Klein. Tübingen: Mohr.

———. 2005. *Das Johannesevangelium*. HNT 6. Tübingen: Mohr.

———. 2007a. "Die Erzählung von den bethanischen Geschwistern (Joh 11,1–12,9) als Palimpsest über synoptischen Texten." Pages 182–212 in *Studien zum Corpus Johanneum*. Edited by H. Thyen. Tübingen: Mohr.

———. 2007b. "Die Erzählung von Jesus und der Ehebrecherin (Joh 7,53–8,11)." Pages 306–22 in *Studien zum Corpus Iohanneum*. Edited by H. Thyen. WUNT 214. Tübingen: Mohr.

———. 2007c. "μονογενης und die frühe Rezeptionsgeschichte des Lexems." Pages 429–33 in *H. Thyen, Studien zum Corpus Iohanneum*. WUNT 214. Tübingen: Mohr.

Tiedemann, H. 2005. "Sexualität." Pages 21–25 in *Neues Testament und Antike Kultur*. Vol. 2. Edited by K. Erlemann and K. Scherberich. Neukirchen-Vluyn: Neukirchener Verlag.

Tilborg, S. v. 1993. *Imaginative Love in John*. BiblIntSer 2. Leiden: Brill.

Tömmel, T. N. 2013. *Wille und Passion: Der Liebesbegriff bei Heidegger und Arendt*. Berlin: Suhrkamp.

Tornau, C. 2008. "agathon." Pages 10–14 in *WaPh*.

Treu, K. 1972. "Freundschaft." Pages 413–34 in *RAC* 8.

Troeltsch, E. 1981 [1908]. "Über historische und dogmatische Methode in der Theologie." Pages 729–53 in *Gesammelte Schriften*. Vol. 2: *Zur religiösen Lage, Religionsphilosophie und Ethik*. Aalen: Scientia.

———. 1991. "Historical and Dogmatic Method in Theology (1898)." Pages 11–32 in *Religion and History*. Edited by E. Troeltsch. Translated by J. L. Adams and W. F. Bense. Edinburgh: T&T Clarke.

Urban, C. 2005a. "Hochzeit, Ehe und Witenschaften." Pages 23–30 in *Neues Testament und Antike Kultur*. Vol. 2. Edited by K. Erlemann and K. Scherberich. Neukirchen-Vluyn: Neukirchener Verlag.

———. 2005b. "Die Rollen der Familienmitglieder." Pages 17–21 in *Neues Testament und Antike Kultur*. Vol. 2. Edited by K. Erlemann and K. Scherberich. Neukirchen-Vluyn: Neukirchener Verlag.

Utzschneider, H. 2009. "Autorenintention." Pages 63–66 in *LBH*.

van der Horst, P. W. 1978. *The Sentences of Pseudo-Phocylides*. SVTP 4. Leiden: Brill.

Veijola, T. 1992a. "Das Bekenntnis Israels: Beobachtungen zur Geschichte und Theologie von Dtn 6,4–9." *ThZ* 48: 369–81.

——. 1992b. "Höre Israel! Der Sinn und Hintergrund von Deuteronomium vi 4–9." *VT* 42: 528–41.

——. 2004. *Das 5. Buch Mose: Deuteronomium; Kapitel 1,1–16,17.* ATD 8,1. Göttingen: Vandenhoeck & Ruprecht.

Vogel, M. 2009. "Einführung." Pages 3–31 in *Joseph und Aseneth.* Edited by E. Reinmuth. Sapere XV. Tübingen: Mohr.

Vögtle, A. 1936. *Die Tugend- und Lasterkataloge im Neuen Testament.* NTA 16/4–5. Münster: Aschendorff.

——. 1994. *Der Judasbrief: Der Zweite Petrusbrief.* EKK XXII. Solothurn: Benzinger.

Vollenweider, S. 1989. *Freiheit als neue Schöpfung: Eine Untersuchung zur Eleutheria bei Paulus und in seiner Umwelt.* Göttingen: Vandenhoeck & Ruprecht.

——. 2002. "Der 'Raub' der Gottgleichheit: Ein religionsgeschichtlicher Vorschlag zu Phil 2.6(-11)." Pages 263–84 in *Horizonte neutestamentlicher Christologie: Studien zu Paulus und zur frühchristlicher Theologie.* Edited by S. Vollenweider. WUNT 144. Tübingen: Mohr.

Waaler, W. 2008. *The 'Shema' and the First Commandment in First Corinthians.* WUNT 2/253. Tübingen: Mohr.

Warnach, V. 1951. *Agape: Die Liebe als Grundmotiv der neutestamentlichen Theologie.* Düsseldorf: Patmos.

Waser, O. 1907. "Eros 1." Pages 484–542 in *PW* 6/1.

Watson, F. D. 2000. *Agape, Eros, Gender: Towards a Pauline Sexual Ethic.* Cambridge: Cambridge University Press.

Watt, J. G. van der. 2000. *The Family of the King: Dynamics of Metaphor in the Gospel according to John.* BIS 47. Leiden: Brill.

——. 2006. "Ethics and Ethos according to John." *ZNW* 97: 147–76.

Watt, J. G. van der, and R. Zimmermann. 2010. *Moral Language in the New Testament* Tübingen: Mohr.

——. 2012. *Rethinking the Ethics of John: "Implicit Ethics" in the Johannine Writings.* WUNT 291. Tübingen: Mohr.

Weinfeld, M. 1991. *Deuteronomy 1–11.* New York: Doubleday.

Weiss, H.-F. 1991. *Der Brief an die Hebräer.* Göttingen: Vandenhoeck & Ruprecht.

Weiss, J. 1970. *Der erste Korintherbrief.* KEK. Reprint of the revised 9th ed. of 1910. Göttingen: Vandenhoeck & Ruprecht.

Weiss, W. 1993. "Glaube—Liebe—Hoffnung." *ZNW* 84: 196–217.

Welsch, W. 1994. "Einleitung." Pages 1–43 in *Wege aus der Moderne: Schlüsseltexte der Postmoderne-Diskussion.* 2nd ed. Edited by W. Welsch. Acta humaniora. Schriften zur Kunstwissenschaft und Philosophie. Berlin: Walter de Gruyter.

Westbrook, R., et al. 1997. "Ehe." Pages 893–99 in *DNP* 3.

——. 2006. "Marriage." Pages 385–93 in *BNP* 8.

Westerholm, S. 2013. "Is Nothing Sacred? Holiness in the Writings of Paul." Pages 87–99 in *Purity, Holiness and Identity in Judaism and Christianity: Essays in Memory of Susan Haber.* Edited by C. S. Ehrlich, A. Runesson, and E. Schuller. Tübingen: Mohr.

Wetz, C. 2010. *Eros und Bekehrung: Anthropologische und religionsge-schichtliche Untersuchungen zu Joseph und Aseneth*. NTOA/StUNT 87. Göttingen: Vandenhoeck & Ruprecht.

Williams, C. E. 2012. *Reading Roman Friendship*. Cambridge: Cambridge University Press.

Wills, L. M. 1995. *The Jewish Novel in the Ancient World*. Ithaca, N.Y.: Cornell University Press.

Wilson, W. T. 1991. *Love without Pretense: Romans 12.9–21 and Hellenistic-Jewish Wisdom Literature*. WUNT 2/46. Tübingen: Mohr.

Wischmeyer, O. 1978. "Vorkommen und Bedeutung von Agape in der außerchristlichen Antike." *ZNW* 69: 212–38.

———. 1981. *Der höchste Weg: Das 13. Kapitel des 1. Korintherbriefes*. StNT 13. Gütersloh: Mohn.

———. 1995. *Die Kultur des Buches Jesus Sirach*. BZNW. Berlin: Walter de Gruyter.

———. 1999. "Herrschen als Dienen—Mk 10,41–45." *ZNW* 90: 28–44.

———. 2003. "Die Neutestamentliche Wissenschaft am Anfang des 21. Jahrhunderts: Überlegungen zu ihrem Selbstverständnis, ihren Beziehungsfeldern und ihren Aufgaben." Pages 245–71 in *Herkunft und Zukunft der neutestamentlichen Wissenschaft*. Edited by O. Wischmeyer. NET 6. Tübingen: Francke.

———. 2004a. "Das Gebot der Nächstenliebe bei Paulus: Eine traditionsge-schichtliche Untersuchung." Pages 137–61 in O. Wischmeyer, *Von Ben Sira zu Paulus: Gesammelte Aufsätze zu Texten, Theologie und Hermeneutik des Frühjudentum und des Neuen Testaments*. Edited by E.-M. Becker. WUNT 173. Tübingen: Mohr.

———. 2004b. *Hermeneutik des Neuen Testaments: Ein Lehrbuch*. NET 8. Tübingen: Francke.

———. 2004c. "Staat und Christen nach Römer 13: Ein neuer hermeneutischer Zugang." Pages 229–42 in O. Wischmeyer, *Von Ben Sira zu Paulus: Gesammelte Aufsätze zu Texten, Theologie und Hermeneutik des Frühjudentum und des Neuen Testaments*. Edited by E.-M. Becker. WUNT 173. Tübingen: Mohr.

———. 2004d. "ΘΕΟΝ ΑΓΑΠΑΝ bei Paulus: Eine traditionsgeschichtliche Miszelle." Pages 162–66 in O. Wischmeyer, *Von Ben Sira zu Paulus: Gesammelte Aufsätze zu Texten, Theologie und Hermeneutik des Frühjudentum und des Neuen Testaments*. Edited by E.-M. Becker. WUNT 173. Tübingen: Mohr.

———. 2004e. "Herrschen als Dienen: Markus 10,41–45." Pages 190–206 in O. Wischmeyer, *Von Ben Sira zu Paulus: Gesammelte Aufsätze zu Texten, Theologie und Hermeneutik des Frühjudentum und des Neuen Testaments*. Edited by E.-M. Becker. WUNT 173. Tübingen: Mohr.

———. 2004f. "Macht, Herrschaft und Gewalt in den frühjüdischen Schriften." Pages 39–53 in O. Wischmeyer, *Von Ben Sira zu Paulus: Gesammelte Aufsätze zu Texten, Theologie und Hermeneutik des Frühjudentum und des Neuen Testaments*. Edited by E.-M. Becker. WUNT 173. Tübingen: Mohr.

——. 2009a. "Das alte und das neue Gebot: Ein Beitrag zur Intertextualität der johanneischen Schriften." Pages 207–20 in *Studien zu Matthäus und Johannes: Festschrift für Jean Zumstein*. Edited by A. Dettwiler and U. Poplutz. AThNT 97. Zürich: Theologischer Verlag.

——. 2009b. "Beobachtungen zur Gedankenwelt von Römer 8,31–39." Pages 799–809 in *The Letter to the Romans*. Edited by U. Schnelle. BEThL CCXXVI. Leuven: Peeters.

——. 2009c. "Erklärung/Erklären II. Neutestamentlich." Pages 147–48 in *LBH*.

——. 2009d. "Die Grundlagen der Autorität des Apostels Paulus." Pages 29–45 in *Autorität in der Kirche / Authority in the Church*. Edited by P. Collins, W. Klausnitzer, and W. Sparn. Munich: Verlag Sankt Michaelsbund.

——. 2009e. "Interpretation/Interpretieren/Interpret II. Neutestamentlich." Pages 291–92 in *LBH*.

——. 2012a. "Kanon und Hermeneutik in Zeiten der Dekonstruktion: Was die neutestamentliche Wissenschaft gegenwärtig hermeneutisch leisten kann." Pages 623–78 in *Kanon in Konstruktion und Dekonstruktion: Kanonisierungsprozesse religiöser Texte von der Antike bis zur Gegenwart; Ein Handbuch*. Edited by E.-M. Becker and S. Scholtz. Berlin: Walter de Gruyter.

——. 2012b. "1 Korinther 13: Das Hohelied der Liebe zwischen Emotion und Ethos." Pages 343–60 in *Deuterocanonical and Cognate Literature Yearbook 2011: Emotion from Ben Sira to Paul*. Edited by R. Egger-Wenzel and J. Corley. Berlin: Walter de Gruyter.

——. 2012c. "'Die Liebe Christi dringt uns . . .': 2 Kor 15,15f und die Liebe Christi bei Paulus." Pages 323–36 in *Der zweite Korintherbrief: Literarische Gestalt—historische Situation—theologische Argumentation; Festschrift für D.-A. Koch*. Edited by D. Sänger. Göttingen: Vandenhoeck & Ruprecht.

——. 2012d. "Romans." Pages 245–76 in *Paul: Life, Setting, Work, Letters*. Edited by O. Wischmeyer. Translated by H. S. Heron, with revisions by D. T. Roth. London: T&T Clark.

——. 2012e. "Römerbrief." Pages 281–314 in *Paulus: Leben—Umwelt—Werk—Briefe*. 2nd ed. Edited by O. Wischmeyer. UTB 2767. Tübingen: Francke.

——, ed. 2013a. *Lexikon der Bibelhermeneutik: Begriffe—Methoden—Theorien—Konzepte*. Berlin: Walter de Gruyter.

——. 2013b. "Wie spricht der Jakobusbrief von Gott? Theologie im Jakobusbrief." Pages 385–409 in *Weisheit als Lebensgrundlage: Festschrift für F. V. Reiterer*. Edited by R. Egger-Wenzel, K. Schöpflin, and J. Diehl. DCSt 15. Berlin: Walter de Gruyter.

——. 2015a. "Anders Nygren and the 'Babylonian Captivity of Agape' Once and Now." *Svensk Teologisk Kvartalskrift* 91: 164–72.

——. 2015b. *Liebe als Agape: Das frühchristliche Konzept und der moderne Diskurs*. Tübingen: Mohr.

——. 2016a. "Gerechtigkeit und Liebe: Das Verhältnis zweier theologischer Konzepte des Paulus im Römerbrief." Pages 61–77 in *Paulus und Petrus:*

*Geschichte—Theologie—Rezeption; Festschrift für Friedrich Wilhelm Horn zu seinem 60. Geburtstag.* Edited by H. Omerzu and E. D. Schmidt. ABG 48. Leipzig: Evangelische Verlagsanstalt.

———. 2016b. "Zwischen Gut und Böse: Teufel, Dämonen, das Böse und der Kosmos im Jakobusbrief." Pages 153–68 in *Das Böse, der Teufel und Dämonen / Evil, the Devil, and Demons.* Edited by J. Dochhorn, S. Rudnig-Zelt and B. Wold. WUNT 2/412. Tübingen: Mohr.

———. 2020. "Ego-Documents on Religious Experiences in Paul's Letters." Pages 181–198 in *Lived Religion in the Ancient Mediterranean World: Approaching Religious Transformations from Archeology, History and Classics.* Edited by V. Gasparini et al. Berlin: Walter de Gruyter.

———. 2021. "Ethical Concepts in Mark and John: A Comparative Approach." In *John's Transformation of Mark.* Edited by E.-M. Becker, H. K. Bond, and C. H. Williams. London: T&T Clark.

———. Forthcoming. *Der Brief des Jakobus.* KEK. Göttingen: Vandenhoeck & Ruprecht.

Wischmeyer, O., and D. Hiller. 2009. "Einverständnis/Zustimmung." Pages 140–41 in *LBH.*

Witte, M. 2012. *Gerechtigkeit.* UTB 3662. Tübingen: Mohr.

———. 2014. "Begründungen der Barmherzigkeit gegenüber den Bedürftigen in jüdischen Weisheitsschriften aus hellenistisch-römischer Zeit." Pages 387–412 in *Anthropologie und Ethik im Frühjudentum und im Neuen Testament.* Edited by M. Konradt and E. Schläpfer. WUNT 322. Tübingen: Mohr.

Wolter, M. 2008. *Das Lukasevangelium.* HNT 5. Tübingen: Mohr.

———. 2013. "Die Liebe." Pages 449–53 in *Paulus Handbuch.* Edited by F. W. Horn. Tübingen: Mohr.

———. 2016. *The Gospel according to Luke—Volume I (Luke 1–9:50).* Translated by W. Coppins and C. Heilig. Edited by W. Coppins and S. Gathercole. 2 vols. BMSEC 4. Waco, Tex.: Baylor University Press.

———. 2017. *The Gospel according to Luke—Volume II (9:51–24).* Translated by W. Coppins and C. Heilig. Edited by W. Coppins and S. Gathercole. BMSEC 5. Waco, Tex.: Baylor University Press.

Wolter, M., K.-W. Niebuhr, and M. Theobald. 2013. "Die Rechtfertigungslehre." Pages 347–65 in *Paulus Handbuch.* Edited by F. W. Horn. Tübingen: Mohr.

Woodward, S. 1981. "The Provenance of the Term 'Saints.'" *JETS* 24: 107–16.

Wright, N. T. 2013. *Paul and the Faithfulness of God: Parts I–IV.* 2 vols. London: SPCK.

Wulf, C. 2013. "Liebe." Pages 966–67 in *Dorsch: Lexikon der Psychologie.* 16th ed. Edited by M. A. Wirtz. Bern: Huber.

Wülfling, P. von Martitz, G. Fohrer, E. Schweizer, E. Lohse, and W. Schneemelcher. 1969. "υἱός, υἱοθεσία." Pages 334–402 in *ThWNT* 8.

———. 1972. "υἱός, υἱοθεσία." Pages 334–99 in *TDNT* 8.

Yarbro Collins, A. 2007. *Mark: A Commentary.* Hermeneia. Minneapolis: Fortress.

Zeller, D. 2010. *Der erste Brief an der Korinther.* Göttingen: Vandenhoeck & Ruprecht.

————. 2012. "Pauline Paraenesis in Romans 12 and Greek Gnomic Wisdom." Pages 73–86 in *Greco-Roman Culture and the New Testament: Studies Commemorating the Centennial of the Pontifical Biblical Institute*. Edited by D. E. Aune and F. E. Brenk. SNT 143. Leiden: Brukk.

Zimmermann, R. 2001. *Geschlechtermetaphorik und Gottesverhältnis: Traditionsgeschichte und Theologie eines Bildfeldes in Urchristentum und antiker Umwelt*. WUNT II/122. Tübingen: Mohr.

————. 2013a. "Das 'Gute' als ethische Norm in Antike und Christentum: Gut, Güter, Güterabwägung in philosophischen und christlichen Ethiken." Pages 53–60 in *Ethische Normen des frühen Christentums: Gut—Leben—Leib—Tugend*. Edited by F. W. Horn, U. Volp, and R. Zimmermann. WUNT 313. Tübingen: Mohr.

————. 2013b. "Körperlichkeit, Leiblichkeit, Sexualität: Man und Frau." Pages 378–85 in *Paulus Handbuch*. Edited by F. W. Horn. Tübingen: Mohr.

————. 2013c. "Pluralistische Ethikbegründung und Normenanalyse im Horizont einer 'impliziten Ethik' frühchristlicher Schriften." Pages 3–28 in *Ethische Normen des frühen Christentums: Gut—Leben—Leib—Tugend*. Edited by F. W. Horn, U. Volp, and R. Zimmermann. WUNT 313. Tübingen: Mohr.

Zobel, K. 1992. *Prophetie und Deuteronomium*. BZAW 199. Berlin: Walter de Gruyter.

Zumstein, J. 2013. "'Gott ist Liebe.'" Pages 154–68 in *Aneignung durch Transformation: Beiträge zur Analyse von Überlieferungsprozessen in frühen Christentum; Festschrift für M. Theobald*. Edited by W. Eisele, C. Schaefer, and H.-U. Weidemann. Freiburg: Herder.

# Index of Ancient Sources

New Testament

# Early Christian Writings

# Index of Authors